The People's Republic of China: A Handbook

Map 1   People's Republic of China

The People's Republic of China: A Handbook

edited by Harold C. Hinton

Westview Press • Boulder, Colorado

Dawson • Folkestone, England

Published in 1979 in the United States of America by
 Westview Press, Inc.
 5500 Central Avenue
 Boulder, Colorado 80301
 Frederick A. Praeger, Publisher

Published in 1979 in Great Britain by
 Wm. Dawson and Sons, Ltd.
 Cannon House
 Folkestone
 Kent CT19 5EE

Library of Congress Catalog Card Number: 78-10306
ISBN (U.S.): 0-89158-419-6
ISBN (U.K.): 0-7129-0886-2

Printed and bound in the United States of America

Contents

Illustrations

Tables

Preface

It has been several years since the last handbook on the People's Republic of China (P.R.C.) was published in the United States, but there are additional reasons for the publication of this one. It has long been a truism that China is an important and interesting country due to physical size, its uniquely large population, the antiquity and complexity of its culture, the massive wars and revolutions through which it has passed in modern times, and its actual or apparent potential for becoming a major world power. These considerations are as valid today as they ever were, or more so. There is today an obvious additional consideration: in 1976 the P.R.C. suffered the loss of its two most important leaders, Mao Tse-tung and Chou En-lai, and entered a new political era in which the quest for stability and modernization appears to have replaced the earlier tendency, powerful if intermittent, toward radical upheavals.

From an American point of view, China has been an important country in various ways since the late nineteenth century and is still one today: the P.R.C. ranks second only to the Soviet Union among the Communist states with which the United States must cope, and the United States has been committed since 1972 to "normalize" its relations with Peking at the full diplomatic level; it succeeded in doing so at the end of 1978, in spite of the difficult obstacle created by its commitment to Taiwan.

The exploitation and even the exploration of China's natural resources have been hampered in the past by political disorder and other problems, and there has been a tendency to underestimate these resources. By now, however, it is reasonably clear that the P.R.C. is at least moderately well endowed, although some of its natural resources, including the apparently large deposits of offshore oil under the East and South China seas, will require much capital and technology (including imported technology) to develop.

No one doubts that the P.R.C. has the largest population in the world, even though its exact size and rate of growth are not precisely known. Chinese agriculture has traditionally been efficient—a major reason why such a high population level has been attained—and it seems likely that the current leadership, plus the farmers, will manage to keep the population at least adequately fed for some time to come, even if the current objective of cutting population growth to 1 percent per year is not achieved. Survival, however, is not enough to make China a great power. For that, assuming it to be possible, a sufficient portion of the total population must be educated and trained to competence in a wide range of modern skills; if this is done, as it has not been (adequately) to date, the law of averages and the well-known innate talents of the Chinese will produce discoveries and innovations that will enable the country to advance scientifically, economically, and culturally, relative not only to its own past but to the rest of the world. This is not to say that China will necessarily ever become a "superpower" or attain a high standard of living for the majority of its population; the base from which it has started may be too low for that.

Three obvious disasters could ruin China's prospects for becoming a truly modern power: a serious failure of the food supply to keep pace with population growth; large-scale political struggle or civil war; or defeat in a major foreign war (presumably by the Soviet Union). None of these disasters appears likely to materialize in the near future, although neither can they be ruled out. The most probable outlook is for continuing but difficult and unspectacular growth and development. Results will appear over decades, not years. If that is the case, China will presumably remain, in relative terms, essentially what it is now: a unique power standing below the two superpowers but in several important respects (notably political dynamism and strategic military power) well above any other nation.

Implicit in this discussion has been the proposition that ideology, whether orthodox Marxism-Leninism or its more radical Chinese variant, the "thought" of Mao Tse-tung, is playing a declining role in the life of China. This has been the case since the end of the Cultural Revolution in 1969, although the survival of Mao and other radical leaders for several years after that time tended to disguise the fact. The point should not be overstressed; ideology is not dead in China, and even if it were its passing could not be officially announced yet, because every country needs some sort of ideology and some degree of continuity— only Mao and his thought can provide these for China. With amazing success, Mao posed for a generation as the symbol of authority and unity for his people, and because he became more radical with age his immense influence was essentially a radicalizing one. Too radical, in fact; the Cultural Revolution was on balance a destructive interlude. Mao may turn out to be worth more dead than alive; like other major historic figures, he can be interpreted in various ways, and the current leadership is reinterpreting him as almost a moderate, in a way that was not possible during his lifetime, while at least implicitly attributing his excesses to the purged and disgraced "Gang of Four."

The foregoing is a brief and necessarily impressionistic sketch from life. But on what authority does it rest? In other words, how do we learn about China? Can we, in fact, really know anything at all about it for sure? These are questions that the China specialist (or Chinawatcher) hears constantly from nonspecialists. The answer to the last question is yes, but the others require a more extended discussion. The problem cannot really be solved through a perusal of the titles in the bibliographies at the end of the contributions to this handbook, or even of the contents of the works listed, helpful and informative though they are, because the bibliographies are designed mainly as guides to further reading for the nonspecialist rather than as aids to true research.

China is neither easy nor impossible to learn about; it is difficult. Most events and data relating to internal affairs must be comprehended primarily from sources emanating from within the P.R.C., meaning for the most part primary official sources. The majority of these are published either in specialized books and other publications, or in more general sources like the *People's Daily* (*Jen-min jih-pao*), the official newspaper published by the Central Committee of the Communist Party of China; *Red Flag* (*Hung ch'i*), the theoretical organ of the same body; the *Liberation Army Daily* (*Chieh-fang chün pao*), which is not supposed to circulate outside the country and must usually be gotten at by reading those of its articles and editorials that are reprinted in some other source; and press releases and radio broadcasts, most of them by the New China News Agency (Hsin hua). This makes a formidable body of material, in quantity if not in quality, for the propaganda content is very high. A surprising amount of it is available in English translation (usually Peking's own) and can be found most readily in the official *Peking Review*, in the series of Chinese press translations published by the American Consulate General in Hong Kong, and in the serial *Foreign Radio Broadcasts* (published by the U.S. Foreign Broadcast Information Service). Authentic documents originating but not published in the P.R.C. are often translated and reprinted in the periodical *Issues and Studies* (Taipei). Developments relating to foreign affairs can and should be followed from foreign sources as well; and these must therefore be assembled from the statistics published by its trading partners. All this means that a great deal of research on China can be done in primary sources, even without a knowledge of the Chinese language.

Primary, or at least official, sources are not enough, however. They are tendentious and difficult to interpret (except on the basis of considerable experience), and they leave important and often intentional gaps. The volume of secondary writings on contemporary China in various languages is great, and the quality has tended to improve over time. Secondary sources contain original information and/or significant interpretations; they should not be overlooked.

Experience (which leads to an understanding of the P.R.C.'s actual record, as distinct from the image it tries to project), plus a good command of the relevant primary and secondary sources, can yield a useful, though presumably incomplete, knowledge of contemporary China, or at least of some significant aspect of it, as well as the basis for intelligent (though of course fallible) prediction. This is the level of expertise of the contributions to this handbook.

The editor's function, apart from writing his own contribution and this Preface as he has defined it for himself, has been mainly to plan the volume and to select the contributors. By agreement with the publisher, he has kept the length down to one that he hopes will make it possible for a sizable number of people to buy and read the handbook; the formidable length and infrequent use of all too many handbooks is proverbial. The eleven topics selected as the subjects of contributions appear to the editor to embrace most of the significant problems in which a general, or even a moderately specialized, reader might be interested. The contributors were carefully chosen on the basis of their expertise and experience from a fairly wide variety of backgrounds and viewpoints and were encouraged to present their topics as they thought best; no effort was made to impose a "line" of any kind on them. Consequently, responsibility for the statements contained in each chapter of the handbook rests with the contributor in question.

The editor would like to thank Frederick A. Praeger of Westview Press and Ian Williams of Dawson Publishing for suggesting and financing the preparation of this handbook, and Mervyn Adams Seldon for invaluable editorial help in preparing the manuscript for publication.

Harold C. Hinton

The Contributors

Judith Banister is visiting research associate at the East-West Population Institute, Honolulu. She received her B.A. in history in 1965 from Swarthmore College and her Ph.D. in demography, agriculture, and economic development in 1978 from Stanford University, where she studied at the Food Research Institute.

King C. Chen is professor of political science at Rutgers University. He is the author of *Vietnam and China, 1938-1954* (1969), editor of *The Foreign Policy of China* (1972), and a contributor to *China: A Handbook* (1973), *The Role of External Powers in the Indochina Crisis* (1973), *Dimensions of China's Foreign Relations* (1977), and many professional journals.

Ralph C. Croizier is professor of history at the University of Victoria, Canada. He is the author of *Traditional Medicine in Modern China* (1968), editor of *China's Cultural Legacy and Communism* (1970), and author of *Koxinga and Chinese Nationalism: Myth, History and the Hero* (1977).

Genevieve C. Dean is a research associate with the United States–China Relations Program at Stanford University. She received her A.B. from Cornell University, her M.A. in public law and government from Columbia University, and her D.Phil in history and social studies of science from the University of Sussex. She has also served as consultant to the Science Policy Division of the Science, Technology and Industry Directorate in the Organisation for Economic Co-operation and Development, Paris.

A. M. Fraser, colonel, United States Marine Corps, retired, served on active duty for twenty-five years in various places, including mainland China and Taiwan. He is a graduate of the British Joint Services Staff College and of the United States National War College. Since retirement, he has served as a consultant to the Smithsonian Institution, the General Accounting Office, and the Department of State. He is the author of *The People's Liberation Army: Communist China's Armed Forces* (1973) and a contributor to *Pacific Community, Asian Affairs, Problems of Communism,* and several military journals.

Harold C. Hinton is professor of political science and international affairs at the Institute for Sino-Soviet Studies of The George Washington University. He received his Ph.D. in modern Chinese history from Harvard University in 1951. He is the author of numerous works on Chinese politics and foreign policy and Far Eastern international politics, including *Communist China in World Politics* (1966), *Three and a Half Powers: The New Balance in Asia* (1975), and *An Introduction to Chinese Politics* (1973, 1978).

Harald W. Jacobson is a United States Foreign Service officer, retired. He saw naval service in China during World War II and later served at the American Consulate General in Hong Kong, the American Embassy in New Delhi, and the Department of State. Since retirement he has been adjunct professor at The American University.

Edwin F. Jones, United States Department of State, retired, served with the Office of Intelligence and Research from 1946 to 1974. His field was the economies of the Asian Communist countries. Since retirement, he has served as a consultant to the Institute for Defense Analyses. He has published numerous articles on the Chinese economy.

Richard Curt Kraus is assistant professor of sociology at the University of Illinois, Urbana, where he is also associated with the Center for Asian Studies. He received his Ph.D. from Columbia University in 1974 and was a junior fellow of the East Asian Institute and of the Research Institute on Communist Affairs at Columbia.

Ramon H. Myers is curator-scholar of the East Asian Collection of the Hoover Institution on War, Revolution, and Peace at Stanford University. He received his B.A., M.A., and Ph.D. degrees from the University of Washington. He has been associated in various capacities with the University of Miami, the University of Hawaii, the Australian

National University, and Harvard University. He is the author of *The Chinese Peasant Economy* (1970) and of numerous articles on the economic and social histories of China and Japan.

Philip A. True is a geographic analyst on China at the National Foreign Assessment Center and an adjunct faculty member at the Institute for Sino-Soviet Studies, The George Washington University.

1
Geography
Philip A. True

The importance of China in Asian affairs results in part from such basic factors as its central location and common borders with most Asian nations, its immense size and population, and ancient cultural ties whose imprint still persists in other Asian countries. Although their importance varies with the strength of the central government and its foreign policy initiatives, these factors remain essential to an understanding of China's historical role in Asia, and they continue today as unspoken but nonetheless recognized forces underlying Peking's relationship with neighboring states.

China's internal policies also reflect a composite of many factors, among which are the character and quality of the physical environment and the size, distribution, and other characteristics of the population. The variety of and interaction among landforms, climate, soil, and vegetation provide the environmental milieu within which Chinese agricultural practices have evolved. The basic characteristics and use—and misuse—of China's land resources have presented Peking with many serious problems and hard choices. Immense efforts have been put into numerous programs over the past twenty-five years to "remake nature" and bring environmental problems under control.

Aside from sheer numbers, China's population is notable for its highly uneven distribution, the cultural unity of the Han (ethnic Chinese) majority of its inhabitants, and the presence of numerous ethnic minority groups whose political importance is far greater than their total numbers would suggest. Despite a population that is nearing 1 billion on a land area only marginally greater than that of the United States, much of China is sparsely populated and large areas in the western provinces are uninhabited. About 80 percent of the people are engaged in agriculture, and rural population densities reflect generally the suitability of environmental conditions for growing crops. Since only 11 percent of China is farmland, extremely high rural population densities occur on the limited number of alluvial plains and lowlands, primarily located in the eastern provinces.

The cultural unity of the Han Chinese (Han derived from the Han dynasty, the first great Chinese dynasty, 202 B.C.–220 A.D.) developed, spread, and was strengthened by the uninterrupted continuity of the scholar-official ruling class whose ability to communicate via a common written language transcended the linguistic fragmentation of the Chinese. Additionally, Chinese culture was able to develop and persist without major or traumatic change because of China's location and its relative isolation from other major centers of civilization. Although limited contacts did exist, the long distances coupled with deserts, high mountains, and generally inhospitable environments provided a buffer and barrier preventing any large-scale impact by alien peoples.

Despite the overwhelming numerical dominance of Han Chinese, the fifty-odd ethnolinguistic groups, termed minority nationalities by Peking and totaling perhaps 55 million or so, remain politically important because of their strategic locations—primarily in sensitive frontier areas in the western and southwestern provinces. Administrative control over these regions and their non-Han people has been an important political objective of the Chinese government. In the past two decades, improved communications have opened up these areas, and the settlement of large numbers of Han Chinese in the remote frontier provinces—particularly Sinkiang and Inner Mongolia—has assisted and given backing to Peking's control and authority.

The most important spatial patterns in China are those related to the basic east-west division of the country. A line following a roughly southwest-northeast alignment drawn from northwestern Yunnan Province along the eastern edge of the Tibet-Tsinghai plateau, across the eastern margins of the Ordos Desert, and then tracing the crest of the Greater Khingan Range north to the Amur divides China into roughly equal parts. To the east and south of this line are 95 percent of the population, nearly all of the agricultural land, most of the major industrial centers, and the bulk of the transportation facilities. In contrast, to the north and west lies largely unpopulated country with only scattered population clusters; most of the inhabitants are non-Han Chinese, economic development has barely begun, and most of the region has a political history of only sporadic and nominal central government control.

Physical Patterns

Most of China's land surface consists of rugged uplands: large areas are at high elevations, and the major mountain ranges, as well as the major streams, trend from west to east. In general, the highest terrain is located in the west, whereas the few sizable alluvial plains and lowlands are mostly concentrated in the eastern coastal provinces. A great variety of landforms—primarily hills and low mountains occasionally interspersed with lowlands and intermontane basins—are located between the eastern lowlands and western highlands. The practical effect of these physical characteristics is a compartmentalized landscape where lowlands, plains, and basins are separated from one another by rough uplands—often preventing easy communication between these core areas. One of the lasting achievements of China's rulers has been the ability to sinicize and maintain control of such a large and physically diverse territory.

The west-to-east alignment of major mountain ranges is important climatically because of the blocking effect of highlands on the movement of air masses and weather systems. In turn, climatic conditions affect vegetation, soil patterns, and how the land is used. Historically, the west-east aligned ranges have isolated key lowlands and basins and made communications between them difficult. This has been particularly true in western China, where some of the world's highest mountains are located. The T'ien Shan, originating in Soviet Central Asia, the Kunluns, and the Himalayas are enormously important determinants of climate and other environmental characteristics. These highlands have long isolated the basins and plateaus of western China, and it has only been in recent decades that air travel and a few highways have begun to open the recesses of Tibet and Sinkiang to one another and to the rest of China. In the eastern half of China, the Tsinling Shan and lesser mountains that extend east from the Tibetan highlands for several hundred kilometers have functioned in a similar manner. The highlands, averaging about 3,000 meters, block much of the cold, dry Asian air masses from penetrating into the Szechwan Basin to the south. The result is sharply contrasting environmental and agricultural patterns north and south of the Tsinling highlands. For example, the growing season is about 100 days longer in the Szechwan Basin than in the Wei basin immediately north of the mountains. In similar fashion, the Nan Ling, a roughly east-west aligned belt of hills and mountains at about latitude 25° N, serves as a significant physical divide. It largely

Map 2   Physical Map of China and Provinces

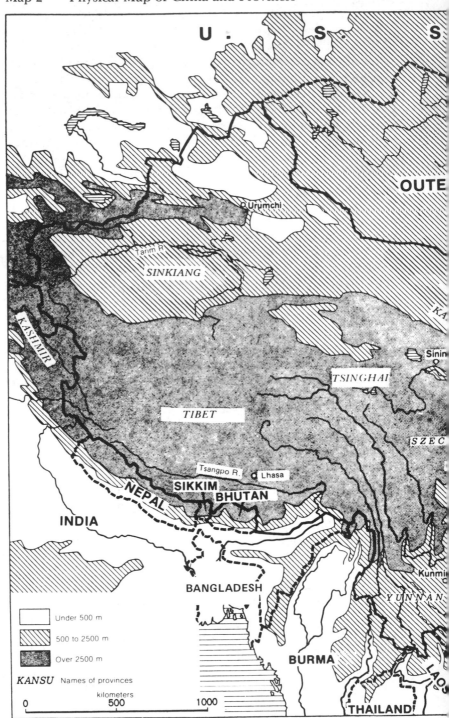

R .

Hailar

Ulan Bator

NGOLIA

HEILUNGKIANG

Sungari R.

Harbin

KIRIN

Kirin

Liao R.

Shenyang

LIAONING

INNER
MONGOLIA

Kalgan

HOPEI

River

PEKING

Tientsin

Dairen

JAPAN

KOREA

Taiyuan

SHENSI

SHANSI

Tsinan

SHANTUNG

Tsingtao

Sian

HONAN

KIANGSU

Huai R.

NANKING

SHANGHAI

HUPEI

Wuhan

Han R.

Yangtze R.

Hangchow

CHEKIANG

CHUNGKING

Nanchang

KIANGSI

OW

Changsha

HUNAN

Foochow

Kweilin

FUKIEN

TAIWAN

KWANGSI

CANTON

Sikiang R.

KWANGTUNG

Hongkong

TNAM

Hainan Is.

PHILIPPINES

prevents the cold, continental air masses that periodically sweep across the Yangtze basin from reaching the subtropical lands of Kwangtung and Kwangsi provinces to the south.

A second, more subdued structural trend consists of a series of southwest-northeast oriented mountain ranges, generally relatively low (2,000 to 3,000 meters), located in the eastern third of the country. These ranges include the Wuyi Shan that isolates Fukien and southern Chekiang provinces from the middle Yangtze lowlands in Kiangsi Province; the Taihang Shan that rises abruptly along the western margins of the North China Plain; and the Khingan ranges of Northeast China. The Taihang and Khingans also serve as important climatic barriers in that their height and location largely blunt the penetration of moisture-laden maritime air masses into the interior of Asia.

All told, about one-third of China's total area is classified as mountains, one-quarter comprises plateaus, and roughly 10 percent is hills. The remaining land is divided between basins and plains, approximately 19 and 10 percent respectively. While limited areas of the hills and plateaus are cultivated, the essential point made by these rough landform percentages is that most of China consists of landforms where growing crops is difficult and the living hard, and only limited areas of China are truly favorable for agricultural purposes. Chinese accomplishments over the long span of history in evolving an intensive agricultural system from a small and environmentally fragile base are testimony to the careful husbanding of limited land resources and the administrative techniques and organizational skills that have mobilized manpower to work on national and regional projects beneficial to the public good.

The basic structural trend of the country also means that most of China's major rivers flow in generally west-to-east aligned courses. This orientation, specifically of the Huang Ho (Yellow River), Yangtze, and Hsi Chiang, is important in terms of erosion, communications, and flooding. Because of the 5,000 meter elevation of the sources of the Huang and Yangtze, there has been immense downcutting through rock and soil, and massive amounts of sediment have been collected as they flow seaward. This has affected navigability and increased the potential for flooding. The directional trend of the rivers' courses also is significant in that major storms follow a similar west-to-east track. Consequently, a major, slow-moving storm or a series of storms may parallel one of the major river systems and thus dump large amounts of rain over long sections of the river and cause severe flooding. A favorable factor, however, is that the west-east alignment permits shipping to penetrate deep into the interior of the China mainland—a situation developed most highly on the Yangtze.

Climate

The importance of rainfall, length of the growing season, temperatures, and the impact of droughts and floods can scarcely be overstated in a country where agriculture plays so vital a role in the economic and political health of the government. The most significant climatic division in China is the west-east separation between western arid and semiarid climates and the relatively humid conditions of eastern China. This climatic division is created by the high mountains and plateaus guarding the interior of China that, coupled with distance, prevent any significant influx of maritime air into the interior. Whereas precipitation averages only 100 to 400 millimeters in the west, between 500 and 1,500 millimeters fall annually in eastern China—sufficient in most areas to sustain forests and to permit the growing of crops without irrigation.

The variety of climatic types in China is the product of a complex interaction of factors that in simplest form begin with the input and exchange of solar energy that fuels the world's atmospheric system. The basic patterns revolve about air mass exchanges—the periodic surge and flow of the air masses that originate, or are strengthened, over the Asian continent and the maritime air masses whose sources are the nearby oceans. These air masses are triggered by the differential rate of heating and cooling of land and water. In the cooler half of the year, continental air dominates over almost all of China, and cold, dry air masses periodically surge south and east, bringing in their passage clear skies but little precipitation. In the warmer half of the year, continental air is displaced with moist maritime air masses that, as they periodically move inland, are lifted when they contact cooler continental air or terrain features to produce rainfall. In practice, maritime air masses are present for a significantly longer time in the south of China than in the north and northeast; the reverse is true for dry, continental air masses. The result is a steady increase of annual precipitation from north to south and a very pronounced concentration of rain in the June-September period in the northern half of China, but a considerably longer rainy season in the southern provinces.

Temperatures in China for stations comparable in latitude and

Table 1.1 Selected Climatic Comparisons

Station	Latitude °N	Mean Temperature (C°) Jan.	July	Mean Annual Precipitation (mm)
Harbin	45	-19.7	23.6	574
Minneapolis		-11.1	22.5	633
Peking	40	-4.2	26.7	627
Washington		3.6	25.6	1,036
Wuhan	30	4.4	29.7	1,255
New Orleans		13.1	28.9	1,364
Kwangchow (Canton)	23	13.9	28.9	1,615
Miami	26	19.4	27.8	1,522
Ai-hui	50	-23.6	21.4	513
London	51	2.8	17.8	582

elevation with those in the United States and England are given in Table 1.1. Although the comparability in summer temperatures is close, winter readings in China are significantly lower—a result of the larger and colder high pressure cells that form over the Asian mainland. Despite the lower winter temperatures, the dryness of the air—particularly in north and northeast China—compensates to some extent in individual perceptions of cold. Temperatures expressed in terms of frost-free seasons show the expected lengthening from north to south, but with significant modifications caused by mountain barriers, of which the Tsinling and adjoining highlands are the most important. North of the Tsinling Shan, the frost-free season is about 225 days, but the blocking effect of the highlands allows a nearly year-round frost-free season in the Szechwan Basin immediately to the south.

The Asian air circulation patterns are modified in western China by elevation, mountain ranges, and distance from sources of maritime air. A lack of precipitation is the most significant characteristic: least amounts (100 to 250 mm) fall in the deep desert basins in Sinkiang and in the high northern plateau of Tibet. Precipitation gradually increases to the east, and 250 to 500 mm normally are received in the southeastern and eastern portions of the Tibetan Plateau, the eastward margins of Inner Mongolia, and in the higher elevations of the T'ien Shan. Grasslands have formed under such conditions and provide forage for large numbers of sheep, goats, and other animals. Temperature ranges are extreme in western China because of the great differences in elevation. In the highest portions of the Tibetan Plateau, freezing

Map 3   Agriculture

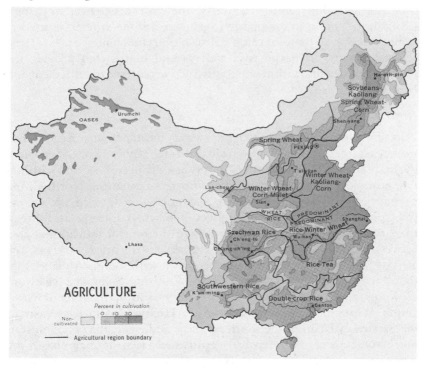

temperatures and snow flurries occur even in mid-summer, while in the Turfan Depression (150 meters below sea level) temperatures may reach as high as 45° C in summer.

Regional Divisions

The major regional divisions of China are defined principally by climatic patterns and major landform features, and to a lesser extent by a combination of cultural features, accessibility, economic patterns and development, and historical factors. Five major regions are commonly recognized. The scantily populated western half of China contains the Tibetan highlands and Northwest China, each with about one-quarter of China's area but with a combined population of no more than 5 percent of China's total. Desolate high mountains and plateaus, desert basins, and grasslands are the characteristic landscapes of the west. Eastern China is subdivided into three traditional regions: Northeast,

North, and South China. Each possesses distinctive environmental qualities and dimensions; culturally, the main differences in eastern China from region to region are linguistic, but the differences are less important overall than common cultural traits and bonds. Each of these regions centers on fertile river valleys and basins that provide the physical framework within which distinctive patterns of settlement and land use have evolved.

North China

In many ways North China retains today its ancient historical role as the key region in China. Though small in area (about 12 or 13 percent of the mainland), much of North China is densely populated and within it live approximately a third of the Chinese population. North China normally is defined to the north and northwest by climatic factors (precipitation amounts), a good reflection of which is the positioning of the Great Wall. In general, the wall is in the zone or transitional area between semiarid steppe lands, where grazing is the principal economic activity, and land where crops can be grown with some confidence that the harvest will be adequate. The Tsinling Shan, its eastward offshoots, and the Huai River valley form the southern border of North China. While the transition between the Huang Ho drainage basin to the Szechwan Basin to the south is sharp and clear, the changes from north to south in the intensively cultivated Huai drainage basin are much more gradual. Historically, the Huai country was a mixture of forest and swamp, and it served until the ninth century or so as a recognizable barrier to north-south communication.

Within North China, two distinct major physical subdivisions are found: the North China Plain and the Loess Plateau (or uplands). The Huang Ho cuts through the Loess Plateau, collecting massive amounts of silt from its numerous tributaries before flowing onto the North China Plain. The plain is a product of the Huang Ho and its deposition of alluvial materials, and Chinese historical records note that the river has swung across the North China Plain, occupying for lengthy periods of time widely separated channels.

Chinese civilization originated, developed, was nurtured in, and expanded from the loess-covered uplands of North China. The present landscape in this portion of China is often forbidding, particularly in the uplands away from major stream valleys. Most of the hilly areas are extensively eroded and commonly slashed by deep, steep-sided ravines. Many village paths and roads are worn below the level of surrounding fields, and vegetation is largely absent, except for scattered plantings of trees and shrubs—a program pushed vigorously by Chinese authorities. The bleakness of the landscape is accentuated during winter and early spring by strong, gusty winds that envelope and coat the landscape with a fine layer of yellow dust. During the past century in particular, and in earlier times as well, the area has been ravaged by drought and flash floods that annually destroy crops, villages, and human life.

In spite of its unpromising physical environment, particularly the scanty and unreliable precipitation (about 500 to 700 millimeters annually), several natural advantages favored early settlement of the area. The wind-carried loessial deposits are of recent origin, geologically speaking, fertile, unusually homogeneous in texture, and porous. The soil was easily tilled by primitive wooden digging tools. Natural vegetation in much of the area apparently was grass, and the scanty rainfall appears to have developed only a comparatively sparse forest cover that presented only minor problems to early man armed with simple tools. Whatever the exact circumstances leading to early settlement, Chinese culture evolved in the loessial area of the north; in time, political institutions and administrative techniques were perfected that eventually led to a consolidation of petty states and the founding of the first dynasty about 221 B.C. (the Ch'in) that unified and controlled most of the key areas of modern-day China.

The North China Plain is the largest area of compact agricultural settlement in China, accounting for 20 percent of China's farmland. Almost everywhere the land is cultivated. Exceptions include low-lying coastal areas (some of which are in the process of reclamation), some poorly drained depressions in the northern section of the plain, and scattered areas elsewhere—usually where past flooding has left deposits of sand and gravel. Villages are compact, often fairly large, and sited at regular intervals over the plain. The monotony of the landscape is relieved by clumps of trees around villages and trees planted along the major roads. During much of the year the plain is dry, dusty, and barren in appearance, but in spring the greening of fall-sown crops like wheat and barley, joined later by various summer crops—corn, millet, sorghum, vegetables, and cotton—combine to give the plain a rich, fertile appearance. The traditional uncertainty of agricultural production has been relieved to some extent in the past decade by a rapid increase in the amount of land under irrigation.

Although some areas are supplied by small impoundments and use of river water, more important has been the tapping of underground supplies through digging wells. Around the western margins of the plain particularly, where alluvial deposits from nearby mountainous areas occur, wells provide nearly all of the water for the fields. The increased availability of water has not only meant a more dependable harvest but has allowed an increase in multiple cropping—growing two or more crops on the same plot of land during a year—and in the variety of crops grown. Rice, for example, is increasingly planted on the North China Plain because of dependable supplies of water. Finally, the plain is benefiting from large-scale water and soil conservancy projects that have been underway during the past two decades—specifically the Huang Ho and Hai Ho river projects that have reduced flooding, permanently drained and protected large tracts from waterlogging, and increased supplies of irrigation water. While the threat of flooding remains (and some localized flooding is common each year), massive, destructive floods by the Huang Ho—whose bed is elevated several meters above the plain—have thus far been avoided.

The Loess Plateau comprises the western and northwestern half of North China. The dominant character of the area is its blanket of fine yellow, loessial soil that covers the underlying landforms to depths of 50 to 100 meters. A few mountains rise above the loessial mantle, particularly in Shansi Province, but elsewhere much of the land consists of rounded hills interspersed with occasional basins and river plains. Despite the historic significance of much of this region in the development of Chinese civilization, it is today a hard land, torn and cut by countless ravines and gullies knifing through the porous soil and long stripped of its vegetative cover. A cruel climate frequently withholds even the limited amount of precipitation (300 to 500 millimeters) normally received. Bitter cold winters combined with blowing dust add to the hard-bitten character of the area. Some of the most devastating famines in the world have depopulated large areas in Shensi, Shansi, and Kansu; and revolts and revolutions have often germinated in these barren hills.

Despite the hardships and climatic uncertainties, the Loess Plateau is relatively well populated, with very high population densities in fertile river plains and basins. The soil fertility is renowned, and the amount of land under irrigation is increasing. In the more favored areas, winter wheat is extensively grown; in the hilly areas and the drier northern and western portions of the subregion the major crops are corn, millet, and sorghum; there also are important cotton growing areas. In the drier, hilly areas agricultural income is supplemented by keeping sheep and goats. Many of the loessial hillsides are terraced into narrow fields to supplement the meager amounts of level land found in the stream valleys. It is probably no coincidence that in this most difficult of agricultural environments in China is located the famed Tachai Production Brigade, the agricultural exemplar for China, and the slogan "Learn from Tachai" is reiterated in the press and emblazoned throughout the country on walls and hillsides. "Self-reliance," the original slogan identified with Tachai, heralded the virtues of selfless dedication to back-breaking land improvement tasks no matter how difficult the physical obstacles.

North China is an industrially important region based on plentiful supplies of energy (coal and oil), a fairly good transportation network, and a variety of industrial crops, like cotton, to supply the textile industry. In addition, extensive Chinese projects over the past two decades to improve the river systems and expand irrigation provide a major market for electric pumps, irrigation/drainage equipment, and related products.

Extensive coal deposits were an important stimulant to early development of industry in North China. Although coal production continues to be important, the recent discovery of major oil deposits in North China has given the region an added energy boost. Several fields are being developed along the low-lying coastal area of Hopeh from the mouth of the Huang Ho north to near Tientsin; in addition, a start has been made in exploiting offshore deposits in the shallow waters of Po Hai. Good deposits of coal are located in many areas ringing the North China Plain, in the foothills in Shantung Province, and in Shansi. Very large coal reserves are present in Shensi Province, though little coal there has yet been mined.

North China ranks high nationally in industrial production, particularly in transportation equipment, iron and steel, chemicals, and textiles. Industry developed earliest in the coastal cities of Tientsin, Tsingtao, and Tangshan. Since the Chinese Communists came to power, however, inland cities like Loyang, Chengchow, and Kaifeng along the western margins of the North China Plain have expanded greatly and produce a wide range of agricultural machinery and related products, plus textiles; Taiyuan, capital of Shansi Province, is a major center of heavy industry; and a wide range of industries are found in Peking and its environs.

14

Map 4   Selected Resource Sites

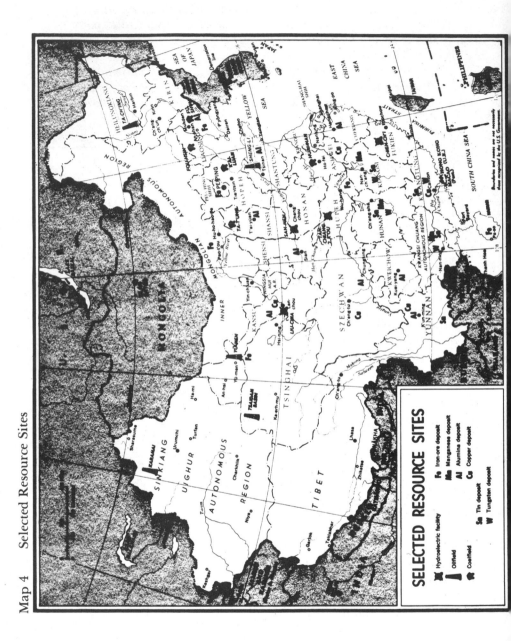

South China

South China, twice the size of North China, contains approximately half of China's population. This huge and diverse region, which stretches eastward from the Tibet-Tsinghai plateau and south from the Tsinling Shan–Huai River divide, encompasses densely populated lands, and large areas of sparsely populated hill and mountain country. The three major regional subdivisions of South China are: the middle and lower Yangtze plain; the Szechwan Basin; and the Yunnan-Kweichow plateau.

The major difference between North and South China is a visible one: the long growing season in South China coupled with considerably greater rainfall gives it a green, summer-type landscape for most of the year. Its flooded ricefields, villages surrounded by clumps of bamboo, and nearby hills with terraced lower slopes coincide with the mental picture that many people have of China. Water is present in most of South China's agricultural countryside—in small ponds and larger impoundments, in irrigation ditches lacing the fields, and in canals or streams that connect rural villages to provide transport links and the means to transport goods to market. The long growing season in the south is conducive to multiple cropping systems, and commonly two or three crops are harvested yearly. Rice dominates almost all the various cropping combinations; about 70 percent of the rice is double-cropped. Wheat, peanuts, sweet potatoes, oilseed crops, and a great variety of other crops and vegetables also are grown.

In contrast to the relatively homogeneous ethnic composition of North China, South China presents much greater ethnic and linguistic diversity—a result of repeated migrations and mixings over many centuries and much local isolation. The many southern dialects or languages, like Cantonese, Wu, Min, and others, are incomprehensible to northern Chinese who speak one of the northern, or Mandarin, dialects. The Chinese Communists are attempting, however, to popularize a national spoken language based on northern speech. In the more rugged uplands, particularly in the southwestern provinces of Kweichow and Yunnan, live large numbers of non-Han peoples who over the centuries have been displaced from more favored agricultural areas by the pressure of Han Chinese settlers.

The historical development of South China and its political integration proceeded along considerably different lines than in the north. Although groups based in the Yangtze lowlands and elsewhere in the south likely made significant contributions to Chinese civilization as it evolved in North China, political development was slow in South China and hampered by the high proportion of uplands, forests, and swamps that retarded large-scale agricultural development, allowed only poor communications, and delayed regional integration. While much of the south was nominally under central government control during the Han dynasty, only a few key areas and routes leading to them were directly administered. In succeeding dynasties Han settlement of the south proceeded at a pace that slowed or quickened with political events and economic conditions in the north. Increasing population pressures in North China led to clearing of additional agricultural land—primarily in the fertile plains of the lower Yangtze area. About 600 A.D., the Grand Canal was built to transport grain and other products of the area to the Chinese capital, then located in the western margins of the North China Plain. Population in South China grew rapidly, particularly after the ninth century when invasion and warfare in the north spurred major southward population shifts. By the time of the Yuan (Mongol) dynasty in the thirteenth century, the population balance had swung decisively to South China—a regional dominance that continues.

Although South China contains China's largest industrial and commercial center, Shanghai, the region lags behind North and Northeast China industrially. Traditionally, industry was concentrated in the cities along the lower Yangtze. While industry has continued to prosper there, expansion has been greatest in the middle Yangtze area, and Wuhan and the Changsha-Hengyang area in Hunan Province are rapidly growing metallurgical and machine-building centers. Both Chungking and Chengtu in Szechwan are major industrial centers; light industry—paper, sugar, and textiles—is well developed in the Kwang-chow (Canton) area. Energy supplies generally are meager in most provinces of the south, though locally important supplies of coal are scattered in the middle-lower Yangtze area and in Szechwan; very large hydroelectric resources exist in the South, however, and several major sites have been developed or are scheduled for future development. A variety of minerals and metals occurs in South China, and nationally important mines are worked supplying tin, tungsten, antimony, manganese, and mercury. Deposits of iron ore in the Yangtze valley provide the basis for a growing iron and steel industry there.

The middle and lower Yangtze plain is the key economic region of South China. Its dominance results from fertile alluvial soils, which permit an intensive agricultural economy to flourish and support very high rural population densities, and from the Yangtze waterway network. The lowlands extend upstream about 1,000 kilometers from the mouth of the Yangtze, narrowing where mountains intersect the river and widening in other areas—principally where major tributary streams join the main stream. Below Nanking the lower Yangtze widens and merges imperceptibly to the north with the Huai River plain. An important physical feature of the middle Yangtze is sizable but fluctuating lakes (Poyang and Tungting Hu) that act as natural flood reservoirs during the summer rainy season. Dikes and levees have been expanded and strengthened to protect valuable farmland and the cities adjoining the river. This region is the major rice growing area in China. North of the Yangtze the common cropping pattern is rice followed by a winter crop of wheat or barley; south of the river double-cropped rice increasingly is grown, often in combination with a winter grain or vegetable.

The importance of the Yangtze waterway system, which permits ocean-going vessels to move upstream to the Wuhan cities, to the economic growth of the Yangtze basin is difficult to overemphasize. The link to Shanghai downstream and to world shipping, coupled with a fecund agricultural hinterland, makes this region potentially one of the most important in all of the People's Republic of China. Shanghai, Nanking, and Wuhan are the major cities and centers of industrial growth, but there are numerous lesser urban centers serving the vast Yangtze hinterland. Shanghai retains its rank as the premier industrial city in China. Mineral deposits, particularly iron ore deposits at Tayeh and Maanshan, provide raw materials needed for continued growth of the metallurgical industries.

The Szechwan Basin (sometimes referred to as the "red basin" because of the color of its soil) has been integrated into the main currents of Chinese civilization and political developments since early times, despite a location deep within China and an encircling belt of forbidding mountains. Economic and political ties were established early with North China, principally a connection with the Chengtu plain (located in the northwestern corner of the basin), where a reliable irrigation system had been built permitting a prosperous agricultural society to develop based on growing irrigated rice. Although the Chengtu plain and a few favored river valleys elsewhere in the basin have long supported large agricultural populations, most of the basin remained forested and lightly populated until about 500 years ago. Savage peasant revolts in the seventeenth century devastated and depopulated large areas, and it took massive immigration from other provinces during the eighteenth and nineteenth centuries, spurred by

Map 5   People's Republic of China: Major Transportation Routes

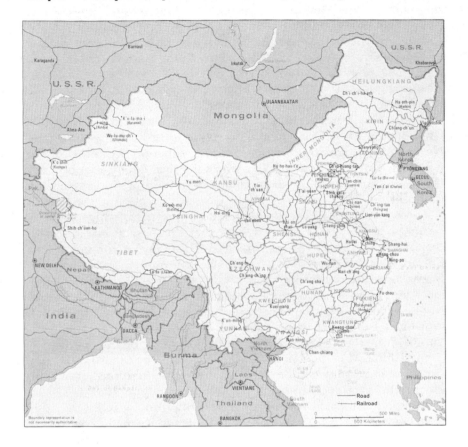

tax incentives, to clear and bring under cultivation most of the land now tilled. Much of this later settlement expanded from the limited lowlands and valleys—possibly no more than 5 percent of the land surface—onto the gentle slopes of the many hills in the basin. Typically, lower terraces are irrigated and planted to rice and upper terraces are devoted to dryfield crops.

The Szechwan Basin is able to support a very high population, estimated presently at about 100 million, because of its famed agricultural productivity—an abundance based on favorable climate (hot summers, mild winters, adequate rainfall, and near year-round growing season) and fertile soil. The amount of rain received in much of the basin is a bit less than for many areas in South China. But the topography and location of the basin are conducive to much cloudiness and high humidity levels—factors that make the Szechwan Basin a disagreeable area to visit or live, but enhance precipitation effectiveness and hence agricultural output. A single crop of rice is the major crop, followed by wheat, rape, or a legume; corn and sweet potatoes are planted in unirrigated fields; and various other crops, fruit, and vegetables also are harvested.

The earlier isolation of Szechwan was broken during the 1950s by a railroad from North China, and later other rail links were completed to provinces to the south and east. The two major cities of the Szechwan Basin, Chungking and Chengtu, are important industrial centers; both cities received industrial impetus from the moving of the Chinese Nationalist government capital to Chungking during the Sino-Japanese War (1937-1945). The energy resources of the basin—sizable amounts of coal and natural gas, and a little oil—are being developed to further economic growth.

The Yunnan-Kweichow plateau region differs markedly from the densely settled Yangtze lowlands and the Szechwan Basin: overall population densities are relatively light; most of the area consists of rough, highly dissected uplands; and a large non-Han Chinese population is scattered throughout parts of the subregion.

Administratively, this region includes all of Kweichow Province and the eastern half of Yunnan, plus some adjoining areas in neighboring provinces. Elevations are highest in the northwest (about 2,000 meters) and gradually lower to about 1,000 meters in the southeast. Higher mountains intersect the plateau surface; most of the higher population concentrations are in river valleys and mountain basins. In Yunnan a series of ancient lake plains with fertile soils provides the proper environment for multiple cropping practices based on growing rice. Parts of the plateau consist of karst topography—a landscape of stone pinnacles, sinkholes, underground streams, and caverns—created from belts of limestone that underlie the land surface. The uneven rate of erosion has in some places created areas so rugged and difficult that they are virtually uninhabited. Even where erosion is less severe, the porosity of the limestone subsurface creates agricultural problems—primarily in maintaining soil moisture and impounding water for irrigation.

The proportion of the non-Han Chinese population ranges from 20 to 30 percent; most of the uplands are settled by Miao, Yi, and lesser groups, and various Tai-related groups inhabit many of the more isolated lowlands. (The best and more accessible lowlands and upland basins, however, usually are occupied by Han Chinese.) Nearly all of these non-Han groups have filtered into these remote and difficult areas during the past several centuries as a result of military and political pressure exerted by Han Chinese who dislodged them from the more fertile lands in other areas of South China.

Major economic development is limited and largely confined to provincial capitals (Kunming and Kweiyang) and a few mining centers. The completion of railroads into both provinces during the past fifteen years is an important factor for a fuller political and economic integration of this formerly backward and isolated region with the rest of China.

In Kwangtung and Kwangsi, the southernmost provinces, the Hsi Chiang (West River) and its tributaries are navigable and provide access deep into the interior. Kwangchow (Canton) is the major port and urban center, and its function is similar to that of Shanghai in terms of trade and access to the interior, though comparable urban and industrial development upstream in the hilly Kwangtung-Kwangsi area is lacking. Canton, however, was the first port opened by the Chinese to world trade; after very early contacts with Arab and other traders, the Portuguese (1516) and other Europeans followed. Canton's "window on the world" role finds expression in the old Chinese saying that "everything new begins in Canton." The remainder of South China consists primarily of a mosaic of narrow river valleys, steep-sided hills and mountains, pockets of alluvial coastal lowland, and small upland basins. In general, the landscapes become more rugged, higher, and less densely populated from east to west. Nearly all of the lowlands and basins are in crops, often with villages huddled on the edge between slopes and valley flats. The unused uplands would appear to be ideal areas for forestry, but a long history of indiscriminate cutting and burning has left few timbered areas, though some progress in reforestation has been made.

Northeast China

Northeast China is a mix of old and new, of lightly populated plains and very large industrial cities, of more pronounced foreign influence than other major regions of China but with ancient cultural and political ties with the Chinese heartland. A major reason for the contrasts and apparent paradoxes of the northeast is that almost all of the settlement, economic development, and foreign influence has been crammed into a brief time frame of less than a century—essentially after

1900. Russia and Japan coveted the fertile and largely empty plains, the forested mountains, and the varied and accessible mineral resources, and both of these countries have had a significant role in the development of the northeast.

Northeast China is about the size of North China but contains less than one-quarter of its population—about 8 or 9 percent of the China mainland total. The broad physical outlines of the northeast are simple: a large northeast-southwest aligned plain, where the bulk of the population lives, surrounded by a horseshoe of relatively low mountains. Although the northeast adjoins North China, a wedge of steppe and rugged uplands extending from the Mongolian Plateau to the sea limits easy access to a narrow strip of coastal plain. Administratively, the northeast consists of the three provinces of Liaoning, Kirin, and Heilungkiang, though physically the western margins of each consist of rolling steppe country more properly part of the Mongolian Plateau region.

Throughout most of China's history the southern margins of the Northeast Plain, essentially the lowlands where the meandering Liao River empties into Po Hai, have been under some form of direct Chinese influence or control and Han settlement. But despite the physical proximity to North China, the remainder of the northeast remained until recent times frontier territory: forbidding, sparsely populated, and only nominally under Chinese dominion. The thin population of the region ranged from small groups who inhabited the forested mountains to more numerous nomadic groups who roamed the rich grasslands of the plains.

The political significance of the northeast has been historically related to locational factors. The western plains and grasslands of the northeast are physically linked to the Mongolian steppe; from this extensive base area nomadic groups frequently threatened, and occasionally controlled, adjacent areas of North China. The Manchus, for example, consolidated their control in the lower Liao Plain, allied themselves with various steppe and forest-based groups, and in time deposed the Ming dynasty and established the Manchu (Ch'ing) dynasty in 1644. During most of the Manchu period, the northeast remained officially a Manchu preserve and a series of edicts banned Chinese settlement in much of the region until late in the nineteenth century. Some Chinese migration had, in fact, taken place earlier, but the lifting of settlement prohibitions resulted in a vast migration of Han Chinese in the early decades of the twentieth century. From a few million at the turn of the century, the population increased rapidly to nearly 50 million by mid-century, and to an estimated 95 million by 1976.

The other major factor in development of Northeast China has been its pivotal location between Russia and Japan. Returning to the Amur-Ussuri frontier in the mid-nineteenth century and regaining the vast Amur basin explored and claimed earlier in the seventeenth century, Russia rapidly developed its Far Eastern territories and began to look south to the largely empty lands and rich resources of China's northeast. An initial Russian goal was to shorten the long haul of the Trans-Siberian Railroad circling the Amur-Ussuri valleys to the port of Vladivostok; hence the investment in and construction of railroads through Chinese territory to shorten this route. Japan, victorious in the Russo-Japanese War (1904-1905), assumed an increasingly important role in development of the northeast. By 1940 the only significant industrialized area in China was in the southern portion of Northeast China centered at Shenyang (Mukden), at that time controlled and occupied by Japan and its products oriented toward Japanese needs.

The core of this region is the Northeast Plain, the largest lowland in all China, which extends north-south for nearly 1,000 kilometers and from east to west for 200 to 400 kilometers. Most of the population and agricultural land, many of the raw materials needed for industry, and the best communications are located on the plain. Although agriculture is hampered by frequent spring droughts and a short growing season, the rich black soil and the availability of land have made the northeast an important grain producer—principally corn, spring wheat, kaoliang, and soybeans. Because of the short growing season and the limitations on the type of crop grown, the amount of land required to feed a farm household is several times greater than in the more productive ricelands of South China. Although the Chinese estimate that several million hectares of additional agricultural land can be put into cultivation, a lack of rainfall deters cultivation along the western margins of the plain and poor drainage is a drawback along the northwestern and northern portions. The opening of additional land to the plow thus will be costly and require significant capital investment to provide for irrigation and drainage facilities. Because of the recent opening and expansion of farmland, the northeast is one of the few areas in China where extensive farming practices—state farms and use of heavy agricultural machinery—are practicable.

The low mountains surrounding the Northeast Plain contain the primary remaining timber reserves in the country. Much of the southeastern uplands adjacent to North Korea were cutover during the

Japanese occupation; to the north, however, the forests of the Greater and Lesser Khingan ranges had barely been exploited prior to 1949. Since then logging rail lines have been pushed into the remote mountains and much timber has been cut.

The marked contrast between the still lightly populated Northeast Plain (except for the southernmost part)—compared to other major agricultural regions—and the string of large industrial cities is one of the more striking features of the northeast. Northeast China is the most urbanized region in China; most of Liaoning Province, for example, is administratively attached to one of several large industrial cities of the province. (The Chinese incorporate sizable rural areas in their major municipalities, primarily to assure food supplies to the city and to aid in industrialization of the countryside.) Though most of the cities have origins as ancient settlements and trading centers, all have mushroomed dramatically in size during the twentieth century. Their appearance is a mixture of influences. Many are well planned with tree-lined avenues and separate industrial and worker housing districts. Much urban growth occurred during the Japanese era, though the architectural legacy of the period is perhaps best forgotten. Russian influence can be seen in the occasional onion-shaped domes of Russian Orthodox churches, a few monuments, and Chinese versions of Russian names for some streets. Russian influence is most noticeable in Luta—the Dairen–Port Arthur area developed by Russian and Japanese capital—and in Harbin, the major city of the northern portion of the Northeast Plain.

Northeast China today retains its primacy as China's major industrial area and as its leading center of heavy industry. Early development of industry was made possible by large deposits of coal, development of hydroelectric power resources, and the availability of various ferroalloys and other minerals. In most cases, reserves are small, but accessibility made them highly important in the initial industrial buildup. Iron and steel, machine tools, structural steel, turbines, generators, and chemicals represent some of the industrial output of the northeast. The industrial importance of Northeast China has been bolstered by the renowned Tach'ing oil field, located northwest of Harbin, which began operating in the early 1960s. Tach'ing probably produces nearly half of China's crude oil. The economic advancement and exploits of Tach'ing workers have been widely publicized in China as the example for all Chinese industry.

Northwest China

Northwest China, sometimes termed the Sinkiang-Mongolia region, is similar to the Tibetan highlands in its size, the low density and non-Han Chinese composition of its population, and lack of direct Chinese rule throughout much of its history. In physical terms, however, the two regions differ greatly. Northwest China includes nearly all of the deserts of China—most of them located deep in basins surrounded by arid mountains. Life in the deserts is concentrated around the rims of the basins where mountain-born streams flow down and supply precious irrigation water needed for agriculture. Exceptions to these generalizations occur in the flanks and intermontane basins of the T'ien Shan and in the eastern and southeastern border lands of the northwest (administratively, Inner Mongolia) where precipitation is sufficient for grazing animals.

The population of the northwest historically has been a mixture of non-Han Chinese peoples, though population pressures elsewhere and large-scale resettlement programs have seen millions of Han Chinese move into areas formerly dominated by minorities. The bulk of Sinkiang's non-Han population consists of Turkic groups, Islamic in religion. The majority are Uighurs, who mostly live in the oases as agriculturalists. The Kazakhs, the second most populous group, are primarily herders. Both Kazakhs and Uighurs, together with lesser numbers of other Turkic groups, are part of a large block of central Asian peoples whose traditional homelands extend across the mountain and steppe country of both China and Russia—an issue exploited in the Sino-Soviet border dispute. The Mongols, another sizable minority group, are scattered along the northern rim of China from Inner Mongolia to Sinkiang. Chinese Muslims, termed Hui, are numerically important, and many live in the province of Ningsia and in the urban centers of the northwest.

Sinkiang (properly the Sinkiang Uighur Autonomous Region) is the key subregion of Northwest China, and it consists physically of two large basins—the Tarim and Dzungarian—separated by the high peaks of the T'ien Shan. The Tarim Basin, the larger of the two, is rimmed by oases with the larger and more productive located in the western and higher end of the basin. The Tarim River collects most of the streams from the western and northern flanks as it meanders eastward towards the lower eastern end of the basin. The Tarim terminates in Lop Nor, a shallow lake of fluctuating size and location, now noted as a site for the testing of atomic weapons. The lake has contained little water in recent years because of the increasing use of the Tarim's water upstream for irrigation. A striking feature of the Tarim Basin is the presence of old, abandoned watercourses, marked by dead or dying trees and shrubs, which extend down into the desert heart of the basin. Some of these old stream valleys have been reclaimed in recent years as new underground water sources have been tapped and small dams and other water control facilities have been built to maximize the available surface water. Grain (wheat and corn) is the principal crop, but locally important amounts of cotton, fruit, and sugar beets also are grown.

The northern (Dzungarian) basin is smaller than the Tarim and contains less desert area; somewhat greater precipitation (upward of 250 mm) in the west and north supports grasslands suitable for grazing. Additionally, the somewhat better resource base of Dzungaria has resulted in a much greater population growth rate than in the Tarim; probably half of Sinkiang's population now lives in the north. The economic development of northern Sinkiang has been fostered by the Karamai oil field and deposits of coal. The major city, Urumchi, is the capital of the province, the only significant industrial center, and the terminus of the railroad connecting Sinkiang with the remainder of China. During the 1950s when China and the Soviet Union were close allies, the trans-Sinkiang railroad was planned to meet with the Soviet rail system at the border—a connection unlikely to be made in the near future. The T'ien Shan and associated mountains that separate the two basins are shaped like a V, with the broad, open end—the agriculturally rich Ili Valley—facing west toward Soviet Central Asia. Because of its largely Kazakh and Uighur population and natural orientation to the west, the Ili area traditionally was (and remains today) one of the most politically sensitive border areas.

The eastern third of Northwest China also consists mainly of deserts, primarily in the western half, and some grasslands in the south and east. Administratively, most of this subregion consists of the Inner Mongolia Autonomous Region (where Han Chinese outnumber Mongols ten to one), the Ningsia Hui Autonomous Region, and part of Kansu Province. The grasslands vary in their use; some of the pasturelands, particularly the more remote, are grazed by nomadic Mongol groups as in the past, but increasingly the nomadic population has been stabilized in permanent settlements where forage crops can be raised, health facilities for man and beast are available, and communication links to more settled areas have been built. Cutting through the Inner Mongolian deserts is the Huang Ho, and from its great northern bend the river is tapped to irrigate sizable areas of farmland settled by Han Chinese. Construction of a railroad linking Paotow, one of the earliest planned industrial bases of the Peking regime, with Lanchow to the west has stimulated additional industry and the economic growth of the entire Yellow River corridor.

The Kansu Corridor, a narrow belt of oases and small settlements, connects the populated centers of North China and the desert basins of Sinkiang. Along this northern flank of the Nan Shan wound the ancient silk route; today the oases of the corridor are connected by road and railroad to provide quick access to China's western frontier. Much of the capital equipment and other supplies needed to upgrade the northwest economically are produced in Lanchow at the eastern entrance to the corridor—a city that has grown enormously from a sleepy frontier town several decades ago to a modern, industrial giant today sprawling for many kilometers along the Huang Ho.

Historically, the northwest has been the most important frontier of China. The Great Wall and other fortifications that date to the earliest years of the Chinese state were attempts to stabilize the frontier and to regulate movement and trade of "barbarian" groups of the inner Asian steppes—groups that periodically threatened the Chinese core area in North China. Farther west in Sinkiang, Chinese frontier policies were twofold. On the one hand there was an interest in maintaining trade links that led through central Asia and eventually to the Mediterranean world; but of even greater import was the need to secure the northwestern frontier from potential invaders. Chinese strategy was to control the grasslands of Dzungaria and to secure the passes over the eastern end of the T'ien Shan that provided egress from central Asia to the Kansu Corridor.

Northwest China presently is a fast-growing region that has witnessed considerable modernization and economic development based on a scattering of energy and mineral resources and aided by modern communications. The paucity of agricultural land and limited water resources, however, will most likely slow and restrict future growth to a more modest pace.

Tibetan Highlands

The Tibetan highlands make up the most distinctive region in China: it is a huge region that comprises nearly a quarter of China's territory; elevations average 4,000 meters, and higher mountains reach heights of 6,000 to 7,000 meters and above; population density is very low, and large areas are uninhabited; communications, though improved, are still difficult and time-consuming; and the Tibetan area has had the least direct central government rule of any of China's major regions.

The Tibetan highlands, which essentially comprise the Tibet-Tsinghai plateau, contain some of the world's most spectacular terrain. The eastern rim of the plateau is crossed by several of the great rivers of Asia—the Huang, Yangtze, Salween, and Mekong—which have entrenched and progressively deepened their courses as they have flowed to the southeast. In places their gorges have knifed down to the 2,000 meter level or lower while, above, the ridges and peaks between the rivers, representing the ancient plateau surface, are at 5,000 to 6,000 meter heights. Since the Yangtze, Mekong, and Salween flow in parallel, northwest-southeast aligned valleys that are less than 50 kilometers apart in some areas, east-west communication across the grain of the topography has been extremely difficult. This belt of formidable terrain has traditionally shielded southern Tibet, including the locus of Tibetan culture and political power centered at Lhasa. The northernmost and highest part of the Tibetan highlands averages some 5,000 meters in elevation. Here the terrain is gently rolling with numerous large basins dotted by brackish lakes—many fringed with salt flats. Rocky outcrops and ridges and a few mountain masses seem relatively low in terms of the relative relief, but in absolute terms peaks occasionally reach 6,000 to 6,500 meters. Only in slightly lower and more favored areas is there sufficient forage to tempt a few nomads with their flocks and herds. High winds sweep across the plateau almost daily, and even in mid-summer sudden storms with hail and snow flurries are not uncommon. Winter cold is intense, and temperatures as low as 40° C have been recorded.

An initial Chinese objective after taking control of Tibet in 1951-1952 was to shorten drastically the journey to Lhasa from Chinese bases in neighboring provinces. By late 1954 two roads generally following ancient caravan trails had been hacked across the mountains and plateau, enabling Chinese truck convoys to reach Lhasa in several days (instead of the previous three-month journey by pack animals). In addition, the Chinese have greatly expanded the road network throughout the Tibetan highlands and most settlements can now be reached by vehicles. The maintenance and upgrading of the network remains a priority effort.

The bond of Tibetan Buddhism and the temporal and spiritual powers embodied in the Dalai Lama traditionally provided a loose form of control over all Tibetan groups, though political control from Lhasa was exercised over only that territory now administratively the Tibetan Autonomous Region. Throughout most of its history, Tibet successfully resisted the yoke of Chinese administrative and political control. Nevertheless, some Chinese influence and presence existed at times, specifically during the eighteenth century when Lhasa's requests for military help to combat external threats or internal dissension led Peking to appoint *ambans* to Lhasa who represented the Chinese central government. Whatever Chinese authority that existed vanished with the demise of the Manchu dynasty in 1911, and from 1912-1951 Tibet was for all practical purposes a de facto independent state.

The bulk of the Tibetan population is concentrated in southern and southeastern Tibet in somewhat lower valleys at elevations between 3,000 and 3,800 meters. Crops grown include barley and a few hardy root crops. The Chinese have experimented with other crops and have attempted to improve farming methods. Grain production has increased; wheat and other crops are raised in increasing amounts; and improvements have been able generally to keep pace with a growing population. Despite this, however, rice and other foodstuffs are shipped to Tibet for use principally by Chinese military, administrative, and other personnel. The extensive grasslands of the Tibetan highlands produce wool, hides, and other animal products for local needs.

Only recently have the basic economic and social patterns of Tibet begun to shift. By the early 1970s communes had been introduced and traditional Tibetan institutions were being gradually modified or supplanted. Small-scale industries, established in Lhasa and a few other locations, and improved communications have introduced a growing variety of consumer goods, which will hasten the decline of the traditional self-sufficient Tibetan economy based on local resources. Some survey work in the Tibetan highlands suggests mineral resources of significance, but any large-scale exploitation awaits further improvements in communications—specifically a railroad now under construction in Tsinghai Province and scheduled to reach Lhasa in the 1985-1990 period.

Transforming the Environment

China has exerted a peculiar fascination on Westerners. Early visitors were impressed by the tidy Chinese rural landscape, by the seeming harmony and symbiotic relationship existing between man and nature as expressed through carefully tended fields of irrigated rice and terraced hillsides. Despite impressions of a "timeless" character to the Chinese landscape, reinforced by paintings of manicured fields and peaceful villages visible through morning mists, China's environment has witnessed dramatic change at the hands of man.

Probably deforestation has been the most pervasive action induced by the works of man. By the late nineteenth century almost no stands of forest remained in the northern provinces, and much of the South China uplands also were largely cut over. Population pressures caused hillsides to be cleared for crops, but timber needs for construction, fuel, and charcoal were contributing factors. The end result was serious erosion that damaged or destroyed both upland fields and lowland plots. Rivers, overburdened with increased loads of sediment, more frequently broke through their protective dikes, causing flooding, crop losses, and famine. The ancient proverb "How old will you be when the Yellow River is clear?" was applicable to a large number of China's rivers.

Landscape Modification Programs

Probably no Chinese government of the past faced greater environmental challenges than did that of Mao Tse-tung in 1949. Decades of civil strife and war and the breakdown or absence of governmental control had left their mark: irrigation systems and flood control facilities were in disrepair, erosion was increasing, and no centrally coordinated planning existed to redress environmental damage. After a brief period of repair and restoration, Peking launched a variety of programs in the early 1950s designed to improve environmental conditions; exhortations to "remake" and "transform" nature were the rallying cry to millions of Chinese peasants.

Chinese environmental programs have involved both large-scale, capital-intensive programs and small, local works requiring little state funding. Chronically troublesome rivers received initial priority. The Huai, whose natural outlet to the sea had long been blocked by silt, was tackled first. Outlets to the sea were constructed, upstream dams built, flood control protection strengthened, and irrigation extended. Basic control of the Huai has been achieved and agricultural benefits derived, but basic problems have not been completely overcome; repair, rebuilding, and additional water conservancy measures continue.

More publicity was generated over the 1955 Yellow River plan. Drafted with the help of Soviet advisors, this ambitious plan called for a series of dams to produce· electricity, provide irrigation water, halt flooding, and improve navigability of China's most destructive river. The major achievement of two decades of work has been the most important: no major flood has taken place on the lower course.

Realization of other objectives of the plan, however, has been less successful. The key Sanmen Dam project, for example, has had serious problems caused by failure to control upstream erosion: the dam has been redesigned, only limited electricity can be generated, supplies of irrigation water are restricted, and use of the reservoir is limited. Several other upstream dams, however, particularly those near Lanchow, are in operation, and electricity produced has been a major factor spurring the immense growth of industry in the Lanchow area. Nevertheless, permanent control of the Huang Ho awaits a solution to the long-term erosion problem in the middle reaches of the river where it flows through the barren loess-mantled hills of Shansi and Shensi provinces.

A third river basin project has been control of the Hai, a short but unruly stream receiving the flow of several tributaries draining the central and northern portions of the North China Plain. Heavy flooding of the northern half of the plain in 1963 led to renewed efforts at control. During the last decade new channels and outlets to the sea have been built, and the flood discharge of the Hai system increased about six times. As with the Huai project, the magnitude of the problem has made difficult the achievement of lasting results, though conditions have improved markedly and the threat of flood damage has greatly lessened.

From the beginning, small-scale projects suitable for villages or groups of villages have been emphasized—improving existing facilities, building small impoundments, digging new irrigation canals, planting trees, and similar tasks. The results of these efforts are evident in almost all parts of China. The countless small ponds and reservoirs, when coupled with the 2,000 large and medium-sized reservoirs built with provincial and state capital, have markedly improved the amount and dependability of water for irrigation. Tree-planting campaigns have been particularly effective in urban areas and along roadsides, but less successful are reforestation efforts in the uplands. Here areas of success are mixed with evidence of limited progress or failure. Selective concentration on key areas has been less apparent than mass campaigns to involve all rural inhabitants. A major problem has been lack of follow-up after planting—watering, treatment of disease, pruning, and similar efforts.

Agricultural Modernization

Peking is now packaging its multiple environmental projects within an overall program of rapid economic modernization. The publicity given over many years to "Learn from Tachai" with its emphasis on self-reliance is being downplayed and subordinated. Policy shifts introduced during 1977-78 stress the acquisition of Western technology and finance and an emphasis on capital intensive projects that can in time make significant contributions to the agricultural sector. For example, Peking planners have revived plans that would transfer surplus water from the lower Yangtze to North China; a number of medium-sized and large key water control projects will be initiated on China's major rivers; and there are renewed plans to reclaim large tracts of land, primarily in the northeastern provinces.

In addition to these major undertakings, China continues to emphasize small-scale, local efforts lumped under a "farmland capital construction" program that includes a variety of tasks ranging from traditional activities like reforestation, irrigation, and drainage to carving out new fields from the hillsides (as in Tachai), enlarging and leveling old fields to permit use of mechanized equipment, and increasing the productivity of existing fields. The goal of mechanizing agriculture is directed primarily at the basic problem of limited land resources. Mechanization reduces peak-period labor needs; in turn it permits labor to be freed to meet the greater demands of an intensified cropping system. Additional irrigation and drainage equipment will help in reducing crop losses caused by drought and flood and aid in expanding the amount of "high and stable yield" farmland.

China's environment has undergone noticeable change. The building of countless storage impoundments, irrigation canals, and new river channels, and the widespread use of pumps to move water to (and from) fields have permitted significant improvements and modifications in Chinese agricultural patterns. Millions of trees planted over twenty years have made urban areas more pleasant and habitable, protected fields from wind and blowing sand damage, provided for construction and fuel needs, and helped in some places to control erosion. Although much waste and replanting was characteristic during the early years, more attention has recently been paid to sound forestry practices. Some of the more extreme landscape modification schemes where hillsides have been torn apart and rebuilt may be questioned as to the economic end result considering the expenditure of labor. More lasting and nationally useful will be the continuation of long-term programs in water and soil conservancy work, with concentration on existing areas of good productivity. All of these environmental modification programs reiterate the pressing need to protect, preserve, and enhance China's scant physical assets. Significant accomplishments have been made in improving China's physical environment, but the task is immense and much still remains to be done.

Bibliography

Atlas: People's Republic of China. Washington, D. C.: Government Printing Office, 1972.

Dreyer, June T. *China's Forty Millions.* Cambridge, Mass.: Harvard University Press, 1976.

Lattimore, Owen. *Inner Asian Frontiers of China.* Boston: Beacon Press, 1962.

Murphey, Rhoades. "Man and Nature in China." *Modern Asian Studies* 1, pt. 4 (October 1967):313-334.

Nickum, James E. *Hydraulic Engineering and Water Resources in the People's Republic of China.* Report of the U.S. Water Resources Delegation (August-September 1974). Stanford, Calif.: United States–China Relations Program, 1977.

Orleans, Leo A. *Every Fifth Child: The Population of China.* Stanford, Calif.: Stanford University Press, 1972.

Plant Studies in the People's Republic of China: A Trip Report of the American Plant Studies Delegation. Washington, D.C.: National Academy of Sciences, 1975.

Richardson, S. D. *Forestry in Communist China.* Baltimore: Johns Hopkins Press, 1966.

Shabad, Theodore. *China's Changing Map: National and Regional Development, 1949-71.* New York: Praeger, 1972.

Tuan, Yi-fu. *China.* Chicago: Aldine Press, 1970.

Wang, K. P. *Mineral Resources and Basic Industries in the People's Republic of China.* Boulder, Colo.: Westview Press, 1977.

2
Recent Population Changes in China

Judith Banister

Population and Development

Population growth and spatial population distribution are very important factors in the development process of any country, including the People's Republic of China (P.R.C.).[1] In the early phases of development, historical mortality levels are greatly reduced, but fertility levels remain high, causing a period of very rapid population growth. For example, it is common today for the population of a developing country to increase at a rate of 2 percent a year or more. China's population size has increased at approximately this rate since the early 1950s. A 2 percent annual population growth rate doubles a country's population size in thirty-five years.[2] If the country has managed to double production in all sectors of the economy during the same thirty-five-year period, a difficult feat, per capita production levels would not have increased at all. Therefore, any developing country faces the challenge of increasing production levels much faster than population growth, so that popular living standards may be increased and the historical poverty cycle may be broken. The P.R.C. has faced this challenge by emphasizing rapid increases in agricultural and industrial production, while trying to reduce the country's rate of population growth through fertility control.

As the population of a developing country increases rapidly, it is typical for the agricultural sector to be unable to provide enough employment for everyone living in the countryside. Therefore people move toward the big cities seeking work. The usual result is a phenomenon called "overurbanization." Large numbers of rural dwellers migrate to the cities to live in makeshift squatters' settlements and attempt to make enough income to survive. It is not unusual for 20

Map 6   China: Population Density

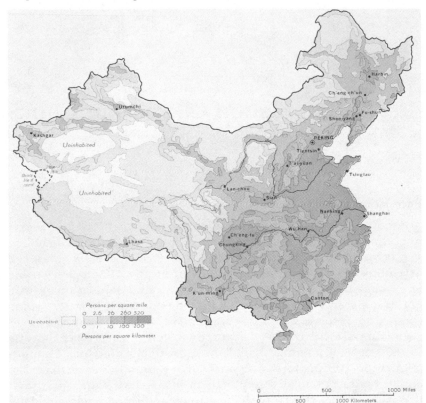

to 50 percent of a city's labor force in a developing country to be
underemployed, doing either no paid work or extraneous tasks that
bring them some food or a little money. China has vigorously attacked
this process by attempting to provide employment for everyone in the
countryside, by trying to prevent rural-to-urban migration, and by
moving urban dwellers to border regions or to wherever they might be
more fully employed.

Since 1949, the population of the P.R.C. has gone through a rapid
transformation. Mortality levels declined very quickly during the 1950s,
but this trend was reversed during and after the Great Leap Forward of
the late 1950s. Since the Great Leap period, infant as well as overall
mortality levels have declined to those attained only by the more
advanced countries of the developing world. Fertility in China remained

at or above traditional levels right up to 1963. Most developing countries still retain such a high birth rate. Since the early 1960s, however, China's rapid societal transformation combined with one of the world's most thorough family planning programs has caused a fast reduction in fertility, particularly in those populous provinces that are leading in their birth rate declines. In addition, China has managed to limit, control, and direct internal migration to avoid or reverse over-urbanization in the major cities, while population growth has been unusually rapid in some of China's sparsely populated regions.

A Brief History of China's Population

There is very little statistical information available on pre-1949 patterns of marriage, fertility, and mortality in China. One of the best sources of such information was a survey of rural agricultural households in many provinces of China during 1929-1931. The demographic data from this survey were recently reanalyzed by a group of demographers at Princeton University, who reported the following generalizations about rural agricultural families in the China of 1929-1931:[3] marriage was early and universal in rural Chinese society; women married at age 17.5 on the average, men at age 21.3; almost no men or women remained single. One might expect that, since almost everyone married at a young age, reproduction would have begun early and resulted in very high total fertility levels for each woman. Contrary to expectation, fertility was only moderately high in these Chinese rural farm families. Each woman had, on the average, only 5.5 births in her lifetime if she lived through her reproductive years. It is unclear why fertility was not much higher in such households. One theory suggests that poor nutrition and endemic diseases resulted in sterility and subfecundity in a significant proportion of the population. Another possible explanation is that social norms or temporary economic conditions encouraged sexual abstinence or the use of primitive birth control and abortion techniques to keep down the number of births to each couple.

The Princeton analysts also concluded that mortality levels in rural Chinese society were very high during 1929-1931. They found that the expectation of life at birth was very low, only 23.7 years for females and 24.6 years for males.[4] Infant mortality was extraordinarily high, about 300 deaths during the first year of life per thousand live births. Such high mortality levels resulted in an estimated crude death rate of 41.5 per thousand population. This high death rate was balanced by an estimated crude birth rate of 41.2 per thousand population.[5] In other words, these data suggest that the rural agricultural part of China's population in about 1930 existed in a state of traditional population equilibrium, a situation of approximately zero population growth with high mortality balancing the traditional fertility level.

The Princeton demographers speculated that these data from 1929-1931 actually give us a glimpse into China's more remote past, because rural agricultural families were the most traditional sector of China's population during this century. Indeed, this picture of early and universal marriage, moderately high fertility, and very high mortality may be typical of many periods in China's past. There were also many centuries, however, when China's population grew rapidly in size, which means that fertility levels exceeded mortality levels to a significant degree. Overall, China's total population size grew slowly and sporadically from about 40 to 50 million in 1000 A.D. to a count of 583 million in 1953. This averages out to an annual population growth rate of about 0.27 percent. Therefore the long-term trend during this millenium was not zero population growth but rather a slight excess of births over deaths.

As of 1949, when the P.R.C. was founded, China was still a traditional society with high mortality and at least moderately high fertility levels. Since then, its people have been experiencing rapid "demographic transition" from high fertility and mortality levels to low ones. In the thirty years since 1949, some of China's cities and provinces have almost completed this transition, while others have reduced mortality but retain traditional fertility practices.

China is the world's most populous country. Between one-fifth and one-fourth of the world's total population lives on the China mainland. Therefore China's rapid achievement of vastly improved mortality conditions and very marked fertility reduction is significant on a world scale. P.R.C. population policies are beginning to serve as a model for other developing countries.

Changing Population Policies in China

During the earliest years of the P.R.C., Chinese leaders believed that there would be no population problem in China. They followed the Marxist theory that "overpopulation" is really a condition brought about by the exploitation of workers and the contrived unemployment common in capitalist economic systems. It was felt that the P.R.C., being a socialist system, would have no problem providing food, employment, and other basic human needs for its population, even if the country's population began increasing rapidly due to reduced mortality.

The P.R.C. government, however, inherited the world's most populous country. Its people were densely populated on the arable land and already pressing hard on the agricultural resource base. This realization dawned on Chinese leaders during the 1950s, as the country's death rate declined precipitously and the already huge population began increasing at a rate of more than 2 percent per year. During several years in the mid-1950s, increases in agricultural production did not keep pace with increases in population, and the continuing risk of food shortages during bad crop years became obvious.

In addition, the best count ever made of China's population took place during 1953-1954. It was discovered, once the census was completed, that the P.R.C. had about 100 million more people than had been estimated by the Nationalist government prior to 1949 and by various population experts. The enormity of China's population and the prospect of its rapid increase caused a reversal of the early P.R.C. pronatalist population policy. In 1956, the country's first family planning program began. This initial attempt to reduce fertility used the media to teach about contraceptive methods and to change traditional attitudes regarding birth control. Laws that had prohibited abortion and sterilization were abolished. Factories began or expanded production of condoms, diaphragms, and spermicides, while research and field trials were conducted on intrauterine devices (IUDs) and on the world's first vacuum aspiration abortion apparatus. An attempt was made to set up local and provincial committees to promote birth control.

The first family planning program was short-lived, however. At the beginning of the Great Leap Forward, launched in 1958, Chinese leaders thought that they had found the key to overcoming bottlenecks in China's economic system. They believed that growth in all kinds of production would finally "leap forward" ahead of population growth and that rapid population growth would cease to be a problem. Therefore they abandoned the birth control promotion campaign and cut back on the production of contraceptives.

The Great Leap failed to attain its immediate goal of rapid increases in agricultural and other kinds of production. Population growth continued while production levels fell. A period of food shortages and economic depression resulted during 1959-1961.

In 1962, when the economy began to show signs of recovery, a new birth planning program was launched. This time province-level birth control committees were set up to guide the program. The media campaign emphasized the importance of late marriage as well as birth control. Sterilization, abortion, and IUDs were popularized in addition to the barrier birth control methods.

The second birth control campaign was visible in the P.R.C. press for four years, but family planning publicity suddenly ceased in 1966 as the Cultural Revolution escalated. After a short period of policy confusion, all factions of the government reemphasized their dedication to promoting late marriage and birth planning. As the Cultural Revolution wound down in about 1969, the family planning program was accorded the top priority status that it has retained ever since. Not even the recent deaths of Chou En-lai and Mao Tse-tung and the leadership shifts that followed have weakened government resolve to reduce China's rate of population growth as quickly as possible.

The current family planning campaign is guided by a national birth planning committee in Peking, in addition to provincial, county, city, and local birth planning groups. The birth control pill has been added to the list of available birth control techniques, and since about 1971 the government has provided the pill, IUDs, abortion, and sterilization free of charge. The media promote late marriage and birth control, especially by popularizing the successes of some of the leading communes, cities, prefectures, and provinces in birth control work.

Population Data Collection and Reporting

The People's Republic of China has emphasized the collection and calculation of certain kinds of population data and indices. Because of the government's concern with reducing mortality to low levels, death registration is required and crude death rates are frequently calculated at local levels and periodically calculated at the provincial and national levels. Because of the desire to raise marriage ages as a means of fertility reduction, marriage age targets are set locally and the proportions marrying at or above those ages are often recorded. To monitor the effects of the vigorous family planning program, contraceptive use data are collected at the local level and contraceptive use rates by birth control method are occasionally calculated. Because of the urgency and high priority given to reducing crude birth rates and rates of natural population increase, national, provincial, and local targets are set and frequent compilations from the birth and death registration systems monitor the success or failure of family planning efforts. Finally, because of the emphasis on strict control of internal migration, local areas are required to maintain a system of permanent population registration, which is coupled with the rationing system. From these registers, periodic counts of the population can be made.

The P.R.C. government is extremely secretive about its ongoing population data collection efforts and their results. Any discussion of population matters tends to cause uneasiness among Chinese leaders because of their reversal, in practice, of Marxist population doctrine. Only a tiny proportion of the collected population data has been reported in the P.R.C. press, in radio broadcasts, in official briefings to visiting foreign delegations, and in speeches at international meetings. The data thus reported tend to come from the most advanced provinces, cities, counties, and rural communes, and only occasionally from more ordinary units. Nevertheless, my compilation and analysis of such data has enabled me to assess the progress so far in the demographic transitions of a large number of China's provinces.

The P.R.C. has not taken a second census since that of 1953-1954, perhaps because the task is enormous, expensive, and time-consuming. The P.R.C. government, however, is not known to shrink from important tasks just because they are difficult. A more likely reason for the lack of a second census is that the taking of a census would have to be publicized so that the Chinese people would know what was expected of them, and after the census, China's leaders would be bombarded with the question, "Well, how many people did you count in China?" Government leaders are afraid of a large count and its implications for per capita production and consumption figures in many sectors of the economy. The government does not like to give ammunition to detractors of the new China, who might use the census total to point out that per capita grain production has hardly increased at all since 1953, and that general per capita living standards are still very low.

Though no actual census count has been taken since 1953 for all of China, two registration counts have apparently been taken from the permanent population registers, both times with utmost secrecy. Throughout the late 1960s, there were "rumors" that a national population count had been taken in 1964, which included the collection and compilation of birth and death registration data as well as population totals. Finally in 1972, Chou En-lai confirmed that such a count had been taken in 1964. Similarly, there are now "rumors" that a national count was taken about 1972, and that this count also included a compilation of birth and death registration data.[6] It can be predicted that within the next five or ten years, some P.R.C. leader will confirm that this count was taken. So far, the government seems to have taken a count of the population about once each decade, in 1953, 1964, and 1972. These decennial registration counts may provide the groundwork for a future true census in China every ten years.

In both 1964 and 1972, local areas were apparently required to report their total population size as of a particular day, broken down by sex, age group, nationality, and occupation, and the total number of births and deaths registered during the one-year period preceding the count. These data were successively compiled at the county and municipal level, the provincial level, and the national level. The crude birth rates, crude death rates, and natural population increase rates recorded for each political unit were then used as the base point for monitoring subsequent results of the family planning campaigns in progress. For example, during the Fourth Five-Year Plan of 1971-1975, the national government reportedly stipulated that all cities and municipalities should strive to reduce their natural population increase rates to 10 per thousand population (1.0 percent annual population increase), and all counties, communes, and provinces should aim for a nat- ural population increase rate of 15 per thousand (1.5 percent) by 1975. Vital rates were calculated for 1972 from the registra- tion count, and subsequent compilations were made to monitor any progress from the 1972 rates toward the 1975 target. In many provinces, annual province-wide meetings of local family planning personnel were held to assess the previous year's progress and to upgrade the persuasive skills of the birth control motivators from all the less successful units.

It is incorrect to argue that the P.R.C. government does not have any good idea, and does not care to know, how many people there are in China or what the birth and death and natural population increase rates are for the whole country and all its subunits. Such information is of vital concern at all levels of China's government and is gathered and monitored frequently. Furthermore, the government believes these data to be correct as an order of magnitude, and planning at all levels is based partly on the population data so collected. Nevertheless, it is possible to use demographic techniques on the reported population data to demonstrate that there is some underregistration of births and deaths in China, and that the Chinese government is therefore underestimating its present levels of fertility and mortality. It also appears that the P.R.C. government undercounted its population in the 1964 and 1972 counts.[7] Though the recorded and collected P.R.C. population data are imperfect, they are very useful for monitoring changes from one time to another. For example, even if births are always underregistered by 10 percent, recorded annual birth rate declines usually reflect a genuine decrease in the actual birth rate of a commune or city or province.

Health and Mortality

Among developing countries, the P.R.C. has an unusually good preventive health care network, which emphasizes the prevention of epidemics through vaccination, personal and public hygiene, control of human waste, and the interruption of disease vector cycles. This public health work was begun in earnest during the early 1950s. Periodic patriotic health campaigns exhorted everyone to take part in cleaning up the environment and killing pests like mosquitoes and flies. By about 1957, China's death rate may have been halved from pre-1949 levels.

During the Great Leap Forward and the early 1960s, however, some aspects of the preventive public health system languished for lack of funds and personnel. Some diseases, such as schistosomiasis, which had been vigorously attacked during the 1950s, staged a temporary resurgence. Most important, people's resistance to disease was lowered by malnutrition during the food shortages and economic dislocations. As a result, the death rate probably rose for a few years. The extent of the rise is unknown, perhaps even to China's government, since the country's statistical system broke down along with the economic and public health systems.

Since the early 1960s, the P.R.C.'s preventive health network has become pervasive. Vaccination programs have spread to more areas of the countryside. Remote areas that were hardly touched by the public health campaigns of the 1950s have now been incorporated into the disease prevention programs. In particular, minority group areas and sparsely populated border regions have now been included.

Tibet is the last area of China to introduce basic public health measures. As of late 1975, the Tibetan region still had a crude death rate of around 20 per thousand population, very similar to the death rate of Nepal just across the border.[8] A crash program to reduce Tibet's death rate was belatedly introduced in 1973, but much remains to be done. The following radio broadcast from late 1976 indicates that basic environmental sanitation and preventive health care are only now reaching beyond Lhasa in Tibet:

> There are some 8,000 barefoot doctors, health workers, and midwives in Tibet. Following the establishment of cooperative medical service, some

100 cooperative medical service stations have been built in various parts of
Tibet on a trial basis. A movement to control water and nightsoil, to
rebuild wells, latrines, stables, and cooking stoves and to improve
environmental hygiene has just begun in the countryside and pastoral
areas.[9]

Curative medical care has become available to China's people much
more slowly than public health programs. Even today, the P.R.C. still
has a shortage of fully trained doctors. During the 1950s, only some
urban residents had access to modern medical care, while other urban
people and almost all rural residents were without doctors. As a result,
city death rates declined much faster than rural mortality levels.

During the 1960s, under Mao Tse-tung's prodding, there was a radical
shift in China's medical system toward meeting the needs of rural
people. In 1965, he directed that highest priority for health care should
be given to rural areas. Immediately thereafter, the training of "barefoot
doctors" began. Now, only fourteen years later, there are 1.5 million of
these paramedics in China. Their job is to provide primary medical care
to all rural people.

A barefoot doctor is usually a young person who has achieved
a medium educational level, such as graduation from junior middle
school. These young people are trained for a short period of time,
perhaps six months, in a county hospital or training center, or in the
health center in their own commune. They are full members of their
village production teams, where they return after this minimal training
to do part-time agricultural work and part-time medical work. They
receive frequent refresher courses and additional medical training, often
given by visiting medical teams from the cities. The barefoot doctor is
the entry point into China's rural medical system today. A sick or
injured person goes to the barefoot doctor first, except in cases of dire
emergency, and the barefoot doctor handles most cases and refers some
patients to the commune medical center. A commune of 50,000 people
may have just a few doctors who work at its hospital, so the paramedics
send to these doctors only the cases needing expert medical care.

The number of rural medical personnel has also been expanded by the
very minimal training of volunteer health workers who staff village or
production brigade health stations. In addition, midwives have been
trained in great numbers to provide safe delivery in normal childbirths
and to give pre- and postnatal care.

Paramedical workers have been trained to supplement the small number of fully trained doctors, but, in addition, the availability of skilled medical doctors in the countryside has been expanded by several means. First, the P.R.C. greatly shortened the number of years of training for doctors, from seven years for all doctors during the 1950s down to two, three, or four years for doctors during the early 1970s.[10] Though many of China's doctors still work primarily in city hospitals, the policy in effect since 1965 is that every urban hospital should have between one-fourth and one-third of its doctors in the countryside at any one time, either on assignment to mobile medical teams or to a rural commune hospital. The urban doctors work in rural areas on a rotating basis.

The availability of curative medical care in the countryside has also been expanded by the incorporation of traditional Chinese doctors into the medical system and their training in advanced traditional and modern medical techniques. In 1958, traditional and Western medicine were decreed to have equal status. Then Mao's directive in 1965 called for the full integration of Chinese and Western medicine, in part through the barefoot doctors who are trained in the use of acupuncture and herbal medicine.[11] When barefoot doctors refer patients to the commune hospital, these patients often prefer to be treated by a traditional Chinese doctor. Practitioners of traditional Chinese medicine handle a large proportion of the total volume of medical complaints in China today.

The great majority of people in China's countryside now have some access to curative medical care. One method of evenly distributing medical care has been the development of production brigade cooperative health plans. The production brigade is an intermediate level of organization between the production team, or natural village, and the commune. Using this system, brigade members pay a few dollars a year for full medical care, which is heavily subsidized by communally earned income from the sale of grain and other products. The following radio broadcast describes the progress made in the spread of cooperative health plans and in the training of barefoot doctors and other paramedical personnel:

> A health network that includes mother and child health care centres at the county, people's commune and production brigade levels and midwifery centres at production teams covers the 80% of the Chinese population that lives in the countryside. China's constitution stresses State protection of mothers and children, who account for 70% of the population. More than 85% of the production brigades have set up their own cooperative medical service today, particularly since the start of the Cultural Revolution in

1966. Of the 1,500,000 "barefoot" doctors in the countryside, one-third are women. In addition, there are 3,900,000 part-time rural medical workers and midwives. Some 1,000,000 city doctors have gone to the countryside in the past few years to help with rural medical service.[12]

Due to the continuing emphasis on preventive public health measures and to the slowly increasing provision of curative medical care throughout China, rates of mortality and morbidity declined during the 1960s and have certainly continued to decline in most rural areas during the 1970s. After the apparent attempt to gather nationwide data on the number of births and deaths recorded in local areas, the P.R.C. reported a 1972 national crude death rate of 7.6 per thousand population.[13] Though there is still some underregistration of deaths in China, particularly neonatal deaths, it is reasonable to assume that the P.R.C. has achieved a crude death rate of 10 per thousand population during the 1970s. Many other countries in Asia have attained a similarly low death rate, but these are often small countries, while the other populous Asian countries continue to have higher death rates than that of China.

Fertility

During the 1950s, fertility rates stayed at their historical levels. In fact, it is possible that the crude birth rate, along with other fertility measures such as the period total fertility rate and the net reproduction rate, increased above traditional levels. I hypothesize that this happened, partly because China probably had a postwar baby boom after decades of war had forced the postponement of many marriages and births. Also, it is likely that the rapid improvements in health and length of life decreased sterility and subfecundity in the general population and increased the length of time that couples lived together before one of them died. In addition, social and economic changes weakened some customs that had limited fertility, such as traditional restrictions on the remarriage of widows. In some other developing countries, fertility rose as mortality declined during the early phase of the demographic transition, and China may have followed this pattern.[14]

Officially reported P.R.C. birth rates for the 1950s were 37 per thousand in 1952-1953 and 34 per thousand in 1957, with some vacillation during the intervening years.[15] The early estimate came from sample surveys, and the 1957 estimate may have come from vital registration data. These reported birth rates are far too low for the 1950s, when China's population was still basically a noncontracepting population. It must be assumed that underregistration and under-reporting of births continued to be serious throughout the decade.

There is very little evidence that the first fertility reduction campaign of 1956-1958 had any immediate impact on fertility, even in China's cities. Toward the end of the campaign, it was stated that the supply of contraceptives then available was sufficient to meet the needs of only about 2.2 percent of all couples in the childbearing ages.[16] The medical establishment waged a battle against performing abortion and sterilization operations even when these operations had been legalized. In practice, the availability of birth control services and the organization of personalized motivational work for fertility control never reached beyond a few cities during the 1950s.

During the Great Leap Forward and its aftermath, there may have been some temporary dip in the birth rate due to economic depression and malnutrition. The population retained its traditionally high fertility right up through 1963, however, according to recently reported data for a few scattered locations.[17] Only Shanghai city proper has reported a very significant birth rate decline by 1963. But both Peking and Sian municipalities reported crude birth rates of more than 40 per thousand for 1963. Except for one county near Canton, no suburban or rural areas had claimed tangible fertility decline by 1963.

The second fertility reduction campaign of 1962-1966, however, had a powerful impact on the birth rates of some cities, according to the reported information. Some suburban areas also reported rapid birth rate declines between 1963 and 1966. Rural areas experienced a lag time before their fertility rates began declining. Evidence from interviews of Hong Kong refugees from the P.R.C. in 1965 indicated that rural women, at least in Kwangtung Province next to Hong Kong, had been affected by the propaganda campaign for birth control.[18] Of the small sample of 125 refugee women, 95 percent claimed unequivocally to approve of birth planning, and 60 percent knew about the IUD. But only one-fourth of these women knew of any family planning services available in their own villages, and only 2 percent reported any known use of birth control in their villages. The interviewees were still producing babies at the traditional rate. As a result of this apparent rural lag between attitudinal changes and the practice of birth control, China's overall fertility level stayed fairly high at least through 1965.

During the Cultural Revolution period, there was seemingly no attempt at nationwide population data collection, so there is a big gap in reported vital rate data between 1965-1966 and 1971-1972. But those few rural localities and whole provinces that have now reported vital rates for both before and after the Cultural Revolution all claimed a significant drop in their birth rates or natural population increase rates.[19] What was the cause of this apparent fertility decline in relatively progressive rural areas during the Cultural Revolution period?

The solution to this puzzle seems to lie in the rapidly expanding network of rural medical services after 1965. I suggest that the second fertility reduction campaign during 1962-1966 reached many rural areas, raising people's motivation to control their fertility and creating a receptive climate for family planning services. It was not until the expansion of the rural medical system, however, that such family planning services actually became available in the villages and production brigade clinics. This process happened gradually during the late 1960s and is continuing today in more remote areas. One of the main skills required of barefoot doctors is that they be knowledgeable about birth control techniques and able to perform at least outpatient surgical birth control procedures.

During the Cultural Revolution years, while many rural areas and even whole provinces were experiencing birth rate declines, some of the most advanced urban and suburban areas reported a slight rise in their crude birth rates from the low levels in 1965 or 1966. The apparent cause of the temporary birth rate increases was a rush to "get married early," once the extreme pressure to delay marriage experienced during 1962-1966 was relaxed. The Communist Party was unable to enforce the late marriage policy during early Cultural Revolution years because of struggles and disarray among the leadership. When postponed marriages are carried out all at once, a rush of first births soon follows, especially in the P.R.C. where it is still the custom to use no contraception between marriage and the first birth.

During the 1970s, the P.R.C. is in a state of very rapid demographic transition, characterized by a huge range of birth rates, death rates, natural population increase rates, contraceptive use rates, infant mortality rates, and ages at marriage from one geographical area to another. Therefore it is very risky to extrapolate from experiences in one part of China to the country as a whole. Reported crude birth rates (or birth rates derived from other reported rates) range from under 17 per thousand population in the most advanced provinces of Kiangsu and Hopeh up to more than 40 per thousand in Tibet. In some parts of China, the current vigorous family planning program seems to be doing very well in encouraging late marriage and high rates of contraceptive use, resulting in rapid declines in recorded birth rates and natural increase rates.

The national government in Peking is very circumspect about reporting estimated national crude birth rates for different years during the 1970s, but data from several official briefings to foreign scholars and officials suggest the following generalization: the national government estimates that China's national crude birth rate declined from about 26 to 27 per thousand population in 1972 to "a little over 20 per thousand" in 1974 and 1975.[20] My computer projections of China's population from the 1953 census to the present indicate that China's actual crude birth rate is likely to be higher than this during the 1970s. If China's birth rate were actually this low, then the country would be heading steadily toward the achievement of replacement level fertility in about 1980.[21] I estimate that this projection based on official birth rate data is too optimistic, given the considerable number of populous provinces in China that are reporting slow progress and many difficulties in their efforts to reduce fertility. Therefore I conclude that the P.R.C. still has a problem of underregistration of births, which produces an underestimate of the birth rate calculated from vital registration data.

In spite of some underregistration of births and deaths, the general picture of China's demographic transition is clear. The country's death rate declined drastically during the 1950s, rose somewhat during about 1958-1961, and has declined to a comparatively low level at the present time. China's birth rate stayed high through 1963 and has declined in a wavelike pattern since then, beginning with the cities, followed by suburban areas, then nearby rural areas, and finally more remote rural areas. Some sparsely populated border and minority regions of China continue to have traditionally high birth rates today.

Population Growth

The growth of China's population since 1949 has been due primarily to the difference between births and deaths, because international migration has been negligible compared to the huge total size of China's population. During the 1950s, China's rate of population growth rose to more than 2 percent per year, due mostly to the rapid mortality decline during that decade. The economic and food supply problems experienced during 1958-1961 may have increased mortality levels enough to reduce the rate of population growth to less than 2 percent annually for a year or two.

During the 1960s, the P.R.C. may have reached its peak rate of population growth. Three provinces, now some of the most advanced ones in their demographic transitions, reported natural population increase rates in the 2.5 to 2.95 percent range for about 1965.[22] In these leading provinces, death rates had declined after the Great Leap, but birth rates had declined significantly only in some cities by 1965, while fertility remained high in rural areas. Thereafter, birth rate declines in these provinces were extremely rapid, especially during 1972-1976. The natural increase rates of these provinces are now reported to be in the range from under 1.0 percent to 1.5 percent. In the short period of fourteen years, at least three populous provinces have essentially completed their demographic transitions from high fertility to low fertility, and more provinces are following close behind, according to the data available.

It was reported to a visiting group in 1973 that China had lowered its rate of population growth to 1.9 percent a year.[23] This estimate may have come from the nationwide compilation of vital registration for 1972. Since then, many populous provinces have claimed steadily declining natural population increase rates, which they have recorded in the process of monitoring annual provincial vital rates. Nevertheless, many other provinces have not reported any declines in their natural population increase rates, which should dictate caution in assuming that the P.R.C. as a whole is experiencing a current population growth rate below about 1.5 percent annually.

Age Structure

China was and still is a developing country with a young population, in contrast to those developed countries where greater and greater proportions of the population are now in the older ages. A "young" population can attain a much lower crude death rate than an "old" population, simply because old people are more likely to die than young people, especially after infant mortality levels are greatly reduced. If a developing country with a young population provides reasonably high levels of preventive and curative medical care for the general population, it is potentially able to achieve a crude death rate as low as the 5 per thousand population regularly recorded in Taiwan. A crude death rate in the 7 to 10 per thousand range for the P.R.C. during the 1970s is not an unreasonable estimate, given China's still-young age structure and rapidly improving rural medical system. Low crude death rates like these contribute to rapid population growth, because it is very difficult if not impossible to reduce a developing country's crude birth rate to such low levels.

Detailed data on China's age structure today are almost totally unavailable, except for the age structure of one district of Shanghai for 1971. It is possible, however, to derive a plausible current P.R.C. age structure by beginning with the reported 1953 census age structure or an adjusted one, and using a computer population projection package to project the population forward every year up to the present. Many guesses and assumptions have to be made in this process, because China's exact fertility and mortality conditions for every year since 1953 are not known. These data must be estimated from officially reported data for some years with interpolations in between, and with the use of model schedules of age-specific fertility and mortality rates.

Very interesting patterns of changing age distribution emerge from this projection. During the 1950s and early 1960s, generally speaking, China had high fertility but fast-declining mortality at all ages, especially at young ages. Thus, for about fifteen years, most of the enormous numbers of children being born were continuing to live, instead of dying before reaching adulthood as many of them would have done in previous decades. This produced a bulge in the age structure composed of young children. As China's overall fertility began declining after 1963, each year's new cohort of births became a smaller proportion of the population than previous birth cohorts, and the bulge in the age structure receded among young children with each passing year.[24] Since then, however, the large number of people born between about 1952 and about 1965 are growing up. The oldest of these, born in 1952 or 1953, began childbearing in the mid-1970s. Not until 1995 will these huge cohorts have completed their childbearing. Thus, even if China attains replacement level fertility very soon, the birth rate will continue to be much higher than the death rate, and China's population will continue growing at a rate of about 1.4 percent a year through 1995. The only way that China can reduce its rate of population growth much below that rate, except for some catastrophe that would raise the death rate, is to persuade people to lower their fertility below replacement level. In other words, the one-child and the childless family would need to become much more popular, and other life-styles, like nonmarriage and homosexual relationships, might need to become more acceptable.

It does not seem likely that such changes will happen during the next decade, but China's government is so determined to reduce the country's population growth rate that it may begin encouraging greater tolerance of low fertility life-styles.

Total Population Size

Ever since the early 1960s, the P.R.C. government has consistently used low population totals in its press reports. The disparity between China's actual population size and the rhetorical total used in its press has reached absurd levels. Usually, whenever a newspaper article or radio broadcast needs to use some number for China's total population size, the figure "800 million" is used. Yet no sensible projection of the mainland China population since the 1953 census can come up with a total population of less than 980 million for year-end 1978. To keep the total that low, one must assume a population growth rate just below a reasonable range for every year since the 1950s. It is more likely that China's population has already passed 1 billion people.

Though the P.R.C. government has not taken a true census or anything resembling a true census since 1953, it has apparently attempted a nationwide count of the population based on the permanent population registers as recently as 1972 and perhaps even more recently. Unless the population registration system is hopelessly nonfunctional, the government in Peking knows that its population now totals well over 950 million people.

Due to the unwillingness of P.R.C. leaders to overcome their ideological biases on population matters, however, they have so far been unable to deal openly and rationally with the actual size of China's population. Rather, in order to maintain the fiction that China has 100-200 million people fewer than the actual number, it has apparently been necessary to forbid provincial leaders to reveal the true population size of their provinces. Otherwise any intelligent person could add up the current provincial population totals to get a more correct current national population total.

The leaders of most of China's populous provinces regularly understate their provincial population size. Occasionally some signal seems to be given that allows provincial leaders to raise the rhetorical population totals they use publicly. For example, when Mao Tse-tung died in late 1976, the published formal condolences sent in from many provinces revealed much higher population totals than these provinces had previously used. My theory is that provincial leaders were told, as Mao's death approached, that they could use that occasion to release their 1972 population counts. Many provinces did so, while others have not yet released their 1972 population totals, and some seem to have released their true current population totals instead. It is not clear why some provinces have released 1975 or 1976 population totals while most others have not. Incidentally, the silliness of the population numbers game played by the P.R.C. government is illustrated by the fact that the provincial population totals released after Mao's death added up to over 910 million while the newspaper articles and speeches releasing these totals had titles like "800 Million People Deeply Mourn Our Great Leader and Teacher Chairperson Mao, and Vow to Carry His Future Work of Proletarian Revolution Through to the End."[25]

Population Distribution

Published data documenting internal migration within China are very scarce. In general, the government attempts to prevent people from moving their residences unless such a move is specifically planned and organized by the government. The mechanisms for preventing internal migration are the location-specific rationing of cotton cloth and some staple foods, and the requirement that a person be offered a job in another place and have the permission of her or his present work unit to leave before the move will be allowed. It is so difficult to move that the P.R.C. has remained a geographically immobile society in which most people continue to live where they were born or very nearby.[26]

The government allows and encourages certain types of internal migration, however. Ever since the early 1950s, there has been some movement from densely populated areas of China to the more sparsely populated border, mountainous, and desert regions. This movement has not made much of a dent in the provinces that the migrants have left, but has strongly affected the receiving areas. In the first place, most such migrants are members of the dominant Han Chinese nationality, which comprised an overwhelming 94 percent of China's population as of the 1953 census. These Han Chinese migrants go to areas where minority groups live, steadily shifting the ethnic balance toward Han numerical superiority in China's border regions. In addition, the migrants are usually young, educated, and dedicated to socialism, so they tend to run the governments, schools, factories, and development projects in the areas to which they move. Therefore this government-sponsored migration flow to the sparsely populated areas of China serves to consolidate government and Party control over these regions and promotes rapid social and economic development and urbanization in previously backward areas. The influx also causes resentment among the more than fifty different minority groups whose cultural identities, languages, religions, and control of their former territories are threatened.[27]

The other major type of migration flow in the P.R.C. has occurred within each province or to nearby provinces. There has been constant pressure from rural residents who want to move to cities, because living standards are still much better in the cities. During the 1950s, city populations mushroomed, and city governments began the policy of forcing the in-migrants to return to the countryside. This policy continues in China's biggest cities, some of which claim to have stabilized or almost stabilized their population sizes. Meanwhile, however, some rural-to-urban migration has been permitted into newer or smaller cities where factories are being built and workers are needed.

The other major intraprovincial movement has been the migration of young adults just after they finish middle school from the cities where they were born and raised to the countryside. This was an unpopular policy that was formally rescinded in January 1979. Those young adults for whom city jobs were not available were required to move to rural communes. Many of them settled down there, while others moved on, often to other towns or cities where the job market was expanding. This controlled migration flow showed very little respect for people's preferences about where they wanted to live, but it did have some positive results. Overurbanization of China's major cities has so far been largely prevented or minimized. China's population has remained spread out in the countryside, rather than becoming concentrated in cities. The movement of educated city youth to rural areas has helped to lessen the differences between the city and the countryside, because the city youth help to change local attitudes, develop the local economy, raise the educational level, and expand cultural life in the villages.

China's geographically immobile society and the recent urban-to-rural population flows have probably contributed to the reduction of rural fertility levels in China. Each people's commune and, within that, each village, is a political and geographic unit whose boundaries are usually fixed. Local leaders and local residents now know that there is little hope for reducing population pressure in the commune through out-migration. Indeed, the commune may be required to accept in-migrants from the city. This knowledge may be persuading rural leaders to urgently promote late marriage and birth control in order to reduce the village's natural population growth rate.

Conclusion

The P.R.C. was in extremely rapid demographic transition toward low mortality and low fertility levels during the 1970s, according to population data massively collected in China but only spottily reported. These data are faulty, as shown by province-by-province analysis, which picks up occasional contradictions between one datum and another. There is some evidence of underregistration of neonatal deaths, overestimation of the proportions of couples contracepting, under-counting of the number of local residents, and a few cases of a minimally functioning vital registration system, which records only about half of the local births and deaths. In spite of these statistical weaknesses in some geographical areas, reported P.R.C. population data are in general remarkably consistent, show clear patterns of change over time, and duplicate trends found in some other developing countries. When China's leaders at any level report a birth rate, a death rate, a natural population increase rate, a list of contraceptors by type of contraceptive, marriage age data, or infant mortality rate, these officials appear to be telling the truth based on the data they have collected. They do not lie. Rather, if officials are ashamed of a particular datum, they simply do not report it. The only exception to this general rule is that the total population size of the whole country or a populous province is usually seriously underestimated, and the officials know that they are doing this. No officially reported total for China's population size or for any province's population size should be considered a current total, unless it can be shown that the reported population figure is consistent with all the other reported population data on that province or the whole country.

So far China has done very well in reducing mortality levels, in the countryside as well as in the cities. During the last decade, the process of mortality decline was speeded up by the training and deployment of millions of paramedics and health workers to take care of primary medical care. A referral system for difficult cases channels the patients needing more expert care to the few available fully trained doctors. This system is paid for, in more than 85 percent of the rural production brigades, by a cooperative medical insurance system heavily subsidized by communal income. The other 15 percent of the brigades, at last report, are still without any such cooperative medical plan, which may leave their members more vulnerable to illness because they cannot afford to pay for medical care. The urban medical system, by contrast, is more advanced than the rural system. Paramedics also work there, but the supporting network of hospitals and doctors is more extensive.

Fertility decline during the 1970s proceeded very rapidly in some provinces, slowly and haltingly in others. Some provinces still have traditional levels or higher-than-traditional levels of fertility, but in general these are border provinces with large minority group populations. Also, the total number of people living in the provinces with the highest birth rates is small, compared to China's total population size.

Two key changes contribute to the current fertility decline. One is rising proportions of married couples contracepting. All forms of birth control appear to be available and in use almost everywhere in the country, except for some minority group areas, border regions, and very sparsely populated provinces. The variety of methods available contributes to popular acceptance of one method or another. In addition, the motivation for large families seems to be changing, due to socioeconomic development, the communal rural economy, rising educational levels, women's role changes, as well as social and political pressure against high fertility. An example of a province with high rates of contraceptive use is Kwangtung, which reported for 1974 that 60 percent of married women of reproductive age were using birth control throughout the province.[28] Local areas of Kwangtung are using some kind of family planning accounting system that tends to exaggerate the proportion of couples currently contracepting, so this 60 percent figure is also a slight exaggeration. Nevertheless, the achievement of a contraceptive use rate of more than 50 percent in a province of about 58 million people is remarkable in the experience of currently developing countries. Kwangtung is not alone in this achievement. Several other populous provinces have reported lower birth rates or natural population increase rates than Kwangtung and therefore presumably have similarly high rates of contraceptive use.

The other means by which China has been reducing its birth rate and natural population increase rate has been a rising age at marriage for women and men. This trend is poorly documented, but in some local areas whole cohorts of youth have been "mobilized" to postpone their marriages during the 1970s. Local officials sometimes refuse to issue marriage licenses to couples considered "too young" to marry and try to persuade the young adults to postpone their planned marriages. The target marriage ages for women and men vary from locality to locality, from as low as twenty-two for women and twenty-four for men to as high as twenty-seven for women and thirty for men. Some urban areas stipulate that the combined age of two persons planning to marry should be fifty years or more.

To the extent that the pressure to raise age at marriage has succeeded, it has resulted in short-term as well as long-term fertility decline. Later marriage lengthens the time between generations, gives couples a longer time to lower their desired number of children, and cuts out some of the most fertile years from the reproductive period of a couple. In the short run, whole cohorts of first births are postponed when cohorts of marriages are postponed. Some local areas have reported extreme birth rate declines following mass postponement of marriages. While some of these data are faulty, the trend toward higher marriage ages and the resulting downward pressure on the birth rate is clear. Even in some minority group areas, there are anecdotal reports of rising marriage ages.

Until very recently, China's population was growing at a rate of more than 2 percent per year, in some years at perhaps 2.5 percent a year. Now the country's population growth rate is probably less than 2 percent annually, and dropping to an equilibrium level of around 1.4 percent a year, which can be expected to continue through 1995, if replacement level fertility is reached and maintained. So far, the P.R.C. has had great difficulty keeping production increases in some sectors of the economy well ahead of population growth rates. Agricultural production, particularly grain production, has increased at a rate roughly equivalent to or only slightly faster than the population growth rate since 1953. Fortunately, rapid fertility decline has prevented China from experiencing a 3 percent annual population growth rate for a long period, an experience common in many developing countries. Rather, the P.R.C. now has the chance for regular modest increases in per capita production and consumption of essential items like food, in spite of its present age structure, which is unfavorable to a low birth rate and low natural population increase rate. Within the foreseeable future, after today's teenagers and young adults finish their childbearing period,

China should be capable of stabilizing its population size. Few other developing countries have such a prospect clearly in view.

Notes

1. Parts of this chapter are excerpted from Banister (forthcoming). For this book, Dr. Banister collected officially reported data on fertility, contraceptive use, age at marriage, mortality, age structure, migration, and total population size for the People's Republic of China and all its subunits. As much as possible, she tested these data for accuracy and consistency and reasonableness, before using reported population statistics to describe recent population changes in each province and in the P.R.C. as a whole. Using a computer population projection technique, she simulated the changes that China's population had experienced since the early 1950s, and predicted a likely pattern of population growth during the next twenty-year period.

2. In contrast, developed countries generally have a population growth rate of around 1 percent a year or less, and some have achieved a situation of zero population growth.

3. Barclay et al. (1976).

4. This does not mean that everyone died before age twenty-five but that the average life span was around twenty-five years.

5. The rate of natural population increase is calculated by subtracting the crude death rate from the crude birth rate.

6. See Banister (1977):68-69, and Banister (forthcoming) for the piecemeal evidence indicating that a national population count was taken in 1972.

7. A computer population projection for China based as much as possible on official national population data produces very low levels of fertility and mortality for the 1970s, levels that are inconsistent with reported data and qualitative information from China's provinces. See Banister (1977), chapters 4-13; and Banister (forthcoming).

8. "Han Suyin Discusses Her Visit to Tibet" (Hong Kong *Wen-hui Pao* in Chinese, November 11, 1975), *U.S. Joint Publications Research Service* no. 66480 (January 2, 1976):7. (Translations on the People's Republic of China no. 334.) Also see Banister (1977):449-452, 466; and Banister (forthcoming).

9. "Tibet Holds Conference on Health Work" (Lhasa Tibet Regional Service in Mandarin, October 16, 1976), *Foreign Broadcast Information Service Daily Report—PRC* 1, no. 205 (October 21, 1976):J1.

10. Rogers (1974):15; and Wolfson (1975):7-8.

11. Rogers (1974):13-14.

12. "Medical Services" (NCNA in English, March 7, 1977), *Summary of World Broadcasts, Part 3: The Far East, Weekly Economic Report,* Second Series, FE/W920/A/1 (March 16, 1977):1.

13. "Public Health" (NCNA in English, September 24, 1973), *Summary of World Broadcasts, Part 3: The Far East, Weekly Economic Report,* Second Series, FE/W744 (October 3, 1973):1.

14. See Davis (1956):318; United Nations Department of Economic and Social Affairs (1965):5-6; and United Nations Department of Economic and Social Affairs (1973):76.

15. Aird (1961):46-49; Pressat (1958):570; and Chandrasekhar (1960): 53-54.

16. "Strengthen the Work of Supplying Contraceptives," *Ta Kung Pao* (Peking), February 5, 1958.

17. See Banister (1977):268-273; and Banister (forthcoming).

18. Worth (n.d.), cited in Parish (1976):7.

19. See data from Kiangsu, Hopeh, Honan, and Kwangtung provinces in Banister (1977); and Banister (forthcoming).

20. Sources for this generalization are given in Banister (1977): 454-464; and in Banister (forthcoming).

21. Replacement level fertility means that women in the reproductive ages have just enough daughters to replace themselves. If a country achieves replacement fertility and continues this fertility level indefinitely, the population size will eventually stabilize (ignoring migration). The achievement of replacement level fertility, however, does not mean that the population immediately stops growing, because there may be a large number of women of childbearing age in the population.

22. They are Kiangsu, Hopeh, and Kwangtung provinces.

23. "China's Birth Rate Now Under Control, Congress Unit Told," *New York Times,* May 6, 1973, p. 5.

24. A cohort includes all those people born in the same year.

25. *Jen-min jih-pao,* September 20, 1976, p. 1, and Aird (1978):1.

26. It is impossible to document this assertion except from the impressions of visitors to China and from interviews with refugees about their home villages or neighborhoods. For instance, William Parish and Martin Whyte estimate from refugee interviews that 90 percent of the young males in the countryside of Kwangtung Province are still in their home villages, frequently living with or next door to their parents. See Parish and Whyte (1978):54.

27. Orleans (1972):93-119.

28. "Population: Kwangtung" (Canton City Service in Cantonese,

April 23, 1975), *Summary of World Broadcasts, Part 3: The Far East,
Weekly Economic Report,* Second Series, FE/W824 (April 30, 1975):1;
error in original translation corrected in "Population: Kwangtung,"
SWB-WER FE/W825 (May 7, 1975):1.

Selected Bibliography

The following short bibliography is limited to the secondary sources
referred to in the text, plus a few works that will give the reader more
detailed information on China's population than this article has been
able to cover. No primary sources are included here.

Aird, John S., "Population Policy and Demographic Prospects
in the People's Republic of China," in *People's Republic of
China: An Economic Assessment.* U.S. Congress, Joint Economic
Committee. Washington, D.C.: Government Printing Office, 1972.
Pp. 220-331.

————. "Recent Provincial Population Figures." *The China Quarterly*
(March 1978):1-44.

————. *The Size, Composition, and Growth of the Population of
Mainland China.* U.S. Bureau of the Census, International Popula-
tion Statistics Reports, Series P-90, no. 15. Washington, D.C.:
Government Printing Office, 1961.

Banister, Judith. *China's Pattern of Population Growth.* Stanford,
Calif.: Stanford University Press, forthcoming.

————. *The Current Vital Rates and Population Size of the People's
Republic of China and Its Provinces.* Ph.D. dissertation. Food
Research Institute, Stanford University, 1977. 566 p.

————. "Mortality, Fertility, and Contraceptive Use in Shanghai," *The
China Quarterly,* no. 70 (June 1977):255-295.

Barclay, George W., Ansley J. Coale, Michael A. Stoto, and T. James
Trussell. "A Reassessment of the Demography of Traditional Rural
China." *Population Index* 42, no. 4 (October 1976):cover and 606-635.

Chandrasekhar, S., *China's Population, Census and Vital Statistics.* 2nd
ed., revised. Hong Kong: Hong Kong University Press, 1960.

Chen Pi-chao. "China's Population Program at the Grass-Roots
Level." *Studies in Family Planning* 4, no. 8 (August 1973):219-227.

————. *Population and Health Policy in the People's Republic of China.*
Occasional Monograph Series no. 9. Washington, D. C.: Smith-

sonian Institution Interdisciplinary Communications Program, 1976.

Chen Pi-chao and Ann Elizabeth Miller. "Lessons from the Chinese Experience: China's Planned Birth Program and its Transferability." *Studies in Family Planning* 6, no. 10 (October 1975):354-366.

Davis, Kingsley. "The Population Specter: Rapidly Declining Death Rate in Densely Populated Countries—The Amazing Decline of Mortality in Underdeveloped Areas." *American Economic Review* 66 (May 1956):305-318.

Djerassi, Carl. "Fertility Limitation Through Contraceptive Steroids in the People's Republic of China." *Studies in Family Planning* 5, no. 1 (January 1974):13-30.

Durand, John D. "The Population Statistics of China, A.D. 2-1953." *Population Studies* 13, no. 3 (March 1960):209-256.

Faundes, Anibal and Tapani Luukkainen. "Health and Family Planning Services in the Chinese People's Republic." *Studies in Family Planning* 3, no. 7, supplement (July, 1972):165-176.

Han Suyin. "Population Growth and Birth Control in China." *Eastern Horizon* 12, no. 5 (1973):8-16.

Ho Ping-ti. *Studies on the Population of China, 1368-1953*. Cambridge, Mass.: Harvard University Press, 1959.

Horn, Joshua S. *Away with All Pests: An English Surgeon in People's China, 1954-1969*. New York: Monthly Review Press, 1971.

Johnson, Elizabeth and Graham Johnson. *Walking on Two Legs: Rural Development in South China*. Ottawa: International Development Research Centre, 1976.

Lampton, David Michael. *The Politics of Medicine in China: The Policy Process, 1949-1977*. Boulder, Colo.: Westview Press, 1977.

Orleans, Leo A. "China's Population: Can the Contradictions be Resolved?," in *China: A Reassessment of the Economy*, U.S. Congress, Joint Economic Committee. Washington, D.C.: Government Printing Office, 1975. Pp. 69-80.

_____. "Chinese Statistics: the Impossible Dream." *The American Statistician* 28, no. 2 (May 1974):47-52.

_____. *Every Fifth Child: The Population of China*. Stanford, Calif.: Stanford University Press, 1972.

Parish, William L. "Birth Planning in the Chinese Countryside." Paper presented at the annual meeting of the American Sociological Association, New York, August 1976.

Parish, William L. and Martin K. Whyte. *Village and Family in Con-*

temporary China. Chicago: University of Chicago Press, 1978.

Pressat, Roland. "La Population de la Chine et son Economie." *Population* 13, no. 4 (October-December 1958):569-590.

Report of the Medical Delegation to the People's Republic of China, June 15-July 6, 1973. Washington, D. C.: National Academy of Sciences Institute of Medicine.

Rogers, Everett M. "Communication for Development in China and India: The Case of Health and Family Planning at the Village Level." Paper prepared for the Summer Program of Advanced Study on Communication and Development, East-West Communications Institute, Honolulu, Hawaii, July 1974.

Sidel, Ruth. *Women and Child Care in China, A Firsthand Report*. Baltimore, Md.: Penguin, 1973.

Sidel, Victor W., and Ruth Sidel. *Serve the People, Observations on Medicine in the People's Republic of China*. New York: Josiah Macy Jr. Foundation, 1973.

Taeuber, Irene B. "China's Population: Riddle of the Past, Enigma of the Future," in *Modern China*, edited by Albert Feuerwerker. Englewood Cliffs, N.J.: Prentice-Hall, 1964. Pp. 16-26.

Taeuber, Irene B., and Nai-chi Wang. "Questions on Population Growth in China," in *Population Trends in Eastern Europe, the USSR, and Mainland China*. New York: Milbank Memorial Fund, 1959. Pp. 263-302.

————. "Population Reports in the Ch'ing Dynasty." *Journal of Asian Studies* 19, no. 4 (August 1960):403-417.

H. Yuan Tien. *China's Population Struggle: Demographic Decisions of the People's Republic, 1949-1969*. Columbus: Ohio State University Press, 1973.

————. "The Demographic Significance of Organized Population Transfers in Communist China." *Demography* 1, no. 1 (1964):220-226.

————. Fertility Decline Via Marital Postponement in China." *Modern China* 1, no. 4 (October 1975):447-462.

United Nations Department of Economic and Social Affairs. *The Determinants and Consequences of Population Trends, Vol. 1*. Population Studies, no. 50. New York: United Nations, 1973.

————. *Population Bulletin of the United Nations, no. 7, 1963*. New York: United Nations, 1965.

Wegman, Myron E., Tsung-yi Lin, and Elizabeth Purcell. eds. *Public*

Health in the People's Republic of China. New York: Josiah Macy Jr. Foundation, 1973.

Wolfson, Margaret S. *Serving the People, Some Impressions of Social Development in China; Report of a Study Mission to the People's Republic of China.* Paris: OECD Development Centre, 1975.

Worth, Robert M. "Health Trends in China Since the 'Great Leap Forward'." *American Journal of Hygiene* 78, no. 3 (November 1963): 349-357. Reprinted in *The China Quarterly*, no. 22 (1965):181-189.

———. "Recent Demographic Patterns in Kwangtung Province Villages." Unpublished manuscript, n.d.

3
History

Harold C. Hinton

The People's Republic of China has already existed for more than a generation. Clearly it is more than the "passing phase" that Secretary John Foster Dulles once predicted. It has accumulated a historical record that is important, interesting, and basic to an understanding of all other aspects of the history of modern China and, although complex, is quite comprehensible.

Background

Like most other traditional non-Western societies, China experienced in the nineteenth century the profoundly unsettling impact of the dynamic ideas, organization, and technology of the West. Unlike most others, China was too big and too tough to become the colony of a single Western power, although all the major powers including Japan acquired a degree of influence over it such that China was sometimes humiliatingly labeled a semicolony. Unlike a few of the others, notably Japan, China lacked an existing political elite capable of reinvigorating and modernizing the country so that it could contend with the West on roughly equal footing.

Since reform on a grand scale was not possible, the alternative to subjugation or collapse had to be revolution. The necessary ideology was evolved, as a curious mixture of Chinese and Western ideas, in the early twentieth century by the idealistic but naive patriot Sun Yat-sen, who labeled it the Three People's Principles. Existing Chinese models of political organization and action being inadequate to the needs of his Kuomintang (National People's Party), Sun formed in 1923 an alliance with Lenin's Comintern on a platform of antiimperialism and took over to a degree the authoritarian and effective Communist organizational and functional model, known officially and somewhat euphemistically as democratic centralism. As a by-product of his alliance with the Comintern, Sun also formed one with the young (founded in 1921) but vigorous Communist Party of China (CPC).

At first this three-fold alliance was highly successful against its adversaries—the "imperialist" powers and the forces of domestic reaction (principally the "warlords")—and in mid-1928 the Kuomintang proclaimed, somewhat unrealistically, that it had acquired legitimate power over the whole of China. In the meantime, however, the death of Sun in 1925 had removed the main cement holding the revolutionary alliance together. His successor, Chiang Kai-shek, was a military man and far more conservative. He regarded the Comintern (by then under the control of Stalin) and the CPC with profound suspicion and feared, with much justification, that they were trying to take over the Kuomintang and, through it, China. He sought to deal with this problem through two coups, one (1926) directed at limiting the Communists' presence in the Kuomintang's leading bodies and the other (1927) directed at annihilating their mushrooming labor and peasant organizations in the Kuomintang's heartland, the lower Yangtze valley.

The Rise of the Chinese Communist Movement (1927-1949)

At the cost of a complete disruption of the revolutionary alliance, Chiang was largely successful, except that the CPC, although rendered temporarily harmless, had not been destroyed. While the Kuomintang more or less controlled the cities, there emerged in the rural areas of central and southern China a half dozen Communist-controlled base areas ("soviets"). For a variety of reasons, including personality and luck, the most important of these turned out to be one in southern Kiangsi led by a young Hunanese named Mao Tse-tung. Using a number of appeals and techniques, including land reform (i.e., redistribution of landlord-owned land among the poorer elements of the local peasantry) and a highly politicized version of guerrilla warfare, Mao and his colleagues there and elsewhere succeeded in rendering their bases viable enough to attract much hostile attention from Chiang Kai-shek's government in Nanking. By October 1934, heavy governmental military pressures had dislodged the Communists from their base areas and set them in motion on their famous Long March to Northwest China.

There they established a new, much poorer, base area and continued to face Nationalist military pressures, although in a less severe form. By 1931-1932 the Imperial Japanese Army had seized Manchuria (known to Chinese as the Northeast). The CPC tried to undermine the Nationalists' efforts against the Party by appealing to some elements among them, and to Chinese public opinion as a whole, to stop the civil war and unite to resist further Japanese encroachments. This line had considerable appeal and was supported, in essence, by Stalin and the Comintern. Chiang Kai-shek himself came to endorse it, outwardly at any rate, after being kidnapped by two of his own commanders at Sian in December 1936; in turn he was accepted by the CPC, again outwardly and largely because of Stalin's insistence, as the head of the prospective nationwide anti-Japanese resistance.

Since neither side was acting in good faith, and since each came to believe that Japan would be defeated eventually by other powers regardless of what happened in China and that it could therefore afford to put its own interests first, the new alliance did not long survive the outbreak of a major Sino-Japanese war in 1937. The next eight years proved to be decisive for the outcome of the struggle for power in China. The Japanese invasion created enormous disruption in eastern China, which had been the Kuomintang's power base, and forced the Nationalists back into remote and backward southwest China. There, in spite of substantial American aid and support, they largely vegetated and deteriorated until the Japanese collapse in 1945, by which time they were too inept, corrupt, and reactionary to save themselves. The Communists, on the other hand, drew on their experience in rural organization and guerrilla warfare to establish about twenty base areas, some of them behind Japanese lines, and to expand the Red Army.

By V-J Day (September 2, 1945), the Communists were in both a mood and a position to again challenge the nominally stronger Nationalists. The beginning of the final round was delayed, however, by the fact that until the spring of 1946 both the United States and the Soviet Union had significant military presences in China (in the Soviet case, in Manchuria), and that both wanted their clients to avoid a civil war that might involve themselves. The United States, with tacit Soviet approval, engaged in a complex effort to stave off civil war in China and through mediation to bring the Nationalists and the Communists into a political and military coalition with each other. The effort foundered on mutual hostility and suspicion, and after the spring of 1946 the irrepressible conflict began to escalate. For a variety of political and military reasons implicit in the history of the two adversaries, as already summarized, the Kuomintang became in 1949 the first but not the last non-Communist Asian regime to fall victim to a Communist insurgency. It then moved its base to Taiwan, where it remains. The victors, acting through a nominally representative but actually handpicked and Communist-dominated body known as the Chinese People's Political Consultative Conference, proclaimed the People's Republic of China (P.R.C.), with its capital at Peking, effective October 1, 1949.

Consolidation and Reconstruction (1949-1952)

At the time of the Liberation of 1949, the CPC was understandably in a confident mood. As a result of its resounding victory, it was accepted by most Chinese as their new leadership and was actively supported by many, probably a majority. There was no realistic possibility, at least for the time being, of a successful challenge to its control from either inside or outside the country. The new regime was strong enough at the beginning of 1950 to allow Mao Tse-tung to work out a relationship with Stalin in which China held the role of junior partner and ally rather than satellite.

On the other hand, there were abundant problems. Decades of civil and foreign war had left the country exhausted, its modest rail network and industrial system barely functioning, and an astronomical inflation raging. There were pockets of resistance here and there, and Tibet and Taiwan remained to be "liberated."

In essence, the CPC tackled these and other problems with its tested methods of ideology and organization. The "thought" of Mao Tse-tung, a heavily sinicized version of Marxism-Leninism, was industriously propagated as the new national ideology, and Mao himself was increasingly built up in the media, school textbooks, and elsewhere as a kind of father or even emperor figure, the personal symbol of the desired new national unity and dynamism. As such he was accepted by most Chinese, including of course CPC members, who were tired of China's disunity and weakness and the troubles these had brought. On the organizational side, the CPC extended throughout the country its network of cadres, committees, bureaus, and so on, which had been perfected in North China by Liu Shao-ch'i and P'eng Chen during the anti-Japanese war. Under the supervision of the Party apparatus, a network of "people's governments," mass organizations (labor unions, peasants', women's, youth, and other organizations), and the like proliferated rapidly, with CPC members in the controlling positions.

According to Mao's thought, China immediately after the Liberation was not yet "building socialism" but rather was completing the "new democratic" stage of its revolution, under the leadership of the working class and the CPC rather than the bourgeoisie ("old democracy"). Mao labeled his regime a "people's democratic dictatorship": democracy for the people (under Communist leadership), dictatorship for the "reactionaries." According to the principles of Leninism, one of the most important and urgent tasks was land reform, as an essential half-way house between the old "feudal" agrarian system and the desired socialist countryside of the future. Accordingly, in the spring of 1950 the CPC inaugurated a nationwide agrarian reform campaign (except in national minority areas) modeled on similar but smaller-scale agrarian reforms earlier in its history. Since one of its objects was the physical elimination of actual or potential anti-Communist elements in the countryside, thousands of people who were not actually (absentee) landlords, as well as others who were, were tried and convicted, and sentenced, often along with their families, to death or imprisonment; their lands of course were confiscated and redistributed. Similar, but smaller and less violent, campaigns were launched at about the same time in the urban areas against non-Communist businessmen and intellectuals, as well as against Communist cadres accused of corruption and other evils.

The outbreak of the Korean War in June 1950 paralleled the CPC's armed "liberation" of Tibet and resulted in the extension of American military protection to un-"liberated" Taiwan. China's entry into the war the following fall opened a major, although undeclared, war between it and the obviously more powerful United States. This was a dangerous situation for the CPC, which, however, characteristically saw it also as an opportunity. The CPC's propaganda helped to create a "siege mentality" in the light of which still more vigorous action at home appeared justifiable and even necessary. For about two years, beginning in the last months of 1950, the CPC conducted a massive campaign against actual and alleged "counterrevolutionaries," thousands of whom were executed, sent to forced labor ("reform through labor"), or imprisoned. A reasonable estimate of the total number of people executed at the instigation of the CPC during the three years immediately following the Liberation would be three quarters of a million.

As early as March 1949, the CPC had begun planning for the economic rehabilitation of the country, especially its battered urban sector. Liberation brought the CPC physical control over many of China's economic assets, much more than the Kuomintang had ever possessed. This control facilitated many tasks, notably the struggle against inflation, which was brought rapidly under control by expressing prices in terms of "parity units," computed as fixed quantities of certain basic commodities, rather than money. With the aid of several thousand Japanese engineers and technicians who had remained in China after 1945, railway lines and industries, many of them originally built by the Japanese, were restored to usefulness with remarkable speed. In this way the CPC's economic timetable, announced by Mao Tse-tung in 1950 as beginning with three years of reconstruction to be followed by a series of five-year plans designed to make the P.R.C. a modern state and major industrial power by the end of the twentieth century, was kept at least approximately on schedule.

The "Transition to Socialism" (1953-1955)

At the beginning of 1953 the CPC announced the inauguration of the First Five-Year Plan and of the P.R.C.'s "transition to socialism." The plan covered both industry and agriculture and in the former case was based on a hopeful assumption about Soviet aid. This was to a considerable extent only an assumption and, together with inadequate data and a shortage of skilled personnel, it put the plan on a decidedly shaky basis. Although during the 1950s the Soviet Union was to provide the P.R.C. with a total of about $2 billion of (reimbursable) economic and military aid, in early 1953 the Kremlin was coping with the succession to Stalin and was in a poor position to make definite or generous commitments to Peking. Largely as a result, the plan was not put into final shape until February 1955 and was not made public until July of that year. In spite of these problems, the industrial aspect of the plan, which in the Soviet manner stressed heavy industry, performed very well. It was largely in other areas that the most serious difficulties of the period arose.

One of these was elite politics. Kao Kang, a high-ranking Politburo member, was also Chairman of the State Planning Committee and regional boss of Manchuria, which contained China's greatest concentration of heavy industry. He was too close to the post-Stalin Soviet leadership, as he had been to Stalin, for the comfort of his more nativist colleagues; he favored continued stress on Manchuria (where

Soviet influence was strong) as against the development of new industrial centers elsewhere; and he supported a relatively moderate approach to agriculture (in essence, mechanization before collectivization). In all these respects Kao was out of step with the mainstream of the Party leadership, including Mao, and his arrogant personality only exacerbated the differences.

At the end of 1953 Mao fell seriously ill for several weeks, and Kao took advantage of the apparent opportunity to lobby for his policies and seek support—with little or no success—among the army leadership. In addition, he allegedly formed an alliance with Jao Shu-shih, the regional boss of eastern China, where China's major light industrial center, Shanghai, was located, and sought the second place in the Party and state hierarchies to the possibly dying Mao. But Mao recovered by March 1954, and Kao's plot, or alleged plot, was foiled at about the same time; Kao was later said to have committed suicide.

Kao's fall was accompanied by the breaking up of the regional centers of power that had existed for the past few years in the three major hierarchies—the Party (the regional bureaus of the Central Committee), the government (the regional governments), and the army (the field armies). As a further measure of modernization and centralization, the P.R.C. received from the CPC as the former's fifth birthday present (October 1, 1954) its first real state constitution. According to the more important and innovative of its provisions, Mao Tse-tung became chairman of the P.R.C. (i.e., chief of state), a quasi-legislative body analogous to the Soviet Union's Supreme Soviet and known as the National People's Congress was created, a Ministry of Defense headed by the P.R.C.'s senior active soldier (P'eng Teh-huai) was established within Premier Chou En-lai's State Council (cabinet), and the State Planning Committee was also subordinated to the State Council.

The agricultural aspect of the First Five-Year Plan centered on "step-by-step" socialization. Like most other Communist parties in power, the CPC has preferred in practice the collective farm (referred to in China as the agricultural producers' cooperative), in which the land is cooperatively owned and the members have residual claims on its products, to the theoretically superior state farm, in which the state has ownership and is the residual claimant since it has contracted to pay fixed wages to the workers on the farm. The CPC knew what disasters Stalin's brutal approach to collectivization had inflicted on agriculture and the peasants in the Soviet Union and was determined to avoid anything of the same kind. Accordingly, as it had done in parts of North

China before Liberation, it began, after land reform, with the formation of supposedly voluntary and seasonal "mutual aid teams," in which tools and labor were pooled but land titles and land use were not. The First Five-Year Plan called for the creation of lower level ("semisocialist") cooperatives, in which land use but not land titles would be "cooperativized"; these were to be followed in time by higher level ("fully socialist") cooperatives, in which land titles would be "cooperativized"—collective farms in the usual (Soviet) sense except for the presumable absence of farm machinery.

By 1954 lower-level cooperatives were being formed in sizable numbers, with some adverse but not catastrophic effects. There was something of a "blind influx" of peasants into the cities, which combined with serious Yangtze floods to produce urban food shortages by the end of 1954. All this in turn helped to evoke another campaign against counterrevolutionaries, although not on the scale of a few years earlier, and a major policy debate within the party leadership. Mao, whose impatient and imperious tendencies appeared to have grown since his illness of the year before, found himself opposed to a majority of the Politburo and the Central Committee. They, or at least some of them, wanted to slow the rate of cooperativization envisaged in the First Five-Year Plan. Mao, in opposition, wanted to accelerate it, on the doubtful theory that the peasant's temperament was much more "socialist" than his opponents supposed.

Instead of bowing to an adverse majority as a thoroughly orthodox "democratic centralist" would have done, Mao decided to get his way by means outside the Party constitution. At the end of July 1955, only a few weeks after the First Five-Year Plan had been unveiled before a session of the National People's Congress, he convened an ad hoc meeting of first secretaries of the provincial Party committees and persuaded them to accept his demand for faster rather than slower cooperativization. Mao's position was also energetically supported over the ensuing months by the party's massive propaganda machine, over which he maintained close personal control. As a result, cooperativization was indeed accelerated in the fall of 1955; in fact, once momentum had been attained, the lower level cooperatives were upgraded to upper level ones, so that by the end of 1956 most peasants had been fully cooperativized. At the same time similar, but less important and less traumatic socialization campaigns were conducted in two other sectors, private business and handicrafts. After his triumph, Mao was not likely again to accept frustration willingly at the hands of an adverse majority of his colleagues.

The Hundred Flowers and the East Wind (1956-1957)

The cause of "democratic centralism" in the CPC received a powerful stimulus from the Soviet Party's Twentieth Congress in February 1956, and in particular from Khrushchev's heated denunciation of Stalin at the end of it in the famous Secret Speech. Mao, although not dead like Stalin, was his Chinese equivalent, if only a rough one, and Mao's position was inevitably affected by Khrushchev's campaign against the memory and policies of the departed dictator. Evidently deriving some inspiration from this, a few of Mao's colleagues in the Party apparatus, notably Liu Shao-ch'i, moved to curb his political role, although in a far more tactful manner than Khrushchev's. At the CPC's Eighth Congress (September 1956), a number of innovations adverse to Mao's position and to his "cult of personality" were introduced into the Party constitution. By remarkable coincidence, those leaders who failed to support Mao publicly during the congress were to fare badly during the Cultural Revolution, a decade later.

Meanwhile Mao had begun a political campaign on his own behalf, using as before the Party propaganda machine to achieve much of the effect he wanted. Determined to vindicate his leadership and statesmanship against the implied criticism of his more bureaucratically inclined colleagues, and to put them and the impetuous Khrushchev down, Mao launched in the spring of 1956 the famous Hundred Flowers Movement. Its essence was an invitation to intellectuals and specialists, whether members of the CPC or not, to "bloom and contend," or in other words to speak their minds freely on matters of public interest. Mao evidently believed that the result would be an outpouring of praise and support, tempered by constructive criticism, for himself and the regime he had done so much to create.

The campaign got off to a slow start. Understandably, the Party apparatus was not enthusiastic about it, and the intellectuals were not sure they would be safe if they spoke their minds on controversial questions. The Hungarian crisis of October-November 1956 helped by suggesting to the Party apparatus the possibility that a similar explosion might occur in China unless a safety valve were provided in the form of free public discussion of public issues. Mao undertook to encourage the intellectuals to loosen their tongues through an important speech on "contradictions among the people" that he delivered on February 27, 1957.

The outcome was a delayed outpouring of comment and criticism in the late spring, some of it by CPC members. Once convinced that they had been promised immunity, the critics, considered as a whole, denounced every imaginable aspect of the CPC's rule, including Mao Tse-tung's *personalismo*. This unpleasant result, which was un-expected at least to Mao, placed the CPC in an excruciating dilemma: it could either tolerate the criticism and allow it to continue, in which case (by its own totalitarian standards) it would risk the collapse of its legitimacy and control, or it could silence and punish the critics, in which case it would violate its pledge of immunity to them. It chose the second alternative, and by way of justification it published on June 18 an admittedly edited version of Mao's previously unpublished speech of February 27, after inserting in it some restrictions on freedom of speech that the critics were then accused of having ignored.

All this represented a major emotional and political crisis for the regime, and above all for Mao himself as the sponsor of the Hundred Flowers Movement. While the vacationing Mao pondered what to do, the apparent answer materialized in an unexpected quarter. During the summer the Soviet Union became the first power to test an intercontinental ballistic missile, and on October 4 the first to orbit an earth satellite. These spectaculars, and still more the sensation they created in the United States (the "missile gap"), made Mao believe, or at least claim to believe, that the "socialist camp" led by the Soviet Union was achieving an irreversible ascendancy over the "imperialist camp" led by the United States, or in his own more picturesque language that "The East wind has prevailed over the West wind." Mao evidently hoped that the impulsive Khrushchev, now that he had purged some of his more conservative (in foreign policy) colleagues including Defense Minister Zhukov, could be persuaded to put Soviet power and prestige fully at the service of a more or less worldwide politico-military offensive against "imperialism" to be designed by Mao. The main early results to be hoped for were Taiwan for the P.R.C., West Berlin for the Soviet Union (or, more accurately, for East Germany), and a badly needed boost for Mao's prestige at home and abroad. This militant strategy, to be sure, threatened to arouse not only the opposition of the supposedly decadent "West wind" but also the alarm of the neutral countries; Mao had already decided that the latter were basically "soft" on "imperialism" in any case and that their goodwill was of little practical value to the "socialist camp."

Mao began to press this line on Khrushchev when he visited Moscow in November 1957 on the occasion of the fortieth anniversary of the October Revolution and the convening of a major international conference of Communist parties. Khrushchev, who had a keener appreciation than Mao of international realities and knew very well that the "missile gap" actually favored, or would soon favor, the United States, in effect declined Mao's proposal as too risky. If there was to be a great international offensive against "imperialism," the P.R.C.'s role in it would have to be greater than Mao had originally envisioned. Already convinced that the centralized, bureaucratic Soviet approach to economic development was not suited to Chinese conditions, Mao now began to think of Khrushchev as "revisionist" (unduly moderate) in his domestic and foreign policies and as under the influence of the still more "revisionist" Tito, who in 1958 began to denounce Mao as a threat to world peace and to the autonomy of individual Communist parties.

The Great Leap Forward (1958-1960)

Largely in response to Mao's current mood and views, the pendulum of Chinese domestic politics and foreign policy began to swing to the left in the fall of 1957. During the ensuing winter Mao succeeded in winning at least the qualified support of the Party apparatus, whose leaders were apparently unwilling to face a major debate with him so soon after the fiasco of 1957, for a galvanic effort at "self-strengthening" (a favorite term of nineteenth-century Chinese reformers) to be known as the Great Leap Forward.

Although it had some urban and industrial aspects, the Great Leap Forward was primarily a rural and agricultural movement. Mao and his fellow radicals in the Party leadership unrealistically assumed an almost unlimited substitutability of labor for the other factors of production. More specifically, the supposedly socialist Chinese peasant, if properly motivated, organized, and led, was considered capable of a labor output sufficient to move the country rapidly in an "uninterrupted revolution" to a higher plane of economic development and to the brink of, if not actually into, the ultimate stage of "communism," which not even the Soviet Union had claimed to have entered.

The organization through which this dream was supposed to come true was known as the "people's commune," and it began to make its appearance in the spring of 1958. In essence, it was a new headquarters superimposed, on the average, over a dozen of the old agricultural producers' cooperatives, which were now renamed production brigades. In principle, at least, each commune was to be as self-sufficient as possible and was not only to plan agricultural operations over this relatively large area but to operate local industries including heavy ones (the famous "backyard furnaces"), communal kitchens and nurseries (to release female labor power for other tasks), communal schools, and militia organization. The commune was given the Party leadership's official and public approval in the summer of 1958 and rapidly became universal except in national minority areas.

The Great Leap Forward, as symbolized by the commune movement, encountered serious obstacles and problems. The peasants were worked to the point of exhaustion. The small private plots that they had enjoyed until then were mostly taken away, and they were expected to be content with ideological rather than material incentives. "Close planting" and "deep plowing" of the fields made good propaganda, but they were bad for the land. The "steel" produced in the "backyard furnaces" proved to be good for almost nothing. Normal economic activity, including the Second Five-Year Plan (1958-1962), was seriously disrupted.

The Party leadership aggravated these problems in unnecessary ways. The talk about an imminent attainment of "communism" aroused exaggerated expectations in some quarters and profoundly irritated the Kremlin. For propaganda purposes, the leadership overstated the achievements of the Great Leap Forward and urged local cadres to do the same with respect to the results of their own efforts. The outcome, among other things, was a series of gross statistical exaggerations; the regime claimed a 1958 harvest of 375 million tons, as against 185 million tons actually produced the year before.

Parallel with its galvanic effort at home, Peking undertook an external initiative in a relatively controllable area, the Taiwan Strait, designed to foster an all-out effort in the Great Leap Forward and to compensate for what was deemed Moscow's insufficient dynamism abroad. Over obvious Soviet objections, Peking in August-October 1958 tried to blockade the Nationalist-held offshore island of Quemoy with artillery fire and air action, so as to score if possible a success against the Nationalists and their American patrons. But the other side's response was unexpectedly firm, and Soviet support being almost purely verbal, Peking felt compelled to call off the crisis and initiate contacts with the United States at the ambassadorial level at Warsaw. This episode imposed a serious strain on Sino-Soviet relations and contributed, together with Peking's general assertiveness, to Khrushchev's termination in mid-1959 of a unique program designed to help the P.R.C. to produce its own nuclear weapons and surface-to-surface (offensive) missiles that he had previously agreed to in the fall of 1957.

In the fall of 1958 the Chinese leadership began to modify the most obviously excessive features of the Great Leap Forward, like the "backyard furnaces." This policy was formally announced at a Central Committee meeting in December. At the same meeting, it was also announced that Mao would not succeed himself as chairman of the P.R.C. when his current term expired, as it was soon to do. The available evidence on the motivation for this somewhat puzzling move suggests that, rather than being eased out by his colleagues, Mao had voluntarily decided some time before to give this office up while retaining his more important chairmanship of the Party Central Committee, partly in order to save time and energy but also because the post resembled one held by the despised "revisionist" Tito, whom the Chinese press had begun to attack in the spring of 1958. Accordingly, at a session of the National People's Congress held in April 1959 the chairmanship of the P.R.C. was assumed by Liu Shao-ch'i.

In March 1959 the situation in Tibet, which had been serious for at least three years, erupted. The warlike Khampa tribesmen were already in revolt, and the Dalai Lama, who had become thoroughly disenchanted with Peking, had been persuaded by his countrymen to escape to India. Intensified activity by the People's Liberation Army (PLA) in Tibet and along the Sino-Indian border, as well as increasingly repressive political measures against the Tibetan population, produced a stream of refugees to India and Nepal, several thousand of them being male Khampas of military age (who in many cases acquired weapons from foreign sources and later returned to Tibet to fight). Indian sympathy for the Dalai Lama and the Tibetan refugees, as well as the fact that the proper location of much of the Sino-Indian border was in dispute, created something of a crisis between Peking and New Delhi, in which Khrushchev clearly sympathized with the Indian side.

By this time Defense Minister P'eng Teh-huai had become convinced that the Great Leap Forward was endangering the P.R.C.'s long-term development and the modernization of its armed forces, as well as Soviet military aid and protection. The fact that the Soviet leadership agreed with him weakened his position in Peking rather than strengthening it. In June 1959, after returning from a trip to the Soviet Union and Eastern Europe, he launched a challenge to the Great Leap Forward and to Mao's leadership. In this he was completely unsuccessful, and in August he was purged and succeeded as Defense Minister by his rival Lin Piao who, although a brilliant soldier on the record, was as much a radical Maoist in outlook as P'eng was a pragmatic modernizer.

At that time the Party leadership was preparing to celebrate the P.R.C.'s tenth anniversary. It decided to scale down the claim for the 1958 harvest to 250 million tons (still too high by about 50 million tons), this being the highest figure that it thought would command belief, and to readjust the targets for 1959 accordingly. This did not indicate any bearishness on Peking's part. On the contrary, believing that the mediocre harvest of 1959 would be followed and compensated for by a good one in 1960, the CPC placed heavy orders for industrial equipment in Moscow and entered its second decade in power in an optimistic mood.

Unfortunately for Peking, its optimism at home was matched by its assertiveness abroad. Fed up with what it considered Khrushchev's softness on American "imperialism," especially his visit to the United States in the summer of 1959, Peking launched a propaganda attack on him in April 1960, although without using his name in public, and began to denounce him in June at various international Communist meetings. Understandably angered, Khrushchev overreacted by cancelling the Soviet economic aid program in the P.R.C. and withdrawing the Soviet technicians (1,390 in all) in the summer of 1960. This was a serious and probably intentional blow to Peking's industrial development program.

Even worse was the fact that the 1960 harvest turned out to be still smaller than that of the year before. This problem was complicated by a considerable disruption of transport produced by the Great Leap Forward. As a result, a serious food shortage, approaching famine in some areas, developed in 1961. Peking had no choice but to call off the Great Leap Forward, in fact although unadmittedly; this it did at the end of 1960.

Recovery and Controversy (1961-1965)

In lieu of the Great Leap Forward, Peking inaugurated a program of retrenchment and recovery at the beginning of 1961, largely under the supervision of the Party apparatus. Grain imports were initiated, although without being publicly mentioned. Heavy industrial expansion was virtually stopped, and emphasis was placed instead on industry that supported agriculture, like chemical fertilizers. Most important of all, the peasants were again permitted a reasonable level of material incentives and private plots were restored, while the communes were reduced in size.

Under this policy, conditions rapidly improved, one of the first clear signs of recovery being the good winter wheat harvest gathered at the beginning of 1962. Through 1965, the same pragmatic policies and relative prosperity continued to obtain, always under the supervision of the Party apparatus.

This seemingly idyllic situation aroused profound concern on the part of Mao, who feared a slide into "revisionism" and from the beginning of 1962 on urged a return to something like the Great Leap Forward. Unable to achieve this, he had to settle for a succession of ineffective half measures. Later in 1962 he persuaded his colleagues to agree to the Socialist Education Movement, aimed mainly at enhancing the political consciousness and performance of Party cadres in the rural areas; however, increasing differences developed between Mao and Liu Shao-ch'i as to how the campaign should be conducted. In 1963 and 1964, Mao launched some other campaigns, notably one to "learn from the People's Liberation Army," which under Lin Piao's leadership had supposedly become a model of Maoist militancy, and one to "train a generation of revolutionary successors" among the youth.

Recovery at home coincided with some dramatic developments abroad. In the spring of 1962, Peking found itself confronted with crises on four fronts. A flareup of fighting in Laos brought American troops to Thailand. Some 60,000 Sinkiang nomads fled to Soviet Central Asia, apparently with Soviet connivance if not at actual Soviet instigation. Worse still, the Nationalists appeared to be girding for an attack across the Taiwan Strait. The evaporation of the latter threat, if it ever was one, in late June left Peking free to concentrate on the fourth crisis, on the Sino-Indian border. Indian troops were moving into a disputed area known as Aksai Chin, across which Peking had built a military road linking western Sinkiang with western Tibet. After repeated warnings failed to stop this process, Peking launched a brilliantly successful offensive (October 20–November 20, 1962) that pushed the Indian army well away from the road and humiliated New Delhi in the eyes of the world. Peking was shielded to a degree by the simultaneous Cuban missile crisis, which focused the attention of the superpowers on the Caribbean. Chinese propaganda branded the withdrawal of Soviet missiles from Cuba as an act of betrayal by Khrushchev, who in turn made his sympathy for the Indian side in the Sino-Indian border crisis reasonably clear.

Sino-Soviet relations grew still worse as a result of Khrushchev's signature in the summer of 1963 of the nuclear test ban treaty with the

United States and Great Britain. For a number of reasons, Peking regarded this as another act of betrayal by Khrushchev, and it retaliated by escalating its propaganda polemic against him and his "revisionism." By the time of his fall from power in mid-October 1964, Sino-Soviet relations were very tense indeed.

Although Khrushchev himself probably had no friends at all in Peking by that time, the same did not necessarily apply to his successors led by Brezhnev, who of course had been responsible for his ouster. Indeed, the new Soviet leadership offered the Chinese a sweeping accommodation in February 1965, while at the same time proposing "united action" in connection with the escalating war in Vietnam. There is some reason to believe that some of Mao's colleagues, probably including Liu Shao-ch'i, felt some interest in this proposal, but Mao himself wanted no part of it, since he claimed to believe that the entire Soviet leadership was ineradicably infected with "Khrushchev revisionism." He had come to believe the same about Liu Shao-ch'i, and in January 1965, he decided to get rid of Liu somehow—easier said than done.

The Cultural Revolution (1965-1969)

As Mao indicated in an interview with Edgar Snow in January 1965, he felt a concern that was even stronger and broader than his desire to be rid of Liu Shao-ch'i and curb the "revisionism" of the Party leadership. This was his worry that the future of revolution in China might be in danger if its youth were insufficiently revolutionary. Mao evidently decided that the young people should be ideologically energized through an experience replicating insofar as possible that of himself and his colleagues, notably the heroic days of the Kiangsi soviet and the Long March. In the course of this "great upheaval" (a term used by Mao in August 1966 as the Cultural Revolution was moving into high gear), the "revisionist" elements in the Party could be "rectified" or eliminated. Mao also wanted to silence and get rid of "revisionist" elements in the country's cultural and academic life, some of whom had been criticizing him in print under thin allegorical disguises since 1961 for his "cult of personality," the Great Leap Forward, the purge of P'eng Teh-huai, and so on. There is good reason to believe that Mao was incited to launch the "great upheaval" by his wife Chiang Ch'ing, who felt a strong sense of dislike and rivalry for Liu Shao-ch'i's wife Wang Kuang-mei and wanted an opportunity to play an active role in politics.

The beginning of the Cultural Revolution was probably delayed for about six months by a crisis that focused the attention of the leadership elsewhere. This was the escalation of the war in Vietnam beginning in February 1965 and the ensuing strategic debate in Peking over its meaning for China. To the extent that the debate had an overt aspect, its two main spokesmen were Peking's two most conspicuous soldiers, Chief of Staff Lo Jui-ch'ing and Defense Minister Lin Piao. Writing in May 1965, Lo maintained that Hanoi was correct in moving its regular forces into South Vietnam, that China should give active support to the point of sending troops of its own if so requested by Hanoi, that such a strategy would create a risk of an American strategic attack on the P.R.C., and that this risk in turn required the reestablishment of a close working relationship with the Soviet Union, at least in the military field. Writing in the following September, and presumably speaking for Mao, Lin insisted on the contrary that the war in South Vietnam should be fought by the Vietcong on as "self-reliant" a basis as possible, that by the same token China should restrict its own role in the war to a low level that would minimize its risks and costs, that if in spite of this caution an American attack on China occurred, it would take the form of a conventional invasion that could be defeated in a "people's war," and that it was neither necessary nor desirable for Peking to improve its relations with the "Khrushchev revisionists." Lin's formulation, which essentially governed Peking's role in the Indochina war after Lo Jui-ch'ing's purge early in 1966, was the first open indication that Lin might be seeking to be, and might be under consideration as, Mao's heir instead of Liu Shao-ch'i.

There is considerable evidence that Mao did not foresee in full the course that the Cultural Revolution would take nor did he plan a strategy for managing the revolution. On the contrary, the strategy bore, as it unfolded, the mark of extemporization.

In September-October 1965, Mao convened a special meeting to consider the first stage: an ideological and political housecleaning within the cultural and academic communities. This idea was of particular concern to P'eng Chen, the powerful municipal boss of Peking, China's main cultural center; some of Mao's intended targets were among P'eng's colleagues and protégés. At the most, P'eng was prepared to, and subsequently did, conduct the campaign as an exercise in improving the historical accuracy and literary quality of the intellectuals' published output, rather than as the ideological and political campaign that Mao had desired. P'eng's attitude, which was evidently shared by a considerable number of the Party leadership, angered Mao and led him to withdraw from Peking to the Yangtze valley, where he spent the next six months (November 1965–May 1966). There, and especially in Shanghai, the radicals among the leadership, and Chiang Ch'ing in particular, had established a political base since the spring of 1965. There Mao pondered how to purge P'eng Chen and tried to gather strength for that purpose while watching P'eng conduct the first stage of the Cultural Revolution in his halfhearted manner.

One of Mao's problems apparently was that he lacked at first a solid majority on the Party's key body, the seven-man Standing Committee of the Politburo (Political Bureau of the Central Committee). Chou En-lai supported him for devious reasons, chief among which was probably a desire to salvage from the impending "great upheaval" as much as possible of his State Council and the economy; he chose to give qualified cooperation to Mao, rather than risk everything through opposition. Lin Piao was sympathetic but on account of his sense of military responsibility evidently withheld his full support until after Peking concluded with the United States, in March 1966, what amounted to a tacit agreement that neither would escalate the war in Vietnam in such a way as to endanger the other. Teng Hsiao-p'ing apparently wavered, torn between his closeness to Liu Shao-ch'i and his probable rivalry with P'eng Chen, his immediate junior on the Party Secretariat. The other members of this Politburo Standing Committee, Liu in particular, were opposed to any further escalation of the Cultural Revolution. Sensing a threat to his position, Liu engaged in some clumsy and ultimately unsuccessful maneuvers to protect it, such as a trip to South and Southeast Asia in the spring of 1966 in his capacity as chairman of the P.R.C. (i.e., chief of state). Some of Mao's other targets, notably Chief of Staff Lo Jui-ch'ing, appear to have engaged in a "February plot" in 1966 against Mao, perhaps under the impression (widely shared in Peking for a time) that he was dying; if so, the plot was frustrated and the plotters purged.

Early in May 1966, Teng Hsiao-p'ing came over to Mao's side, and by the end of the month Mao had returned to Peking, and P'eng Chen had been purged in a bloodless coup executed by forces loyal to Mao and to Lin Piao. During this period there emerged at universities and secondary ("middle") schools in Peking, and later throughout the country, organizations of militant Maoist students known as Red Guards. With Mao's increasingly obvious approval, and with the active political encouragement and logistical support of the People's Liberation Army and its political arm (the General Political Department of the General Staff), the Red Guards set about denouncing and demonstrating against the "power holders" in their own institutions (i.e., deans and others) and later those in the Party leadership (i.e., Mao's opponents in the Party apparatus).

This exceedingly unruly phenomenon was bound to present serious problems, political as well as practical, for the Party hierarchy, and notably for its senior statesman Liu Shao-ch'i and its active leader Teng Hsiao-p'ing. Realizing this, Mao withdrew once more to the Yangtze valley, leaving Liu and Teng to weaken their political positions by embroiling themselves in controversy with the Red Guards, as they promptly proceeded to do.

At the beginning of August, after Mao's return to Peking for the second time that year, the Party Central Committee held a plenary session for which both sides had been girding themselves for some months past. The hall was evidently packed, most irregularly, with Mao's supporters, including Red Guards. Lin Piao, claiming at least implicitly to speak on behalf of the armed forces, gave Mao strong and perhaps decisive support. Even so, there was enough in the way of countercurrents and outright opposition that the Maoist triumph was less than complete. The meeting did not formally endorse the Red Guards or purge the opposition; rather, the Politburo and its Standing Committee were enlarged so as to increase, although not overwhelmingly, the Maoist majority. Chou En-lai managed to secure the adoption of some safeguards, which were to prove less than adequate, for intellectuals and technicians against the full force of the Cultural Revolution and the Red Guards.

If the Red Guards were not formally sanctioned at this meeting, they were soon afterward. For about three months beginning in mid-August, eight giant rallies of Red Guards, a total of about 10 million, were held in Peking so that they could see Mao, be greeted by him, and get a look at Lin Piao, who now began to be cast publicly, although still informally, in the role of Mao's heir. Many of the Red Guards had traveled to Peking from relatively remote parts of the country, often in transport provided or at least coordinated by the People's Liberation Army. While in Peking, the Red Guards through turbulent demonstrations virtually put out of action the Party's allegedly "revisionist" Secretariat and its subordinate departments, which have never since recovered their full pre–Cultural Revolution importance.

It was a different story, however, when in the fall the Red Guards were told in effect to perform a similar job on the "power holders" in the Party apparatus at the regional and provincial levels. These targets were not only tough and experienced but had close ties of long standing with the local military and police leaderships. They not only resisted effectively but fought back, in some cases by forming their own Red Guard units to resist the onslaught of the genuine, or Maoist, ones. The only major area where the latter made any real gains at first was Shanghai, the radical headquarters. There a "commune" was proclaimed in February 1967, but it soon gave way to a more structured organization known as a Revolutionary Committee, in which power was shared by representatives of "revolutionary mass organizations" (mainly Red Guards), military personnel, and "loyal" cadres who had actually or nominally deserted the "power holders" and declared their loyalty to the Cultural Revolution.

Seeing that the Cultural Revolution was not making much progress at the local level and that the country was in some danger of sliding into anarchy, which in spite of his bombastic pronouncements about "great upheavals" and the like he did not really want, Mao in late January 1967 ordered the People's Liberation Army, his only remaining reserve, into the fray. Before agreeing, Lin Piao probably bargained to confirm his own status as Mao's heir and to ensure that the Cultural Revolution within the People's Liberation Army would be an internal affair rather than being conducted from without by the Red Guards.

The army's explicit mission was to "support the left," or in other words the Red Guards and other "revolutionaries." But it also had, or thought it had, an implicit mission to prevent chaos. The two were in conflict because the main threat to public order was the Red Guards, but Mao's "proletarian headquarters" in Peking did not acknowledge this fact fully. The Red Guards were hardly less unpopular with the local army commanders than they had been with the "power holders" of the Party apparatus. In practice, the army emphasized order and tended to repress the Red Guards, who referred to February 1967 as the month of the "adverse current." Their protests moved Peking to order the army on April 6 to ease up; when it did so, several months of serious Red Guard violence followed. Meanwhile, at about the end of March, Liu Shao-ch'i and other "revisionists" were purged, irregularly, from the Party leadership, and a propaganda campaign began in the official press against Liu, labeling him "China's Khrushchev." Because of these various problems, only six revolutionary committees (including the one for Shanghai) were formed at the provincial level through the summer of 1967.

During that summer Red Guard violence, which sometimes took the form of seizing weapons from military personnel, aroused increasing opposition from the army. Friction of this kind was particularly serious in the important industrial complex of Wuhan. When two delegates from Peking came there in July to investigate and mediate, the Wuhan

Military Region Commander Ch'en Tsai-tao had them seized. He soon released them under threat of military action from forces loyal to Peking and became briefly the target of a major propaganda offensive. The radicals seized on the so-called Wuhan Incident to demand the launching of a campaign to "drag out the power holders in the People's Liberation Army" and generally radicalize the armed forces. Not only was this campaign abortive, probably on account of the united opposition of the military region commanders, but a number of radicals were purged, including the director of the General Political Department of the General Staff.

This trend to the right was reinforced by the after effects of the temporary seizure by radicals of the Foreign Ministry on August 19, and the burning of the British mission three days later in reprisal for the imprisonment of some leftist journalists in Hong Kong. Shortly afterward, statements by Mao and Chiang Ch'ing, the only leaders who could hope to make the Red Guards accept unwelcome directives, suggested at least a qualified mandate for the army to suppress Red Guard violence. Fortified in this way, the army formed and dominated eighteen provincial-level revolutionary committees during the last quarter of 1967 and the first half of 1968.

As long as the Red Guards remained in existence, however, their violence, some of which was directed against each other, continued to be a serious problem. In the summer of 1968 some of it took the form of raids on trains carrying arms to North Vietnam. With the proceeds, rival Red Guard units in Kwangsi fought and killed each other, probably angering Hanoi and unquestionably enraging Peking. Convinced at last that the Red Guards had outlived their usefulness and become a major problem, Mao authorized their suppression at the end of July 1968. This was accomplished by the army during the next few months with the support of teams of workers. Thus the Cultural Revolution came to an end in all but name. Officially, it was a great success; a great rally on September 7 celebrating the formation of the remaining provincial-level revolutionary committees pronounced the entire country "red" and the Cultural Revolution victorious. By 1969, the Cultural Revolution had effectively ended.

The Ascendancy and Fall of Lin Piao (1968-1971)

Lin Piao emerged from the Cultural Revolution in a strong position. To outward appearances, he enjoyed the full support of Mao Tse-tung and the radical elements of the Party leadership in his new role as Mao's heir, and he was China's senior soldier with personal followers in many key military positions in Peking and the provinces. He was the object of a "cult of personality" second only to Mao's. He was, however, despite his own ambition, a man of very little political intelligence and great ideological dogmatism. He was in poor health and physically unimpressive, lacking Mao's imposing presence. It is possible that Mao may have been privately antagonized by Lin's drive for power. It is certain that Chou En-lai, a man far abler than Lin, regarded him as a threat to his own position and policies and as unfit to be Mao's successor.

One of Lin's most serious shortcomings was the fact that, as his pronouncements at least as far back as 1965 indicate, he was still wedded to what is sometimes called the "dual adversary strategy": advocating, for ideological reasons, simultaneous struggle against American "imperialism" and Soviet "revisionism." This demanding and dangerous outlook had arisen during the quarrel with Khrushchev but had become obsolete just as the Cultural Revolution was ending; conditions then began to indicate a return to the classic and commonsense Maoist strategy of combining tactically with the less dangerous adversary in order to cope with the more dangerous one. In August 1968 the Soviet Union unexpectedly invaded Czechoslovakia, and this crisis was rendered especially threatening in Peking's eyes by the fact that since the previous spring the Soviet press had been engaged in an unusually powerful anti-Chinese campaign. Speaking on August 23, Chou En-lai coined the term "social-imperialism" to describe Moscow's current behavior. On November 25 he proposed talks at the ambassadorial level with the incoming Nixon administration to begin on February 20 of the following year. During the winter, however, radical elements probably led by Lin Piao convinced Mao to oppose the talks, which were accordingly cancelled by the Chinese side on the eve of their scheduled commencement.

With incredibly simpleminded logic, Lin evidently prepared to match this blow at "imperialism" with one at "revisionism." He was to be formally elected Mao's heir at the forthcoming Ninth Party Congress, which after many postponements was scheduled to open in mid-March. He apparently wanted to emphasize his own role as leader of the People's Liberation Army, and that of the PLA as defender of the fatherland. This may have been partly to counter a tendency on the part of his civilian colleagues to believe that the PLA had acquired too much power and needed to be pruned back now that it had played the essential giant killer's role of suppressing the Red Guards; the 1969 New Year's Day editorial had contained much less praise for the PLA than had similar documents during the previous several years.

It was apparently Lin who, encouraged by the fact that the Soviet Union appeared to be involved in a crisis of sorts over West Berlin, organized an ambush of a Soviet patrol on a disputed island (Chenpao to the Chinese, Damansky to the Soviets) in the Ussuri River on March 2, 1969. The Soviet response was unexpectedly strong, at least to Lin; Moscow had its own domestic and external reasons for wanting to teach Peking a lesson. In addition to making a great deal of propaganda, the Soviet side struck back on the same island in greater strength and with devastating effect on March 15. Peking and the Chinese public flew into a virtual panic that lasted for several months, and the Party congress was postponed again, probably in order to remove an irritant in Soviet eyes and to give the leadership time to look for ways of coping with the new crisis. It appears that Lin's blunder on the Ussuri set in motion a slow political decline on his part; at any rate, he was relatively inconspicuous from then on, while Chou En-lai, who alone could manage the vital task of coping with Moscow on the diplomatic level, was highly conspicuous. Fortunately for Peking, Soviet counsels were also divided; in late March, Premier Kosygin, speaking for the doves, proposed talks to resolve the border issue.

While evading this proposal, which was unacceptable to the radicals, Peking drew enough encouragement from it to open the Ninth Party Congress on April 1. As usual, efforts were made to avoid giving an appearance of crisis. Lin Piao gave the major speech, in the course of which he denied that Peking actually claimed more than a modest amount of territory currently held by the Soviet Union; he was also elected sole vice chairman of the Party Central Committee and named formally as Mao's heir. This appointment was a logical extension of earlier developments, and to have done otherwise might have appeared as an undignified appeasement of Moscow, where Lin was highly unpopular.

In mid-May Chou En-lai began to normalize Peking's external relations, which had been severely damaged by the frenzy of the Cultural Revolution, by sending ambassadors back to Chinese embassies abroad and by seeking diplomatic recognition from countries that had not yet extended it on condition that they break all official ties with Taiwan. The first country to do this was Canada (October 1970); others followed in rapid succession. The biggest prize of all, the United States, of course remained uncaught, but there was hope inasmuch as President Nixon was clearly interested in better relations with Peking. In any event, this improvement of China's external position was helpful as partial insurance against a Soviet attack, which then appeared to be a distinct possibility.

During the last three quarters of 1968, and for about three years thereafter, the Soviet Union built up its conventional and nuclear forces near the Chinese border at an alarmingly rapid rate. It also initiated a number of border clashes, presumably to remind Peking of its vulnerability and prod it in the direction of the conference table. Unwilling to tolerate indefinite evasion, Moscow on June 13, 1969, demanded border talks within two or three months. These pressures, supplemented by pleas from Hanoi and by discussions between Chou En-lai and Kosygin in Peking on September 11, convinced Mao and largely silenced the radicals; Sino-Soviet border talks began in Peking on October 20 and have continued intermittently ever since. Some progress has been made toward agreement on the proper location of the border, but very little toward easing the military confrontation across it. Peking has unsuccessfully demanded a ceasefire agreement, a mutual troop withdrawal, and a Soviet admission that the nineteenth century border treaties were "unequal," i.e., unjust. (On November 6, 1974, a Chinese statement on the border issue appeared to drop the demand for a new treaty.) Moscow has unsuccessfully proposed a nonaggression pact, as well as a general normalization of Sino-Soviet relations that would place it in the position of senior partner once more.

In view of the persistent threat from the Soviet Union, Chou En-lai continued to favor an improvement of relations with the United States. Lin Piao and the other radicals, still wedded to the dual adversary strategy, were opposed; after the American intervention in Cambodia at the end of April 1970 Mao inclined to their side, but only for a short time. The two sides clashed, on both domestic and foreign issues, at an important Central Committee meeting in August-September 1970. Lin pressed for a reversion to a radical agrarian policy similar to the Great Leap Forward but lost. The fact that Party committees began to be reestablished at the provincial level in December was only one of a number of signs that moderate policies of stabilization were essentially in the ascendant during this period.

At the same Central Committee meeting, Lin probably also expressed opposition to Chou's proposed opening to the United States; if so, he lost again. Over the next ten months, a series of Sino-American contacts via third parties resulted in Henry Kissinger's famous secret visit to Peking in July 1971 and the extension of an invitation to President Nixon. Lin Piao and his supporters had been outmaneuvered, but their views had not changed.

Domestic politics were even more important than foreign policy in bringing the Lin Piao affair to a head. Lin's ambition led him to demand installation as chief of state in succession to Mao, corresponding to his already attained position as Mao's heir in the Party leadership. Since Mao had given up the chairmanship of the P.R.C. in 1959, Lin pressed Mao to resume it and then turn it over to him at a session of the National People's Congress to be held in the near future. Chou, who had probably already decided to purge Lin and was looking for an opportunity, opposed this demand; Mao evidently did too.

What happened next is not entirely clear, but what is reasonably certain is that Peking's later official version of this episode is unlikely to be correct. The official version is that Lin, having plotted unsuccessfully to assassinate Mao, tried to flee to the Soviet Union but was killed in a flaming airplane crash in the Mongolian People's Republic. A much more likely version is that Lin, taking advantage of Mao's absence from Peking in early September 1971, attempted a coup against his nemesis Chou En-lai that failed, and was killed by security forces; the airplane crash in Mongolia on the night of September 12-13 was probably contrived in order to blacken Lin's reputation by seeming to establish the otherwise highly implausible charge that he, alone among high-ranking Chinese Communists since 1949, had been so pro-Moscow as to try to defect to the Soviet Union.

The Ascendancy of Chou En-lai (1971-1975)

After Lin Piao's death, Mao Tse-tung continued to play an essentially elder statesman role, and practical power, as Mao stated privately to Edgar Snow as early as December 1970, passed to Premier Chou En-lai, the main architect of Lin's overthrow. This was not to be for very long, however; Chou was terminally ill with liver cancer in 1972, although he remained fully active for two years after that.

Since Lin Piao had been a military man, some of the most important effects of his fall were naturally felt in the military field. His closest military supporters in Peking and in the military regions were purged. His policy, which had emphasized the opposite extremes of progress toward an expensive and provocative intercontinental ballistic missile capability and (for ideological reasons) small-unit tactics and guerrilla warfare, was sharply modified. Instead, the emphasis was now on creating in the shortest possible time a minimum nuclear deterrent against the Soviet Union, consisting of medium- and intermediate-range ballistic missiles—there are indications that this may have been achieved as early as 1973—and on the more difficult task of modernizing the conventional forces. The threat of regional military power ("warlordism") that had emerged during the Cultural Revolution was dealt with expeditiously in December 1973. Probably at the initiative of Chou En-lai and the recently rehabilitated Teng Hsiao-p'ing, Mao summoned the eleven military region commanders to Peking and informed the eight most powerful that they were being transferred. Although in their former regions they had also held top political posts, in their new regions their powers were to be strictly military.

Meanwhile the Party apparatus, the state system, and the armed forces, in streamlined form, were being restored to working condition after the near-chaos of the Cultural Revolution. Success in this required the rehabilitation of many cadres (including high-ranking ones) who had been purged during the Cultural Revolution. Chou did not shrink from this step, even though it was highly objectionable to the radicals and probably none too welcome to Mao. By far the most important and controversial of the rehabilitations was that of the blunt, able, and pragmatic Teng Hsiao-p'ing, who was evidently intended by Chou En-lai to succeed him as premier—Teng did in fact function informally as acting premier during much of Chou's illness. In effect, Chou was trying with considerable success to build a broad centrist coalition that would even include the more reasonable of the radicals—the two main exceptions among the latter being Chiang Ch'ing and her protégé Yao Wen-yuan—to manage Mao and to ensure stability during the impending period of leadership succession. In addition, Chou and Teng promoted economic modernization, with emphasis on the import of foreign (including American) industrial equipment and technology and the acquisition of additional foreign exchange through increased exports of coal, petroleum, and cotton textiles. On the vital rural front, a Central Committee directive of December 26, 1971, promised the peasants that they could retain their private plots.

Probably Chou's most spectacular success was his opening of the P.R.C. to the United States. Although he rationalized it at home to some extent as a move to cope with an allegedly resurgent Japan, it was actually intended primarily as a means of constraining the Soviet Union. With Lin Piao out of the way, the Nixon visit proceeded smoothly in late February 1972; although the resulting Shanghai communiqué did not fully "normalize" Sino-American relations, it went a considerable distance in that direction. Full diplomatic relations could not be established because of the continuing American relationship with Taiwan, but liaison offices—embassies in everything but name—were set up in Peking and Washington in the spring of 1973. Chou established full diplomatic relations with Japan in September 1972. These successes enhanced his already enormous power and prestige, but he wisely refrained from taking the risky step of trying to be proclaimed Mao's heir.

Although Chou had dealt effectively with one major threat to his policies, regional military power, he was unable to do the same with the other, the radical minority in the Party leadership, because it was supported and protected—or at least widely believed to be so—by Mao Tse-tung. Indeed, as Chou's program moved ahead the radicals grew increasingly vocal in opposition to it. Fortunately for the radicals' enthusiasm for the "newborn things" of the Cultural Revolution, Mao had announced in August 1966 that China needed a "great upheaval" every seven or eight years. Accordingly, in early August 1973, shortly before the Tenth Party Congress convened virtually under the auspices of Chou En-lai, the radicals launched a program of what it pleased them to call "going against the tide" with a press campaign against Confucius, who was clearly intended to symbolize Chou but was less likely to retaliate. The following month, the radicals founded in Shanghai a propaganda journal entitled *Study and Criticism*, in which they aired their views. Lacking a mass power base since the suppression of the Red Guards, the radicals tried to construct a new one in the form of an armed urban militia under the control of the radical-dominated mass organizations (principally the labor unions). Except in Shanghai, this threat was quietly but effectively fended off by the moderates, and what did emerge in the way of an urban militia was only lightly armed and was controlled by the local army headquarters (again, with the exception of Shanghai).

Chou En-lai by no means remained on the defensive against the radicals. In February 1974 he achieved two master strokes of psychological warfare: he linked the anti–Lin Piao and the anti-Confucius propaganda campaigns, so that any one attacking the sage could be held to be criticizing Lin rather than Chou; and he launched a brief campaign against Western culture, especially music, of which Chiang Ch'ing was widely known to be paradoxically fond. Sometime during the next year he arranged key appointments for some men he trusted: his old military friend and colleague Yeh Chien-ying, who had been conspicuous during the Nixon visit, became defense minister. Teng Hsiao-p'ing, having already rejoined the Central Committee and the Politburo, became the first civilian chief of staff of the People's Liberation Army. The little known but obviously able Hua Kuo-feng, who had cultivated good relations with Mao while serving as a Party official in Hunan (Mao's native province) and had acquired a bureaucratic specialization in agriculture, became minister of public security (agriculture and security being a fairly common combination of specialties for leaders in Communist countries). Chou may have intended the much younger Hua (born in 1920 or 1921) to become premier after Teng (or instead of Teng in the event that radical opposition prevented Teng from succeeding Chou).

It appears that Mao had a stroke in June 1974; in any event, he left Peking and stayed away until April 1975. For his part, Chou entered a military hospital in Peking the following month (July 1974) and thereafter reemerged only rarely—though he still played a supervisory role. Increased authority inevitably devolved on Teng Hsiao-p'ing as the most influential of the vice premiers. Chiang Ch'ing, who hated both Chou and Teng, also became correspondingly more active, at least as measured by her public appearances.

The zenith of Chou's career, ill or not, was probably a long-delayed session of the National People's Congress in January 1975, preceded by a Central Committee meeting at which Teng Hsiao-p'ing was elected a vice chairman of the Central Committee and a member of the Standing Committee of the Politburo. At the congress, Chou announced his commitment to what came to be called the "four modernizations" (of agriculture, industry, national defense, and science and technology), which although attributed by Chou to Mao irritated the radicals for an essentially negative reason: the absence of any express interest in ideology, in "red" as against "expert." The radicals were also angered by guarantees in the new state constitution adopted by the congress that they termed "bourgeois right," like private plots for the peasants. During the spring, accordingly, major articles by two leading radicals, Yao Wen-yuan and Chang Ch'un-ch'iao, attacked by implication the political thrust of the congress and stressed hoary themes like "proletarian dictatorship." Possibly more significant was the fact that Mao had stayed away from the congress and the preceding Central Committee meeting, probably to show disapproval rather than for reasons of health since he received some foreign visitors during the same period.

Because Teng Hsiao-p'ing was much more acerbic and even more ideologically unacceptable to the radicals than was Chou En-lai, political tensions rose rapidly during his stewardship. In the summer of 1975 he sent troops to suppress strikes and demonstrations in the Hangchow area by workers, who by definition were ideologically sacred. He clashed openly with Chiang Ch-ing at an important conference on agriculture held from mid-September to mid-October; Hua Kuo-feng "summed up" the conference in at least a nominal effort to mediate. At about the same time the radicals, allegedly at Mao's initiative, launched a propaganda attack on certain characters in the famous traditional novel *Water Margin (Shui hu chuan)*, under which guise they denounced Teng for his "capitulationism" toward "revisionism" at home and abroad. He did nothing to help on this score by releasing on December 27, with an apology, the crew of a Soviet military helicopter who had been held since March 1974 on a charge of espionage. Another propaganda campaign that began in the fall of 1975 attacked Teng for his nonideological views on education. The tension between the two sides was so great that it was impossible to hold a normal National Day (October 1) celebration in 1975 or even to publish the usual editorial on that occasion.

The Succession (1976)

It seems that Mao was content to leave the succession question, like most others at that time, largely to Chou, except that Mao apparently could not stomach Teng Hsiao-p'ing as Chou's own successor. Chou's plan evidently included the passing of Mao's title as Party chairman to a young member of the Shanghai radical group, Wang Hung-wen, whom Chou had made nominally third in the Party at the Tenth Congress and whom he presumably expected to be a figurehead, with real authority devolving on Teng Hsiao-p'ing at least for a time.

Chou died on January 8, 1976. Teng delivered the eulogy a week afterward and appeared certain to succeed Chou at least as acting premier. Later in the month, however, the Politburo Standing Committee, now composed of six men, apparently deadlocked on the question of whether Teng or the radicals' candidate, Vice Premier Chang Ch'un-ch'iao, should have the acting premiership. They accordingly reached into the regular (non–Standing Committee) Politburo membership and bestowed the acting premiership on the only vice premier who also held a political portfolio: Minister of Public Security Hua Kuo-feng.

Chou's death had made Teng vulnerable, and the radical campaign against him mounted in intensity during February and March. This campaign alarmed the moderates, who were probably willing to sacrifice Teng if absolutely necessary but not the substance of Chou's policies, with which Teng of course had been closely associated since 1973. They accordingly made a festival for the dead in early April the occasion for a demonstration in Chou's honor. On the morning of April 5, their supporters were infuriated to find that wreaths bearing inscriptions praising Chou (and sometimes criticizing Chiang Ch'ing) had been removed from the main square in Peking, T'ien An Men Square, evidently at the initiative of the radical elements of the leadership and probably of Chiang Ch'ing in particular. The result was a riot lasting several hours.

This episode strengthened the radicals, who were able to make the plausible although dubious case that the demonstration had been organized by supporters of Teng (rather than of the unassailable Chou). On April 7, accordingly, there appeared two major announcements: one proclaimed the removal of Teng from all his Party and state posts, the other the appointment of Hua Kuo-feng not only as premier (no longer acting premier) but as first vice-chairman of the Party Central Committee (a new title, and one that clearly made him heir presumptive to Mao). At the same time, an understanding was apparently reached within the leadership to the effect that, since the Party chairmanship and the premiership had never been held by the same person, when Hua inherited Mao's Party title he should turn over the premiership to Chang Ch'un-ch'iao, the ablest member of the Shanghai group.

During the next few months the radicals intensified their political campaign through propaganda, strikes, and demonstrations—not only against Teng but against the moderates as a whole, whom they labeled the "bourgeoisie in the Party." The radicals' sense of urgency was apparently enhanced by a feeling that they had little time left; it was announced in mid-June that Mao would no longer receive foreign visitors, obviously because his health was failing rapidly. There is a lack of contemporary evidence, and therefore of credibility, for later assertions that Mao had wanted for some time past to purge the leading radicals, including Chiang Ch'ing.

The radicals showed a characteristic and dangerous tendency toward the dual adversary approach in their external behavior; there was a bomb blast at the Soviet embassy in late April, and in early July there were extensive and provocative maneuvers in the Taiwan Strait. (It should be remembered that Teng Hsiao-p'ing was no longer chief of staff of the People's Liberation Army.) In these and other ways the radicals, who were already widely unpopular, made still more enemies; Premier Hua Kuo-feng's attitude at that time is not clear, but he was probably inclining increasingly toward the moderates.

In traditional China, the approaching end of a dynasty that had lost the right to rule (the "mandate of heaven") was thought to be signaled by natural disasters. This belief lent an additional dimension to a powerful earthquake (8.2 on the Richter scale) that on July 28, 1976, virtually destroyed the industrial city of Tangshan, near Tientsin; perhaps as many as three quarters of a million people were killed. The radicals did their cause no good by insisting that what the situation required was still more intensive study and application of the thought of Mao Tse-tung. In reality, the massive task of earthquake relief required transport, supplies, and organization that only the army could provide, and that only Premier Hua Kuo-feng could coordinate. It was probably significant that the membership of a high-level earthquake relief delegation (presumably picked by Hua) that visited the stricken area at the end of July included none of the senior radicals. During the period of the earthquake and its aftermath a powerful and determined antiradical coalition between Hua and the moderates, including the security forces and most of the military leadership, was apparently completed. The radicals had little to protect them but their (incomplete) control over the media and the presumed support of the obviously dying Mao.

Mao's death occurred shortly after midnight on September 9 but was not announced for sixteen hours. This delay almost certainly reflected disagreements between radicals and moderates over the disposition of the body and over the proper distribution of power. The radicals very likely demanded that Hua honor the bargain of the previous spring by turning the premiership over to Chang Ch'un-ch'iao before the funeral. If so, Hua, with the support of the moderates, refused. A week later radical editorials began to appear with a probably spurious quotation from Mao, "Act according to the principles laid down," which was evidently intended not only to have general application but to refer to the bargain. Hua conspicuously failed to use this quotation in his eulogy for Mao, delivered on September 18. The issue was joined, behind the scenes although not yet in public.

The radicals must have realized that their position was serious; they were far weaker than their opponents, and the death of their patron had exposed them to attack in much the same way that Chou's death had exposed Teng Hsiao-p'ing. But there was an important difference: Teng, a moderate with excellent organizational ties, had not been the object of police sanctions; the leading radicals were not to be so fortunate. It is very unlikely that, as later charged, the radicals attempted to have Hua Kuo-feng, still minister of public security in addition to his other functions, assassinated on October 6. It is much more probable that Hua, with the support of the moderates in the leadership and after waiting almost until the end of the mourning period for Mao, had elements of the principal security force, the so-called 8341 unit under Wang Tung-hsing, place the "Gang of Four" (Wang Hung-wen, Chang Ch'un-ch'iao, Chiang Ch'ing, and Yao Wen-yuan), as they began to be called, under house arrest. Pockets of support for them, notably in Shanghai and Manchuria, were similarly contained or crushed by military and police power. On October 9 Hua began to be identified informally, in wall posters, as chairman of the Party Central Committee and as "head" of the Politburo and the Central Military Commission; these titles were subsequently formalized in a series of stages culminating in the Eleventh Party Congress (August 1977).

Evidently the victorious moderate coalition was prepared to accept Hua's continued retention of the premiership as well, but there was substantial support for the rehabilitation of Teng Hsiao-p'ing and in fact some support for making him premier. On the other hand, his rehabilitation also presented some problems, especially for Hua, and it was not finally agreed on until March 1977; a Party Central Committee meeting in July, the first since Mao's death, announced Teng's restoration to all the posts he had held before April 1976, including that of chief of staff of the People's Liberation Army. At the ensuing Eleventh Party Congress, he was elected the third-ranking member of a five-man Standing Committee of the Politburo (Hua Kuo-feng, Yeh Chien-ying, Teng Hsiao-p'ing, Vice-Premier Li Hsien-nien, and Wang Tung-hsing).

The new leadership was clearly dedicated to stability, economic development, and military modernization; however, the possibility of further political turmoil could not, of course, be ruled out. The thought of Mao Tse-tung was skillfully reinterpreted to emphasize its moderate aspects and to dismiss its radical ones as aberrations somehow attributable to the Gang of Four who were blamed for everything imaginable. Hua Kuo-feng became the object of a cult of personality resembling Mao's although less intensive; it was officially insisted that Hua was Mao's legitimate successor and indeed had been appointed by

Mao. The role of the security forces and the maintenance of order through police controls were stressed, but not to excess. Science and technology were fostered by means that included somewhat greater freedom from political pressures and continued importation of foreign technology. Efforts were made to raise wage levels, an important incentive for the labor force. It even appeared that China might be beginning to move in the direction of "market socialism" of the kind practiced in some East European countries.

Teng Hsiao-p'ing, the most dynamic figure in the new leadership, appeared to be very much an old man in a hurry, as Mao had been before him. Presumably conscious that he might not have much longer to live and convinced that the P.R.C. had lost years of development on account of Mao, the other radicals, and the Cultural Revolution, he moved as fast as he could to promote Chou En-lai's "four modernizations." To this end he did his best to put his personal supporters in key positions, rather than gradually building a broad coalition as Chou had done. It seemed probable that he was interested in even more offices for himself, like premier or possibly chairman of the P.R.C. It also appeared possible, although far from certain, that a stop-Teng movement might form around the much younger Hua Kuo-feng.

In foreign affairs, the new leadership followed in essence the policies of Chou En-lai, but without his brilliantly creative touch. Peking continued to insist that the United States must abandon Taiwan if it wanted to "normalize" relations with the P.R.C., but the absence of normalization until 1978 did not spoil what had been achieved in Sino-American relations. Peking continued to maintain a vigorous adversary relationship with the Soviet Union, neither accommodating with it nor provoking it to a dangerous degree but rather managing in a competent manner the threat from the colossus to the north. Japan was cultivated as before as China's leading trading partner and as a valuable counterweight to the Soviet Union. Peking continued to encourage anti-Soviet vigilance in Europe and to deprecate détente between the United States and the Soviet Union, which might free Moscow to concentrate still more of its forces near the Sino-Soviet border. In the Third World, the anti-Soviet emphasis was also foremost; in order to conciliate governments, Peking reduced its support for insurgency ("revolution") somewhat, but not to the point of abandoning it entirely.

Bibliography

Barnett, A. Doak. *China on the Eve of Communist Takeover.* New York: Praeger, 1963.

————— . *Communist China: The Early Years, 1949-55.* New York: Praeger, 1964.

Clubb, O. Edmund. *Twentieth Century China.* 2nd edition. New York: Columbia University Press, 1972.

Domes, Jürgen. *The Internal Politics of China, 1949-1972.* New York: Praeger, 1973.

Guillermaz, Jacques. *A History of the Chinese Communist Party, 1921-49.* New York: Random House, 1972.

————— . *The Chinese Communist Party in Power, 1949-1976.* Boulder, Colo.: Westview Press, 1976.

Harrison, James Pinckney. *The Long March to Power: A History of the Chinese Communist Party, 1921-72.* New York: Praeger, 1972.

Hinton, Harold C. *An Introduction to Chinese Politics.* 2nd edition. New York: Holt, Rinehart and Winston/Praeger, 1978.

Hucker, Charles O. *China's Imperial Past: An Introduction to Chinese History and Culture.* Stanford, Calif.: Stanford University Press, 1975.

Karnow, Stanley. *Mao and China: From Revolution to Revolution.* New York: Viking, 1972.

Lin Piao. *Long Live the Victory of People's War.* Peking: Foreign Languages Press, 1965.

MacFarquhar, Roderick. *The Origins of the Cultural Revolution.* Vol. 1, *Contradictions Among the People, 1956-1957.* New York: Columbia University Press, 1974.

Mao Tse-tung. *Selected Works of Mao Tse-tung.* 5 vols. (covering through 1957). Peking: Foreign Languages Press, 1965-1977.

Meisner, Maurice. *Mao's China: A History of the People's Republic.* New York: Free Press, 1977.

Oksenberg, Michel. "Mao's Policy Commitments, 1921-1976." *Problems of Communism* 25, no. 6 (November-December 1976):1-26.

Rice, Edward E. *Mao's Way.* Berkeley: University of California Press, 1972.

Schurmann, Franz. *Ideology and Organization in Communist China.* 2nd ed. Berkeley: University of California Press, 1969.

Solomon, Richard H. *Mao's Revolution and the Chinese Political*

Culture. Berkeley: University of California Press, 1971.

Thornton, Richard C. *China: The Struggle for Power, 1917-1972.* Bloomington: Indiana University Press, 1973.

Walker, Richard L. *China under Communism: The First Five Years.* New Haven, Conn.: Yale University Press, 1955.

4
The Political System
Harald W. Jacobson

The system of government developed in the People's Republic of China (P.R.C.) is a centralized, one-party system, a self-styled "dictatorship of the proletariat,"[1] in which the Communist Party of China (CPC), through an intricate network of administrative agencies, exercises virtually total control over the lives of China's 950 million people. In addition to the CPC, this network consists of a formal state apparatus, the judicial and security organs, the People's Liberation Army (PLA) and militia, and an array of mass organizations that embrace in their collective functions every citizen of the P.R.C. The system as it functions today has evolved progressively over the relatively few years since the P.R.C. was formally established on October 1, 1949.

The motivating force behind this system is a sinicized form of Marxism-Leninism officially referred to by the Chinese as "Marxism–Leninism–Mao Tsetung Thought," which is described as the "highest form of Marxism-Leninism in the present era" and is claimed by Peking's leaders to be the most orthodox form of Marxism practiced anywhere today. The major objective placed before the system at present is, in the words of the late Premier Chou En-lai, the building of China "into a powerful, modern socialist country" before the end of the present century.

Maoist Thought on the Transformation of Chinese Society

Well before the Communists came to power in China, Mao Tse-tung foresaw China moving toward the ultimate goal of communism through two distinct revolutionary stages: a democratic revolution, followed by a socialist revolution.[2] Though official commentary on the transition to a socialist society has been blurred somewhat since the

Communists came to power, the general trend of social development since 1949 has conformed closely to the scheme outlined by Mao in a series of articles written in the 1930s and 1940s.

During the democratic revolution, Mao visualized the transformation of the "semicolonial" society of China—his description of the pre-1949 status of Chinese society—into an "independent democratic society." This was not to be a "bourgeois democracy," which he considered prevailing democracies to be, but a new and special "Chinese type" of democracy, a people's democracy, or as he termed it, a "New Democracy," in which vestiges of capitalism would be tolerated and bourgeois elements willing to cooperate in the building of a new China would be invited to participate. Acceptable social classes were to be workers, peasants, petty bourgeoisie (small merchants, handicraftsmen, professionals, intellectuals, and some upper peasants), and national bourgeoisie (middle capitalists and rich peasants). Only landlords, "big capitalists," and other classified as counterrevolutionaries were to be excluded. Industry and commerce would include a private, capitalist as well as a state-owned sector.

The democratic revolution was to be followed by a socialist revolution, marking the transition to socialism. During this period, residual capitalism would be phased out, remaining bourgeois elements basically eliminated, traditional culture replaced by a "new culture," and society placed on a socialist, egalitarian base. From that stage China would move eventually into a state of communism, the nature of which CPC theoreticians, like their fraternal political thinkers elsewhere, have studiously avoided discussing and a goal for which no schedule has yet been set.

In line with Mao's concept, the P.R.C. was formally established on October 1, 1949, by an assembly convened in Peking by the CPC in late September 1949, composed of delegates of the CPC, representatives of several small political parties and groups that had been active in China during and shortly after World War II, and a number of independent political figures who had opposed Kuomintang (KMT) rule in the country. This assembly took the name "Chinese People's Political Consultative Conference" (CPPCC), presumably to suggest continuity with the Political Consultative Conference that had met in Chungking in early 1946, during the abortive effort of General George C. Marshall to assist in forming a coalition government in China in the hope of averting civil war. Indeed, several of the non-Communist as well as CPC delegates to the CPPCC had also participated in the earlier forum. Such continuity would impart legitimacy to the new regime, while the exploitation of a multiparty forum would suggest a broad political base and popular support and would harmonize with Mao's concept of the New Democracy.

Although Chinese Communist theoreticians began in the mid-1950s to describe the period immediately following the establishment of the P.R.C. as a period of transition, implying transition to socialism, the period from 1949 to 1953-1954 was in fact a period of political consolidation and economic rehabilitation, and its social and economic characteristics were those attributed by Mao a decade earlier to the period of the New Democracy.

Consolidation and rehabilitation were essentially completed by the end of 1952, and preparations were launched for the promotion of national economic plans and the socialization of China. Thus the period of transition to socialism can be said to have commenced about 1953-1954. This period lasted approximately twenty years, or from 1953-1954 to 1973-1975.

The transition of Chinese society through the revolutionary stages is clearly reflected in the series of revisions of Party and state constituents since 1949. Thus, in 1973 and 1975, successive constitutions were adopted by the Party and state, respectively, in which the former inferentially and the latter specifically[3] acknowledged the attainment of socialism. Earlier, shortly after the inauguration of the commune program in 1958, some Chinese leaders had prematurely declared that China had entered the socialist stage and stood on the threshold of communism but such assertions had soon disappeared from CPC rhetoric.

Paralleling the reflection of the socialization process has been a step-by-step unveiling in the constitutions of the Party's changing position from that of acknowledged leader of a united front to that of undisguised dictatorship. The united front of the early 1950s was of considerable importance to the CPC for more reasons than those noted in connection with the significance of the CPPCC. Prior to 1949, the experience of the CPC had been limited largely to rural areas of China. With the acquisition in relatively short time of vast territories in 1948 and 1949, and particularly with the occupation of large urban industrial centers, the Party was confronted with immense new problems requiring the attention of personnel possessing managerial and technical skills, of which the CPC was either in short supply or totally lacking. It was therefore essential for the CPC to retain large numbers of such skilled personnel already on station until they could be replaced by cadres trained under Communist guidance, or until the former skilled personnel successfully underwent programs of ideological remolding.

As Communist cadres increased in numbers and in skills, and as the capitalist sector was progressively squeezed out, the remaining bourgeoisie became decreasingly useful to the CPC and its members were gradually weeded out. They became a major target for attack during the Cultural Revolution and in the major political campaigns that followed, and, in line with Mao's warning that the bourgeoisie will continue to pose a threat to the Party and to its objectives even after the attainment of socialism, the "elimination" of the bourgeoisie came to be identified by the Party constitution as one of the "basic programs" of the Party during the period of socialism.[4]

Political Geography, Constitutions, and Elections

To avoid repetition in the sections that follow, it is useful at this point to discuss briefly the territorial subdivisions of the P.R.C. as they relate to the functions and operations of the Party and state. Similarly, brief summaries of constitutional developments in the P.R.C., CPC theory of constitutions, and its concept of elections will obviate the need to deal with these subjects separately under Party and state.

Administrative and Electoral Subdivisions

For administrative purposes, the P.R.C. is territorially subdivided at four levels—the provincial, prefectural, county, and subcounty. Except for the prefectures (autonomous prefectures excluded), these are classified by the regime as levels of "state power" and serve as electoral units. Although there have been changes over the years in the territorial organization and in the names given to territorial subdivisions, the counties have remained relatively constant since 1949, and in most cases have remained intact since imperial times. Though most provinces have retained traditional names and many have remained unchanged in area, there has been considerable reorganization of the structures of frontier provinces through the elimination by merger of some and the shifting of the subordination of some counties back and forth from one province or autonomous region to another. Most conspicuous has been the establishment of the autonomous regions. Above the province, the CPC has experimented from time to time with larger provincial groupings for various administrative purposes, as noted below, while below the county level the country has experienced major territorial reorganization with the promulgation of the people's communes.

At the provincial level, there are at present 21 provinces, 5 autonomous regions, and 3 municipalities—Peking, Shanghai, and Tientsin—directly under the central government (one province, Taiwan, claimed by the P.R.C. is presently beyond its control). The provinces and autonomous regions are divided into counties, autonomous counties, and metropolitan cities. The municipalities under the central government and the cities under provincial authority generally include neighboring rural counties as well as the urban districts into which they are subdivided.[5] At the county level, at the end of 1976 there were 2,136 county or county-equivalent units and 186 cities subordinate to provincial-level governments.[6]

In the early 1970s, an intermediate administrative level between the province and the county was revived by the introduction of prefectures, consisting of a combination of several counties into a larger administrative unit. Created primarily for economic administration, the prefectures essentially correspond to the special districts that functioned at an earlier period of Communist control and that had roots in traditional Chinese territorial organization. At the end of 1976, there were 217 units at the prefectural level in the country,[7] but at the Fifth National People's Congress (NPC) in early 1978, Premier Hua Kuo-feng pointedly remarked that revolutionary committees would not be established at the prefectural level, except in autonomous prefectures, inasmuch as the "organ of state power at the prefectural level is an agency of the provincial authorities."

In some cases, two or more ancient cities have been joined for administrative purposes. Examples are Luta, a combination of former Port Arthur and Dairen; Wuhan, a combination of Wuchang, Hanyang, and Hankow; and Siangfan, the merger of Hsiangyang and Fancheng in Hupeh Province.

Below the counties are some 50,000 people's communes and an indefinite number of towns. (In the 1960s, there were some 70,000 communes.) The people's communes are divided into production brigades and these in turn are divided into production teams. The production team is the basic rural accounting unit, while most rural institutions are maintained at the commune and town levels; urban institutions are maintained at district and neighborhood organization levels.

The autonomous areas—regions, prefectures, and counties—are

Map 7   Administrative Map of China

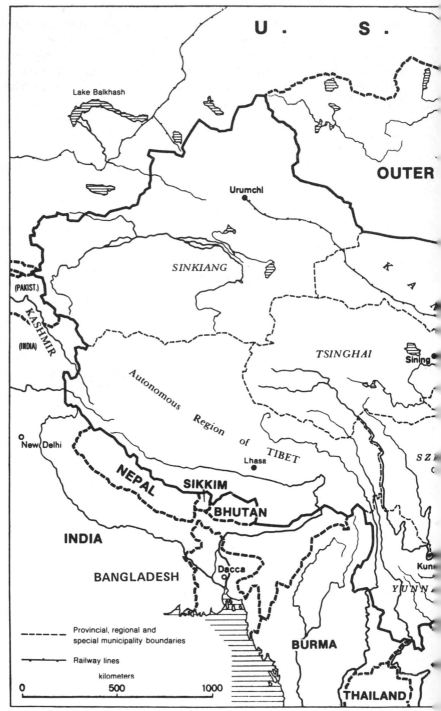

geographical areas in which one or more of China's fifty-odd ethnic and cultural minorities,[8] numbering some 55 million, are heavily concentrated. These areas were set apart initially from basically Han-populated areas in order to induce cooperation by allowing a modicum of self-government and to take into account traditional cultures and institutions in the planning of political, economic, and social programs. The term "autonomous" does not imply political independence but rather a limited degree of self-government and the tolerance of local cultures, practices, and the use of indigenous languages while the areas are steadily directed, under Han tutelage, toward the ultimate goal of integration with the rest of the country. The distinction between the political system of the Han and that originally obtaining in the autonomous areas has been essentially abolished; consequently, the political apparatuses of the autonomous areas now correspond generally to those in Han areas, except that at the autonomous prefecture level there are political institutions that are absent in nonautonomous prefectures.

In areas of high Mongol concentration in the Inner Mongolian Autonomous Region and in western parts of Heilungkiang, Kirin, and Liaoning provinces, "leagues" correspond to prefectures and "banners" to counties. These names derive from the traditional terms used by the Mongols in reference to units in their nomadic tribal organization.

The P.R.C. has from time to time grouped provinces in various combinations for special purposes. Immediately after the establishment of the regime, for purposes of consolidation and military control, the provinces were grouped into six large administrative areas—the northwest, north, northeast, central-south, southwest, and east China areas. These were abolished in 1954, but are now being restored under the same designations, according to Party Chairman and Premier Hua Kuo-feng, in order to facilitate the planning and administration of the ambitious modernization program to which the Party is committed.

For military administration (discussed in Chapter 10), the P.R.C. is divided into eleven large military regions. Shantung Province constitutes a military region by itself; Sinkiang Military Region is composed of Sinkiang Province and part of western Tibet; Chengtu Military Region is composed of the remainder of Tibet and Szechwan Province; the remaining eight military regions consist of two of more provinces and autonomous regions, each of which constitutes a military district. The military commands of the three municipalities are designated as garrison commands and are attached to two of the military regions.

Structures of the major nonmilitary organizations in the P.R.C.—the Party, the state, and the mass organizations—are all built on a pyramidal model, generally with five or six tiers of organs ascending from the base units through administrative organs at subcounty, county, and provincial levels to the national executive-administrative body at the apex.

Nature and Function of Constitutions

Party and state constitutions are promulgated by the P.R.C. for the purposes of defining Party policies and programs for the short term as well as the long term and of providing operational guidance and rules for Party functionaries and the public. They are therefore considered neither sacrosanct nor permanent but as documents to be altered with relative ease in accordance with the requirements of a rapidly changing society.

Each national Party congress (Party congress hereafter) that has met since the Party came to power has adopted a revised Party constitution—the Eighth Party Congress in 1956, the Ninth in 1969, the Tenth in 1973, and the Eleventh in 1977.[9] The 1956 constitution was a lengthy document of sixty articles grouped under nine chapter headings. It included fairly extensive discussions of Party principles and objectives, procedures for acquiring membership and membership obligations, and contained detailed information about Party structure and the powers and functions of Party organs at each level. Subsequent constitutions have all been brief, focusing on matters of primary interest and concern to the Party at the time of promulgation. In these, Party structure has been dealt with only in the barest outline. The 1969 constitution, for instance, adopted after the Cultural Revolution at a time when the military were in a particularly strong position, contained a clause naming Lin Piao as Mao's successor in the Party. The 1973 constitution, produced after Lin Piao's abortive coup d'etat and demise, eliminated the clause but otherwise retained much of the text of the 1969 draft. The most recent Party constitution of 1977, promulgated after a major Party purge and after a decade of internal dissension, placed emphasis on the importance of Party unity, discipline, and the practice of democratic centralism. It also reorganized the system for maintaining surveillance over the performance and behavior of Party members.

State constitutions show a similar history. A provisional state constitution, actually consisting of three documents, namely, the "Common Program of the Chinese People's Political Consultative Conference," the "Organic Law of the Central People's Government of the People's Republic of China," and the "Organic Law of the Chinese People's Political Consultative Conference," was adopted by the CPPCC in 1949. This was replaced by a formal "Constitution of the People's Republic of China" enacted by the First National People's Congress (NPC)[10] in 1954, which in turn was revised at the Fourth NPC in 1975, and then supplanted by one adopted by the Fifth NPC in 1978.

As in the case of the Party constitutions, the 1954 state constitution was a lengthy document of 106 articles that dealt in detail with government organization and with the principles that were to guide the government, while the 1975 constitution was brief, noting the attainment of socialism and acknowledging the supremacy of Party over state but touching only lightly on organizational matters. Following the Ninth Party Congress and the promulgation of the Party constitution that designated Lin Piao as Mao's successor in the Party, the draft of a revised state constitution was circulated throughout the country for study and comment. This draft provided for the restoration of Mao Tse-tung as chief of state and commander of the armed forces and named Lin Piao as Mao's successor in the state apparatus. The draft, however, provoked heated dispute and was never acted upon, partly because Lin Piao's death had rendered one of the most controversial points and the central objective of the draft obsolete, but it did provide much of the rationale for the 1975 constitution. The 1978 version glorifies Mao as the founder of the P.R.C., rededicates the regime to hold high and defend the "banner" of Mao Tse-tung, and restores much of the detail about the organization of the state apparatus that had been deleted from the 1954 version.

The Electoral System

An election in the Chinese Communist system, whether Party or state, national or local, is a consensus-seeking process—a process in which agreement on candidates to be elected to Party or state organs at all levels is reached through discussion and negotiations. Both Party and state constitutions[11] stipulate that all elections must be by secret ballot after "democratic consultations" and that they be in accordance with the "three-in-one" principle of combining "the old, the middle-aged, and the young." A communiqué released at the conclusion of the Tenth Party Congress in 1973 described the process of "democratic consultations" by stating that the delegates to that congress had been elected after "repeated deliberations and consultations" about the candidates, and after solicitations of the opinions of the masses both inside and outside the Party in the areas or organizations to which they belonged.[12] The requirement that the three age groups be represented in all elected Party and state organs is a product of the criticism levied during and after the Cultural Revolution against the perpetuation of power monopoly by veteran revolutionaries. While an increased number of young functionaries have been elected to the large bodies of the Party and state since the Cultural Revolution, the most important permanent organs of Party and state continue to be dominated mostly by veterans and senior middle-aged personnel, with relatively few young persons in positions of real power. Application of the principle is thus a relative matter.

In 1968, Hsieh Fu-chih, minister of public security at the time, told the Twelfth Plenum of the Eighth Central Committee that delegates to the Eighth Party Congress in 1956 were the first to have been elected to a Party congress; participants of preceding congresses, except the First, at which the Party was organized, had all been appointed.[13] The present Party constitution calls for the election of delegates to the national Party congress every five years and elections to provincial and county Party organs every three. But the Party constitution allows for both prior or delayed elections in either case. At each level of Party organization, preparations for elections are the responsibility of the Party committees at the corresponding level, and the composition of Party committees elected by Party congresses at any level is subject to the approval of committees at the next higher level.

Election of deputies to the NPC is also called for every five years, but elections to provincial and lower-level state organs vary from two to five years, depending on the level. The state constitution also provides for early or postponed elections. It grants electoral units and electors the power to supervise the deputies they elect and to replace them at any time according to provisions of law.[14] It grants the right to vote and to stand for election to every citizen eighteen years of age, regardless of sex, who has not been legally deprived of such rights.

The Party

As of August 1977, the Communist Party of China had a membership of more than 35 million,[15] representing an increase of 7 million over the 28 million claimed by Chou En-lai at the Tenth Party Congress in 1973. This number exceeds the total population of all but twenty-one countries in the world, excluding China, and makes the CPC the largest political organization ever formed. The management of such an enormous entity is obviously a task of major organizational and administrative proportions.

The experiences of the Cultural Revolution and the political infighting in the post–Cultural Revolution period have caused the Party to focus new attention on matters relating to membership selection, training, and discipline. The Party constitution provides that membership is open to "any Chinese worker, poor peasant, lower-middle peasant, revolutionary soldier, or any other revolutionary" eighteen years of age who is acceptable to his peers and to Party organizations at the basic and immediately superior levels, who possesses the proper political outlook, and who successfully passes through a rigid selection process. The term "Chinese" includes the ethnic minorities as well as the Han residents of the country.

Party membership provides status, career opportunities, and personal influence and is therefore highly sought after, particularly by talented and ambitious youth. But with less than 4 percent of the population possessing Party membership, despite the size of the Party, it is a goal not readily achieved. Sources of recruitment are production units (factories, mines, and communes), schools, mass organizations, the PLA, and particularly, the Communist Youth League, in all of which aspirants have the opportunity to demonstrate talent, leadership qualities, industry, and political rectitude.

In order to preserve the revolutionary qualities of the CPC, Mao advanced five principles that must characterize "successors" to the revolution in China: (1) they must be genuine Marxist-Leninists, not revisionists like Khrushchev; (2) they must wholeheartedly serve the majority of the people of China and the whole world; (3) they must be proletarian statesmen, capable of uniting with the overwhelming majority, including those with whom they do not agree and even those who have opposed them; (4) they must be models in applying the Party's principle of democratic centralism and masters of the leadership principle of dealing with and listening to the masses; and (5) they must be modest and prudent, must guard against arrogance and impetuosity, and must be imbued with the spirit of self-criticism, having the courage to correct mistakes and shortcomings in their work.[16]

In line with these principles, the constitution has laid down a strict code of conduct with which Party members are expected to comply. In addition to carrying out the tasks assigned by the Party, this code calls for a commitment to the conscientious study of Marxism-Leninism-

Mao Tsetung Thought; avoidance of the pursuit of private interests; honesty, truthfulness, and openness; upholding Party discipline and unity; abstention from factional activity; service to the people; and maintenance of close ties with the masses. To insure adherence to these principles and better performance by Party members, the 1977 Party Congress reemphasized the need for Party organs at all levels, including those in units within the PLA, to implement the standing requirement of establishing commissions for inspecting Party discipline and to vigorously enforce these inspections.

Members who fail to meet standards of conduct and performance are subject to disciplinary action ranging from an initial warning to reeducation through labor and even expulsion. In recent years, expulsion has been resorted to even in cases of leading members of the Political Bureau—Liu Shao-ch'i, for instance, who was expelled in October 1968 after more than a year of criticism for alleged counterrevolutionary activities, and the "Gang of Four" (Wang Hung-wen, Chang Ch'un-ch'iao, Chiang Ch'ing, and Yao Wen-yuan), all Political Bureau members, in July 1977 for conspiracy to seize Party and state power. Liu had at one time been considered Mao's eventual successor, while Wang had ranked third in the Party after being catapulted forward at the Tenth Party Congress as the leading member of a new generation of CPC leaders.

The National Party Congress

Theoretically, the highest organ of the Party is the national Party congress. Real power, however, rests with the Political Bureau of the Central Committee and, more precisely, with the Standing Committee of the Political Bureau, the ultimate decision-making body in the system. The number of delegates to the congress is not fixed by the constitution but, together with questions relating to procedures governing their election and replacement, is left to the Central Committee to determine. The communiqué announcing the conclusion of the Eleventh Party Congress, held August 12-18, 1977, stated that 1,510 delegates had attended that congress and that they had been elected by Party organizations "in different areas and units"—presumably meaning by the Party committees of the provinces, autonomous regions, and municipalities directly under the central government and by Party organizations at Party headquarters in Peking and at the top echelon of the PLA.

Four Party congresses have been elected since the Party came to

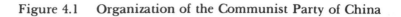

Figure 4.1 Organization of the Communist Party of China

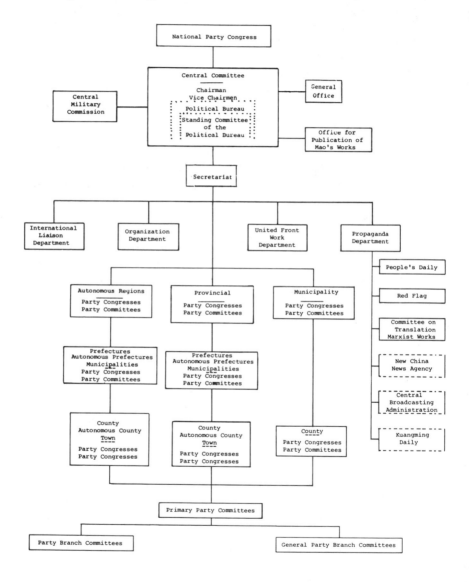

Table 4.1   National Party Congresses and Party Growth

Congress	Venue	Date		Delegates	Party Strength
First	Shanghai	July	1921	12	57
Second	Shanghai	June–July	1922	12	123
Third	Canton	June	1923	27	342
Fourth	Shanghai	January	1925	20	950
Fifth	Hankow	April–May	1927	80	57,900
Sixth	Moscow	July–September	1928	118	40,000
Seventh	Yenan	April	1945	752	1,210,000
Eighth	Peking	September	1956	1,021	10,734,000
Ninth	Peking	April	1969	1,512	20,000,000
Tenth	Peking	August	1973	1,249	28,000,000
Eleventh	Peking	August	1977	1,510	35,000,000

Data in this table have been drawn from several sources. The data on Party growth
are mostly taken from Winberg Chai, The New Politics of Communist China: Modernization of a Developing Country (Pacific Palisades, Calif.: Goodyear, 1972) p. 42;
and from P.R.C. sources. The figure for the Third Congress, however, is taken
from Jacques Guillermaz, A History of the Chinese Communist Party 1921-1949 (New
York: Random House, 1972), p. 83. Considerable uncertainty exists in respect to
the number of delegates present at the first six Party congresses. The figures
used for the first three are those that appear to be most commonly accepted. The
figure for the Fourth Congress is taken from Warren Kuo, Analytical History of
Chinese Communist Party (Taipei: Institute of International Relations of the
Republic of China, 1966), vol. I, p. 136; for the Fifth, Guillermaz, A History of
the Chinese Communist Party 1921-1949, p. 133; and for the Sixth and Seventh,
James P. Harrison, The Long March to Power, A History of the Communist Party,
1921-1972 (New York: Praeger Publishers, 1972) pp. 156 and 359, respectively.
For the Sixth, Harrison states that the congress was attended by 84 voting and
34 nonvoting delegates.

power: the Eighth in 1956, Ninth in 1969, Tenth in 1973, and the
Eleventh in 1977. Data pertaining to these and to previous congresses are
included in Table 4.1. The Party congress is elected for a term of five
years, but this period can be extended or reduced by the Central
Committee, whose duty it is to convene the congress. While the 1956
Party constitution called for annual sessions of the congress, subsequent
constitutions appear to contemplate only one session for each congress.
Despite the earlier requirement, however, only one Party congress since
1949, the Eighth, has been convened more than once, and over the
thirteen years of its life that congress met only twice, in 1956 and 1958.
Thirteen years elapsed between the initial meeting of the Eighth and the
convening of the Ninth Party Congress, but only four years between the

Ninth and Tenth and between the Tenth and the Eleventh, indicating a possible trend toward more regular convening of the congress but nevertheless reflecting a liberal interpretation of the Central Committee's power to extend or to reduce the life of a congress.

The proceedings of the Eighth Party Congress, to which representatives of Communist parties of both Communist and non-Communist countries were invited to attend as observers, were reported extensively by the P.R.C. media during its sessions. The attendant publicity rendered that congress a valuable platform from which to publicize Party programs, policies, and achievements, and to mobilize the masses for action. Subsequent congresses, however, have been convened in secrecy, no foreign observer has been invited to attend, and though rumors and speculations that they were in session or were about to be convened have circulated on each occasion, no publicity was released until each congress had adjourned.

The Ninth Party Congress, which met for twenty-four days, held plenary sessions at the beginning and end, and in between divided the delegates into smaller groups to discuss problems and issues. The same procedure may have been adopted at the following two but official releases give no indication. The Eleventh Party Congress held a one-day preliminary meeting on the eve of its formal opening, at which a presidium of 223 delegates was elected to guide the congress sessions, an agenda adopted, and credentials of the delegates certified.

Greater attention has been given to the inclusion of women, youth, and minority representation in the election of delegates to the last three congresses—the Ninth, Tenth, and Eleventh. The communiqué of the Eleventh Party Congress stated that middle-aged and young Party members (bracketed in one group) made up 73.8 percent of the delegates (leaving the veteran contingent at 26.2 percent), women 19 percent, and ethnic minorities 9.3 percent; 72.4 percent of the delegates were workers, peasants, and soldiers, 6.7 percent revolutionary intellectuals, and 20.9 percent revolutionary cadres. The proportion of minority representation is considerably above the proportion of the minority in the total population (about 5.8 percent), and the representation of workers, peasants, and soldiers rose from 67 percent in 1973 to 72.4 percent in 1977, but that of women declined from 20 percent in 1973 to 19 percent in 1977. Delegates credited to Taiwan, but living elsewhere, were included for the first time at the Tenth Party Congress.

A large percentage of the revolutionary elements elected to the Ninth

Party Congress, following the Cultural Revolution, failed to gain reelection to the Tenth or the Eleventh congresses, probably due, in most cases, to association with fallen leaders. On the other hand, a number of veterans, who had come under criticism during the Cultural Revolution and who had been dropped by the Ninth Party Congress, were restored to Party congress membership at either the Tenth or Eleventh congress.

Though described by the constitution as "the highest leading body," the actual power of the Party congress is limited. The 1956 constitution assigned the Party congress four tasks: (1) to hear and examine reports of the Central Committee and other central organs; (2) to determine the Party's line and policy; (3) to revise the Party constitution; and (4) to elect the Central Committee—its most important function. The present constitution contains no article dealing with the powers and functions of the Party congress but refers to the subject obliquely in stating that the Central Committee is elected by the Party congress. No other power or function is mentioned. The congress communiqués issued after the 1969, 1973, and 1977 congresses, however, indicate that the congress continues to perform the functions granted by the earlier constitution although the performance has become essentially pro forma. While the functions may have become pro forma, the congress nevertheless serves some useful purposes. It provides the Party leadership an opportunity to deal directly with regional functionaries and activists and to instruct them on Party policy and motivate them for action; it also offers regional leaders, particularly young, rising leaders, an opportunity to meet with leaders of the Party center so that they will return to their posts charged with responsibilities by the Party's highest authorities.

The Central Committee and the Party Chairman

The Central Committee is composed of two categories of personnel, members who possess voting rights and alternate members who may speak but not vote. The number of members and alternates is subject to determination by the Political Bureau in consultation with the Central Committee, and the trend has been a steady increase in each category since the Central Committee was first formed (see Table 4.2).[17]

The Central Committee elects its Political Bureau, the Standing Committee of the Political Bureau, and the chairman and an unspecified number of vice chairmen of the Central Committee. The Central Committee is the highest organ of the Party when the Party congress is not in session, which under present procedures, as noted, is

Table 4.2   Seventh to Eleventh Central Committees

Central Committee	Members	Alternates	Total
Seventh	44	33	77
Eighth-1956	97	73	170
Eighth-1958	91	89	180
Ninth	170	109	279
Tenth	195	124	319
Eleventh -1977	201	132	333
Eleventh-1978	210	132	342

from the conclusion of one congress to the convening of the next. And when the Central Committee is not in session, "its functions and powers" are exercised by the Political Bureau and its Standing Committee. These functions are not defined, nor are they limited; consequently, depending on the personal influence, prestige, and power of its members, they can be absolute and unlimited.

The Central Committee elected at the Eleventh Party Congress, composed of 201 members and 132 alternates, is the largest Central Committee elected to date. Of the 333, 26 members and 2 alternates have served continuously as members or alternates of the Central Committee since the Seventh or Eighth Party congresses (two were first given Central Committee appointment at plenary sessions of the Sixth Central Committee). Thirty-six members and 3 alternates were first elected at the Eighth Party Congress but were dropped by either the Ninth or Tenth, most because of adverse criticism during the Cultural Revolution, and rehabilitated at the Tenth or Eleventh Party Congress. The bulk, however, 139 members (69 percent) and 127 alternates (96 percent), had never served on the Central Committee prior to 1969, and of these, 53 members (26 percent) and 75 alternates (57 percent) were elected to the Central Committee for the first time in 1977. At the Third Plenum of the Eleventh Central Committee, held in November 1978, nine new members, all Party veterans mostly in their 70s, were added to the Central Committee, five of whom had been members and two alternates of the Eighth Central Committee but subsequently dropped.

Despite the last additions, the general trend reflected by these figures is the acceleration of the rate at which veteran revolutionaries are being replaced by a new leadership generation. Most conspicuous has been the passing, between the 1973 and 1977 Party congresses, of Mao Tse-tung and Tung Pi-wu, the two remaining founding members who were still associated with the CPC, and of veteran stalwarts Chu Teh, Chou En-lai, Li Fu-ch'un and K'ang Sheng and the rise to Party chairmanship of Hua Kuo-feng, who first attained Central Committee status at the Ninth Party Congress in 1969.

The 201 full members of the Eleventh Central Committee include all surviving members of the Tenth Political Bureau who were not purged plus the first secretaries of all provincial level Party committees and most subordinate secretaries, chairmen of all provincial level revolutionary committees, commanders of all military regions and districts, the first political commissars of these commands, and the national and some provincial leaders of major mass organizations. Alternates of the Central Committee include additional members of national and provincial level Party organs and military figures, plus model workers, peasants, and miners, and cultural and intellectual figures. (Military representation on the committee, however, declined from 32 percent on the Tenth Central Committee to less than 30 percent on the Eleventh.) In view of the obvious intention of including these categories on the Central Committee, the "consultation" involved in the election must, in this case, refer both to the process of familiarizing congress delegates with the identity of persons nominated by the Political Bureau for inclusion and to the exchange of views regarding models and other local figures to be honored by selection.

Prior to the Cultural Revolution, ranking alternates were elevated to full membership when vacancies occurred. This is no longer the practice. The growing tendency has been to reserve full membership for the principal Party functionaries in all organizations, both at the national and the provincial levels, and to elect as alternates rising Party and military figures and workers, peasants, soldiers, and others whose performances merit recognition.

Rank within the Party is a matter of importance. Whereas rank was determined by the number of votes received in the election of the Central Committee at the Seventh (1945) and possibly the Eighth Party Congress, it now appears to be decided by the Political Bureau. Rank is made public by the positions taken by Party members on public occasions relative to the location of the Party chairman, or it is indicated in the official rank listing of leaders attending various functions (these lists, however, may also deliberately avoid revealing rank by listing members according to the number of strokes in the Chinese character for their family names).

The chairman of the Central Committee is the de facto chairman of the Party and commander of the armed forces of the P.R.C. In contrast to most other Communist parties, in which the general secretary is the most powerful figure, the chairman is the principal official in the CPC. The post of Party chairman was created at the Seventh Party Congress in the first major effort to create a cult of Mao Tse-tung.[19] Prior to this, Mao's power had been consolidated around his role as chairman of the Military Affairs Committee (now Military Commission) of the Central Committee, a position he gained at the expense of Chou En-lai at the Tsunyi conference in 1935.

In the early days of the CPC, the most senior position in the Party was also that of general secretary.[20] When Mao was elected chairman of the Military Affairs Committee at the Tsunyi conference, he was apparently not strong enough to gain the general secretaryship, which went to one of his adversaries, Chang Wen-t'ien. The Comintern, however, became disenchanted with Chang and urged that he be dropped as general secretary, whereupon Mao seized the opportunity to abolish the post.[21]

Not only did the creation of the office of chairman contribute to the building of the cult of Mao, but Mao's occupancy of the post from its establishment until his death made the chairmanship what it became. The role of Party chairman was institutionally strengthened when the office of chairman of the P.R.C. was abolished by the Fourth National People's Congress. The chairman of the P.R.C. had, constitutionally, been concurrently commander-in-chief of the armed forces. The latter role was formally transferred to the Party chairmanship by the 1978 state constitution.

Hua Kuo-feng was elevated to the Party chairmanship after the death of Mao, and an intensive campaign was immediately launched to make his relatively unfamiliar name known throughout the country. The campaign sought to cloak Hua with the qualities of Mao and to begin a new cult of his personality. While focus has been placed on the aging of the Chinese leadership, it should be noted that Hua Kuo-feng, a relatively newcomer to top CPC leadership, at fifty-six years of age is the third youngest head of a Communist country at present.[22]

The Central Committee does not sit in continuous session, nor is it required to convene with any regularity. The 1956 constitution required it to meet twice a year, but subsequent constitutions simply state that it will meet when convened by the Political Bureau. The Central Committee elected by the Seventh Party Congress held seven plenums, the Eighth held twelve, the Ninth and Tenth three each, while the Eleventh had already held three plenary sessions as of December 1978. These figures, however, are somewhat misleading as indicators of Central Committee work inasmuch as the Central Committee has also been convened in meetings and conferences that are not included in the numbered plenum series, some of which are referred to as "working conferences." Some regular sessions of the Central Committee have been "enlarged sessions," meaning that people other than members and alternates have been invited to participate. These enlarged sessions have been convened, at times, in order to bring in specialists who are able to contribute to the primary topic to be considered; on other occasions they have been brought in to pad the attendance for political expediency, as in the case of the Eleventh Plenum of the Eighth Central Committee, which met in August 1966 to push through Mao Tse-tung's program for the Cultural Revolution and to demote Liu Shao-ch'i and Teng Hsiao-p'ing (not yet to remove them from office).

The Political Bureau

Because of its size and composition, the Central Committee is impractical as a policymaking or legislative organ. Most of its members reside outside of Peking and have local responsibilities, hence it cannot sit frequently or meet for extended periods. The important functions of forming policy and directing Party affairs fall, therefore, upon the Political Bureau, a more manageable body, most of whose members reside in Peking. In the recent past, the Political Bureau has consisted of twenty to twenty-seven members and three to six alternates, with a Standing Committee of five to nine of its most influential members functioning as an "inner cabinet" (see Table 4.3).

Meetings of the Political Bureau are not ordinarily reported but, since the autumn of 1976, decisions of the Political Bureau have been mentioned by the P.R.C. media with increasing regularity, and on occasion a directive has even been reported in full. In 1977, the Political Bureau began to function again much as it did during the period of leadership harmony in the early and mid-1950s, when it constituted a deliberative body in which members spoke freely and debated issues but, practicing the principle of democratic centralism, presented a united front on decisions taken. That cohesiveness, to whatever degree it actually obtained, was later destroyed by the deep differences on policy that emerged toward the end of the 1950s and continued with varying

Table 4.3   Eighth to Eleventh Political Bureaus

Political Bureau	Year	Members	Alternates	Standing Committee
Eighth	1956	17	6	
"	1958	20	6	6
Ninth	1969	21	4	5
Tenth	1973	22	4	9
Eleventh	1977	23	3	5
Eleventh	1978	27	3	5

The figures above refer to the number elected at the Party Congress sessions and do not reflect changes made at plenary sessions of the Central Committee between congress sessions.

degrees of intensity until the winter of 1976-1977. With the fall of the "Gang of Four," a leadership more united on policy matters emerged, though important differences still remain. This new leadership is led by the Political Bureau's Standing Committee, which is composed of Party Chairman Hua Kuo-feng and Vice-Chairmen Yeh Chien-ying, Teng Hsiao-p'ing, Li Hsien-nien, Ch'en Yun, and Wang Hung-wen. The new leadership has written into the Party constitution a provision that Party committees at all levels must operate on the principle of collective leadership "with individual responsibility under a division of labor."[23]

The Political Bureau elected by the Eleventh Central Committee is composed of twenty-three members and three alternates, of whom twelve are serving on the Political Bureau for the first time, while only three had attained Political Bureau status prior to the Cultural Revolution (Table 4.4). Though this may suggest a fresh leadership, almost all members of the Political Bureau are veteran cadres, with an average age of 68.5 years for those for whom the date of birth is known. Six members have served on the Central Committee since 1945 and two more since 1956, while only one had never been elected to either the Central Committee or the Political Bureau as member or alternate before 1977. Four more members were added at the committee's third plenum, including Ch'en Yun, who was also named a vice-chairman, and Chou En-lai's widow, Teng Ying-ch'ao.

Decisions of the Political Bureau are issued in its name or in that of the Central Committee, take the form of resolutions, directives, and circulars, and are commonly referred to simply as Political Bureau decisions or Central Committee documents. They are normally sent to Party committees at the provincial level for information and further dissemination when they relate to Party matters and to the State Council for action when they relate to general state affairs. Military decisions are coordinated through the Military Commission of the Central Committee. All decisions and directives, however, appear to be processed through one or another of the specialized Central Committee organs.

The new leaders have embarked on policies of marked change from those that prevailed until Mao's death. While continuing to wave the banner of Mao Tse-tung, they have in face repudiated many of his fundamental policies and tactics and in some fields have reintroduced elitist policies highly criticized by Mao. At the core is their comprehensive policy objective of transforming China into a "modern, powerful socialist country" by the end of this century through the modernization of, and the advancement to world levels in, agriculture, industry, national defense, and science and technology. These objectives, first enunciated by Chou En-lai at the Fourth NPC in 1975, do not in themselves contravene aims sought by Mao, but some courses of action outlined for their attainment negate or violate principles preached by Mao. This comprehensive policy is being promulgated under the slogan of "a new Long March toward the four modernizations and to catch up with and surpass world levels."

Organs of the Central Committee

The constitution authorizes the Central Committee to establish "a number of necessary organs, which are compact and efficient" to attend to the day-to-day work of the Party, the government, and the PLA. The work of these organs falls under the direction and supervision of the Political Bureau. The organs have varied somewhat over the years; several were immobilized during the Cultural Revolution—some of these have since been reactivated, others have not. They include at present a Secretariat, a General Office, the Military Commission, a Propaganda Department, Organization Department, United Front Work Department, International Liaison Department, and several bureaus and offices connected with communications and publications matters.

Prior to the Cultural Revolution, the most important of these organs was the Secretariat, which was the housekeeping organ of the Central Committee. It transmitted directives and orders of the Central Committee to the proper executive agencies, was involved in developing

Table 4.4 Political Bureau Elected by the Eleventh Central Committee [1]

Standing Committee of the Political Bureau
(listed by rank)

Hua Kuo-feng
Yeh Chien-ying
Teng Hsiao-p'ing
Li Hsien-nien
Wang Tung-hsing

Members
(listed alphabetically)

Names	Approximate Age	Native Province	Central Committee Membership	Political Bureau Membership	Standing Committee	Specializations and Primary Posts
Chang T'ing-fa	(60)		11CC	11PB		M: Commander, Air Force
Ch'en Hsi-lien	64	Hupeh	A8CC 9/10/11CC	9/10/11PB		M: Commander, Peking Military Region; member, MilCom, CC; vice premier
Ch'en Yung-kuei		Shansi	9/10/11CC	10/11PB		F: Model peasant of the Tachai Brigade; vice premier
Chi Teng-k'uei		Honan (?)	9/10/11CC	A9PB 10/11PB		B: Vice premier; First PolCom, Peking Military Region
Fang Yi	68	Fukien	A8/9CC 10/11CC	11PB		B: Vice president, Chinese Academy of Sciences
Hsu Hsiang-ch'ien	75	Shansi	7/8/9/10/11CC	11PB		M: Vice chairman, MilCom, CC; vice chairman, NPC
Hsu Shih-yu	71	Honan	A8CC 9/10/11CC	9/10/11PB		M: Commander, Canton Military Region
Hua Kuo-feng	56	Shansi	9/10/11CC	10/11PB	11PB	B: Chairman, Central Committee, CPC; chairman, MilCom, CC; premier of State Council
Keng Piao	68	Hunan	9/10/11CC	11PB		B: Director, International Liaison Department, CC
Li Hsien-nien	72	Hupeh	7/8/9/10/11CC	8/9/10/11PB	11PB	B: Vice chairman, CC; vice premier; Economic Affairs and Finance
Li Te-sheng			9/10/11CC	A9PB 10/11PB	10PB	M: Commander, Shenyang Military Region; member, MilCom, CC
Liu Po-ch'eng	85	Szechwan	7/8/9/10/11CC	8/9/10/11PB		M: Inactive former field general; member, MilCom, CC; vice chairman, NPC
Ni Chih-fu		(Hopeh)	9/10/11CC	A10PB 11PB		W: Model worker; trade union activity
Nieh Jung-chen	78	Szechwan	7/8/9/10/11CC	11PB		M: Vice chairman, MilCom, CC; vice chairman, NPC
P'eng Ch'ung	(60)	Fukien	A9/10CC 11CC	11PB		B: Third secretary, Shanghai Municipal CPC Committee; second vice chairman, Shanghai Municipal Revolutionary Com.
Su Chen-hua	68	Hunan	A8CC 10/11CC	11PB		M: First PolCom, navy; deputy commander, navy

Names	Approximate Age	Native Province	Central Committee Membership	Political Bureau Membership	Standing Committee	Specializations and Primary Posts
Teng Hsiao-p'ing	73	Szechwan	7/8*-*10/11CC	8*-*10/11PB	8*-*10/11PB	B: Vice chairman, CC; vice chairman, MilCom, CC; vice premier; chief-of-staff, PLA
Ulanfu	71	Inner Mongolia	A7CC 8/-/10/11CC	A8PB 11PB		B: Director, United Front Work Department, CC; vice chairman, NPC
Wang Tung-hsing			9/10/11CC	A9PB 10/11PB	11PB	B: Vice chairman, CC; director, General Office of the CC
Wei Kuo-ch'ing	70	Kwangsi	A8CC** 8/9/10/11CC	10/11PB		B: First secretary, Kwangtung PPC; chairman, Kwangtung PRC; First PolCom Canton Military Region
Wu Te	63	Hopeh	A8CC 9/10/11CC	10/11PB		B: First secretary, Peking MPC; chairman, Peking MRC
Yeh Chien-ying	78	Kwangtung	7/8/9/10/11CC	9/10/11PB	10/11PB	M: Vice chairman, CC; vice chairman, MilCom, CC; vice chairman, CPPCC; minister of national defense
Yü Ch'iu-li	63		9/10/11CC	11PB		B: Vice premier; minister, State Planning Commission

Alternate Members

Names	Approximate Age	Native Province	Central Committee Membership	Political Bureau Membership	Standing Committee	Specializations and Primary Posts
Chao Tzu-yang			10/11CC		A11PB	B: First secretary, Szechwan PPC; chairman, Szechwan PRC; First PolCom, Chengtu Military Region
Ch'en Mu-hua			10/11CC		A11PB	B: Minister, Ministry of Economic Relations with Foreign Countries
Saifudin	61	Sinkiang	A8CC 9/10/11CC		A10/11PB	B: First secretary, Sinkiang PPC; chairman, Sinkiang PRC; First PolCom, Sinkiang Military Region; vice chairman, NPC

- Teng Hsiao-p'ing was attacked by Red Guard bulletins in early 1967 and was branded a counterrevolutionary by People's Daily in 1968. In the interim he had ceased to appear publicly. He was discharged from all his positions but rehabilitated in April 1973 and restored to most of his previously held posts by January 1974, only to be dismissed for a second time in April 1976. For a second time he was rehabilitated and returned to all posts held in January 1976 by the Third Plenum of the Tenth CC in July 1977.

** Wei Kuo-ch'ing was elected as an alternate member of the Eighth CC in 1956 and as a full member at the second plenary session of the Eighth CC in 1958.

Abbreviations: A   Alternate
                 B   Bureaucrat, Party or state
                 CC Central Committee
                 CPPCC   Chinese People's Political Consultative Conference
                 F   Farmer
                 M   Military

MilCom   Central Military Commission
PB   Political Bureau
PPC   Provincial Party Committee
PRC   Provincial Revolutionary Committee
PolCom   Political commissar
W   Worker

1 This table does not reflect the addition of Ch'en Yun as a vice-chairman and member of the standing committee, or of Teng Ying-ch'ao, Hu Yao-pang, and Wang Chen as Politburo members by decision of the Third Plenum of the Eleventh Committee in December 1978.

operational procedures, exercised a role in security matters, and maintained general surveillance over policy implementation. In carrying out its tasks, it was able to influence personnel appointments. The Secretariat disintegrated when its general secretary, Teng Hsiaop'ing, and several other members came under attack during the Cultural Revolution; it had not been referred to by P.R.C. media until January 1979, when a newly appointed member of the Political Bureau, Hu Yaopang, was identified as secretary general of the Central Committee,[24] a title initially held by Teng when he headed the Secretariat. In the interim, the functions of the Secretariat appeared to have been taken over by the General Office of the Central Committee, headed by Party vicechairman Wang Tung-hsing, and first mentioned by the media in November 1966, about the time reference to the Secretariat ceased.

The Propaganda Department, like the Secretariat, was a casualty of the Cultural Revolution but was restored in October 1976. Propaganda work has been recognized from the time of the founding of the Party as an important Party function. At that time, because of the smallness of the Party, only three officers were appointed by the First Party Congress to serve as permanent Party functionaries. One was to serve as Party secretary, responsible for overall party activity, a second was to oversee organizational work, and a third was to direct propaganda activity. The Propaganda Department has responsibility for developing and supervising ideological training, for promoting the correct ideological line in the field of culture, and for the correct interpretation of the Party line in the domestic and international informational programs of the P.R.C.

The Central Military Commission, headed by the Party chairman and composed of senior PLA officers, is the organ responsible for basic military planning and development (see Chapter 10).

Relations with other Communist parties in good standing with the CPC, as distinct from government-to-government relations, are conducted through the CPC's International Liaison Department. Much of the bickering between Peking and Moscow in the early days of the Sino-Soviet controversy was conducted through this channel, but, with the further deterioration of relations between the P.R.C. and the Soviet Union, ties through the channel were severed.

The mission of the United Front Work Department is, as the name suggests, to promote national policies by securing the support and involvement of the masses in Party projects and movements. It deals with the various mass organizations, like the trade unions, the women's federation, and the peasants' and youth organizations, and with the "democratic parties" active in the CPPCC, which are now being revitalized in connection with the modernization drive. In addition, it appears to have some responsibility in the field of domestic intelligence[25] and directs limited activity beyond the frontiers of China, particularly in neighboring Hong Kong and Macau.

A number of Central Committee bureaus and subordinate committees deal with publications and media activities. *People's Daily (Jen-min jih-pao)* and *Red Flag (Hung ch'i)*, the Party's newspaper and theoretical journal, respectively, are published by organs that appear to function directly under the Propaganda Department. Of two committees directly subordinate to the Central Committee, one is charged with collecting and publishing works of Mao Tse-tung and the other with translating and publishing works of Marx, Engels, Lenin, and Stalin.

A few recent indicators suggest that the New China News Agency (NCNA), the Central Broadcasting Administration, and the *Kuangming Daily* may have been transferred from State Council to Central Committee control. NCNA collects and disseminates news at home and abroad and has primary responsibility for media content in the P.R.C., while the Central Broadcasting Administration maintains networks of radio and television broadcasting stations. Radio broadcasts reach both domestic and foreign audiences, while television is limited in range to a domestic audience, though its Canton broadcasts can be monitored in Hong Kong. The *Kuangming Daily*, a national newspaper, which in the early days of the regime was considered to be the organ of the democratic parties, continues to carry domestic news items intended to appeal to their membership and to intellectuals in general, but carries foreign news identical to that found in *People's Daily*. One of the techniques employed by the Gang of Four in its effort to gain control of Party and state was to plant its journalistic agents in the directorates of key informational organs and to remove those opposed to it. Transferring the control of these organizations to the Central Committee would presumably reduce the prospects for the recurrence of such maneuvers and would conform with other measures taken to centralize and strengthen Party controls.

Local and Primary Party Organs

Party members are distributed throughout the bureaucracy, the mass organizations, various production units, institutions, the military and security establishments, and other local bodies. Each Party member is associated with a "primary Party organization," usually located within the member's employment unit, and there he or she has the twofold responsibility of performing the tasks required by the employment unit and carrying out his or her Party assignment. Basic Party units formed in factories, mines, schools, shops, offices, neighborhood organizations, agricultural production units, lower echelons of the PLA, and other establishments are classified by the CPC as "primary Party organizations"; those formed at county, autonomous prefecture, and provincial levels are referred to as "local Party organizations."

Executive bodies of primary Party organizations are of three types, namely, primary Party committees, general branch committees, and branch committees. The type established is determined by the size of the Party membership of the unit within which the committee is formed. In a unit with more than 100 members, a primary Party committee is elected either directly by the members at a general membership meeting or, if the membership is exceptionally large, indirectly at a meeting of delegates of the membership. Depending again on membership size, and on labor and residence factors, as for instance on a commune where members may be scattered in villages far apart and may be engaged in widely divergent labor activities, the primary Party committee may establish a number of general branch committees or branch committees subordinate to it. In employment units of 50 to 100 members, general branch committees are elected, as in the case of the primary Party committees, either at general membership or at delegates' meetings, while in units with fewer than 50 members, Party branch committees are elected only at general membership meetings. Only at the general membership meetings do Party members as a whole find opportunity to exercise their right to vote or to stand for election in Party affairs.

Party committees at the primary level elect their secretary or secretaries and other officials as dictated by local needs and serve as Party organs most directly in touch with the masses. The committees also elect delegates to the county Party congresses and thus serve as the basic building blocks in the Party pyramid that rises through organs at the county, the autonomous prefecture, and the provincial levels to the Central Committee at the apex.

At the county, autonomous prefecture, and provincial levels, Party congresses are theoretically convened every three years, at which they elect Party committees to serve as the permanent organs at corresponding levels. Since provincial Party congresses were initially established at different times, are elected for shorter terms than the national Party congress, and are convened irregularly, their numerical designations have no relevance to each other or to that of the national Party congress. The Party committees elect their standing committees, secretaries, and deputy secretaries. At the provincial level, a Party committee normally consists of a first secretary, several secretaries, and members. The committees of the more populous provinces may also elect a second secretary. Below the provincial level, Party committees are headed by a secretary. At each level, including the primary, Party committees also elect delegates to the Party congresses at the next higher level and all elections at a given level are subject to the approval of the Party committee at the next higher level.

Local Party committees direct the activities of several subordinate departments patterned after the structure of the Central Committee, generally including departments of organization, propaganda, and united front work, and a local office of the Young Communist League. Primary Party organizations are responsible for guiding the Party members of their units in political and ideological study, for educating members on Party policy, for directing their Party work, maintaining Party discipline, and recruiting new Party members. All members of the Party within a locality are expected to maintain close contact with the masses, report their views on various matters—their attitudes, complaints, and reactions—and to provide leadership by example. To strengthen surveillance over Party members, the Eleventh Party Congress called on all Party committees to enforce vigorously the constitutional provision directing Party committees to set up committees to inspect Party discipline and a Central Commission for Inspecting Discipline, composed of 100 members headed by Party vice-chairman Ch'en Yun, was appointed at the Third Plenum of the Central Committee.

The State

The state constitution describes the People's Republic of China as "a socialist state of the dictatorship of the proletariat led by the working class and based on the alliance of workers and peasants." It is a "unitary multinational state," in which all nationalities are equal. All power in the state "belongs to the people," who, under the leadership of the Communist Party of China, exercise this power through the National People's Congress and the local people's congresses at various levels.[26] The apparent contradiction between the concepts of people's power and Party dominance is rationalized by the declaration that the power of the people is mobilized through the agency of the Party which, as the "vanguard" of the working class, provides "the core of leadership for the whole Chinese people."[27]

The trend of constitutional development from the promulgation of the Common Program of the CPPCC and the Organic Law of the

Central People's Government of the P.R.C. in 1949 through the revision of the state constitution in 1975 had been a piecemeal acquisition by the Party of powers and functions previously granted the state. This trend was partially reversed in 1978 when the newly revised state constitution restored to the state a few of the powers and functions that it had ceded to the Party in 1975; these will be noted in the appropriate sections below. Despite these reversals, however, the general trends have been toward the increased concentration of power, initiative, and policy determination in the Party and the progressive transformation of the state apparatus into an executive, administrative agency of the Party. Strengthening of the Party role has been further enhanced by the virtual elimination of the earlier practice of assigning non-Party personnel to leadership positions in certain selected state organs, including certain ministries of the State Council.

The National People's Congress

At the apex of a pyramid of people's congresses, paralleling the Party congress structure, is the National People's Congress, the "highest organ of state power."[28] The NPC is composed of deputies elected by the provinces, autonomous regions, municipalities directly under the central government, and by the PLA. Provisions in earlier constitutions for the participation in the NPC by deputies elected by Chinese residents abroad[29] or by specially invited "patriotic personages"[30] have been deleted from the 1978 state constitution.

The Organic Law of the CPPCC, adopted in September 1949, provided for the eventual election of an All-China People's Congress to serve as the supreme organ representing the people. Pending the enactment of an election law and the election of that body, the CPPCC was empowered to exercise the functions and powers delegated to the All-China People's Congress. Accordingly, until the First NPC (elected in accordance with an election law that became effective on March 1, 1953) convened on September 15, 1954, the CPPCC had served in that capacity. When the new people's congress convened, it took the name "National People's Congress," by which it was identified in the constitution adopted by that congress.

Deputies to the NPC are elected for five years, terms that may be extended under special circumstances, or shortened. Contrary to the National Party Congress, the state constitution calls for annual sessions of the NPC but allows these sessions also to be "advanced" or "postponed." Five NPCs have been held to date (see Table 4.5). While the first two NPCs met in annual sessions, except for a 1961 session missed by the Second, the Third and Fourth NPCs met only once each, and that despite the fact that the Third, which covered the period of the Cultural Revolution and the Lin Piao affair, had a life of ten years.

Slightly more than 1,200 deputies were elected to the first two NPCs, while the number for the next three jumped first to about 3,000 and then to 3,500, representing an increase of roughly 250 percent—a far greater percentage than that of the interim population growth and suggesting a significant change in the proportionate representation provided for in the original election law. In addition to the accredited deputies to the Fifth NPC (the credentials of three were annulled), leading members of the Central Committee of the CPC, the State Council, and the PLA, who had not been elected as deputies, and all members of the Fifth National Committee of the CPPCC attended that NPC as observers. They also took part in discussions but undoubtedly did not vote.

Deputies to the NPC need not be members of the CPC, though the majority of those elected to recent NPCs probably have been. Indeed, some of the leading members of the NPCs have been "democratic personages," like Soong Ching Ling, the widow of Sun Yat-sen, who has been a member of every NPC and who, as a vice chairman of the Standing Committee of the Fourth NPC, became the ranking member of the Fourth NPC following the deaths of Chu Teh, chairman of the Standing Committee, and Tung Pi-wu, its senior vice chairman.

Constitutionally, conducting the election of deputies and convening the NPC sessions are the responsibilities of the Standing Committee of the NPC. In practice, however, all matters relating to the NPC, including its timing, the content of documents and reports to be submitted, and the nominees for major state offices, are previously determined by the Political Bureau and approved by the Central Committee.[31]

Theoretically, the NPC possesses both legislative and executive powers and exercises limited functions in the judicial process. In practice, however, its operations are confined to the discussion and endorsement of actions initiated by the Political Bureau, approved by the Central Committee in plenums convened to make final preparations for the NPC session, and endorsed by the elected NPC members in preliminary meetings immediately prior to the formal opening of its session.

Specific powers granted the NPC by the constitution are to amend the state constitution; make laws; supervise the enforcement of the constitution and the law; "decide on the choice" of the premier

Table 4.5 The National People's Congress

| Congress | Duration | Deputies | Percent Women | Minorities Representation | Officers Elected | | | |
					P.R.C. Chairman	P.R.C. Vice Chairman	Chairman NPC Standing Committee	Premier
First	Sept. 15 – 28, 1959	1,226			Mao Tse-tung	Chu Teh	Liu Shao-ch'i	Chou En-lai
Second	April 18 – 28, 1959	1,226	12.2	14.6 percent	Liu Shao-ch'i	Tung Pi-wu Soong Ching Ling	Chu Teh	Chou En-lai
Third	December 21, 1964 to January 4, 1965	3,040	17.8	12.27 percent	Liu Shao-ch'i	Tung Pi-wu Soong Ching Ling	Chu Teh	Chou En-lai
Fourth	Jan. 14-17, 1975	2,885	22 +	"54 minorities" Represented	Abolished	Abolished	Chu Teh	Chou En-lai
Fifth	Feb. 26-March 5, 1978	3,500	21.2	"All 54" Represented	---	---	Yeh Chien-ying	Hua Kuo-feng

(nominated by the Central Committee) and other members of the State Council (nominated by the premier);[32] elect the president of the Supreme People's Court and the chief procurator of the Supreme People's Procuratorate;[33] approve the national economic plan, the state budget, and the final state accounts; "confirm" changes in the configuration of major territorial subdivisions; decide on questions of war and peace; and exercise such other functions and powers as the NPC may deem necessary. With power to elect, the NPC is also empowered to remove from office the members of the State Council,[34] the president of the Supreme People's Court, and the chief procurator of the Supreme People's Procuratorate. Finally, the NPC elects a Standing Committee of the NPC.

The Standing Committee of the NPC is composed of a chairman, a number of vice chairmen, a secretary general, and an unspecified number of members. Elected by the NPC, officers and members of the Standing Committee are also subject to recall by the NPC. Its powers and functions are to conduct the election of deputies to the NPC and to convene its sessions; to interpret the constitution and laws and to enact decrees; to supervise the work of the State Council, the Supreme People's Court, and the Supreme People's Procuratorate; to appoint and remove members of the State Council upon the recommendation of the premier when the NPC is not in session; to appoint and remove vice-presidents of the Supreme People's Court and deputy chiefs of the Supreme People's Procuratorate; to "decide on" the appointment and removal of P.R.C. plenipotentiary representatives sent abroad; to "decide on" the ratification and abrogation of treaties concluded with foreign states; to "decide on" the institution and conferment of titles of honor; to grant pardons; to "decide on" the proclamation of war in the event of an armed attack when the NPC is not in session; and to exercise any other function or power vested in it by the NPC.

Under the new state constitution, the chairman of the Standing Committee is assigned a set of specific functions, which symbolically at least elevates that office above the role of simply presiding over meetings of the Standing Committee. The most conspicuous of these functions is that of receiving foreign diplomatic envoys, a function generally associated in the international community with the head of state. Though this function has been performed before by the chairman of the Standing Committee, it had not been one constitutionally assigned to that office. The chairman is also charged with the task of formally executing decisions taken by the Standing Committee on matters for which the latter has the constitutional power to act, like formally ratifying treaties approved by the Standing Committee, dispatching and recalling P.R.C. plenipotentiary representatives abroad, and conferring state titles of honor.

The Standing Committee elected at the Fifth NPC consisted of a chairman, Party veteran Yeh Chien-ying, 20 vice-chairmen, and 175 members, of whom 3 vice-chairmen and 35 members are women.

As in the case of the Eighth Party Congress, the first three NPCs were attended with publicity before, during, and after the sessions. A background report, for instance, released by the NCNA on the eve of the Third NPC gave a brief summary of the previous two NPCs, indicating the number of delegates elected to those and to the Third NPC, and outlining the functions and powers of the NPC. Other preliminary reports listed the deputies to the Third NPC by name, grouped according to representational areas, while the sessions of the NPC were reported daily, with texts of the principal speeches, resolutions, proclamations, and orders, and with the results of the elections. The Fourth NPC met and adjourned before any reference had been made to it by the P.R.C. media.

Treatment of the Fifth NPC, however, reverted to the earlier pattern. The date for the convening of the congress was announced by national media eight days before the opening session. Pre-congress preliminary meetings of the Central Committee and of the congress deputies were reported with brief summaries of the lines the congress would take. These were followed by daily coverage of the congress sessions, though less comprehensive or detailed than reports issued during the first three congresses. An innovation, however, was the very brief television coverage of the opening and closing sessions of the NPC, and especially a three-minute film report that was transmitted to Tokyo by satellite.

Elimination of the Office of Head of State

The 1954 state constitution provided for the election by the NPC of a chairman and a vice-chairman of the People's Republic of China. The chairman of the P.R.C. served as the official head of state and assumed the functions normally associated with such an office, including that of accepting the credentials of foreign ambassadors assigned to China. While the office was widely viewed as a ceremonial one, the 1954 constitution granted the chairman powers well beyond purely symbolic functions. He was the designated commander of the armed forces and chairman of the now-abolished Council of National Defense; with the approval of the NPC, he had the power to appoint and remove the premier, vice-premiers, and other members of the State Council; and he had the power to convene on "important affairs of state" the Supreme State Conference, an advisory body composed of the chairman and vice-chairman of the P.R.C., the chairman of the Standing Committee of the NPC, the premier of the State Council, and others whom the chairman might wish to invite (questions of the number and identity of those additionally to be invited were left entirely to the discretion of the chairman). An ambitious incumbent might well have exploited the constitutional powers of the P.R.C chairmanship to make of that office a potential alternate focus of power to that of the Party chairmanship.

In fulfilling its constitutional obligation, the first NPC elected Mao Tse-tung chairman and Chu Teh vice-chairman of the P.R.C. Either for personal reasons or because he was forced to do so, Mao withdrew his candidacy for the chairmanship before the Second NPC, which was scheduled to meet in 1959, convened. Although the constitution did not grant the Party a role in the nomination of candidates for these offices, the Party's hand in the matter was clearly reflected by the fact that when Mao decided not to stand for reelection he made his decision known at the Sixth Plenum of the Eighth Central Committee, which was held in Wuchang in late 1958.

With Mao's withdrawl, Liu Shao-ch'i, who had been chairman of the Standing Committee of the NPC, was elected chairman of the P.R.C. The number of vice-chairmen was increased to two and the posts were filled by Tung Pi-wu and Soong Ching Ling; Tung, together with Mao, was one of the two founding members still active in the CPC. Chu Teh, formerly vice-chairman, was elected chairman of the Standing Committee of the NPC. This entire configuration was preserved at the Third NPC.

So long as Mao concurrently held the chairmanship of both the P.R.C. and the Central Committee, which was obviously the intent of the framers of the 1954 constitution, power rivalry between the two offices was absent. But when Mao withdrew and Liu assumed the office of state chairman, a potential for conflict developed and did indeed materialize. After Liu fell from power in 1967, the P.R.C. chairmanship was left vacant for a period of time, since Liu was not officially removed from his various posts until October 1968. In the interim, Tung Pi-wu assumed most of the representational functions of the office and, after Liu's removal, was given the title of "acting chairman."

The chairmanship of the P.R.C. then became an issue in the Lin Piao affair. After managing to have his name inscribed in the 1969 Party constitution as Mao's designated successor, Lin moved to improve his future power position by pressing for the adoption of a new state constitution that would declare Mao to be the "chief of state" and the "supreme commander of the whole nation and the whole armed forces," presumably for life, and himself as "Chairman Mao's close comrade-in-arms and successor."[35] This provoked a heated controversy within the Party, which was resolved only with the death of Lin Piao and the promulgation of the 1975 state constitution, which abolished the offices of chairman and vice-chairman of the P.R.C. by the simple expedient of deleting reference to them. The question of restoring the P.R.C. chairmanship appears to have risen again prior to the convening of the Fifth NPC, but there is no public record that it was discussed at that session.

The powers formerly granted the P.R.C. chairman were divided, the appointive powers going to the NPC but requiring Central Committee or Political Bureau approval and the commandership of the armed forces going to the chairman of the Party, while the protocol functions were transferred to the chairman of the Standing Committee of the NPC. The abolition of the state chairmanship rendered the Supreme State Conference obsolescent. In the heyday of its exploitation by Mao, it had been used for some highly important matters. It was at a session of the Supreme State Conference in February 1957, attended by 1,800 persons from all parts of the country, that Mao spoke on internal contradictions. A much revised version of this informal speech was published several months later under the title, "On the Correct Handling of Contra-dictions among the People," now considered by the CPC as one of Mao's major theoretical contributions. At another Supreme State Conference in September 1958, Mao analyzed the domestic and international situations and Chou spoke on the Taiwan Strait situation. While the session was in progress, Chou issued a statement asserting the right of the P.R.C. to take military action to "liberate" Taiwan and the coastal islands held by the Kuomintang but offered to resume the ambassadorial talks with the United States, an offer that was accepted and resulted in the defusing of the Taiwan Strait crisis that had developed. The Supreme State Conference was also used by Liu Shao-ch'i periodically through 1964 but was neglected after leadership differences became deep.

The State Council

The State Council "is the central people's government."[36] It is the "executive organ" of the NPC, to which it is responsible and accountable, and the "highest organ of state administration."[37] It is composed of the premier (nominated by the Central Committee) and a number of vice-premiers, ministers in charge of ministries, and ministers heading commissions (nominated by the premier), all confirmed by the NPC.[38] The functions and powers of the State Council are to formulate administrative measures, issue orders and decisions, oversee the execution of state policies, prepare the national economic plan and the state budget for submission to the NPC, propose laws and other matters for consideration by the NPC, and to perform the many incidental tasks that fall to the administration of a large bureaucracy.

The executive responsibilities entail not only supervision of headquarters operations in Peking but the exercise of administrative direction over the work of the entire state apparatus from the national to local levels, including supervision of operations of P.R.C. missions abroad. Most, if not all, of the ministries, commissions, bureaus, and agencies attached to the State Council are represented in some or all provincial level administrative units. In many cases, their operations reach down to the county and commune levels.

While the functions and powers of the State Council may appear to be exceptionally broad, its basic courses of action are largely predetermined by the Central Committee and the Political Bureau, to both of which it is closely linked by concurrent memberships, as indicated below. With the overt consolidation of power in the Party, much of the initiative originally left to the State Council has progressively eroded through practice or constitutional changes, but some of the functions and powers that were constitutionally taken away in 1975 were restored in 1978. Nevertheless, the State Council continues to be primarily an executive body to which only limited policy-originating powers have been granted.

Functioning in the universal manner of bureaucracies, the State Council expanded rapidly during the 1950s and early 1960s, proliferating both in personnel and component units. By the late 1960s, according to Chou En-lai,[39] these units had burgeoned to 90 in number with a complement of 60,000 in central administrative organs. With the growing number of units, it had become necessary to create intermediate offices between the State Council and the ministries, commissions, bureaus, and agencies to supervise their work. These intermediate organs, referred to as "staff offices," numbered variously from 4 to 8, and each was given supervisory responsibility over a group of units, generally engaged in related activity. The staff offices were invariably headed by Political Bureau or Central Committee members.

The bureaucracy, state as well as Party, came under severe attack during the Cultural Revolution, and a number of ministries, including the ministries of education and culture, ceased to function. In the process of rebuilding the State Council after the Cultural Revolution, Chou En-lai consolidated its operations and reduced the number of its units; consequently, by 1971, the ministries had been decreased to 26 and the central government complement to 10,000.[40] The staff offices were no longer necessary and were abolished. Gradually, however, Parkinson's Law again took effect. By 1978, ministries under the State Council had increased from 26 in 1975 to 29 and commissions from 3 to 6, while other subordinate organs—bureaus and agencies—despite the apparent transfer of some of the Central Committee, had also increased in number.

The State Council organized at the Fifth NPC is composed of Premier Hua Kuo-feng, thirteen vice-premiers, led by Teng Hsiao-p'ing and Li Hsien-nien, twenty-six ministers heading ministries and six heading commissions, plus the president of the People's Bank of China and the director of the All-China Federation of Supply and Marketing Cooperatives. Heads of the latter two organizations were elevated to State Council status for the first time. Six of the council's members perform dual functions as concurrent vice-premiers and heads of ministries, leaving a State Council of forty-five members. Of these, three are members of the Standing Committee of the Political Bureau, seven others are members and one is an alternate member of the Political Bureau, twenty are full and five are alternate members of the Central Committee, and only nine have no affiliation with the top organs of the CPC. The latter appear to be specialists, appointed to head ministries for their particular knowledge and skills. (For the structure of the State Council, see Figure 4.2.)

Until his death in 1976, Chou En-lai had served continuously as premier since the founding of the P.R.C. For the first decade, he had served concurrently as minister of foreign affairs. During his final illness, Teng Hsiao-p'ing and Li Hsien-nien had alternated as his stand-in, but Teng was clearly the person tapped to succeed him as premier. Teng, however, lost out in the power struggle that followed Chou's death and sustained the second political fall in his career, while Hua

Kuo-feng, passing over several higher ranking Political Bureau and State Council members, was initially named acting premier and then in April 1976 was appointed premier on Mao's urgings. Hua was reconfirmed in this position at the Fifth NPC in 1978, despite earlier rumors that he might yield the premiership to Teng, who had been rehabilitated for the second time. In practice, however, Teng appears to be the person taking charge of day-to-day operations of the State Council, particularly of matters relating to the modernization programs.

Ministries carried over from the previous administration deal with foreign affairs, national defense, public security, foreign trade and other international economic relations, agriculture and forestry, water conservancy and power, railroads, communications, posts and tele-communications, finance, commerce, education, culture, public health, and a variety of specific industries. In conformity with general Communist practice, the P.R.C. has a number of machine-building industries—seven in all. A development worthy of note has been the trend toward replacement of military by civilian heads in these ministries. The increase of ministries, from twenty-six to twenty-nine decided upon at the Fifth NPC, results from the division of the former Ministry of Petroleum and Chemical Industries into two separate ministries to deal with each of the industries, and the creation of two new ministries, a Ministry of Civil Affairs and a Ministry of Textile Industries. Being very new, the field of responsibility of the Ministry of Civil Affairs and its relations to the Ministry of Public Security and some other ministries are not yet clear.

To the three former commissions—the State Planning Commission, the State Capital Construction Commission, and the State Physical Culture and Sports Commission—have been added a State Economic Commission, State Scientific and Technological Commission, and a Nationalities Affairs Commission. The appearance of the Nationalities Affairs Commission, charged with dealing with China's fifty-four ethnic and cultural minorities, represents the reemergence of a commission that went into eclipse during the Cultural Revolution.

The expansion of units under the State Council can in large measure be attributed to the regime's determination to move vigorously in pursuit of its ambitious development objectives. The additions and reorganization of subordinate organs, including the elevation of the two existing bodies to State Council level, can almost all be related to this effort. Moreover, the assignment of vice-premiers to head the four

Figure 4.2   The State (Government)

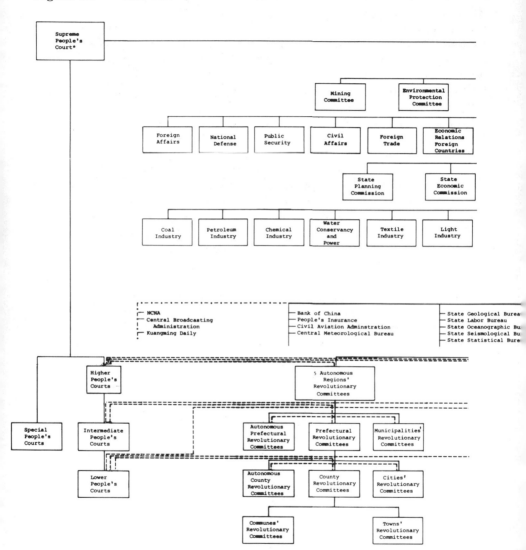

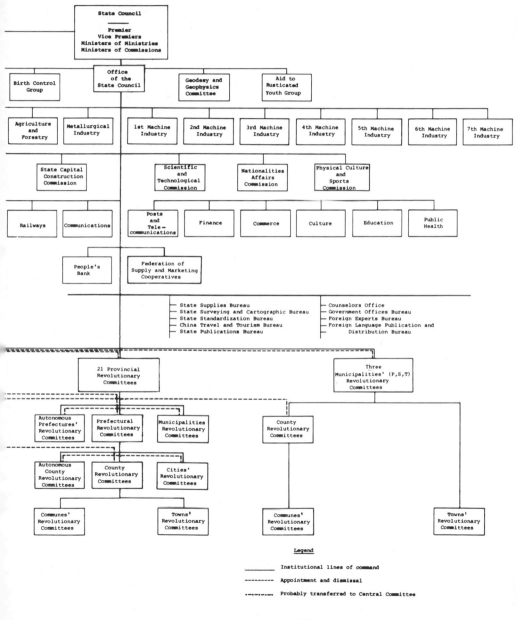

State Council

Premier
Vice Premiers
Ministers of Ministries
Ministers of Commissions

Office of the State Council

Birth Control Group

Geodesy and Geophysics Committee

Aid to Rusticated Youth Group

Agriculture and Forestry

Metallurgical Industry

1st Machine Industry

2nd Machine Industry

3rd Machine Industry

4th Machine Industry

5th Machine Industry

6th Machine Industry

7th Machine Industry

State Capital Construction Commission

Scientific and Technological Commission

Nationalities Affairs Commission

Physical Culture and Sports Commission

Railways

Communications

Posts and Tele-communications

Finance

Commerce

Culture

Education

Public Health

People's Bank

Federation of Supply and Marketing Cooperatives

— State Supplies Bureau
— State Surveying and Cartographic Bureau
— State Standardization Bureau
— China Travel and Tourism Bureau
— State Publications Bureau

— Counselors Office
— Government Offices Bureau
— Foreign Experts Bureau
— Foreign Language Publication and
   Distribution Bureau

21 Provincial Revolutionary Committees

Three Municipalities' (P,S,T) Revolutionary Committees

Autonomous Prefectures' Revolutionary Committees

Prefectural Revolutionary Committees

Municipalities Revolutionary Committees

County Revolutionary Committees

Autonomous County Revolutionary Committees

County Revolutionary Committees

Cities' Revolutionary Committees

Communes' Revolutionary Committees

Towns' Revolutionary Committees

Communes' Revolutionary Committees

Towns' Revolutionary Committees

Legend

—————— Institutional lines of command

---------- Appointment and dismissal

.—.—.—.—. Probably transferred to Central Committee

*Structure repeated for people's procuratorate.

commissions most directly involved—the State Planning, Capital Construction, Economic, and Scientific and Technological commissions—attests further to the importance attached to this effort, while the reactivation of the Nationalities Affairs Commission suggests the value placed on the mobilization of a large and inclusive united front.

Bureaus and agencies under the State Council deal with matters relating to civil aviation, tourism, geology, meteorology, seismology, oceanography, cartography, statistics, labor, and insurance. A State Museum and Archaeological Data Bureau, also known as the Cultural Relics Administrative Bureau, was established in 1973, probably as a result of the impressive archaeological finds during and after the Cultural Revolution. A Language Reform Committee continues to press for the standardization of the spoken language, simplification of characters, and for the promulgation of an alphabetized form of written Chinese.

Directly attached to the State Council is a General Office, which appears to be a housekeeping organ, corresponding to the Secretariat of the Central Committee. It probably handles the routine work of the State Council and coordinates the work of that office with the ministries, commissions, bureaus, agencies, and committees mentioned above. In addition to the General Office, a number of specialized offices, subordinate directly to the State Council, deal with diverse matters such as science, environmental protection, mining, birth control planning, and problems relating to the youth sent to the countryside.

A State Council Office of Overseas Chinese Affairs has been referred to recently by the P.R.C. media and appears to be a staff office. It probably takes the place of the Commission for Overseas Chinese Affairs that was abolished in 1967, and the restoration of such an organization reflects a renewed interest in cultivating both returned overseas Chinese now residing in China and persons of Chinese origin living abroad, particularly scientists and technologists who can contribute to the modernization effort.

Local Government

The principal organs of local government are established at the provincial, county, and commune levels. These are referred to in the state constitution as local organs of "political power."[41] Except in autonomous prefectures, administrative units at the prefectural level are agencies of provincial governments.[42]

The organs of political power at these levels are the people's congresses and revolutionary committees, the former serving as local representative bodies and the latter as permanent executive bodies of the people's congresses and the local organs of state administration at their respective levels.

People's congresses in communes and towns and in other basic electoral areas—cities not further divided into districts and districts of municipalities directly under the central government—are elected directly by the voters and, according to standard procedure, by secret ballot after democratic consultations. People's congresses and revolutionary committees in these basic units of local government are considered to be organizations of political power at the "grass-roots level,"[43] and only in elections at this level are the masses offered the opportunity to exercise their franchise.

People's congresses elected by the communes and towns elect deputies to the people's congresses at the county level; people's congresses at the county level, including those in cities and in the municipal districts, elect deputies to people's congresses at the provincial level; and people's congresses at the provincial level, as noted in the preceding section, elect deputies to the NPC. These together with the deputies elected through the PLA electoral system compose the NPC. Organs of "self-government" are established in autonomous regions, autonomous prefectures, and autonomous counties, which, with the passage of time, tend to conform more and more in structure and function with the standard institutions of local government.

People's congresses of provinces and municipalities directly under the central government, which generally consist of 800 to 1,200 deputies, are elected for terms of five years; those of counties, cities, and municipal districts for three years; and the congresses of people's communes and towns for terms of two years. The people's congresses at all levels are convened by the revolutionary committees at the corresponding level and are expected to hold sessions at least once a year. Elections of local people's congresses are determined by the Central Committee and conducted by the Standing Committee of the NPC and are geared to the election of new NPCs. Provincial-level people's congresses, therefore, are uniformly numbered and carry numerical designations corresponding to that of the NPC. Local people's congresses are charged with the responsibility of enforcing the constitution and the laws, of making plans for local economic and cultural development, and of rendering decisions on matters within the limits of their authority as prescribed by law.

People's congresses at each level elect and are empowered to recall members of the revolutionary committees at the corresponding level. At the county and provincial levels they also elect and have the power to recall the president of the people's court and the chief procurator of the people's procuratorate at their respective levels. Deputies to the people's congresses at the various levels have the right to address inquiries to the revolutionary committees, the people's courts, the people's procuratorates, and the organs under the revolutionary committees at the corresponding levels, to which inquiries the addressees are under constitutional obligation to respond.

A revolutionary committee is composed of a chairman, a number of vice-chairmen, and other members. The committees have the power to establish necessary administrative bodies and to appoint and remove personnel of state organs. At the provincial level, the revolutionary committees, which normally consist of 90 to 120 members, including the chairman and 10 to 14 vice-chairmen, also have the power to establish and supervise the work of administrative offices as their agencies in their respective prefectures.

Duties and responsibilities of revolutionary committees are to ensure that orders and decisions of the people's congresses and of the organs of state administration are duly carried out. They direct the administrative work in their respective areas and exercise powers of initiative within defined limits. Revolutionary committees at all levels are responsible and accountable to the people's congresses at the corresponding level and to organs of state administration at the next higher level. They function under the centralized leadership of the State Council.

Prior to the Cultural Revolution, people's councils functioned in the place of the revolutionary committees. Local people's councils in a province were composed of a governor, deputy governor, and members of the council; in a municipality they consisted of a mayor, deputy mayor, and members of the municipal council; while in a county the council was made up of a county head, a number of deputy county heads, and other members of the county council. The size of the council depended on the population and the extent of territory under the council's supervision.

The nationwide local government structure, however, collapsed during the Cultural Revolution as local revolutionary elements, taking advantage of Mao's advocacy of revolution from the bottom, overthrew local authorities, intimidated government cadres, and launched a period of intrafactional struggles for power. By the winter of 1966-1967, chaos reigned in many parts of the country and the PLA was invited to restore order. In January 1967, several revolutionary groups in Shanghai combined to seize power and formed an administrative body elected through a process modeled on that used to form the Paris Commune of 1871. This experiment, however, proved to be short-lived. Meanwhile, in Heilungkiang Province, revolutionary elements proclaimed on January 31 the establishment of a Red Rebel's Revolutionary Committee. The committee was composed of representatives of three revolutionary groups: revolutionary elements of the provincial military command, revolutionary Party cadres, and revolutionary masses. The revolutionary committee was highly praised by Party authorities and quickly became a model for other provinces, autonomous regions, and municipalities. By February 5, Shanghai had replaced its Paris-type commune with a similarly organized revolutionary committee, featuring the "three-way alliance" of revolutionary masses, cadres, and army men. The same month, revolutionary committees were established in Kweichow and Shantung, and by September 5, 1968, in a little more than twenty months, despite factional struggles, revolutionary committees had been installed in all provinces, autonomous regions, and in the municipalities under the central government.

Although revolutionary committees were initially considered to be temporary institutions, they have now been written into the state constitution as a permanent element of local government. Revolutionary committees also became the standard form of administrative-executive bodies, not only for government at all levels below the national, but also for virtually all other enterprises—factories, mines, schools, shops, hospitals, rural production teams, and even for crews of ships on the high seas. At the Fifth NPC, however, Premier Hua Kuo-feng announced that revolutionary committees would no longer be established in such enterprises, except those factories, mines, and others in which government administration is integrated with management, inasmuch as they do not constitute a level of government.

The early provincial revolutionary committees were fairly evenly represented by the three constituent elements but, as time passed and chaos increased, the PLA assumed an increasingly active role and became more strongly represented in the revolutionary committees. By September 1968, several of the last formed were staffed almost wholly by the PLA and military personnel—the commandant of a military region or military district—presided as chairmen over most revolutionary committees. This situation continued until after the fall of Lin Piao in 1971 and the massive rotation of regional PLA commanders in December 1973.

Subsequent action to reduce the role of the military in civil affairs has completely reversed the situation. Thus, as of early 1978, no military commander headed any provincial revolutionary committee, while every chairman of the twenty-nine revolutionary committees at this level was a member of the Party's Central Committee and concurrently chairman of the local Party committee. Though revolutionary committees are government organs, except for Kwangtung and Peking, no provincial-level revolutionary committee chairman was concurrently a member of the Standing Committee of the NPC.

The Judicial System and Law Enforcement

The judiciary and law enforcement establishments in the P.R.C., consisting of the people's courts, people's procuratorates, and the public security organs, which have overlapping functions and responsibilities, are essentially organs of state power designed primarily to enforce Party and state policies and regulations rather than to protect individual rights; in the past few years they have been brought under closer state control and direction, under Party supervision, than obtained before the Cultural Revolution.

At the top of a three-tiered people's court structure is the Supreme People's Court, "the highest judicial organ"[44] in the P.R.C. Below it are the higher people's courts established at the provincial level and the lower people's courts (formerly termed "basic people's courts") at the county level. The higher and lower people's courts are collectively known as "local people's courts." A level of "intermediate people's courts" between the higher and lower people's courts, present before the Cultural Revolution, appears to have been abolished. The three-tiered courts are supplemented by a series of "special people's courts," consisting of the military, the railway, and the water transportation courts.

The constitution refers only to the method of appointment of presidents of the courts at each level. Appointment of other members presumably continues to follow the general procedure set forth in the "Organic Law of the People's Courts" of 1954, although that law has obviously required amendment to conform with changes in local government organization. The constitution provides for the election of the president of the Supreme Court by the NPC, but no mention is made of a nominating authority (in contrast to the constitutional provisions that the premier be nominated by the Central Committee and other members of the State Council by the premier).[45] Presidents of the higher and lower people's courts are elected and subject to recall by the people's congresses at the corresponding levels. Other members of the respective courts are appointed, according to the 1954 law, by the permanent state organs at each level—by the NPC Standing Committee in the case of the Supreme People's Court and by the revolutionary committees ("people's councils" in the 1954 law) of the provinces and counties in the case of the local people's courts. The Supreme People's Court is responsible and accountable to the NPC and its Standing Committee, while the local people's courts are responsible and accountable to local people's congresses at the corresponding level.

The Supreme People's Court serves not only as the court of last resort but is also empowered by the constitution to supervise the administration of justice by the local people's courts and the special people's courts. Higher people's courts are likewise empowered to supervise the work of lower people's courts, though the Supreme People's Court exercises overall supervision. Administration of the court system was originally the responsibility of the Ministry of Justice, under the State Council, but when that ministry was abolished in 1959 the function was transferred to the Supreme People's Court.

Procuratorial organs, like the people's court system, consist of a Supreme People's Procuratorate, higher people's procuratorates at the provincial level, and lower people's procuratorates at the county level. Special people's procuratorates function in conjunction with the special people's courts. Presiding over the entire structure is the chief procurator of the Supreme People's Procuratorate. Procuratorial organs conduct investigations, prepare indictments, and prosecute the cases before the courts.[46] They are empowered to exercise supervisory authority to ensure observance of the constitution and the laws by all organs of state, including the State Council, government officials, and citizens.[47] They also have the right to review and challenge judgments by the courts at their respective levels, the Supreme People's Procuratorate, however, being empowered to challenge the rulings of courts at all levels, including the Supreme People's Court.

The third establishment involved in the law enforcement process, the public security system, is in many respects the most important and has the greatest and most immediate impact on the people. Its ubiquitous organs function under the direction of the Ministry of Public Security, one of the principal ministries under the State Council and its subordinate agencies in the provinces, counties, and the local communities. Public Security organs command the local police and direct policing operations, including investigation, arbitration of minor disputes and disagreements, maintenance of records of local residents, and the making of arrests; their functions overlap those of the people's procuratorate.

The courts and the procuratorate came under attack during the Cultural Revolution. While the court system survived, procuratorial organs vanished from reference in the P.R.C. media and their functions were taken over by public security. In 1975, at the Fourth NPC, they were formally transferred to public security by the simple process of omitting reference to the procuratorate in the new constitution and by assigning its former responsibilities to public security organs. At the Fifth NPC in 1978, however, the procuratorate was restored and given most of its original functions but its status was changed.

In its earlier existence, the procuratorate had been structured so as to appear to function relatively independently of state organs. While the chief procurator (so named before the title was changed to president) of the Supreme People's Procuratorate was elected and subject to recall by the NPC, as were its other members by the NPC Standing Committee, local people's procuratorates at each level in the chain were organized by and subject to their immediate superior procuratorial body, with the Supreme People's Procuratorate exercising overall administrative and supervisory control. Moreover, while the Supreme People's Procuratorate was responsible to the NPC and its Standing Committee, no linkage was made between lower level procuratorial and corresponding state organs. On the contrary, the "Organic Law of the People's Procuratorate" of 1954 stated specifically that the local people's procuratorates "are independent in the exercise of their authority and are not subject to interference by local state organs."[48] At the same time, they were not empowered directly to annul, change, or stop the execution of directives issued by state organs even if they contravened the law.[49]

Before the Cultural Revolution, the procuratorate and public security organs at local levels and "political and legal committees" of local Party committees coordinated the work of the courts by bringing into their memberships the local heads of the three organizations.[50] Thus, under Party leadership, conflicts of function and jurisdiction could be locally resolved. This practice may have been restored, thereby giving the Party as well as the state a direct supervisory role over juridical and law enforcement activities.

Relatively little is known about court procedures or the handling of court cases. Immediately after the regime was established in 1949, the prevailing judicial system, including the legal codes in force, was abolished. Since no new code, civil or criminal, was adopted and the system of people's courts and procuratorates was not introduced until

1954, cases involving espionage, support of the enemy, counter-revolutionary activities, theft of state property, and other antisocial activities were handled in the interim either administratively by public security organs or tried publicly by ad hoc people's tribunals. After the establishment of the people's courts and procuratorates, some progress was made toward the development of legal codes but the movement was interrupted by the Cultural Revolution. Toward the end of 1977, however, efforts were renewed to produce both civil and criminal codes, efforts that had been abandoned in the early 1960s.

Rights and Duties of Citizens

The state constitution contains a lengthy catalogue of citizens' rights and duties.[51] Equality of all citizens, regardless of race, sex, or culture, is guaranteed. Specific freedoms citizens are entitled to enjoy include the freedom of speech, correspondence, the press, assembly, association, procession, and demonstration. All citizens have the right to "speak out freely, air their views fully, hold great debates, and write big-character posters."[52] A new freedom incorporated into the 1975 constitution at the suggestion of Mao Tse-tung, according to Chang Ch'un-ch'iao,[53] and reaffirmed in the 1978 revision, is the freedom to strike. Inviolability of the person and the person's home is promised, and arrest is constitutional only if carried out as a result of a decision by a people's court or with the sanction of a people's procuratorate, and the arrest must be made by a public security organ.

For many of the rights guaranteed, a complementary obligation is placed on the state to make the necessary provisions to enable the citizen to enjoy the rights guaranteed. For instance, citizens have a right to work and the state is obliged to provide labor. Working people have a right to rest and the state must ensure that the worker can enjoy this right by, among other things, arranging for systems of vacations and developing facilities for rest and recuperation. Working people have a right to material assistance in old age, and for their welfare and for those disabled the state must provide social assistance and health and medical services. Citizens have a right to education, for which the state must expand educational and cultural institutions and popularize education. All citizens who have reached the age of eighteen have the right to vote and to stand for election, as noted in preceding sections, except those persons who have been deprived of these rights by law.

Aside from the general guarantee of equality for all citizens, women were specifically guaranteed "equal rights with men" by the 1954 constitution only in respect to the right to vote and to stand for election. The 1978 constitution returns to the language of the Common Program[54] by assuring women equal rights with men "in all spheres of political, economic, cultural, social, and family life";[55] and, ostensibly in response to a well-publicized campaign by the women's federations in the mid-1970s, guarantees equal pay for equal work. The constitution also advocates and encourages family planning.

In respect to ethnic and cultural minorities, the constitutions point subtly to a shift from a deemphasis on cultural differences to an endorsement of the right to preserve local cultures, probably reflecting a transition from a post–Cultural Revolution objective of moving toward cultural uniformity to the more recent effort to mobilize a united front for a national thrust to achieve the regime's modernization goals. The 1954 constitution provided that "All the nationalities have freedom to use and foster the growth of their spoken and written languages, and to preserve or reform their own customs and ways." In the spirit of this pledge, alphabets were devised for several minority languages for which no system of writing existed, literatures were collected and published, minority peoples in their national dress were commonly seen in parades on ceremonial occasions, and their dances and theatrical works were performed in various parts of the country to emphasize domestically and for foreign audiences the multinational character of the state. At the same time, minority peoples were subjected to pressure to conform to the rest of the country, ideologically and institutionally. The 1975 constitution retained the statement granting all nationalities the right to use their own spoken and written languages[56] but dropped the two important phrases allowing them "to foster the growth" of their languages and "to preserve or reform" their customs and ways. The 1978 constitution restored the reference to the preservation or reform of customs and ways but omitted the "foster the growth" clause.[57]

Freedom of religion was a matter of limited interest to the P.R.C. prior to the Cultural Revolution, when Peking found it useful in the conduct of its foreign relations to be able to demonstrate to foreign visitors, particularly visitors from Islamic and Buddhist countries, that such freedom did exist. During the Cultural Revolution, religion came under attack, believers were scorned, practice of religion declined, and institutionalized religion tended to wither away. Though the question of religion has not been an issue, the constitution continues to guarantee freedom of religious belief but also added the "freedom not to believe" and "to propagate atheism."

The 1977 Party constitution grants its members the right to criticize Party organs and leaders at all levels, and to bypass an immediate leader and present complaints to officials at higher levels, including members of the Central Committee and even the chairman of the Central Committee.[58] Special reference is made to the right to question decisions of Party organs. Similar rights "to lodge complaints" against any organ or functionary of the state for transgression of law or neglect of duty are extended to the citizenry by the 1978 state constitution.[59] Both constitutions forbid the suppression of criticism.

Knowledge of the guarantees and exercise of the rights are, however, two separate and distinct matters. In a country that has pressed vigorously for conformity, launched periodic ideological campaigns, conducted organized attacks against leaders who have expressed views approved at one time but rejected at another, and excommunicated formerly venerated leaders for incorrect outlook and alleged antisocialist activity, it is highly unlikely that many citizens will use the right to speak out freely, assemble, demonstrate, or strike on their own initiative without prior assurance that such conduct is desired by the authorities.

Individual action is more likely to be guided by the obligations placed upon the citizens. The fundamental "rights and duties" of the citizens, the 1975 state constitution states, "are to support the leadership of the Communist Party of China, support the socialist system, and abide by the constitution and laws of the People's Republic of China."[60] In more prosaic language, the 1978 constitution reaffirms these obligations placed upon the citizens.

In certain cases, persons convicted of serious crimes may have their rights as citizens legally removed, though the state is obliged to provide them with the opportunity to earn a living in order that they may be rehabilitated.[61] As for those who have responded positively to remolding and reeducation, Yeh Chien-ying told the Fifth NPC that their rights as citizens should be restored and all pejorative labels removed.

Political Dynamics

In large measure, the success of the CPC in consolidating the country, in accomplishing what it has achieved in economic organization and development, and in carrying out radical and fundamental social change can be attributed to its ability to inculcate the people with a sense of purpose, mobilize the masses for collective action, dignify manual labor, shift individual focus from selfish motives and interests to the collective weal, and give meaning to the concept of nationhood.

The Role of Ideology

The motivating force behind the Chinese Communist movement, as noted earlier, is a form of Marxism that the CPC officially refers to as Marxism–Leninism–Mao Tsetung Thought; it is commonly referred to in the West as Maoism.[62] Mao Tsetung Thought is defined as the "highest form of Marxism-Leninism in the present era"[63] and as the adaptation of Marxism-Leninism to the situation in China. The CPC describes the epoch of Marx and Engels as the preparatory stage for the proletarian revolution, the epoch of Lenin and Stalin as the stage of the first socialist victory in a country and the epoch of the breach for the battle against imperialism, and the epoch of Mao as the one in which capitalism and imperialism were "to be sent to the tombs."[64]

Mao Tse-tung's political and economic concepts derive from his early experience with the bitterness and poverty of peasant life in China and his reaction to the humiliation of China by foreign powers. Information about the success of the Bolshevik Revolution in Russia reached China during a period when Mao and other Chinese intellectuals were groping for answers to China's multitude of dilemmas. Disappointed with the West and with Western approaches, he and others became attracted to socialism as the road to take to solve China's problems. Mao, however, read no foreign language, and published material on socialism and Marxism in Chinese was very limited; consequently, his introduction to the new ideology was largely received through secondary rather than primary sources, and since he was more interested in promoting revolution than in developing theories, he was more influenced by Lenin and Stalin than by Marx.[65] His contributions to Marxism were therefore more in the field of the application of theory to practice than in the field of pure theory; indeed, his contributions to theory were minimal.

Mao Tsetung Thought is embodied in his massive output of pamphlets and tracts. Five volumes in a series containing selections from his most important works have been published by the Chinese Communists to date, the fifth having been released hurriedly shortly after his death. The committee under the Central Committee responsible for collecting, selecting, and publishing the works has been enjoined to expedite its work, which includes the scouring of the country for every scrap of Mao's notes, instructions, commentaries, and other written communications. A large portion of the presently published works consists of writings in which he expounded on strategies and tactics employed in the struggles against the Japanese and the Kuomintang and of his expositions on the social order and political system to be installed after the Communists achieved victory in China.

Maoism, however, is not limited to the concepts set forth in his published works but is shaped also by what Communist leaders know about his unpublished works, his elaborations on policy and objectives at Party deliberations, the exegesis of his ideas by his lieutenants, and even the commentaries of those opposed to him. Mao's thought will continue to be interpreted and reinterpreted in terms of the developing situation in China. Consequently, Maoism in the future will increasingly be what Party leaders say it is and will probably resemble less and less what Mao meant it to be.

At the Seventh Party Congress in 1945, Mao Tsetung Thought was written into the Party constitution as the guiding doctrine for the CPC. This declaration was omitted in the revised constitution adopted at the Eighth Party Congress in 1956, which stated simply: "The Communist Party of China takes Marxism-Leninism as its guide to action. Only Marxism-Leninism correctly sets forth the laws of development of society and charts the path leading to the achievement of socialism and communism."[66] Deletion of the reference to Mao Tsetung Thought was much later attributed to the pernicious machinations of Liu Shao-ch'i, even though P'eng Teh-huai had admitted in his confession to having proposed the deletion. The thought of Mao Tse-tung was restored constitutionally as Party guidance at the Ninth Party Congress in 1969 and has been reaffirmed as such by every Party and state constitution subsequently promulgated. The 1977 Party constitution states, "Marxism–Leninism–Mao Tsetung Thought is the guiding ideology and theoretical basis of the Communist Party of China."[67]

Frequently quoted by Party leaders and P.R.C. media is Mao's warning, "The correctness or incorrectness of the ideological and political line decides everything." In this case, the ideological line is the system of beliefs to which the Party subscribes and the political line is the interpretation of the ideological line as reflected in political action. The correct ideological line is Marxism–Leninism–Mao Tsetung Thought and the ultimate arbiter of the correctness of the line is the Party, meaning those within the Party leadership at any single moment able to exercise sufficient authority to propagate their interpretation of the line through the media and through indoctrination of the populace, and to enforce a corresponding course of action. Differences in respect to action compatible with ideology have been at the heart of major intra-

Party controversies since the Party was formed. Officially, eleven major controversies are recognized as having taken place up to the present and, though these have involved a variety of issues, they have been described as "struggles between the two lines," the correct line and the incorrect line.

Ideology has served the CPC in different ways at various stages of the Chinese Communist movement. It has served to point out wrongs in traditional society that the party is determined to correct, has defined the goals to be sought and the value structure to be promulgated, and has outlined the means of attaining the goals and objectives. Ideology has also served to consolidate Party leadership, to supply common language and concepts for communication with cadres and masses, and to provide points of reference for the mobilization of the masses for action.[68]

Mobilization and Participation

A theme persistently stressed by Mao Tse-tung in his writings, incorporated in Party and state constitutions, frequently emphasized in speeches by Party leaders, and commented upon with some regularity by the P.R.C. media is the importance of involving the masses in the revolutionary process. According to Mao, "The people, and the people alone, are the motive force in the making of world history." Mao preached the superiority of man over machines and the essential goodness of the common people. Repeatedly, he asserted that 95 percent of the people or 95 percent of Party members are good and loyal and can be trusted to contribute to the revolution. During the Cultural Revolution, he encouraged revolution from the bottom as a means of attacking institutions and leadership that had gone awry, a procedure that contravened the Party principle of democratic centralism and a practice that was to present the Party with future organizational and theoretical problems. Mao's faith in the masses and in "the mass line" concept derived from his personal experience in effectively involving local peasantry in revolutionary activity during the Kiangsi and Yenan periods of the revolution.[69]

People are China's most abundant resource. Mao recognized that mobilizing, indoctrinating, and motivating and giving the people direction would enable disciplined masses to accomplish much that in richer and technologically more advanced countries would be done by mechanical means. Accordingly, on the eve of the Great Leap Forward he could bemoan the fact that China's massive population, rather than being a burden to the country, was too small for the labor-intensive projects he had in mind.

Mass involvement constitutes a means for extending indoctrination and ideological guidance, for popularizing the new social values espoused by the regime, for educating the populace regarding policies and objectives of the CPC, for political control, for cultivating a sense of mutual responsibility for the behavior and attitudes of each member of the community, and for the mobilization of the masses for participation in specific projects and support on particular issues.

For purposes of mobilization, virtually every citizen of the P.R.C., except the very young, belongs to one or more of the mass organizations or local control groups that have been formed. The most important of these are the trade unions, the women's federation, youth organizations, and peasant associations. There are also mass organizations for those involved in sports and cultural activities for various professions. Prior to the Cultural Revolution, five national religious associations—Taoist, Islamic, Buddhist, Catholic, and Protestant—were actively used to bring their adherents under the control and in line with the policies of the regime. After an eclipse, these have again emerged as instruments used in the formation of a united front. For those for whom no functional organization exists, there are neighborhood associations—street committees and local rural organizations—of which every resident is a member.

Major mass organizations are governed by complicated layers of administrative organs, extending from a national body down through provincial, to county and local organs. The leading figures of these, particularly of the trade union, women's federation, and Communist Youth League, are Party members and are generally elected to full membership of the Central Committee. Most of the mass organizations were dismantled during the Cultural Revolution. In 1973 a drive was mounted to restore the trade union, women's federation, and the Communist Youth League. Though the drive appeared to have been successful, a renewed effort in the summer of 1977 sought to revitalize these organizations.

Techniques employed for mass mobilization include mass campaigns, education and indoctrination, saturated dissemination through communications systems of messages and ideas, emulation drives, and moral compulsion. Campaigns of one kind or another are virtually always under way. They are normally sparked by a summons for collective action on some issue or project (often an "instruction" by the chairman in Mao's day), or by a national conference or an international development. A national conference, to which provincial leaders and activists are invited, is commonly used to launch a major campaign. This will be followed successively by similar conferences at the provincial and lower levels through which plans and guidance are transmitted eventually to local activists and to the masses. Occasionally, one campaign sparks another. Campaigns have been conducted for a wide variety of political, economic, and social purposes. They have been used to unify the public on domestic and international issues, as in the case of the "Resist America, Aid Korea" campaign during the Korean war; to remold wavering ideology, as in the series of rectification campaigns; to promote emulation of successful endeavors and enterprises, as in the Tachai and Tach'ing emulation campaigns; to denounce an opposition, as in the successive campaigns against Liu Shao-ch'i, Lin Piao, and the Gang of Four; to improve work styles, as in the Lei Feng campaign; and to mobilize the public for collective action, as in Hua Kuo-feng's call at the Eleventh Party Congress, repeated at the Fifth NPC, to mount a nationwide campaign to strive to achieve interim targets in the long-term project of transforming China into a "powerful and modern socialist country" by the end of the twentieth century.

For emulation purposes, model workers, peasants, soldiers, and other activists are periodically called to public attention, praised, and set up as examples for others to follow. Models may be individuals or organized groups, like the Tachai agricultural brigade, the Tach'ing petroleum enterprise, or the "Good Eighth Company of Nanking Road" of the PLA. Model workers and peasants have been rewarded by promotions and by election to high office, the highest having gone to Ch'en Yung-kuei, a model peasant of the Tachai brigade, who rose through the Party secretaryship of the brigade to membership on the Political Bureau, of which he has been a full member since 1973. A female textile worker from Sian, Wu Kuei-hsien, also a model worker, was elected alternate member of the Political Bureau in 1973 but was dropped in 1977, although she retained her membership in the Central Committee. Other model workers have been elected either as members or alternate members of the Central Committee at various Party congresses. At the Fifth NPC, Hua Kuo-feng stated:

> The masses have a vast reservoir of enthusiasm for socialism. Socialist labor emulation is a good and important method of bringing the initiative and creativeness of the people into full play and of achieving greater, faster, better and more economical results in developing the economy.

Each and every locality, trade, enterprise, establishment, and rural commune and production brigade should fully mobilize the masses and bring about an upsurge in emulating, learning from, catching up with, and overtaking the advanced units, and helping the less advanced units. . . . The main aim of the labor emulation is to increase production and practice economy. . . .

Indoctrination begins early in the creches and schools and continues through life. Youngsters in creches are imbued with ideological concepts through simple slogans and songs, and play games designed to propagate new Communist values and to inculcate an early recognition of the duties and responsibilities of citizens. Later, throughout life, citizens must participate in regular political study, discussion, and criticism to heighten political consciousness and eradicate misconceptions. Material for these study sessions is carried by the press and other publications, by wired and wireless broadcasting networks, and by television, though still in its infancy.

The state constitution declares, "Work is an honorable duty for every citizen able to work." To encourage greater effort, the constitution endorses the policy of combining "moral encouragement with material reward,"[70] even though the policy of material rewards was strongly disapproved of by Mao Tse-tung. Motivation is also engendered by such practices mentioned above as the honoring of superior workers by naming them labor heroes, the selection of outstanding workers for participation in leadership conferences, and the granting of Party membership to those who excel in leadership qualities. Above all, however, social compulsion may be the strongest motivating factor.

Despite the tightly controlled society, which discourages people from using their constitutional rights to speak out freely, to criticize, and to demonstrate without being directed to do so, there are openings or means for the people to express their views outside of formal discussion sessions. The most popular of these appears to be the writing of big-character posters, a practice sanctioned by Mao himself at the beginning of the Cultural Revolution. It is, of course, impossible to know how many of the posters are self-initiated and express genuine private views.

The Chinese People's Political Consultative Conference

After an extended period of dormancy, the CPPCC was revived in 1977-1978 and transformed into an institution for the mobilization of a united front to promote domestic and international united front activities and, most immediately, to help enlist all domestic elements in the government's ambitious modernization programs. The CPPCC was originally convened in 1949 to formally establish the P.R.C. and was authorized to exercise the functions and powers of the NPC until the latter could be convened. With the promulgation of the state constitution in 1954, CPPCC functions were transferred to the NPC and the CPPCC adopted a constitution defining its role as that of a united front institution. Three additional conferences of the CPPCC were convened before its decline in the mid-1960s. These assembled, according to the provisions of its constitution, as meetings of the National Committee of the CPPCC: the Second in December 1954, the Third in April 1959, and the Fourth in December to January, 1964-1965. The Second met approximately three months after the First NPC but the Third and Fourth held concurrent sessions with the Second and Third NPCs. On the latter two occasions, the policy reports submitted to the NPCs were also reviewed and discussed by members of the CPPCC in session, whose mission it was to return to the provinces to popularize NPC programs and decisions among the masses. When a Fifth National Committee meeting of the CPPCC was not convened at the time of the Fourth NPC in January 1975, substance was lent to a growing belief that the CPPCC had exhausted its usefulness to the CPC and was being allowed to expire through attrition (for some time through the mid-1970s, virtually the only references to the organization were in obituary notices of its deceased members. Meanwhile, other members had been disgraced during the antibourgeoisie campaigns conducted since the late 1950s).

At the Eleventh Party Congress of the CPC in August 1977, however, Chairman Hua Kuo-feng announced that the Fifth NPC would be convened "at an appropriate time" and that the Fifth National Committee of the CPPCC would "go into session simultaneously." Prior to the convening of the Fifth National Committee of the CPPCC on February 24, 1978, NCNA carried a "backgrounder" in which the CPPCC was described as "China's revolutionary united front organization," with the comment that the revolutionary united front was one of the "three magic weapons" with which the CPC had led the Chinese people to victory, the other two being armed struggle and party building.[71] In addition to CPC delegates, it was noted that the National Committee included representatives of other remaining political parties in the P.R.C., of the major mass organizations, and of specialists from various walks of life (see Table 4.6), and that it was a body for

Table 4.6 Composition of Fourth and Fifth CPPCC National Committees

Affiliation of Members	Number of Members	
	Fourth	Fifth
Communist Party of China	60	76
Kuomintang Revolutionary Committee	40	50
China Democratic League	40	50
China Democratic National Construction Association	40	50
Non-Party Democratic Personnel (Patriotic Personages)	20	25
Chinese Association for Promoting Democracy	20	25
China Peasants' and Workers' Democratic Party	20	25
China Chih Kung Tang	8	8
Chiu San Society	20	25
Taiwan Democratic Self-Government League	8	12
Chinese Communist Youth League	10	13
All-China Federation of Trade Unions	38	49
Peasants	16	21
Women's Federation of the People's Republic of China	32	42
All-China Youth Federation	8	10
Cooperatives	11	--
All-China Federation of Industry and Commerce	40	50
Literary and Art Circles	52	65
Scientific and Technical Circles	60	90
Social Science Circles	20	25
Educational Circles	42	63
Sports Circles	--	25
Journalist and Publications Circles	11	14
Medical and Health Circles	40	50
Organizations for Friendship with Foreign Countries	22	28
Social Relief and Welfare Organizations	11	11
Minority Nationalities	36	56
Overseas Chinese	17	
Returned Overseas Chinese		21
Religious Circles	16	16
Specially Invited Personages	439	993
Totals	1,191	1,988

consultation and proposals. On the day following the initial session of the Fifth National Committee, *People's Daily* carried in its prestigious upper right-hand corner a quotation from Mao Tse-tung pertinent to the occasion: "We must do our best to mobilize all positive factors, both inside and outside the Party, both at home and abroad, both direct and indirect, and make China a powerful socialist country."

The Fifth National Committee of the CPPCC was composed of 1,988 members, an increase of 67 percent over the 1,191 members of the Fourth. The organizations and fields of specialization represented on the two occasions remained virtually unchanged, with the exception only of the 1978 deletion of a 1964 representation from cooperatives and the 1978 addition of sports representatives, absent in 1964. The great increase resulted from a moderate rise of 20 percent in most categories but a substantial 50 percent increase of scientists, technicians, educators, and minority representatives and a doubling of specially invited personages, who made up roughly one-half of the total membership (see Table 4.6). The areas of large increase reflect the regime's desire to involve elements who can contribute through proposals and consultations, as well as materially, to the modernization effort and can assist in correcting major errors committed in the past decade in the fields of education and technology.

A new CPPCC constitution, adopted at the Fifth National Committee meeting, promulgates a set of principles that calls for support of the CPC and the socialist system, upholding the line of Mao Tse-tung, adherence to the principles of the CPC, and promotion of patriotism and revolutionary vigilance. Most of these were also in the organization's 1954 constitution; new to the 1978 constitution, however, is a declaration that Taiwan "has been China's sacred territory since ancient times" and "must" be liberated. A major change was the deletion of a 1954 principle dedicating the CPPCC to contribute to the consolidation of the alliance with the U.S.S.R. and to the "unbreakable friendship" with the people's democracies and the substitution of a constitutional task requiring the CPPCC to work for the development of an international united front against hegemonism and "to struggle unremittingly against hegemonism and the war policies of the superpowers."

The new CPPCC constitution also invites the organization, on a voluntary basis, to promote the study of Marxism–Leninism–Mao Tsetung Thought; to hold report and discussion meetings and organize investigations of various situations; to conduct activities in political, economic, cultural, educational, technical, and scientific fields in order to open avenues to new ideas and talents; to collect and compile the history of modern China; to work for the "liberation" of Taiwan; and to conduct international united front activities.

Like other major organizations, the CPPCC has a National Committee that supervises the activities of local bodies on the provincial and, where necessary, lower levels. Groups represented are not constitutionally identified, except the CPC, but have become standardized by practice, as indicated in Table 4.6. The National Committee is elected or appointed for a term of five years, the same as that for the Party congress and the NPC. The National Committee elects its chairman, a number of vice-chairmen, and a Standing Committee, whose candidates have previously been "endorsed" by the Central Committee. The

Standing Committee appoints a number of deputy secretary generals and a Secretariat to conduct the routine work of the organization. The constitution calls for annual meetings of the National Committee but, as in the case of other organizations in the P.R.C., the standing committee is authorized to convene the committee before its due date or to postpone the meeting.

Local CPPCC committees, patterned after the national, are established in the provinces, autonomous regions, and municipalities. They are composed of members of the CPC, other political parties, mass organizations, specially invited individuals, and representatives of "all walks of life." Where pertinent, minority representatives are included. Below the provincial level, CPPCC committees are established only where it is deemed "necessary."

At the meeting of the Fifth National Committee of the CPPCC, held February 24 to March 8, 1978, Teng Hsiao-p'ing, vice-chairman of the Central Committee of the CPC and vice-premier of the State Council, was elected chairman of the committee. Twenty-three vice-chairmen were elected, of whom 10 are full members of the Central Committee, including 3 full members of the Political Bureau—Wei Kuo-ch'ing (a Chuang minority member), P'eng Ch'ung, and Ulanfu (a Mongol). Ch'i Yen-ming was elected secretary general, and a standing committee of 243 members was also elected. Teng's election continues the policy of placing the CPPCC under the direction of a senior member of the Political Bureau, as only Mao Tse-tung and Chou En-lai have preceded him in that office. Mao served as chairman of the First CPPCC, and at the meeting of the Second National Committee he was elevated to a newly created honorary chairmanship, a post to which he was reelected at the Third and Fourth National Committee meetings, while Chou succeeded him as chairman, holding that office until his death. The Fifth National Committee abolished the office of honorary chairman by the characteristic policy of omitting reference to it in the new constitution. New committees of the CPPCC had been elected in the 29 provinces, autonomous regions, and municipalities between October 1977 and February 1978, and these elected representatives to the Fifth National Committee.

The Cadres

A critically important functionary in the Chinese Communist system is the cadre. The term *cadre* is somewhat ambiguous inasmuch as it is commonly used in reference to a wide variety of functionaries:[72] persons of authority in Party and state bureaucracies; leaders in agricultural and industrial production units; officials in schools, hospitals, and other institutions; members of the PLA; and personnel who hold even minor leadership positions.[73] Essentially, a cadre is a person vested with authority or, according to Schurmann, "someone who holds a leadership position in an organization."[74]

According to Mao Tse-tung, paraphrasing Stalin, "Cadres are a decisive factor, once the political line is determined." Mao added,

> The criterion the Communist Party should apply in its cadre policy is whether or not a cadre is resolute in carrying out the Party line, keeps to Party discipline, has close ties with the masses, has the ability to find his bearings independently, and is active, hard-working, and unselfish.[75]

Cadres may or may not be members of the CPC. Acceptance as a cadre, however, can lead to Party membership. Cadres are selected on the basis of ideological correctness, industry, acceptability to colleagues and co-workers, loyalty, and social background. They may be selected as a result of performance in a bureaucracy, or because of special talent demonstrated at school—foreign language or scientific aptitude, for example—or they may be nominated by co-workers at an employment unit on the basis of demonstrated political and leadership qualities.

Lower-level cadres are the regime's primary instrument for direct dealing with the masses. Thus the success of a program or the effectiveness of a policy depends heavily on the overall competence of the cadres. Accordingly, cadres are expected to maintain close contact with the masses, to listen to them, to accept their comments and criticisms, to be able to explain policies and official positions on issues and matters, and to be able to lead them in study, criticism, and self-criticism. They are also expected to lead by example, particularly by their own industry, willingness to participate in labor, loyalty to the Party, social consciousness, freedom from selfishness, and personal perseverance in political study. Chou En-lai cited three qualities cadres should possess: modesty, prudence, and hard work.[76]

Except for those who enter cadre ranks directly from educational institutions, cadre or job-oriented formal training may be slight. Indeed, for most, training appears to be essentially on-the-job training. At the Tenth and Eleventh Party congresses, however, considerable attention was given to the subject of improving the quality of cadre training, with emphasis placed on the need to improve political study and on improving cadre work styles. Following the Eleventh Party Congress, a Central Committee directive called on Party organs at all levels to take action to restore and improve two cadre training systems—the Party schools and the May Seventh cadre schools.

The Party schools, traceable to the Yenan period and earlier, were maintained by Party committees at the various levels but were suspended during the Cultural Revolution and have been tardy in reopening. The Party school in Peking, connected with the Central Committee, did not reopen until October 9, 1977, four days after the Central Committee directive. Since then, Party schools have reopened in several provinces and others can be expected to be reactivated by Party committees at each level of the Party establishment. The instructional emphasis at Party schools will be on ideological and theoretical training, and the emphasis will be on independent reading under tutorial guidance rather than classroom work.

May Seventh cadre schools take their name from a call issued by Mao Tse-tung on May 7, 1966, urging the populace to study military affairs, politics, and culture and to take part in the socialist education movement. The schools, which did not come into being until late 1968, were originally conceived as reeducational or correctional institutions for those found ideologically wanting during the Cultural Revolution. Since then they have been transformed into cadre refresher schools, to which cadres are sent at intervals for periods of political study combined with participation in labor. Stigma is no longer attached to an assignment to a May Seventh school. The type of labor in which the cadre will engage while at school depends on the location of the school. Those assigned to schools in urban areas work in factories, while those assigned to rural schools engage in agricultural activities. The Central Committee directive referred to above stated that May Seventh cadre schools should differ from Party schools. School authorities were urged to organize courses to run in segments, each repeated, in order to permit cadres from the same establishment, in rotation, to alternate between normal work and school attendance, while at the same time being able to complete a systematic course of study. The courses vary in length from a few weeks to several months and consist of political study and participation in labor.

Cadre morale, particularly at lower levels, suffered a serious setback during the Cultural Revolution when they, as symbols of authority, took much of the criticism and attack on the bureaucracy. At the same time, they also became the butt of criticism of higher authority when public discipline and order collapsed.

In addition to routine guidance in the form of directives and circulars, and instructional material appearing in the press, cadres are frequently invited to conferences where their work is discussed and guidance provided. Urgent conferences are sometimes convened by telephone. Occasionally, cadres are given the opportunity to attend conferences in Peking, where they come into the presence of top Party leaders. For general orientation, the cadre has access to certain limited-distribution publications, like *Reference News,* which contains brief reports and commentaries extracted from foreign newspapers and news agency files dealing with international affairs and commentaries by these sources on developments in China, even critical comments. The material is collected and published by the New China News Agency.

Party Control and Public Order

The preceding pages have frequently referred to the horizontal and perpendicular interlocking of the Party organization with other major command structures, including mass organizations as well as the state and military apparatus (see Table 4.7). This practice of placing members of Party organs in positions of control of organs of other establishments at the corresponding levels, and superimposing upon this network a perpendicular Party investigative chain, supplementing the work of public security bodies, has resulted in the creation of one of the most pervasive control systems developed in any society.

The complete dominance of the Party in the system is best illustrated by the concurrent roles played by senior Party leaders. Party Chairman Hua Kuo-feng, for instance, who by virtue of that office is chairman of the Central Military Commission, has since 1976 also served as premier of the State Council and under the 1978 constitution is commander of the armed forces.[77] Veteran Yeh Chien-ying, of the Hakka minority and second ranking in protocol, is a vice-chairman of the Central Committee, chairman of the Standing Committee of the NPC, and a vice-chairman of the Central Military Commission; while Teng Hsiao-p'ing, apparently in charge of day-to-day administration of state affairs, functions as a vice-chairman of the Central Committee, vice-premier of the State Council, a vice-chairman of the Central Military Commission, chief-of-staff of the PLA, and chairman of the National Committee of the CPPCC. Other members of the Political Bureau hold similar across-the-board responsibilities.

At the provincial level and below, the Party suffered serious institutional damage during the Cultural Revolution, as noted in an earlier section, and Party functions were largely taken over by the military. But it must be remembered that the senior military officers who gained initial dominance on the revolutionary committees and the newly reestablished provincial Party committees were also senior Party members. In any event, since 1971, the Party has gradually replaced the military with civilian Party personnel and separated command of the military regions and districts from leadership of provincial Party and state apparatus. Thus, in contrast to the situation that obtained in the early 1970s, when regional or district military commanders headed more than two-thirds of the provincial level Party and revolutionary committees, after the reorganization of Party committees in 1977 and 1978 and the election of local revolutionary committees prior to the Fifth NPC, no commander of a military region or district remains at the senior post in a provincial-level Party or revolutionary committee. Moreover, every one of the twenty-nine provincial-level Party first secretaries is at present chairman of the corresponding revolutionary committee, and twenty-five of these serve concurrently as the first political commissar of the military region or district in which they function.

Such a control system, combined with intensive politicizing of the populace and cultivation of a sense of belonging, resulted in the high degree of discipline and order commented upon frequently by foreign visitors to the P.R.C. prior to the Cultural Revolution. Order, however, broke down during the Cultural Revolution and has not yet been restored to the high level that obtained in the earlier period. Occasionally in recent years, localities have been placed off limits for foreign visitors on account of local disturbances, and periodically foreign journalists have seen wall posters in various cities that listed names of people convicted of crimes, some posters also specifying the nature of the crimes committed and the punishments meted out. In addition to political offenses, crimes have covered a wide spectrum, from homicide to rape, from illegal attempts to escape from the country to the theft of state property.

At the Fifth NPC, Hua Kuo-feng charged that, under the Gang of Four, corruption, embezzlement, and profiteering had become widespread, while Yeh Chien-ying called attention to "new-born bourgeois elements," among whom were "not a few" of the embezzlers, thieves, speculators, murderers, and other criminal elements that had plagued the regime. Meanwhile, the domestic media, over a period of several months, have carried numerous articles exposing corruption and abuse

Table 4.7 Concurrent Offices Held by Members of the Political Bureau

Name	Party Positions	Government Positions	Military Positions	Other Functions
Hua Kuo-feng	Chairman, CPC/CC; Member, Political Bureau; SC, Political Bureau	Premier, State Council	Commander-in-Chief, PLA; Chairman, MilCom, CPC/CC	
Yeh Chien-ying	VChmn, CPC/CC; Member, Political Bureau; SC, Political Bureau	Chairman, NPC/SC	VChmn, MilCom, CPC/CC	
Teng Hsiao-p'ing	VChmn, CPC/CC; Member, Political Bureau; SC, Political Bureau	VPremier, State Council	Chief-of-Staff, PLA; VChmn, MilCom, CPC/CC	Chairman, NatCom/CPPCC
Li Hsien-nien	VChmn, CPC/CC; Member, Political Bureau; SC, Political Bureau	VPremier, State Council		
Wang Tung-hsing	VChmn, CPC/CC; Member, Political Bureau; SC, Political Bureau; Dir, General Office, CPC/CC			
Chang T'ing-fa	Member, Political Bureau		CO, Air Force, PLA	
Ch'en Hsi-lien	Member, Political Bureau	VPremier, State Council	SC, MilCom, CPC/CC; CO, Peking MR	
Ch'en Yung-kuei	Member, Political Bureau	VPremier, State Council; VChmn, Shansi PrRC		
Chi Teng-k'uei	Member, Political Bureau	VPremier, State Council	First PolCom, Peking MR	
Fang Yi	Member, Political Bureau	VPremier, State Council		VPres, ChiAcadSci; DepHead, CPC Core Group, ChiAcadSci
Hsu Hsiang-ch'ien	Member, Political Bureau	VPremier, State Council; Minister, National Defense	VChmn, MilCom, CPC/CC; Minister, National Defense	
Hsu Shih-yu	Member, Political Bureau		CO, Canton MR; 1st Sec, CPC Com, Canton MR	
Keng Piao	Member, Political Bureau; Dir, InterLiaDept, CPC/CC			
Li Te-sheng	Member, Political Bureau		Member, MilCom, CPC/CC; CO, Shenyang MR; 1st Sec, CPC Com, Shenyang MR	
Liu Po-ch'eng	Member, Political Bureau	VChmn, NPC/SC	Member, MilCom, CPC/CC	
Ni Chih-fu	Member, Political Bureau; 2nd Sec, Peking MPC; 2nd Sec, Shanghai MPC	VChmn, Peking MRC; 1stVChmn, Shanghai MRC		Active, Labor Unions

Name	Party Positions	Government Positions	Military Positions	Other Functions
Nieh Jung-chen	Member, Political Bureau	VChmn, NPC/SC	VChmn, MilCom, CPC/CC	
P'eng Ch'ung	Member, Political Bureau; 3rd Sec, Shanghai MPC	2nd VChmn, Shanghai MRC	2nd PolCom, Nanking MR	VChmn, NatCom/CPPCC
Su Chen-hua	Member, Political Bureau; 1st Sec, Shanghai MPC	Chairman, Shanghai MRC	1st PolCom, navy	
Wei Kuo-ch'ing	Member, Political Bureau; 1st Sec, Kwangtung PrPC	VChmn, NPC/SC; Chairman, Kwangtung PrRC	Dir, GenPolDept, PLA; 1st PolCom, Canton MR	VChmn, NatCom/CPPCC
Ulanfu	Member, Political Bureau; Dir, UFWD, CPC/CC	VChmn, NPC/SC		VChmn, NatCom/CPPCC
Wu Te	Member, Political Bureau; 1st Sec, Peking MPC	VChmn, NPC/SC; Chairman, Peking MRC		
Yü Ch'iu-li	Member, Political Bureau	VPremier, State Council Minister, State Planning Com		
Chao Tzu-yang	AltMem, Political Bureau; 1st Sec, Szechwan PrPC	Chmn, Szechwan PrRC	1st PolCom, Chengtu MR	VChmn, NatCom/CPPCC
Ch'en Mu-hua (f)	AltMem, Political Bureau	VPremier, State Council Minister, EconRelForCoun		
Saifudin	AltMem, Political Bureau	VChmn, NPC/SC		

Abbreviations:

AltMem	Alternate member
Chmn	Chairman
ChiAcadSci	Chinese Academy of Sciences
CO	Commanding officer
CPC/CC	Central Committee of the CPC
Dep	Deputy
Dir	Director
EconRelForCoun	Ministry of Economic Relations with Foreign Countries
GenPolDept	General Political Department
InterLiaDept	International Liaison Department
MD	Military district
MilCom	Central Military Commission
MPC	Municipal Party Committee (CPC)
MR	Military region
MRC	Municipal Revolutionary Committee
NatCom	National Committee
PolCom	Political commissar
PrPC	Provincial Party Committee (CPC)
PrRC	Provincial Revolutionary Committee
SC	Standing Committee
SciTechCom	State Scientific and Technical Commission
Sec	Secretary
UFWD	United Front Work Department
VChmn	Vice chairman
VPrem	Vice premier
VPres	Vice president

of power at high levels in both Party and state organs. In part, the public airing of this breakdown in official morality is probably intended to contribute to the campaign launched at the Eleventh Party Congress and endorsed at the Fifth NPC to intensify efforts to restore discipline within both official and public circles.

Though these campaigns to eradicate corruption and mismanagement may improve political morality, and though the effort to eliminate elements within the Party closely linked to purged former leaders may have produced an apparently united, collective leadership, divisive forces are at work and the ingredients of serious policy differences are close to the surface. Success of the ambitious modernization program to which the regime is committed will require pragmatic approaches and departures from the past that will inevitably raise the question of the future role of Maoism, whether the question is raised directly or obliquely. Differences have already surfaced on such fundamental questions as educational reform, the relative importance of redness and expertise, the degree of reliance on things foreign—particularly, at the moment, foreign technology, and conditions under which things foreign might be accepted. In a system that has no fixed procedure for leadership succession other than competition for power, ability to mute these differences will have a significant bearing on future leadership stability.

Notes

1. Article 1, 1978 state constitution.

2. According to Chang Kuo-t'ao, a founding member of the CPC, this concept of a two-stage revolution was already accepted as a line of procedure by most delegates to the First Party Congress of the CPC in 1921. See Chang Kuo-t'ao, *The Rise of the Chinese Communist Party, 1921-1927* (Lawrence: The University of Kansas Press, 1971), Vol. 1, p. 145.

3. Article 1 of both the 1975 and 1978 state constitutions states that the P.R.C. is "a socialist state," while the preamble to the 1978 version adds that "China has become a socialist country with the beginning of prosperity."

4. General Program, 1977 Party constitution.

5. Peking Municipality, for instance, is composed of nine urban districts and nine counties; Shanghai of ten of each; and Tientsin of twelve districts and five counties. See U.S. Joint Publications Research

Service, *Simplified Handbook on Administrative Divisions of the People's Republic of China 1977*, JPRS 71247, June 7, 1978, pp. 5 and 6.

6. The 2,136 county and county-equivalent units consist of 2,013 counties, 66 autonomous counties, 53 banners, 3 autonomous banners, and 1 *chen* (Want'ing in Yunnan). Ibid, p. 1.

7. The 211 prefectural-level units include 174 prefectures, 29 autonomous prefectures, 1 administrative area (Hainan), and 7 leagues. Ibid., p. 1.

8. In reports relating to representation to recent Party and state congresses, the P.R.C. media speak of China's fifty-four minorities. Peking, NCNA, for instance, February 25, 1976, said that the Fifth National People's Congress included representatives of "all the fifty-four national minorities in China."

9. Revision of Party constitutions was also undertaken by several Party congresses before 1956.

10. The initials NPC have become standard in usage for the National People's Congress, and *not* for the National Party Congress, and will be used with that meaning in this chapter.

11. Unless otherwise indicated, reference hereafter to the Party constitution is to the 1977 revision and reference to the state constitution is to that of 1978.

12. "Press Communiqué of the Tenth National Congress of the Communist Party of China," *The Tenth National Congress of the Communist Party of China (Documents)* (Peking: Foreign Language Press, 1973), p. 79.

13. Edward E. Rice, *Mao's Way* (Berkeley and Los Angeles: University of California Press, 1972), p. 464.

14. Recall power was exercised by the electors of Hopeh and Liaoning provinces and of Peking Municipality when they "annulled" the credentials of one deputy from each to the Fifth NPC in 1978, after finding that those elected had "committed serious mistakes." Peking, NCNA, February 25, 1978.

15. Hua Kuo-feng, "Political Report," Eleventh Party Congress, August 12, 1977.

16. Joint editorial, *People's Daily* and *Red Flag*, July 14, 1964, "On Khrushchev's Phoney Communism and Its Historical Lesson for the World: Comment on the Open Letter of the Central Committee of the CPSU," in William E. Griffith, ed., *Sino-Soviet Relations, 1964-1965* (Cambridge: The M.I.T. Press, 1967), p. 350.

17. The Central Committee carries the same numerical designation as

the National Party Congress at which it was elected; thus the Eleventh Central Committee is the Central Committee elected at the Eleventh Party Congress.

18. *China News Analysis,* Number 1093/94; September 16, 1977, contains considerable additional information about the composition of the Eleventh Central Committee.

19. See James P. Harrison, *The Long March to Power: A History of the Chinese Communist Party, 1921-72* (New York: Praeger, 1972), p. 258.

20. Roderick MacFarquhar, *The Origins of the Cultural Revolution,* Vol. 1, *Contradictions Among the People 1956-57* (New York: Columbia University Press, 1974), p. 140.

21. Ibid.

22. Younger leaders are Fidel Castro of Cuba and Gyorgy Lazar of Hungary. In the absence of essential information, Cambodia was not taken into account in this statement.

23. Article 11, 1977 Party constitution.

24. Peking, NCNA, January 2, 1979. The office of General Secretary (*tsung shu-chi*) had been restored at the Eighth Party Congress in 1956 (MacFarquhar, *Origins of the Cultural Revolution,* p. 140).

25. Harold C. Hinton, *An Introduction to Chinese Politics* (New York: Praeger, 1973), p. 211.

26. See articles 1 to 4 of the state constitution. Aside from changes in phraseology and the transfer of some points to other articles, there is virtually no substantive difference between the 1975 and 1978 constitutions on matters covered in this introductory paragraph.

27. Article 2, state constitution.

28. Article 20, 1978 state constitution.

29. Article 23, 1954 state constitution. Under this provision, twelve representatives of Taiwanese living abroad were elected or appointed to serve as deputies from Taiwan at the Fourth NPC (see "Press Communiqué of the First Session of the Fourth National People's Congress of the People's Republic of China"). At earlier NPCs, in the listing of deputies by province, under Taiwan, representation was indicated as "temporarily vacant."

30. Article 16, 1975 state constitution.

31. The Second Plenum of the Tenth Central Committee, for instance, met January 8-10, 1975, to approve all documents to be submitted to the Fourth NPC and the list of nominees for the Standing Committee and the State Council. Similarly, the Second Plenum of the

Eleventh Central Committee met February 18-23, 1978, to perform the same tasks in respect to the Fifth NPC.

32. The process of election of the premier and other members of the State Council has undergone some change. The 1954 constitution provides for the election by the NPC of the premier upon the recommendation of the chairman of the P.R.C. and of the other members of the State Council upon the recommendation of the premier. With the abolition of the office of chairman of the P.R.C., the 1975 constitution transferred the nominating function in respect to both premier and other members of the council to the Central Committee. The 1978 constitution preserves for the Central Committee the right to nominate the premier but returns to the premier the right to nominate other members of the council.

33. While the 1978 constitution speaks only of the power of the NPC to elect the president of the Supreme People's Court and the chief procurator of the Supreme People's Procuratorate, without reference to the nominating authority, the names of the two officials elected to these offices at the Fifth NPC had been "approved" at the Second Plenum of the Eleventh Central Committee, together with the candidate for premier and "other component members" of the State Council.

34. Power of dismissal appears to include the dismissal of the premier as well as of other members of the State Council, though resort to such action without Central Committee approval is inconceivable.

35. Winberg Chai, *The New Politics of Communist China: Modernization Process of a Developing Nation* (Pacific Palisades: Goodyear, 1972), p. 203.

36. Article 30, 1978 state constitution.

37. Ibid.

38. Composition: ibid., article 31; nomination and election: ibid., article 22.

39. Chou En-lai in an interview with correspondents of *Vus* and *Epocha,* reported by Tanjug, March 17, 1971.

40. Ibid. The twenty-six ministries may refer to those later staffed at the Fourth NPC.

41. Article 34, state constitution.

42. Yeh Chien-ying, "Report on the Revision of the Constitution," delivered at the Fifth NPC, March 1, 1978, and reported by NCNA, Peking, March 7, 1978. See also Hua Kuo-feng, "Report on the Work of the Government," delivered at the Fifth NPC, March 5, 1978, and reported by NCNA, Peking, March 6, 1978, and article

33 of the state constitution.

43. Article 34, state constitution.

44. Article 42, 1978 state constitution.

45. The candidacy of the official elected at the Fifth NPC, however, had been approved by the Central Committee.

46. A. Doak Barnett, *Cadres, Bureaucracy, and Political Power in Communist China* (New York: Columbia University Press, 1967), p. 238.

47. Article 43, 1978 state constitution.

48. Article 6, "Organic Law of the People's Procuratorates," 1954.

49. Ibid., article 8.

50. Barnett, *Cadres, Bureaucracy, and Political Power*, p. 195.

51. The guarantee of most of these rights is contained in articles 44 through 55 of the state constitution but references to others are scattered elsewhere in the document. Duties of citizens are listed in articles 56, 57, and 58.

52. Article 45, 1978 state constitution. Big-character posters are described in a following section.

53. Chang Ch'un-ch'iao, "Report on the Revision of the Constitution," in *Documents of the First Session of the Fourth National People's Congress of the People's Republic of China* (Peking: Foreign Languages Press, 1975), pp. 39-40.

54. Article 6 of the Common Program of the CPPCC. The Common Program, however, did not include the reference to family life.

55. Article 53, 1978 state constitution.

56. Article 4, 1975 state constitution.

57. Article 4, 1978 state constitution.

58. Article 12, 1977 Party constitution.

59. Article 55, 1978 state constitution.

60. Article 26, 1975 state constitution.

61. Article 18, 1978 state constitution.

62. As early as February 1942, *Liberation Daily*, an organ of the CPC in Yenan, spoke of *Mao Tse-tung chu-i* ("Maoism," of the "doctrine of Mao"), hence, the term "Maoism" is not, as is frequently stated, a term coined in the West. See Dennis J. Doolin and Robert C. North, *The Chinese People's Republic* (Stanford: The Hoover Institution on War and Peace, 1966), p. 63, n. 30. In the expression "Marxism–Leninism–Mao Tsetung Thought," CPC practice is *not* to insert a hyphen between the last two syllables in Mao's name.

63. See *Peking Review*, no. 51, December 15, 1967, p. 17.

64. Derek J. Waller, quoting from the *Hunan Daily* for February 4,

1966, in *The Government and Politics of Communist China* (New York: Doubleday, Anchor Books, 1971), p. 32.

65. Franz Michael, "Ideology and the Cult of Mao," in Frank N. Trager and William Henderson, eds., *Communist China, 1949-1969, A Twenty-Year Appraisal* (New York: New York University Press, 1970), p. 29.

66. Stated in the "General Program" section of the 1956 Party constitution.

67. "General Program," Party constitution.

68. For comprehensive studies of ideology and the role of ideology in the Chinese Communist system, see Franz Schurmann, *Ideology and Organization in Communist China*, 2nd ed., (Berkeley and Los Angeles: University of California Press, 1972); Richard H. Solomon, "From Commitment to Cant: The Evolving Functions of Ideology in the Revolutionary Process," in Chalmers Johnson, ed., *Ideology and Politics in Contemporary China* (Seattle: University of Washington Press, 1973), pp. 44-77; and John B. Starr, *Ideology and Culture: An Introduction to the Dialectics of Contemporary Chinese Politics* (New York: Harper & Row, 1973), chapters 1 and 2, from which most of the last paragraph is drawn.

69. For discussions of the "mass line" policy during the Kiangsi and Yenan periods, see Ilpyong J. Kim, *The Politics of Chinese Communism: Kiangsi under the Soviets* (Berkeley and Los Angeles: University of California Press, 1973) and Mark Selden, "The Yenan Legacy: The Mass Line," in A. Doak Barnett, ed., *Chinese Communist Politics in Action*, paperback ed. (Seattle: University of Washington Press, 1972), pp. 99-151.

70. Article 10, 1978 state constitution. Article 7 of the constitution permits peasants to farm private plots and to engage in limited household sideline production and allows pastoral people to keep a limited number of livestock for personal needs, while article 5 allows nonagricultural individual laborers to "engage in individual labor." These provisions continue the constitutional protection of incentives, severely criticized by some in the early 1970s.

71. NCNA, Peking, February 23, 1978.

72. John W. Lewis, *Leadership in Communist China* (Ithaca, N.Y.: Cornell University Press, 1963) pp. 186 ff.

73. For discussions on the subject of cadres, see ibid., chapters 5 and 6; Schurmann, *Ideology and Organization*, pp. 162-172; Barnett, *Cadres, Bureaucracy, and Political Power*, pp. 38-47; and Kim, *Politics of Chinese Communism*, chapter 7.

74. Schurmann, *Ideology and Organization*, p. 162.

75. Mao Tse-tung, "The Role of the Chinese Communist Party in the National War," in the *Selected Works of Mao Tse-tung* (Peking: Foreign Language Press, 1965), vol. 2, p. 202 and p. 210, n. 1.

76. Chou En-lai, "Report to the Tenth National Congress of the Communist Party of China."

77. Article 19, 1978 state constitution.

Bibliography

Barnett, A. Doak. *Cadres, Bureaucracy, and Political Power in Communist China*. New York: Columbia University Press, 1967.

Chen, Theodore H.E. *The Chinese Communist Regime. Documents and Commentary*. New York: Praeger, 1967.

Cohen, Arthur M. *The Communism of Mao Tse-tung*. Chicago: The University of Chicago Press, 1964.

Cohen, Jerome A. *The Criminal Process in the People's Republic of China, 1949-1963: An Introduction*. Cambridge, Mass.: Harvard University Press, 1968.

Domes, Jurgen. *The Internal Politics of China 1949-1972*. Translated by Rudiger Machetzki. New York: Praeger, 1973.

Foreign Broadcast Information Service. "Material on the 11th National Congress of the Communist Party of China." *Daily Report: People's Republic of China* 1, no. 180, supplement 9 (September 1, 1977).

Foreign Language Press. *Documents of the First Session of the Fourth National People's Congress of the People's Republic of China*. Peking: Foreign Language Press, 1975.

————. *Eighth National Congress of the Communist Party of China*. Volume I, *Documents;* Volume II, *Speeches;* Volume III, *Greetings From Fraternal Parties*. Peking: Foreign Language Press, 1956.

————. *The Tenth National Congress of the Communist Party of China (Documents)*. Peking: Foreign Language Press, 1973.

Guillermaz, Jacques. *A History of the Chinese Communist Party, 1921-1949*. New York: Random House, 1972.

————. *The Chinese Communist Party in Power, 1949-1975*. Boulder, Colo.: Westview Press, 1976.

Harrison, James P. *The Long March to Power: A History of the Chinese Communist Party, 1921-1972*. New York: Praeger, 1972.

Hinton, Harold C. *An Introduction to Chinese Politics*. 2nd ed., New York: Holt, Rinehart and Winston/Praeger, 1978.

Johnson, Chalmers, ed. *Ideology and Politics in Contemporary China.* Seattle: University of Washington Press, 1973.

Lee, Luke T. "Chinese Communist Law: Its Background and Development." In George P. Jan, ed. *Government in Communist China.* San Francisco: Chandler, 1969.

Li, Victor H. "The Role of Law in Communist China." *China Quarterly,* no. 44 (October/December, 1970), pp. 66-111.

Oksenberg, Michel. "Methods of Communication within the Chinese Bureaucracy." *China Quarterly,* no. 57 (January/March, 1974), pp. 1-39.

Schram, Stuart R. *Authority, Participation and Cultural Change in China.* New York: Cambridge University Press, 1973.

Schurmann, Franz. *Ideology and Organization in Communist China.* 2nd ed., Berkeley and Los Angeles: University of California Press, 1972.

Solomon, Richard H. "From Commitment to Cant: The Evolving Functions of Ideology in the Revolutionary Process." In Chalmers Johnson, *Ideology and Politics,* pp. 47-77.

_____ . *Mao's Revolution and the Chinese Political Culture.* Berkeley and Los Angeles: University of California Press, 1971.

Starr, John Bryan. *Ideology and Culture: An Introduction to the Dialectic of Contemporary Chinese Politics.* New York: Harper & Row, 1973.

Townsend, James R. *Political Participation in Communist China.* Berkeley and Los Angeles: University of California Press, 1969.

_____ . *Politics in China.* Boston: Little, Brown and Co., 1974.

Waller, Derek J. *The Government and Politics of Communist China.* Garden City: Doubleday, Anchor Books, 1971.

5
Agricultural Development

Ramon H. Myers

The Communist government that assumed power in China in 1949 inherited a country with a long agrarian history. For more than three millennia the Chinese people had perfected the art of farming the land. They had developed unusual skills to replenish the soil's fertility and produce extraordinarily high crop yields, often higher than those in Western countries with modernized agriculture. Certain regions of the country like the Chengtu plain in Szechwan Province, the great Canton delta region of Kwangtung Province, and areas westward up the Yangtze valley through Anhwei, Kiangsi, Hunan, and Hupeh provinces had extensive canalized tracts of land providing for remarkable irrigation of crops. In all parts of the country farmers prepared compost piles to fertilize their fields. By conserving water, restoring the soil's fertility, and farming the land with a garden-like intensity and care, the Chinese had managed to produce enough food and fiber by the early twentieth century to support around 500 million people. This achievement occurred on about 107 million hectares of farm land, which represented only about 11 percent of the country's total land.

The land produced a great variety of crops ranging from fruit and tropical products in the south to miscellaneous grains and the ginseng root in the north. By 1936 China was the world's second largest producer of wheat and the world's largest supplier and consumer of rice. Agriculture was the largest industry, gave employment to about 80 percent of the work force, and produced roughly 60 percent of the country's gross national product.

Sometime in the late seventeenth century agriculture began to expand, population steadily grew, and more people migrated to settle in the northwest, the southwest, and the central highlands. Landless families gradually acquired some land to farm, either as tenants or owner-cultivators. But after World War I this process was halted by the outbreak of civil war and the collapse of national and local administrative efforts, which normally provided peace and stability— necessary conditions that the agriculturalist always needs to farm with minimal certainty and security. As a result of warlordism in the 1920s, Japanese military aggression in the 1930s, and civil war in the late 1940s, villages suffered severe shocks and dislocations that increased the financial burden on farmers and reduced many families to utter ruin. Perhaps the worst two consequences of these three decades of instability were the great rise in rural unemployment and the inability of many families to retain their land to farm. As a result, by 1949 the area of cultivated land had greatly declined, rural unemployment had risen, and farm production had fallen. The new socialist government inherited very difficult problems: to revive farm production in the face of rampant inflation, to increase output to support the industrialization of the country, and to develop a distribution system to feed and clothe the country's huge population.

Production Performance

The new government quickly restored peace and order and production began to increase. (For a map of China showing major crops and percentages of land under cultivation, see Map 3 in chapter 1.) As early as 1952 agricultural output had reached the prewar high level of the mid-1930s. We can assess the performance of agriculture between 1952 and 1976 in several ways. We can compare the growth of production of food grain and fibers with population increase to determine if the per capita availability of food and fiber grew, remained constant, or fell. Or we can compare the growth of total farm production, e.g. food grain, fibers, and special crops, with a composite series of inputs such as land, labor, and capital to determine if the productivity of all farming inputs rose, remained the same, or declined. Useful as these assessments are, however, they cannot be undertaken unless sufficient statistics are available. The present government simply has not published enough statistics by which experts can agree upon a comparison of the trend of total farm production with that of total farm inputs. We can discuss with more certainty the long-term trend of food grain and fiber production based upon official statistics and compare these to various estimates of

Table 5.1 Farm Production and Population Growth, 1949-1976

Year	Total Grain[a] Area (mill. ha.)	Total Grain[a] Yield (hg./ha.)	Total Grain[a] Production (mill. tons)	Cotton[b] Production (000 m.t.)	Population (000)[c] High Estimate	Population (000)[c] Medium Estimate
1949	101.6	1,064	108.1	444	-	-
1950	104.8	1,190	124.7	692	-	-
1951	107.0	1,262	135.0	1,030	-	-
1952	112.3	1,375	154.4	1,304	-	-
1953	114.3	1,373	156.9	1,174	576,777	576,049
1954	116.3	1,379	160.4	1,065	589,157	588,429
1955	118.4	1,476	174.8	1,518	603,454	601,175
1956	124.3	1,468	182.5	1,445	618,621	614,735
1957	120.8	1,530	185.0	1,640	634,309	628,831
1958	121.2	1,649	200.0	1,600	650,378	643,315
1959	109.1	1,512	165.0	1,350	666,631	658,056
1960	119.0	1,260	150.0	905	682,104	672,316
1961	118.8	1,364	162.0	890	695,700	685,083
1962	118.9	1,463	174.0	1,000	705,589	695,727
1963	118.7	1,542	183.0	1,100	714,861	706,232
1964	121.8	1,642	200.0	1,500	727,823	719,109
1965	122.6	1,631	200.0	1,650	743,427	733,650
1966	124.0	1,734	215.0	1,810	754,051	749,059
1967	127.1	1,810	230.0	1,940	764,673	764,196
1968	128.0	1,680	215.0	1,810	780,680	779,283
1969	129.1	1,704	220.0	1,770	797,058	794,808
1970	129.8	1,849	240.0	2,000	813,806	810,801
1971	131.3	1,874	246.0	2,220	830,953	827,288
1972	131.5	1,825	240.0	2,125	848,498	844,309
1973	132.5	1,885	250.0	2,550	866,459	861,915
1974	134.7	1,967	265.0	2,500	884,841	880,133
1975	136.5	1,978	270.0	2,400	903,639	898,953
1976	137.5	1,943	267.0	2,350	922,837	917,845

[a] Economic Research Service, U.S. Department of Agriculture, People's Republic of China Agricultural Situation: Review of 1976 and Outlook for 1977 (Washington D.C.: 1977), p. 32. Total grain includes tubers converted on a grain-equivalent basis. Data for 1949-1957 obtained from Ten Great Years (Peking: Foreign Languages Press, 1959); data for 1958-1975 are based on official sources. Data for 1976 are preliminary estimates.

[b] Ibid., p. 7.

[c] See John S. Aird, Estimates and Projections of the Population of Mainland China: 1953-1986 (Washington D.C.: U.S. Department of Commerce, 1968), Appendix: high estimate based upon model 1 (1953-1965) and model A (1966-1976); medium estimate based upon model III and model B for same year intervals.

population growth to roughly estimate the changing food grain and fiber availability on a per capita basis. These data are presented in Table 5.1 and then discussed with some mention of prewar conditions.

Between 1949 and 1957 farm production quickly revived and continued to increase with food grain and cotton output growing at 6.2 and 18.7 percent per year respectively. Meanwhile, the highest population growth estimate shows an annual growth rate of 1.9 percent for the same period. Therefore food and fiber per capita availability rose so that living standards improved and the supply of raw materials for industrialization increased. This trend was reversed between 1958 and 1961 when production for all crops declined. This period of hardship, following upon the steady improvement in food and fiber availability, makes the overall peformance since 1949 less favorable than if there had been at least some gain in supply during these years. Conditions began to improve after 1965. During the next eleven-year period food grain production increased at the annual growth rate of 2.7 percent, with cotton output growing at 3.2 percent. Again, the highest population estimate for these years is 1.9 percent. A comparison of these rates of growth strongly indicates that per capita availability of both food and fibers steadily rose. Therefore if these same conditions continue for another decade or two, living standards will steadily improve and the supply of industrial goods will be increased.

The overall performance since 1949, however, is one where food and fiber production grew just slightly faster than the highest population growth estimate. China is still a poor country. The people are adequately fed and clothed, but they do not live with abundance. This performance is still superior to that of most developing countries since World War II, which at times have suffered from political instability and inflation. It is also a performance more satisfactory than that of the majority of socialist countries, in particular the Soviet Union where living standards remained appallingly low for more than three decades after the collectivization of agriculture. On the other hand Japan, Taiwan, and most of the advanced countries of Western Europe experienced a more rapid growth of rural living standards during their transition period to industrialization than did China.

The development of agriculture after 1949 was associated with an unusually rapid increase in population. Recently the state has taken vigorous steps to reduce population growth. Should the steady modernization of farming of the past decade continue into the future with a growth of farm production of 2 percent per annum or higher, China will have achieved an agricultural revolution. During late imperial times, farm production slowly expanded to match population, probably at an annual growth rate somewhere beneath .5 to .7 percent. After the 1911 Revolution, farm production either declined or fluctuated around a trend showing neither rise or fall. Population still continued its relentless increase, so that for nearly four decades per capita food availability did not rise and at some periods it even fell. It is little wonder that during the 1920s and 1930s food grain imports rose and in certain regions famine broke out. Therefore the post-1965 agricultural performance suggests that a break with the historical trend might be taking place.

In order to understand how this break with the past has begun to occur, it is necessary to trace some of the major reorganizations of agricultural production and distribution and then examine what role certain factors of production such as capital and technology have played in the process of growth.

The Reorganization of Farm Production

The Early Period of Reform: 1949-1962

Although many institutional reforms to reorganize production took place after 1949, not all of these directly contributed to the increase of land and labor productivity. The restoration of peace and order after 1949 certainly was a major factor that enabled the farming population to return to the business of tilling the soil with the certainty that crops could be harvested and marketed. But while law and order did return to the countryside, the Communist Party began to initiate a series of village reforms that in the next twelve years dramatically changed the life-style of hundreds of millions of rural people.

On May 4, 1946, the Communist Party ordered its cadres to wage war against the landlords in the areas under its control. The Party sought to strip away the economic power of the local elite by transferring their land to the poor. Party leaders hoped that this move would pave the way for Party cadres to install local leaders of their own choosing so that the Communist Party at last could effectively control villages. After the defeat of the Kuomintang military armies in 1949, the policy of land reform was carried to all parts of the country. The Party revised the land reform procedures that it had used in areas that it controlled in North China because farming conditions elsewhere in the country greatly differed. Instead of depriving the bona fide, successful farmers of their land, as Party cadres had successfully done in the northern provinces, the Party ruled that these farmers could retain their land to farm. Such farmers typically worked farms of scattered plots amounting to no more than a half a hectare. Although this group rarely made up more than 20 percent of the households in any single village, they normally marketed around 80 percent of what village households sold. The Party recognized that if this farming group reduced its production, rural marketing might be adversely influenced and cities would not obtain enough food and fiber. This conciliatory policy was extended to the rest of the country.

The lineage associations and absentee landlords, however, had to relinquish their claims to village land. These lands were transferred to the new village associations established at the behest of Party cadres to distribute land to the poorer villagers. By late 1952 the new government could report that land reform had been completed. In this momentous redistribution of property rights, the Party had smashed the power of the local elite, which had long depended upon land property as a major financial pillar for their activities. By establishing village associations to replace the old, local elite, the Party had created a new local organization that its cadres could manipulate to control village society. Not since the fifteenth century had the state in China so effectively established its control in the villages.

In late December 1951 the Central Committee of the Communist Party of China published its views on how the village economy would be reorganized. On the one hand the Party stressed that more cooperation had to be established between households if production was to be increased, but on the other hand the Party contended that it wanted "to avoid any violent setbacks in production carried out in this individualistic peasant economy" so that bona fide farming families would be allowed to farm. Cooperation meant three possible courses. First, several households might form mutual aid teams to share labor, land, and farm capital during peak farming seasons. Second, several households could cooperate through the year to farm and engage in nonfarm projects. Finally, a group of households in the same village neighborhood, perhaps as few as eight or as many as fifteen, would pool their land and farm capital, farm as a team, and be rewarded according to the resources contributed by each household. Cadres were urged to persuade villagers to recognize the advantages of these forms of cooperation and to establish them voluntarily. Party leaders seem to have been convinced of the inherent superiority of cooperative farming over family farming, and they merely intended to transform rural society very slowly by making sure at each step that the farming community shared this conviction.

The progress toward cooperation advanced slowly and fitfully. By the end of 1952 cadres reported that three-fifths of all rural households still privately farmed and the remainder had joined seasonal mutual aid teams with only a very small share belonging either to permanent mutual aid teams or to agricultural production cooperatives. Most of the mutual aid teams were located in the north where Communist influence had been strong during the war against Japan and the Civil War. By

1954 the number of mutual aid teams exceeded 10 million, but there were reports that some farmers had slaughtered their livestock in open defiance of orders to cooperate with other families. Severe grain shortages in 1954 and the intensive drive to allocate more resources for industrialization had resulted in the state attempting to extract more food grain and fiber from the villages than the rural people were willing to relinquish.

Meanwhile, several distinct trends had been taking place in rural communities. On the one hand, many of the village leaders who had vigorously supported the Communist Party during land reform were tiring of Party work and were anxious to return to the normal pursuits of making a living and acquiring property. On the other hand, land reform had created conditions whereby some families had received more land than they had labor and livestock to farm, whereas other families were in the opposite circumstance. This imbalance had been corrected by families resorting to age-old practices: the supplying of wage labor for hire, and the renting and leasing of land and farm capital. Communist rural surveys spotted this resurgence of household contractual exchange. Party leaders quickly became aware of this old rural penchant for property accumulation and recognized that ultimately a new rural elite based on new landed property might someday confront it in the villages. The twin problems of finding loyal, efficient, hard-working village leaders and a resurgent rural capitalism along with the acute shortage of grain in 1954 set off a major debate within the top leadership of the Party.

The debate centered on whether to continue the policy of gradually persuading the peasantry to depend more upon cooperative farming than upon private contract, or to take some other action with a view to preventing the rapid revival of a new property-owning elite in the villages while at the same time accelerating the trend toward cooperative farming. Intra-Party dispute on the "peasant question" was resolved in the spring of 1955 by Mao Tse-tung when he rejected gradualism, although it was the majority view at that time. Mao decided to sever the ties between farm families and their land by having the cadres establish village cooperatives. Every household would relinquish its claim to land and farm capital and would receive rewards according to the work it performed in the village cooperative team. This bold step was the most far-reaching reform of the countryside that any government in China had attempted since the seventh century, the early T'ang period, when the state had seized control of all land and given parcels of it to households on the basis of special needs—the famous *chün-t'ien* system of land holding.

The drama of the next eighteen months can be appreciated only if we realize that in late spring of 1955 only one out of ten households participated in any kind of team-farming arrangement. Throughout the fall and into winter, cadres instructed village leaders to form the cooperatives. The Party allowed households to own some land if it did not exceed 5 percent of the average arable area per capita in all the country's villages. By mid-1956 the Party had managed to make six out of every ten households join village cooperatives; by the end of the year, the figure was almost nine out of ten. These cooperatives contained farming teams ranging from twenty to sixty households, depending upon village size. During early 1956, many farmers slaughtered their livestock and refused to join the production teams. In the face of such resistance, the Party retreated by returning some livestock to their former owners, allowing teams to lease land to certain households and collect rent, and reinstating veteran farmers to manage production teams. These concessions were short-lived, for in the late summer of 1958 the Central Committee published another directive ordering cadres to establish even larger village production units. This was to be done by "militarizing" village organizations.

During the next few years the Party tried many different systems of local control, until in 1962 it became clear that it had found what it was seeking. The new system, the outgrowth of considerable experiment and compromise, was structured as follows: below the county administrative level, the Party established a new organizational unit called the commune. In area, the commune roughly approximated a subunit, or district, within the county. It was essentially an old township made up of a market town, sometimes even several small towns, and its satellite villages. There were roughly 74,000 communes, each with an average of 1,600 households, throughout the country. Villages had been renamed brigades and were now referred to as "production brigades." To create them, many villages had been amalgamated into larger units. Within each large village, or brigade, were production teams made up of between twenty and sixty households, depending on the district. Households within certain sections of the village now worked the land as a team. During the nonfarming period, household members might serve on other brigade teams, work in commune industries or services, or farm the garden-size plots around their homesteads.

The period of 1958-1962 was one of great turmoil, accompanied by a frenzy and a fervor not experienced since the land reform. After the fall harvest in 1958 and through the winter of 1959 rural cadres organized the farmers into large labor brigades to construct commune structures such as dining and sleeping quarters, build irrigation facilities, plant trees, and dig up the fields to experiment with new, deep plowing methods. Farmer dissatisfaction with the new cooperative system and the large-scale use of farm labor on such projects instead of on conventional soil preparing and planting activities produced a very poor harvest throughout the country in 1960. Rather than consolidate the gains realized in recent cooperative endeavors, the Party again instructed cadres to resort to labor brigades as in the past with the devastating result that the 1961 harvest also was very poor. Two bad harvests in sequence for a poor country like China can only spell disaster.

Widespread food shortages became severe. A flood of refugees poured into Hong Kong in 1962 and 1963 reporting that near famine conditions prevailed in some parts of the country. Letters from relatives and friends told of acute food scarcity, and secret documents of the People's Liberation Army (*Kung-tso t'ung-hsun*) describe widespread occurrences of edema from poor diet in the Lanchow Military Region. The state had already responded to the crisis. It initiated stringent rationing and control of interprovincial grain shipments. It began to import large amounts of wheat and flour from abroad: 4 million metric tons in 1961 and 1962 and 5.2 and 5.6 million metric tons in 1963 and 1964, respectively, compared to no such imports during the 1950s.

In 1962 and 1963 the Party also initiated many new policies to revive food production. First, it ordered cadres to disband the large labor brigades. Second, the production team became the unit for reckoning incomes, expenditures, and the disposition of farm assets—rather than the brigade as had been the case since 1958. Third, the Party permitted the reestablishment of private markets whereby farmers could sell products that they had somehow produced on their own, either in their private plots or when not participating with production teams. These concessions to the farmers restored sufficient incentives to the villages to produce and market more food grain and fiber, so that by 1965 agricultural production had again reached the high levels of 1956-1957.

In 1962 the three-tier organizational system of production team, village brigade, and commune managed the production and distribution of agricultural output in the countryside. The production team was the basic unit by which land, labor, and capital were organized to farm the land. Production teams embraced as few as twenty to as many as sixty or eighty households, and they typically were made up of households within a certain section of a village or a small village or hamlet. The brigade, which approximated the village in size and number of people, was merely an administrative unit to organize the production teams within each village. The commune—a large or small town and its cluster of fifteen to fifty satellite villages, which approximates the area once covering the local market center—became another administrative unit by which the Party now controls village life. Through this commune system the Party now as then exercises closer control over rural society than any previous Chinese state was ever able to achieve.

The Period 1963-1976

In spite of the Party's success in separating the rural people from their land, the Party faction identified with Mao Tse-tung was still dissatisfied with the rural way of thinking. It therefore attempted to change rural attitudes through a new agrarian policy enacted in 1964. This new policy was aimed at making production teams work harder and accept less remuneration; at encouraging villagers to refuse state aid, and rely instead upon their own resources and skills; and at persuading rural people to make greater sacrifices for community and state, rather than for family or kin. This policy sought to kindle a new moral fervor, a new state of mind among rural people to be self-reliant, to work for the Party and state, and to share and cooperate with each other in an unselfish and nonindividualist way. The Party adopted this new agrarian policy because Mao and his supporters perceived it as the proper way to transform Chinese society so as to bring about desirable life-styles and moral behavior.

The new policy was predicated upon developments in a poor hamlet in northern Shansi named Tachai. In February 1960 the Shansi Communist Party Committee listened attentively to a speech by a peasant named Ch'en Yung-kuei, who headed the Tachai production brigade and represented the farmers from Hsiyang County. Ch'en recounted how Tachai had raised crop yields to unprecedentedly high and stable levels through a new kind of team spirit and organization. As the Tachai story unfolded, it became apparent that what Ch'en had done was to organize groups of farmers to labor without reward during the winter months. Ch'en pointed out that "constructing large embankments in deep ravines that could hold the silt was like chiseling gold slabs. There would then be no runoff of water. Water could be stored, and the village could still plant good fields." Ch'en's charismatic leadership enabled him to mobilize the farmers to build these embankments and fill in dirt behind them. In this way the village expanded its cultivated land and still had a water supply to irrigate the many terraces. Although a five-day rainstorm destroyed the fruits of their labor in August 1963, the villagers refused state assistance and rebuilt the embankments within two years. Through these volunteer efforts, Tachai had increased its production income. From this increased income, the brigade had saved to buy construction materials to rebuild all household structures and even to improve the irrigation system. Thus Tachai had been able to transfer the farming technology used in the irrigated, alluvial plain areas to this arid, windswept foothill area. Crop yields of maize and sorghum had been pushed to unprecedented levels: in 1962 the brigade is supposed to have harvested 6.00 metric tons of grain per hectare compared to 1.80 in 1953.

This example of farmer dedication to community development rather than private or family gain convinced the Shansi Party Committee, and later the Party leadership in Peking, that the thinking of rural people could be changed if all rural communities could be encouraged to follow the example and leadership of the people of Tachai. Whether or not a new spirit had really emerged in Tachai is not clear. The alleged achievements clearly had been accomplished at great cost and sacrifice, and later there were charges that the crop statistics had been falsified and that the state had actually subsidized Tachai's development. Nevertheless, the Party seized upon this strategy as a new step to develop the rural economy. In 1964 Party cadres were instructed to meet with commune and brigade leaders to discuss how the Tachai example could be followed and duplicated. At first, Party cadres insisted that production teams organize special worker brigades to labor without remuneration on projects that would increase the amount of irrigated land, reclaim more land, or develop other sources of rural income. This approach was sometimes combined with making production teams meet to reevaluate their work-point reward system in order to assign fewer work points. The obvious intent here was to have production teams limit household claims to farm income earned by the team so as to increase accumulated reserves for rural investment. The Party abandoned this policy after several years, in the face of vigorous opposition. By the early 1970s, the "Learn from Tachai" policy still remained a cornerstone of Party agrarian thinking. But now it stressed only that production teams should adopt a transformative way of work and thinking and develop greater mechanization to increase production and income. These efforts were to be carried out through the three-tier organizational system of the commune.

The Period 1976-1978

Mao's death in late 1976, Teng Hsiao-p'ing's return to power, and the Party's new commitment for economic modernization reflect the enormous change of this period. More statistical information appeared in 1978. The government announced that food grain production for that year reached 295 million metric tons. As production fell in 1976 and rose only slightly in 1977, this recent increase of 25 million metric tons over 1975 represents some recovery from the turmoil of this period. However, the annual growth rate between 1975 and 1978 was 2.9 percent, still far below the projected 4 percent annual growth rate set by the Party for agriculture between 1978 and 1984.

The Party initiated many steps in 1978 to restore incentives to production teams and ensure that this body would remain the basic decision-maker in farming. The "Learn from Tachai" movement was virtually abandoned except as a model for mechanizing agriculture. The Party placed greater emphasis upon adopting farm machinery to speed up planting and harvesting and to reduce drudgery in the fields. The government took action to raise farm prices in order to increase rural incomes. The numerous national conferences designed to promote an upgrading of science and technology and the revival of higher education may produce a new stream of agricultural technology for the rural communes in the near future.

The System of Team Farming

For three thousand years Chinese rulers and their officials had attemped to promote farming and control rural life through complex organizations. It is within this context that we must view the three-tier control system of the commune and the state. This system enabled the state to intrude into the life and work of the farm family in ways never achieved by any previous government. Commune officials now effectively control population movement from and into the commune. The commune collects what amounts to a land tax and other minor taxes. It specifies that certain quantities of food, fibers, or both will be produced and sold at fixed prices to state marketing agencies. The commune can mobilize village labor at will for large projects on a scale resembling the corvée labor mobilization of the Ming period (1368-1644). Commune officials establish the procedures determining who will work in commune industries and services and what they will receive as pay. Commune officials have considerable bureaucratic expertise, are local residents, and are among the most able and competent commune members. These leaders are in constant telephone communication with the brigades or villages; they organize numerous meetings to discuss administrative matters.

Commune officials receive an annual agricultural plan from the state and assemble brigade leaders to decide on the allocation of production targets among the brigades. The plan stipulates how much of which crops the state will buy at fixed prices. Brigade leaders meet with their production team leaders to discuss how the teams can fulfill the required production quotas. They must plan to pay the state grain tax, set in 1949-1950 as a proportion of major crop yields of each locale. They discuss the capital projects to be undertaken and the funding required, as well as the amount of income for the brigades' welfare fund. This fund is dispensed for charity, special family needs, and to remedy any disasters that might befall the community. Finally, there is a discussion of what steps might be taken by teams to increase the supply of farm production, and of how living standards can be improved. After these lengthy discussions, production team leaders convene team members and discuss these same matters with them.

From twenty to eighty households make up the production teams. In small villages, a team might include all households; in large ones, families living in the same section of the village make up the team. It is not known for certain, but it is very likely that today's teams comprise the same cluster of families that formerly made up the *pao* or *lin* household units in traditional society, which helped local officials to collect taxes, police villages, and organize village defense. Farm tools and animals are distributed among production teams. Brigade and team leaders determine which fields and teams will be responsible for producing the crops or special products to be sold to the state. Households of each production team send members each day of the farming season to work the fields as a team. Team leaders discuss each day's work in advance, and each member labors at specified tasks: hoeing, sowing, irrigating, weeding, harvesting, and so on. After the farming season, some household members may be assigned to special teams to work on brigade projects like reclaiming land, building embankments, expanding the irrigation system, or planting orchards; other members may be assigned to work in commune industries or services. During the slack season, families manage their own garden plots, fishponds, and livestock.

Households receive incomes and bear financial burdens in accordance with their ability to supply labor and assume part of the general financial burden. This ability depends chiefly upon the number of persons who can work. The team income available for distribution among its households is a residual determined by the claims and deductions of the state, the brigade, and the team. First, the state obtains the land tax, paid either in kind or in cash, and purchases a certain quota of food grain or other crops at low, fixed prices. Production teams deposit the receipts from these sales in branches of the state People's Bank and rarely withdraw them for distribution to member households. Second, the brigade deducts income for: (1) its administrative fund to pay the salaries of brigade cadres and secretaries; (2) the welfare fund to be used for households with little or no earning capacity (widows, wives of soldiers, the aged, invalids); and (3) the accumulation fund, which is used to finance capital projects. The production team then deducts grain and income for seed, fertilizer, farm tools, and the like; it also deducts some food grain for the brigade grain reserve. The remaining income, averaging between 40 and 60 percent of total team income, is then divided among team members according to the work points they have earned throughout the year.

Four principal work point systems have been used at different times in various sections of the country. Information is still too scanty to say which system predominates in the mid-1970s. Under the *time-rate system,* team members tabulate the exact number of work days worked by members each month. This arrangement ignores differences in labor productivity as well as differences in types of work. Under the *work-point grading system,* teams classify their members according to three grades of workers, and award points accordingly on the work time. This system had the same problems as the previous one, although it offered more incentives. Under the *labor-norm system,* teams assign work points for each agricultural task and tabulate the points accumulated by members performing these tasks. The difficulty here is to assess the quality of completed work, and to establish the relationship between jobs and work points in a way that made sense to each team member. Finally, the *"learn from Tachai" system* is for all peasants to report individually what they think their daily work performance is worth and to elicit a team consensus on how many work points he or she had truly earned. Although this system was the last to evolve, few teams practice it because of its unpopularity among farm families.

Whatever the basis for determining work points, team earnings are distributed by dividing the total number of team work points into residual team income and determining the value per work point for that year. Two aspects of this distribution system vary in practice. Of the residual team income in cash or kind, a certain basic grain allowance is distributed to each team household, and the final amount is then allocated according to member work points. But many teams have dispensed with this basic allowance and simply distribute income according to the work points earned by each team member. It is clear that, under the system described above, households with many persons able to work on the team will earn more income than other households. At the same time, the deductions by the state, brigade, and team represent a burden on each household that is borne disproportionately by these multiworker households, the more so the smaller the team's residual income. After all, these same households are supporting poor families in the village and also bearing a greater share of state taxes, brigade costs, and the like.

Such was the system that enabled rural communities to finance their schools, local officers, capital projects, and basic charities without funding or support channeled through financial administration at the county level and beyond. This system certainly had its roots in the past. During the Ch'ing (1644-1911) and Republican (1911-1949) periods, large-scale cooperative activities like water control or irrigation were supported by households on an ability-to-pay basis. This was determined according to the size of each household's land. Each made contributions to the project and received rewards commensurate with the amount of land it owned or managed. The village leaders who organized and managed village schools, granaries, crop-watching associations, and village defense measures assessed households on the same basis. The very poor—always a few households in every community—were supported by their kin or through the charity of other villagers. Some farmers could always be found to keep complex accounts of the charges paid by households for irrigation services. Now as then farmers keep equally complex accounts of brigade and team business, including the tabulation of work points.

The transition from family farming to the team farming system was not without difficulties (which still persist). The source of these difficulties was the conflict between family values and preferences and those the Communist Party thought desirable. Traditionally, farm families had worked and cooperated to achieve family goals: the acquisition of land and other property; the attainment of social status; the elevation of the family's rank within the community. Family rituals and ceremonies requiring expense and dependency upon kinship relationships were part of this life-style. The Communist Party, on the other hand, tried to elicit different loyalty and sacrifice from farm families by having them work for activities that often bore no relationship to family concerns or interests. Families were supposed to always put the interest of the state and Party above their private interests. Needless to say, although the Party was able to create a new rural organization of work and reward, conflicts of interest between the farm families and the Party and government organs still exist.

To cite only a few examples, there is continuing conflict between households and team and brigade policies. In some villages, households earn virtually all their income from team activities. In others, however, as little as 80 or even 70 percent of their income may come from the production team because private sources of income are both available and expanding. Among these are raising vegetables, fish, or fruit in private gardens; working in commune industries or services; and private handicraft activities. In the latter case, households with considerable labor power and managerial skill might prefer to use their resources to exploit these nonteam sources of income. Labor absenteeism from daily team work could become a serious problem for team and brigade leaders.

Another conflict involved state agricultural policies that ran counter to the best economic interests of brigades and their production teams. It has been state policy in recent years to increase food grain production everywhere in the country. Team labor, however, has often been in a position to earn more income from products other than food grains, and its allocation to the latter has therefore been a source of economic inefficiency. To give one of many examples found in the Communist press, in 1970, cadres of Chiungyang Commune in Ch'ao County of Anhwei Province learned that production teams in Shanch'iao brigade had constructed kilns to produce bricks for sale. Team leaders had recognized that using their labor to produce bricks rather than food grain would increase team income.

The new state policy of teaching the farmers self-reliance has also clashed with traditional notions of common sense. In Hoshih Commune of Ch'angshu County in Kiangsu Province, farmers asked the commune authorities for permission to use its machinery to remove a large cesspool so that more land could be cleared for farming. Commune cadres instead ordered the farmers to remove the obstacle themselves as a lesson in community self-reliance. The farmers spent days digging a moat 20 meters along the cesspool, hand-carried water to fill the moat, and then floated the obstacle free. Many farmers were probably shrewd enough to calculate the opportunity costs of their efforts, since it was obvious to all that the cesspool could have been removed by simple machinery within a day's time.

From time to time the press exhorts the farming communities to adopt the correct Party line of thought and work. Party leaders still believe that farm families will resort to private contracts in order to maximize their income. Old beliefs and values do not disappear overnight. Even under the present system of cooperative farming, in which the state so far has successfully stabilized production and guaranteed a distribution of food grain and fiber to all households, many families chafe under the pressures and controls to conform to the new work styles and ways of thinking. Individual gain and the improvement of family status and living standards are still important to rural families. Although the overwhelming majority of them conform to the team farming system, it is problematic how many would withdraw to take advantage of other procedures, especially those of time-honored means, if the opportunity should arise.

State Policies toward Agriculture

Prior to 1937 the Nanking government under Kuomintang rule had increased state efforts and funding to plan major water conservancy projects, expand countryside road networks, establish agricultural colleges and research institutes in different parts of the country, and promote rural banking and the creation of village cooperatives to loan to farmers and buy industrial products. These multifaceted schemes had varying success: research institutes and colleges rapidly developed to begin new seed breeding and testing; the conservancy projects scarcely developed beyond the planning level.

This mixed legacy, which the new socialist government inherited in 1949, gradually helped to promote the spread of new farming technology in the countryside. During the 1950s the new government budgeted money to encourage more research and development of new seeds and fertilizers, especially for rice and wheat. Gradually new seeds resistant to major diseases made their entry into regional cropping systems, but the impact of this development seems to have taken full hold only in the late 1960s and early 1970s. Perhaps the reason for this is that during the 1950s the Party was concerned mainly with building a modern industrial complex and reorganizing the economy to establish its control. Very few resources were allocated in state economic plans for agricultural development. Party leaders believed that initially farm production could be greatly increased merely by removing the old fetters of local elite control, which allegedly exploited the farmers, and by cooperativizing the villages. During the 1959-1962 period (see Table 5.1), it became clear to the Party that reorganization of agriculture alone had not released new forces of production.

After 1962, state policy toward agriculture underwent a decisive shift. The state began to supply more resources to the commune system in the hope of both stabilizing production during years of poor weather and increasing it greatly when excellent weather prevailed. The government began importing more chemical fertilizer and increasing its domestic supply so that total supply, which had stood slightly higher than 3 million tons in 1960, had risen to 9.8 million in 1965 and to more than 20 million in 1970. Between January 1972 and May 1974, China contracted to buy thirty chemical fertilizer plants to produce ammonia and urea at a cost of $492 million.

In the late 1960s, research institutes introduced a new strain of rice with a small stalk, few leaves, and a higher yield than previous strains. A variety of new wheat seeds also had been introduced, so that by the late 1960s major wheat diseases like stripe rust and smut had been brought under control. The research institutes, county research stations, and communes became linked as one pipeline to rapidly test and produce supplies of new seeds for commercial production on team farming plots. As each region and province is able to be served by research institutes, seed-breeding work can be rapidly introduced to counties and communes so that within three years new seeds can replace those already in use.

The state has also encouraged communes to establish small-scale industry to produce construction materials for wells, irrigation ponds and sluices, and a variety of farm machinery. Of course, communes purchase some of these same items from companies located in major industrial centers. But the burgeoning commune industry on the one hand replaces traditional rural handicraft production—a natural transition—and on the other provides employment for rural people at all seasons of the year.

The state plans to increase the pace of agricultural mechanization in order to reduce the exhausting work of soil preparation and harvesting crops by hand. Commune leaders are not worried that such substitution of machines for hand labor will create a problem of technological unemployment. At present, when such labor is released, work teams are formed to rebuild community homes and structures to transform them into more comfortable and healthy dwellings for rural people. More brigades than before are now reported to have plans for tearing down old straw, mud, and wood homes and replacing them with new brick apartments. These brigades will also construct new structures for schools, hospitals, and factories, as well as recreation facilities.

The Role of Farming Inputs

Historically, Chinese farmers have increased farm production by bringing new land into cultivation and farming existing land more intensively to obtain two harvests per year instead of one. By selecting the best seeds from the harvested crop, resorting to trial-and-error methods of soaking seeds, and planting with different fertilizer methods, farmers gradually increased crop yields. Such efforts naturally required a greater expenditure of labor, but rewards were high if productivity increased and farmers had selected the proper mix of crops to sell to the market. Households also worked out cooperative schemes to share and exchange their resources in order to construct irrigation systems and reclaim swamp and lake land for cultivating crops. As the rural population expanded, the relationship between output on the one hand and the supply of land, labor, and farm capital (like seeds, fertilizer, irrigation facilities, and tools) on the other was one of farm inputs growing at the same rate as farm output. In other words, the expansion of farm inputs accounted for the gradual growth of farm output. At the same time, Chinese farming became more labor-intensive, and households gradually farmed less land on a per capita basis.

From the crop statistical data of the 1930s, it becomes clear that crop-yield variation was enormous within and even between regions. In areas where the most advanced farming techniques could be used upon good soils in a favorable climate, very high crop yields were obtained, but much of the countryside lacked these special attributes. Consequently, the potential was greatest for raising crop yields in backward areas to the high-yield levels of areas where the best farming techniques prevailed. It is only natural, then, that the Communist Party has been most effusive to praise backward, poor rural communities like Tachai for establishing the necessary preconditions of irrigation and land reclamation to raise crop yields to the levels of the advanced farming areas that have good soil and stable rainfall.

By establishing model brigades and communes with a proven record in irrigation construction, the Party hopes to encourage other areas to follow suit. Pace-setting brigades like Tachai are noted for mobilizing labor during the slack farming seasons to engage in capital projects like reclaiming land, terracing hills, levelling fields, digging wells, building canals, constructing drainage ditches, and preparing fertilizer compost. During the 1960s and 1970s, cadres vigorously encouraged these efforts so that the total irrigated land, only 34.3 million hectares in 1957, increased to an estimated high of between 41 and 47 million hectares. By 1957, 31 percent of cultivated land was irrigated, and by 1976, that figure had risen to between 38 and 44 percent.

The end of the 1960s saw the beginnings of a revolution in the crop rotation system that still continues. Formerly, in central China two crops of either rice or rice and winter wheat had been harvested each year. In the north three harvests every two years based on a combination of summer grain and fiber crops with winter wheat had been harvested. The advent of early maturing rice and winter wheat seeds combined with improved irrigation, drainage, and greater application of fertilizer of the traditional compost type had produced the following new rotations. In central China more land began having three harvests per year with two rice crops and a winter wheat crop. In the north two harvests per year became more common with a late summer harvest followed by a sowing of winter wheat and its harvest in May or early June. These new cropping cycles raised the annual cropping index and increased the total food grain yield per unit of cultivated land each year; they are being adopted in more areas as water, new seeds, and fertilizer become available.

Water Control

The Chinese have a remarkable record of water conservancy achievements. Long before the eleventh century A.D., the state had established offices to manage large-scale hydraulic projects located along the Yellow and Huai rivers. The early Ming rulers initiated water control projects all over the country. The actions taken by the government after 1959 continue in the same tradition.

The state has promoted major projects like dams and reservoirs to control the Yellow and Hai rivers in North China. Between 1963 and 1973, thirty-four main canals were dug and dredged in Hopeh Province alone and 4,300 kilometers of flood control dikes were built. Heavy spring rains that once flooded the central part of this province now are carried by canals to the Gulf of Pohai or are stored in large reservoirs for irrigating fields. A second important development in the north, the most important farming area to perennially suffer drought, has been the construction of tube wells. For example, in the Hai River valley region, which occupies virtually half of Hopeh Province, nearly a half million wells were sunk in the 1960s. Every county has a water conservancy planning and coordinating office to determine how many wells communes should sink so as not to overbuild and lower the ground-water table.

Another important achievement has been the construction of large canal networks to irrigate vast areas that formerly depended solely upon rainfall. A group of University of British Columbia academics had the opportunity in May 1976 to observe water conservancy developments in Hui County of northern Honan. This poor country produced mainly food grains, and farming depended upon rainfall. In 1966-1967 Hui's officials began mobilizing the farmers to construct a network of canals, ponds, underground dams, wells, and pumping stations to irrigate the county's farmland. By 1976 the communes had built 34 reservoirs, 23 underground dams, 3,000 kilometers of stone and concrete water channels, 5,000 pump wells, and 144 pump stations. Moreover, these achievements had been financed mainly out of commune savings with only 17 percent of total costs funded by the state. As a result, food grain yields had risen to 5.8 metric tons per hectare per year, which nearly trebled the national food grain yield average.

The Hai River project and the Hui community canalization schemes represent several of the more successful water conservancy achievements. The Party intends to duplicate these performances elsewhere. If officials are equally skillful in mobilizing commune work teams and can persuade communes to restrain consumption and save more for financing capital projects, other river systems can be controlled and more counties with little irrigation will begin to have an ample water supply. Within perhaps a decade or two, the state will perhaps have succeeded in irrigating roughly half of the existing farmland, which would be a record unsurpassed by any country of comparable size in the world.

New Seeds

Seed research work has been most successful for specific crops like rice, wheat, and cotton. Annual conferences involving seed breeders and technicians are convened to discuss progress and to solve common problems. So far, the major achievements in seed research have been to develop native varieties through selection and testing over several years in order to obtain varieties resistant to major diseases, which produce high yields and have early maturing qualities. Institutes obtain rice and wheat seeds from other countries and test them in trial plots. But the

Chinese have found that most of these are unsuitable for the soil, climate, and rotation systems. Seed breeders strongly emphasize early maturing for adaptability to the new crop rotation cycles now spreading throughout North and South China.

Prior to 1966-1967, seed research work involved testing under controlled conditions to determine yield response to a variety of variables like fertilizer, heat, and water. In the aftermath of the Cultural Revolution of 1966-1969, this research greatly declined, in fact virtually ended for several years. It seems to have revived slowly in the mid-1970s, but not on a comparable scale. As irrigation increases and more chemical fertilizers become available, research testing the response of new seeds to different environmental factors will play a key role in determining if crop yield in the high, stable yield farming areas can be increased substantially. Meanwhile, seed research now shifts to miscellaneous grains like corn, maize, and sorghum. The hope is that higher yields for these crops can be obtained, as well as early maturing, so that intercropping and double- and triple-cropping on a yearly basis can be introduced to all parts of the country.

Fertilizer

In spite of the rapid increase in chemical fertilizer production and importation after 1962, a report by the U.S. Wheat Studies Delegation, which visited China in mid-1976, states that very small quantities of low-grade chemical fertilizer are actually in use. Considering that this delegation visited the most advanced farming areas, the fact that only 150 to 300 kilograms of low-quality chemical fertilizer were applied to a hectare of land, as compared to more than 700 kilograms on a similar basis in Taiwan, suggests that the scope for chemical fertilizer in use remains great and that many areas may receive very little chemical fertilizer at present. Chinese farmers still apply prodigious quantities of organic fertilizer to their fields in amounts reaching 100 to 150 metric tons per hectare in most cases. This fertilizer is still prepared in the traditional manner: in pits and compost piles. The combination of large quantities of organic fertilizer applied with small amounts of low-grade chemical fertilizer has raised crop yields greatly, especially in the high, stable yield farming areas, which account for nearly one-third of the total cultivated area.

By 1978 the chemical fertilizer recently purchased from foreign sources will be producing perhaps as much as 12 million metric tons of high quality chemical fertilizer. This should give China an annual supply of around 30 to 35 million metric tons of chemical fertilizer, of which a large portion could be allocated to poorer soils of the country as they gradually become irrigated. The prospects would then become more favorable for raising crop yields in poorer farming areas closer to those of the high, stable yield farming areas. This development, along with more intensive research on improved seeds for the better farming areas, should continue to increase yields so that the rate of growth of farm production may be sustained at around 2 percent or slightly higher.

Future Prospects

If China can realize a long-term growth rate of farm production of around 2 percent or more, will this performance be sufficient to feed and clothe the population adequately and still support the momentum of industrialization underway? Much depends upon the success of current efforts to lower the birth rate and subsequently bring population growth in the country under control. While little is precisely known about the present size and composition of China's population, the available evidence does strongly indicate that the government has been making vigorous efforts to limit population growth in a variety of ways. Discouraging early marriage, limiting family size, and educating the people to use some of the birth-control procedures available are the key strategies presently used by the state. The commune-brigade-team administrative and organizational structure certainly makes it much easier for China to initiate these strategies in the countryside, as compared to most developing countries where state control in rural areas is weak and ineffective.

If by the 1980s the population growth rate can be stabilized at 1.5 percent per annum or even slightly less, a 2 percent or higher annual growth rate of food grain and industrial crops ought to be sufficient for China to prosper and industrialize gradually for the remainder of this century. Between 1870 and 1937, Japan's population grew at around 1 percent per annum while agricultural production increased at around 1.5 to 1.7 percent annually. Japan's free market economy allowed massive migration of rural people to cities with great reliance upon foreign trade. China, on the other hand, controls population migration through the commune system, and its system of planned economy makes selective use of foreign trade as an instrument to acquire strategic materials and modern technology. China's different organizations and policies might very well produce a similar performance of rapid industrialization with modest gains in welfare for the entire population. Certainly, such an achievement among today's developing countries would indeed be remarkable.

Selected Bibliography

Buck, John L., Owen L. Dawson, and Yuan-li Wu. *Food and Agriculture in Communist China.* Stanford, Calif.: Hoover Institution, 1966. This work traces agricultural development during the 1950s, evaluates performance, and discusses in detail progress in fertilizer production and irrigation development.

Chen, C. S., and C. P. Ridley. *Rural People's Communes in Lien-Chiang.* Stanford, Calif.: Hoover Institute Press, 1969. These unique documents obtained from Fukien Province shed light on rural organizations at the commune level; they are of special value in describing local responses to the agricultural crisis of the 1959-1961 period.

The Committee for Scholarly Exchange with the People's Republic of China. *Report of the Plant Studies Delegation to the People's Republic of China.* Washington, D.C.: National Academy of Sciences, 1976. A gold mine of information bearing upon research and agro-technical activities pertaining to agriculture by a team of U.S. agroscientists that visited the P.R.C. in August-September.

Henle, H. V. *Report on China's Agriculture.* Rome: Food and Agriculture Organization of the United Nations, 1974. An excellent overview of agricultural development, farming conditions, and evaluation of the inputs responsible for farm production development.

Perkins, Dwight H. "Constraints Influencing China's Agricultural Performance." In Joint Economic Committee, Congress of the United States, *China: A Reassessment of the Economy.* Washington, D.C.: U.S. Government Printing Office, 1975, pp. 360-365. This essay provides a sober corrective to the many optimistic reports that China has solved its food production and distribution problems.

Stavis, Benedict. *Making Green Revolution: The Politics of Agricultural Development in China.* Ithaca, N.Y.: Cornell University, Rural Development Committee, 1974. A useful survey of farming improvements in the 1960s with special stress on identifying the key high, stable yield areas and which factors made these achievements possible.

U.S. Department of Agriculture (Economic Research Service). *People's Republic of China Agricultural Situation.* Washington, D.C.: Foreign Agricultural Economic Report no. 137, 1977. This most recent summary of agricultural production statistics for the period 1949-1976 also includes estimates of the 1976 farm situation and prospects for 1977.

6

Economic Development Strategy, Industry, and Trade

Edwin F. Jones

An Overview

The new leaders of the People's Republic of China came to power in 1949 determined to transform China through rapid industrialization into a modernized world power by the end of the twentieth century. Between 1949 and 1976, the year of Mao's death, substantial progress was made toward this goal. During this period, industrial output rose 25 fold, farm output 2.7 fold, and gross national produce (GNP) 6.3 fold. Industry expanded from a little over one-tenth to nearly one-half of the GNP, while agriculture fell from two-thirds to less than one-third.

These dramatic changes in the economy occurred with remarkably little shift of the labor force from the countryside to the cities. Between 1949 and 1971, the total labor force rose by 71 percent; industry increased its share from less than 5 percent to a little over 10 percent, while agriculture's share fell only from 88 percent to 74 percent. Since a significant portion of the new nonfarm labor force was located in rural areas, the urban share of the population rose from 12 percent to something less than 20 percent.

These phenomena reflect in large part the great disparity between labor productivity in agriculture and that in industry. An extreme scarcity of agricultural resources results in very low farm labor productivity and, despite major agricultural investment, has limited a rise in this productivity. In consequence, laborers have been held on the

Statistical note: Much of the data used in this paper were drawn from the publication *China: Economic Indicators*, CIA, National Foreign Assessment Center, ER-77-10508, October 1977. All data not otherwise identified are from this source.

farms to support the necessary rise in farm output, limiting the growth of the nonfarm and industrial labor forces. Despite limited growth in the industrial labor force, its productivity—which exceeds farm labor productivity many fold—supports a substantial and rapid rise in total economic output.

The increasing weight of industry in total economic output has sustained economic growth despite declining rates of growth in industry and agriculture, as shown by a comparison of annual growth rates in the First and Fourth five-year plans:

	1953-1957	*1971-1975*
GNP	7%	7%
Industry	16%	10%
Agriculture	4%	3%

Moreover, since industrial wages, under the influence of agricultural wages, are low, profits and interest comprise a large component of industrial output and accrue to the government for construction and other expenditures. Thus, the increased share of industrial output in total output has facilitated the mobilization of savings and high levels of investment.

The history of Chinese industry since 1949 (see Table 6.1) reveals two sharply contrasting periods of growth. With ideological conviction and confidence, the P.R.C. embarked initially on an eighteen-year (1950-1967), single-minded program to build a large, modern, integrated, and autonomous heavy industrial complex. It secured agreement from the U.S.S.R. to provide 300 large plants costing about $3 billion as the core of this program, together with substantial technical, material, and administrative assistance for transforming the economy. Soviet financial aid was limited, and the P.R.C. was committed to mobilize the slack and surpluses of a reviving economy to support the program. Though strains mounted, the Chinese leadership responded with feverish efforts and institutional change to mobilize necessary resources, firm in the belief that once the heavy industry base had been secured all other problems could be solved.

This initial period ended in the collapse of the frenetic industrial construction drive of the "Great Leap Forward" (1958-1960), as the P.R.C. overstretched and misused its resources, alienating the U.S.S.R. and terminating the Soviet commitment. Average annual industrial

Table 6.1 China's Industrial Growth Pattern

Period	Output Index (1957=100)	Percent of Total Consumer Goods	Producer Goods Machinery	Other	Average Annual Growth (%) Total	Consumer Goods	Producer Goods
1949	20	60.6	4.4	35.0			
1950/52	(Rehabilitation)				33.9	28.9	40.7
1952	48	53.4	7.5	39.1			
1953/57	(1st FYP)				15.8	10.7	20.7
1957	100	42.9	10.9	46.3			
1958/60	(Great Leap)				21.9	4.5	32.4
1960	181	27.0	15.8	57.2			
1950/60	(Heavy industry push)				22.2	13.6	29.1
1961/62	(Readjustment)				-21.7	-14.7	-22.7
1962	111	32.1	12.1	55.8			
1963/65	(Recovery)				21.5	30.2	16.9
1965	199	39.5	14.0	46.5			
1966/70	(3rd FYP)				9.7	8.2	10.7
1970	316	36.9	20.1	43.0			
1971/75	(4th FYP)				9.7	6.2	11.5
1975	502	31.4	25.0	43.5			
1961/75	(Self-reliance)				7.0	8.1	6.6
1950/75	(Total period)				13.2	10.4	15.6
1978/85 Goal					10.0		

growth during 1949-1960 had reached a spectacular 22 percent and had provided China with a substantial modern industrial plant, including about 150 Soviet core plants. But China found itself in the midst of a man-made famine, with a seriously unbalanced industry, and without access to the modern technology that would permit the continuation of its former industrial drive.

In the immediate aftermath of the 1960 disaster, the P.R.C. leadership drew up a new twenty-year program (1960-1980) for "self-reliance," which accepted the necessity for reduced industrial construction and growth to deal with other vital problems and readjustments. The lost Soviet security shield required sharply increased military expenditures to create a credible deterrent and ensure P.R.C. security. The new appreciation of the closing jaws of the Malthusian trap gave agriculture first claim on industrial resources for a comprehensive program of farm modernization. Rural industrialization and industrial dispersion, consistent with the new programs and the limits of existing technology, imposed requirements for substantial infrastructure investments in communications and transport. Industrial consumer goods output received relative priority, both to mitigate disappointed public expectations and to mobilize resources less painfully through industrial profits.

With the period of "self-reliance" now drawing to a close, we may compare its annual industrial output growth rates with those of the period of Sino-Soviet cooperation as follows:

Period	Annual Industrial Output Growth	Annual Producer Goods Growth	Annual Consumer Goods Growth
1949–60	22.2%	29.1%	13.6%
1961–75	7.0%	6.6%	8.1%

The policies of "self-reliance" appear to have been carried out as originally planned—with the major exception of the improvement of domestic technology, originally seen as a program of training, research, and adaptation, accompanied by the acquisition of foreign prototypes and technical materials through trade. Schools designed in the 1950s to staff a very rapid urban industrial growth became anachronistic after 1960. Initial changes greatly restricted enrollments at higher levels by sharply raising academic admission standards and lengthening and intensifying training to identify and cultivate the best minds to become the scientists of the future; the number of run-of-the-mill high school and college graduates was reduced. Research institutes were expanded to analyze, catalogue, and adapt foreign technologies for Chinese use; during 1963-1965, a series of single prototype plants for different products or different processes for the same product was imported from abroad to be analyzed and copied.

Mao branded this system as elitist and contrary to revolutionary politics, and swept it aside in the Cultural Revolution in 1966. Schools and colleges soon were providing only short-term vocational courses with minimum academic content or standards; they had a prime mission of glorifying the worker and the peasant and of indoctrinating the student to expect a life among them. Research institute staff were dispersed to fields and shop floors, where, under the supervision of Party cadres and peasants or workers, they would help solve immediate technical problems. Production organizations were enjoined to use revolutionary "on-the-spot" solutions to technical problems, rather than going at a "snail's pace" in waiting for foreign equipment or technology.

Despite the waning of the Cultural Revolution from 1969 on and the appearance of pragmatic policies elsewhere, Mao's strong position on technology hampered corrective action. Large import orders for industrial plants in the fertilizer, steel, and petrochemical industries appeared in 1972-1973. But these were apparently justified internally as one-time solutions to pressing bottlenecks in vital industries; an attempt to institutionalize the export of oil to finance the import of industrial plant was reportedly rebuffed in the succession politics of the day. Not until 1977, after the death of Mao and the consolidation of the succession government of Hua Kuo-feng, did the P.R.C. in effect repudiate Mao's policy (blaming it on the "Gang of Four"). The Hua government has repeatedly affirmed the academic integrity and mission of the schools, the necessity for scientists to have the appropriate facilities and organization to do their work without harassment or interference, and the intention to import foreign equipment and technology as required.

In early 1978 the government unveiled ambitious (but possibly attainable) and closely related eight-year plans to develop industry, agriculture, and science through 1985. The key goals are to achieve an annual increase of 4 to 5 percent in agricultural output and of 10 percent in industrial output. A grain output target of 400 million tons was set, and steel production is to reach 60 million tons by 1985.

The P.R.C. announced in March 1978 that it intends, by 1985, to narrow the gap between Chinese and world levels of technology to about ten years, thus "laying a solid foundation for catching up with or surpassing world levels in all branches" by the year 2000. By 1976, China had checked population growth, reducing fertility almost to targeted "replacement" levels, although these new family and birth patterns remained to be sustained and consolidated. Farm output rose satisfactorily through expanded farm manpower and a rapid growth of industrial inputs to agriculture, but the goal of releasing farm labor to industry through a rapid growth in farm labor productivity—if in sight—had not yet been realized. Industrial output was successfully restored and expanded on the basis of domestic levels of technology, but China's industry still faced bottlenecks at critical points stemming from the lack of advanced technology or of supporting infrastructure investment.

After Mao died in 1976, renewed emphasis was placed on education, research, and development to pave the entry to a twenty-three-year "modernization" program during 1978-2000. The Hua Kuo-feng succession government has now focused its planning on this "modernization," with an overlap period to 1985 to complete the unfinished tasks of the "self-reliance" period.

Manpower and Employment

While available data on employment, particularly since 1960, has been fragmentary, ill-defined, and imprecise, it is sufficient to suggest some important generalizations on the growth and deployment of China's labor force. Trends in demography and economic development have been the two important influences.

China began its demographic transition—a transition from a stable, slow-growing population with high mortality and fertility to one with low mortality and fertility—with a rapid drop in its death rates. Serious effort to obtain a matching decline in fertility began after the 1959-1961 famine; in the 1960s a successful urban program secured a small drop in fertility, while in the 1970s the organization of the larger rural areas has led to a marked fertility decline.

Fertility is now approaching replacement levels, which is believed to be the Chinese target since their program is framed in the context of universal marriage and a two-child family. At replacement levels, growth would decelerate and the population would stabilize in the first several decades of the twenty-first century; stabilization is achieved first at younger ages and then progressively at older ages until the population fully matures. For example, in Dr. Aird's projection used below, between 1976 and 2000 the population aged 0-14 rises from 361 million to 375 million, showing little growth, while the productive population aged 15-64 increases from 551 million to 873 million, and the 65 and over population doubles from 38 million to 80 million.

In the demographic transition, the productive-aged population, of which the labor force is a function, will increase at different rates than the total population. This differential growth will alter the ratios of productive and dependent age groups; these ratios tend to influence labor force participation rates by the productive-aged population. These influences can be analyzed by constructing a population growth model for China, like Table 6.2. It is based on the age-sex distribution reported in the 1953 census and selects values for fertility and mortality to produce population totals in subsequent years that approximate the registered population totals reported irregularly by the Chinese.

In this model, the productive-aged population grows more slowly than the total population from 1949 to 1963, and more rapidly thereafter, producing a rise and then decline in the dependency ratio. To calculate the labor force, a rule-of-thumb 70 percent participation rate will be assumed for the productive-aged population for the years 1949-1976, but by the year 2000 the sharply reduced dependency ratio should permit a higher, 75 percent, participation rise. The participation rate is

Table 6.2   Ratio Between Productive and Dependent Population, 1949-2000

Year, July 1	Population (million)			Dependent/ Productive Ratio (per 100)	Crude Birth Rate per 1,000
	Total	Dependent (under 15, over 64)	Productive (15-64)		
1949	538	215	323	67	45.4
1953	583	243	340	71	45.0
1957	640	277	363	76	41.3
1963	719	320	399	80	37.6
1970	840	365	475	77	35.7
1976	951	400	551	73	25.5
2000	1,329	456	873	52	22.0

calculated in terms of full-time labor units, and represents a larger number of full- and part-time workers.

The data are available to trace in some detail and with confidence nonfarm employment in the 1950s. During 1949-1953, nonfarm employment grew rapidly from 26 to 39 million, mostly in the modern sector but with some growth in the traditional sector. During 1954-1957, with the imposition of labor controls, nonfarm employment remained stable, reaching 40 million in 1957; but it grew from 18 million to 24 million in the modern sector while declining from 21 million to 16 million in the traditional sector. In 1958, at the start of the "Great Leap Forward," nonfarm employment jumped abruptly to 57 million. Although nonfarm production continued to rise in 1959 and 1960, employment eased off to 53 million as authorities used the huge increments of 1958 more effectively.

Since 1960 there has been little information on nonfarm employment. It declined sharply in the initial years of "readjustment" as the authorities returned most of the workers newly hired in 1958 to the farm areas in the process of reducing the urban population from 130 million in 1959-1960 to 110 million at the beginning of 1964. Despite rapid recovery growth in industrial output to 1965, the emphasis on efficiency and on raising labor productivity limited employment growth.

During the Third and Fourth five-year plans, industrial growth was substantial. However, while there were indications of modest population growth in large and medium cities, the labor markets in these urban locations remained weak. Strong controls over population movements inhibited rural migration to the cities, while large numbers of urban school graduates were directed to rural farm employment in lieu of urban employment in a systematic, long-term government program.

The stress on rural development in the Third and Fourth five-year plans, however, sharply expanded nonfarm employment in the rural county towns and farm areas, as recent partial data are revealing. The Chinese press reported that at the end of 1977 the small rural industries were employing 17 million workers in some one million firms. In 1975, one observer noted that employment in small rural industries was approximately equal to that of the larger modern industries in the cities. Similarly, a Ministry of Education conference on the problems of primary and secondary school teachers noted that "the number of teachers in China has come close to 10 million," a level suggesting a marked expansion in rural educational services.

Programs undertaken also indicate substantial employment growth in certain sectors over the levels of the 1950s. Full-time rural health personnel must have been expanded by a few million in the systematic program to establish small hospitals in each of the 70,000 communes in the 1960s and small clinics in each of the 1 million brigades. (This calculation excludes "barefoot" doctors, who retained the status of farm workers and were volunteer agents of the medical service in the 4 to 5 million production teams, as well as purveyors of emergency first-aid services.) Again, local reports indicate marked growth in county government administrative and planning personnel since the 1950s consonant with expanded development responsibilities. While such information does not permit precise estimates, it is perhaps sufficient to compile an approximate projection of the changes in nonfarm employment from 1957 to 1976 as shown in Table 6.3.

From the 1976 population estimates, the 1976 labor force may be estimated at 386 million. Teng Hsiao-p'ing, in a March 18, 1978, address to the National Science Conference, stated: "Several hundred million are busy producing food. . . . Average annual output of grain per farm worker is about 1,000 kilograms in China." The 1976 grain output estimates would thus indicate a farm labor force of 285 million, consistent and corroborative of the above estimate of a nonfarm labor force of 100 million.

By the year 2000 the labor force will reach 655 million, according to the population estimates (see Table 6.4). Its farm and nonfarm division will depend on the necessary growth in farm output and the accompanying growth in farm labor productivity, which will determine the manpower that can be freed from agriculture. Between 1953 and 1976, farm labor productivity rose by .7 percent annually, but Chinese officials predict a substantial rise under the new agricultural modernization practices.

Table 6.3 Changes in Nonfarm Employment, 1957–1976 (in millions)

Material sectors	1957	1976
Industry	} 7.9	17
Rural industry		17
Handicrafts	6.6	7
Fishing, salt collection	2.0	4
Subtotal, industry categories	16.5	45
Construction, water conservancy	2.3	7
Transport, posts, communications	4.4	8
Trade, food and drink industry	7.8	15
Subtotal, other material sectors	14.5	30
Government and mass organizations	2.9	6
Education, cultural affairs	2.7	9
Medicine and health	1.9	6
Other	1.3	4
Subtotal, nonproductive (service) sectors	8.7	25
Total	39.7	100
Percent of total in industry	42	45

Note: Where specific data are unavailable, 1976 estimates in the material sector have been based on judgments of output and labor productivity trends. For example, there has been a marked expansion in both construction and transport. In transport, a marked increase in the efficiency of modern transport and a displacement of traditional transport has led to a more rapid growth in labor productivity and a slower growth in employment than in construction. Special factors have also been considered; handicrafts have been displaced somewhat by the growth of modern industry, but also expanded in a systematic program to subcontract work from industries to housewives, dependents, and others (so-called street industry); in 1957 trade firms were under strong pressure to minimize employment and transfer workers to industry, while in 1976 there is more emphasis on improving consumer services in a more complex market economy.

Should farm output increase by 3 percent annually and farm labor productivity by 2.5 percent annually, the nonfarm labor force could rise by 5 percent annually, and by the year 2000 account for half the labor force, or 327 million. Such a nonfarm labor force would exceed by far that of any other country, and although its output would depend on its productivity, its size lends plausibility to Hua Kuo-feng's claim in his report to the Fifth National People's Congress that in the year 2000 Chinese "output of major industrial products [is expected] to approach, equal, or outstrip that of the most developed capitalist countries."

Table 6.4   Labor Force Projections, 1949–2000 (in millions)

Year	Population	Labor Force	Non-farm	Farm	Nonfarm Labor % of Total	Nonfarm Labor Ave. Ann. Growth (%)
1949	538	226	26	200	12	
1960	682	266	53	213	20	6.7
1976	951	386	100	286	26	4.1
2000	1,329	655	327	328	50	5.0

Technology and Education

Education is an important long-run factor in the transition from a handicraft society to a modern industrial nation and has had a major role in China's development policy. In all modern societies, education has the two-fold function of training and socialization, i.e., imparting on the one hand academic skills and on the other hand an awareness of common values, ethics, and principles of social organization to permit a cohesive, functioning adult society. The stresses of rapid growth and of attaining an appropriate balance between the goals of "red and expert" have shaped China's educational policies.

The People's Republic of China began with an ambitious goal for a society with roughly 20 percent literacy: to extend universal education first through a six-year primary curriculum and later to a nine-year primary–junior high curriculum over the course of several five-year plans. When attained, selective, highly restricted admissions on the basis of examination to senior high and higher education levels would be scaled to industrial growth and other social needs. Through the 1950s, however, expansion was rapid at all levels, and the growth at higher levels was chiefly limited by the availability of qualified applicants. In this period, enrollments multiplied nearly four-fold at the primary level, ten-fold at the secondary level, and seven-fold at the higher-education level.

After 1960, the education program shifted to a "less but finer" policy, slightly reducing enrollments and sharply increasing academic admission requirements at senior high and higher education levels. This policy was in accord with "self-reliance" austerity. It was also possible because graduates at lower levels were sufficiently numerous to permit highly competitive and restrictive admissions to higher levels based on academic standing. Primary school enrollments were approaching near-universality, and in the cities universal enrollment through junior high was nearly obtained. The program aimed at mobilizing the best minds and at giving them intensive training to meet the technological challenges of the period.

Beginning in 1966 with the Cultural Revolution, the education system ran afoul of Mao's discontent and was dismantled and recast. Mao charged that the system had become a huge, subversive state bureaucracy, run by the educated and tainted with bourgeois thinking. In his view, the quest for academic excellence produced a distorted education unsuited to the lesser needs of many localities, discriminated against the rural areas in favor of the urban areas, and advanced the children of educated bourgeois families (who could pass entrance examinations) over the children of illiterate peasant and worker families.

Formal education ceased during 1966-1968, and then the system was gradually rebuilt over a number of years, moving progressively from primary to secondary to higher education. The new system sought universal education for a ten-year, primary-secondary curriculum for children aged seven to sixteen. This ideal, while not attained, has been approached, with marked increases in total and rural area enrollments but not in urban areas where school facilities were already well developed. Educational policy shifted markedly toward socialization at the expense of academic standards. No student was to be tested, graded, or failed, and authority of teachers was greatly restricted.

Secondary graduates in the new system were assigned to work posts, for college admissions were limited to youths with at least three years' work experience. While formal instruction in the colleges ceased in 1966, the 1965-1966 enrollment of 750,000 remained attached to their respective colleges, and from 1968 to 1970 the various classes were declared graduated on schedule and the "graduates" assigned to work posts. With the colleges emptied at the end of the 1969-1970 year, experimentation began from 1970-1971 on with abbreviated courses ranging from six months to a maximum of three years. Local units— e.g., communes, military units, and enterprises—were assigned quotas for nomination of applicants. Such youths had to have three years' work experience and at least a junior-high educational level. On graduation, the students would be returned to their original work posts. Course work was short on theory, long on practice, and heavy on politics. Though enrollments have not been reported, the uncrowded condition of various campuses described by visitors suggests enrollments significantly below previous levels. Measured by school enrollments, China's educational effort progressed between 1949 and 1976 as shown in Table 6.5.

Table 6.5   School Enrollments, 1949-1976

	Primary	Secondary	Higher Education
	(in millions)		(000)
"Rapid Growth"			
1949/50	24.4	1.27	117
1954/55	51.2	4.19	253
1959/60	90	12.9	810
"Less but finer"			
1964/65	85	12	700
"Cultural Revolution"			
1969/70	-- 140[a]	--	0
1975/76	-- 200[a]	--	500[b]

[a] From fragmentary provincial data, estimated at 70 percent of a school-age (7-16 years) population of 200 million in 1969/70 and at 85 percent of a school-age population of 235 million in 1975/76.

[b] A speculative estimate from descriptive information.

In 1977, the Hua Kuo-feng succession government repudiated the Cultural Revolution educational policies, charging that the Gang of Four radical faction had exaggerated the minor criticisms that Mao had made into a damaging antiintellectual crusade. The new government demanded, and asserted the urgency of, a reemphasis on academic training, although conceding, in its proposed reforms, the difficulty and long-term character of the task.

The primary-secondary system, with an estimated enrollment of 200 million and a teaching staff of nearly 10 million, is to retain its structure, with reforms consisting of restoring the dignity and authority of the teachers, upgrading the teaching staff, and updating and improving texts. With little teacher training now in progress, inputs of new professionally trained teachers will be a long time in coming, and the huge size of the present staff precludes retraining more than a very small fraction on a rotation basis. The main reliance at present must be upon on-the-job training, supplemented by spare-time and correspondence courses. The improvement of textual materials is also impeded by poor student preparation and low teacher qualifications and must proceed experimentally and gradually.

In the colleges, the present short course instruction, while not considered "college" training, has been found useful and will be continued in order to provide local employing units access to quick, specialized training. Regular college education will be reconstructed, operating in tandem. In a September 29, 1977, interview, Vice-Premier

Teng Hsiao-p'ing identified education as the area where the Gang of Four "had created the greatest damage. . . . They turned a whole generation of young people into intellectual cripples." Teng also indicated that the most serious problem was the scarcity of college graduates: "In the twenty-five through thirty-five age group there are very few scientists, research experts, physicians, engineers, biologists, and mathematicians." The problems of reconstructing college-level education suggest that large numbers of fully qualified college graduates will not be secured until about 1983. Teng stated that, to meet the crisis, a two-tier system would be established, in which upper tier of "special project" schools would concentrate on the most needed specialties and would receive the most gifted and talented applicants who would have the support of the best teachers and the most challenging, up-to-date texts, so as to proceed at a faster pace than that of the lower tier. This policy hopes to secure highly qualified graduates without waiting for the full reconstruction of higher education.

The data shown in Tables 6.6 and 6.7 on China's college graduates by year of graduation illustrate the handicaps China faces on entering its period of "modernization." The data show that the rapid expansion of higher education in the 1950s provided more than 1 million new college graduates during 1958-1965, sharply raising their ratio to the nonfarm labor force. The graduates entered the labor market at a time of retrenchment, however, and this led to a downgrading in their employment and eventually to the conditions that permitted the closure of the colleges. The subsequent growth in the nonfarm labor force and the absence of new, fully qualified college graduates have, however, cut the ratio by half during 1965-1976, and are likely to cut it by two-thirds before a reconstructed higher education system begins turning out new graduates in about 1983.

Technology and Foreign Trade

Foreign trade is perhaps one of the quickest and surest avenues for a developing nation to acquire advanced technology through the import of capital goods and technical services. Despite this fact, China over the past decades has been ambivalent over the appropriate role of foreign trade in its development, reflecting autarkic forces in its economic structure and in its politics.

It is an empirical fact that large countries, at whatever stage of development, tend to have a small level of foreign trade relative to their

Table 6.6   College Graduates by Year of Graduation,
1913-1976

Period	Graduates by year of graduation (000)	Age in:[a] 1978	1985
1913-32	51.2	68-87	76-95
1933-47	157.3	53-67	61-75
1948-57	379	43-52	51-60
1958-65	1,067	35-42	43-50
1966-70	(750)[b]	30-34	38-42
1971-76	(500)[c]	24-29	32-37

[a] Assumed graduation at age 23.

[b] With no formal instruction during 1966-70, the 1965/66 enrollment was declared "graduated" with students having received variously from less than one to less than five years instruction in a five-year curriculum.

[c] A speculative estimate of graduates from short-term, substandard college courses.

gross national product. This tendency has been particularly marked in China, where in the peak year of 1959 imports approached only 3 percent of the gross national product and in most years have been less than 2 percent. Even though China has carefully husbanded its foreign exchange resources for essential imports, such ratios severely constrict possible import contents of capital construction or of industrial ouput, and the rapid increase in the share of these sectors in total product/expenditure over the decades has further diluted their import content.

There is a strong strain of autarky in China's politics. China has never been a large trading nation. The national myth of its experience since the Opium War—the century of humiliation—has been one of imperialist plunder through foreign trade. While its development plans acknowledge a need for trade, their aim is to end this dependence through acquiring advanced technology. The operation of China's planned economy, which has emphasized import substitution wherever possible to stretch limited foreign exchange earnings and the export of marginal surpluses when and if they occur, has tended to make China an unreliable market and supplier and has minimized domestically the importance of foreign trade (see Tables 6.8 and 6.9).

During the initial period of the Sino-Soviet alliance (1949-1960), foreign trade flourished as an integrated part of development planning.

Table 6.7   Supply of College Graduates, 1949–1976

| Year | Supply of College Grads | | Nonfarm Labor Force (million) | Grads per 1000 in Nonfarm Labor Force |
	Total Graduated (000)	Est. Alive and Active (000)		
1949	230	180	26	7
1957	589	530	40	13
1965	1,656	1,575	50	32
1976	1,656	1,540	100	15
1985	1,656	1,500	155[a]	10

[a] Projected at 5 percent average annual growth rate indicated for 1976–2000.

By 1952, more than two-thirds of China's trade was with socialist countries (over half with the Soviet Union), and annual trade plans provided for expanding industrial deliveries to China and for Soviet block markets for the exports that China could supply. Soviet purchases initially stressed minerals, then expanded to grains, oilseeds, and food specialties, and finally reached peak levels with large imports of fabrics, clothing, and light industry products. During this period, China's total trade rose from $1.2 billion in 1950 to a peak of $4.3 billion in 1959.

In the 1960s, as famine and an end to the Soviet relation ushered in the "self-reliance" period, there were sharp alterations and fluctuations in trade. Trade was rapidly reoriented from socialist to nonsocialist countries, the latter accounting for more than three-quarters of China's trade by 1966. Trade levels fell sharply, as exports declined with the depressed economy, and imports were further constrained by an accelerated repayment of the Soviet debt. With economic recovery, trade levels rose sharply during 1964-1966, nearly reaching 1959 levels. Trade levels then again declined with the disruptions and autarkic impulses of the Cultural Revolution turning upward at the end of the decade as order was restored. In the 1970s, the Chinese economy entered a new phase, requiring expanded imports and forcing an expansionary approach to foreign trade.

At the end of the 1950s, basic industries like steel, coal, electric power, and transport had been overexpanded, and their 1959-1960 output peaks were not exceeded until 1971 for steel, 1970 for coal, 1968 for electric power, and 1969 for transport (million tons originated). Investment in these capital-intensive sectors had been limited in the 1960s, freeing investment resources for the growth industries of the period, such as petroleum, fertilizer, and engineering industries.

Table 6.8   China's Foreign Trade (in U.S. $, millions)

Year	Total	Exports	Imports	Balance
1950	1,210	620	590	30
1951	1,900	780	1,120	-340
1952	1,890	875	1,015	-140
1953	2,295	1,040	1,255	-215
1954	2,350	1,060	1,290	-230
1955	3,035	1,375	1,660	-285
1956	3,120	1,635	1,485	150
1957	3,055	1,615	1,440	175
1958	3,765	1,940	1,825	115
1959	4,290	2,230	2,060	170
1960	3,990	1,960	2,030	- 70
1961	3,015	1,525	1,490	35
1962	2,675	1,525	1,150	375
1963	2,770	1,570	1,200	370
1964	3,220	1,750	1,470	280
1965	3,880	2,035	1,845	190
1966	4,245	2,210	2,035	175
1967	3,895	1,945	1,950	- 5
1968	3,765	1,945	1,820	125
1969	3,860	2,030	1,830	200
1970	4,290	2,050	2,240	-190
1971	4,720	2,415	2,305	110
1972	5,920	3,085	2,835	250
1973	10,090	4,960	5,130	-170
1974	13,950	6,570	7,380	-810
1975	14,385	7,025	7,360	-335
1976	12,885	6,915	5,970	945

The 1970s required larger across-the-board investments and decisions on developing surpluses and bottlenecks. The spectacular growth in crude oil output after 1968 created surpluses that forced China to resort to low priority usage to dispose of them, while a similar growth in fertilizer output was still inadequate to the immense needs of the farm program, making large supplementary imports of fertilizer necessary. The steel industry was not in a position to provide quickly the large amounts of high quality steels necessary to fulfill the machinery and equipment needs of the 1970s. China did, however, complete several steel plants in the 1960s that had been partially equipped by the Soviets during the previous decade. It was able to rationalize and improve

Table 6.9   Commodity Composition of Trade (%), 1976

Exports			Imports		
Agricultural	36		Foodstuffs	9	
Animals, meat, fish		9	Grain		5
Grain		6	Sugar		3
Fruit and vegetables		5	Other		1
Textile fibers		4			
Crude animal materials		4	Capital goods	31	
Other		8	Machinery		22
			Transport equipment		8
Extractive	12		Other		1
Crude oil		9			
Other		3	Consumer goods	1	
Manufacturing	52		Industrial supplies	59	
Textile yarn and fabric		17	Iron and steel		24
Clothing and footwear		7	Nonferrous metals		4
Other light manufactures		13	Metal products		2
Chemicals		5	Chemicals		10
Metals and metal products		4	Textile fibers		5
Machinery and equipment		4	Rubber		3
Petroleum products		2	Other		11
Total	100		Total	100	

output with limited technical innovations, but did not demonstrate a strong grasp of large-scale mass production. Moreover, by 1973 steel output had reached a plateau at capacity levels in all sectors—raw materials, transport, crude steel, and finishing facilities—requiring huge investments to further expand output.

While trade expanded rapidly in the 1970s, trade policy was a subject of strong debate within the government, affecting growth patterns. The Fourth Five-Year Plan (1971-1975), drawn up in 1970, called for expanded foreign trade, greater investments in transport and basic industry, and a reduction in military expenditures. The plan remained locked in a political impasse until 1972 when, after the demise of Lin Piao, it was approved in revised form with a stronger foreign trade emphasis. Trade growth accelerated in 1973-1974. Plans for continued growth were indicated by whole-plant purchase commitments in excess of $2 billion and by policy decisions in early 1974 to greatly expand crude oil exports.

Despite these developments, the Chinese press indicated that trade policy was still a matter of controversy, which became more heated by mid-1975 under the influence of succession politics, the preparation of the Fifth Five-Year Plan (1976-1980), and a foreign exchange crisis.

Japan, the targeted oil export market, refused to commit itself to greatly expanded imports of Chinese oil, forcing China to cut back oil investment and production targets and eliminating the export earnings that were to finance whole plant imports.

With the consolidation of the Hua Kuo-feng government, a positive foreign trade policy was again affirmed. Hua's report to the Fifth NPC called for expanded foreign trade and the development of export production to support it. Numerous Chinese officials at the National Science Conference and elsewhere have emphasized the importance of imports in learning from abroad and developing technology.

Industry

Between 1949 and 1975, China's industrial output rose twenty-five-fold or an average of 13 percent annually, raising industry from a small to a dominant sector of China's economy. This growth was underwritten by high rates of savings or gross investment in the GNP; such rates had reached 20 percent as early as 1952 and had temporarily exceeded 30 percent in the late 1950s. Though declining in the 1960s as strains and imbalances forced retrenchment and a recasting of development policy, these rates appear to be approaching their former high levels, judging from the resurgent growth in industrial producer goods output in the late 1960s and early 1970s.

With the increased weight of industry and its high accumulation potential, with worker productivity greatly exceeding wages, its contribution to savings has increased. While data do not permit precise calculations, industry is at least financing a much greater share of its own growth than in the 1950s and may be financing the growth of, rather than drawing on, lagging sectors like agriculture. Thus, the dynamic rates of gross investment regained would also appear to be more firmly and securely based than in the past.

Industrial growth has been uneven (see Table 6.10). The ambitious programs and the narrow margins of a near subsistence economy, together with the insistence of Maoist ideology on anticipating and precipitating social and political change, imparted typical cyclical patterns of drive, retrenchment, and consolidation. The 1960 crisis of famine and withdrawal of Soviet technical and material support divided industrial policy into two distinct periods. The 1949-1960 period may be characterized as a "heavy industry push," in which resources were focused on promoting industrial growth and the average annual

Table 6.10   Industrial Production of Selected Goods

Year	Electric Power (billion KWH)	Crude Oil (mil. tons)	Crude Steel (mil. tons)	Cotton Cloth (bil. lin. meters)
1949	4.3	.1	.2	1.9
1952	7.3	.4	1.3	3.8
1957	19.3	1.5	5.4	5.1
1960	47.0	5.1	18.7	4.9
1962	30.0	3.7	8.0	3.5
1965	42.0	11.0	12.5	6.4
1970	72.0	28.2	17.8	7.5
1975	121.0	74.3	26.0	7.6
1985 target	--	--	60.0	--

output of industry rose by a phenomenal 22 percent. This policy was replaced by an interim twenty-year "self-sufficiency" program for 1960-1980, which accepted slower industrial growth while diverting important investment resources to meet critical needs in agriculture and national defense and rationalizing industrial growth within the limits of less available technology. Industrial output grew at an average of 7 percent annually during 1960-1975.

The interim policy, through restoring economic balance and raising technological levels, sought to create conditions for renewed rapid industrial growth from 1980 to 2000. Success in expanding farm output and reducing population growth suggests that nonfarm labor force could increase its share of the labor force from a present level of about one-quarter to perhaps as much as one-half, providing substantial scope for industrial growth. The plans for technological growth in the interim period, however, were disrupted in the 1966 Cultural Revolution, when research institutes were disbanded, college instruction ended, and primary and secondary education shifted from an academic to a low-level vocational track under Mao's insistence that institutions deal wth current realities rather than future hopes. The succession government of Hua Kuo-feng, however, moved quickly to restore research and education, and identified technological growth as a major priority for the coming 1980-2000 period.

Industry and Agriculture

With the limited area of farmland relative to its population,

Map 8   Fuels and Power in China

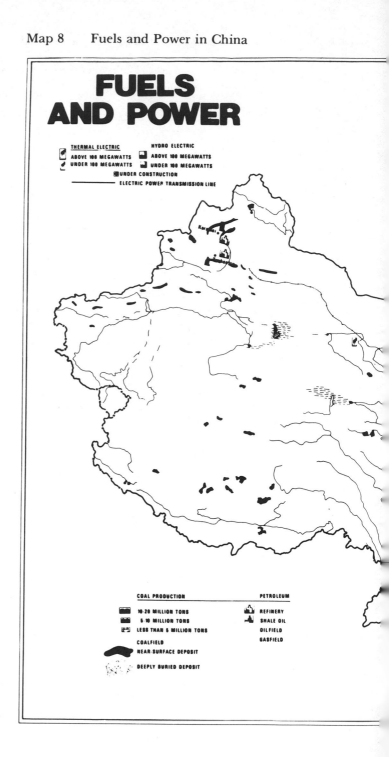

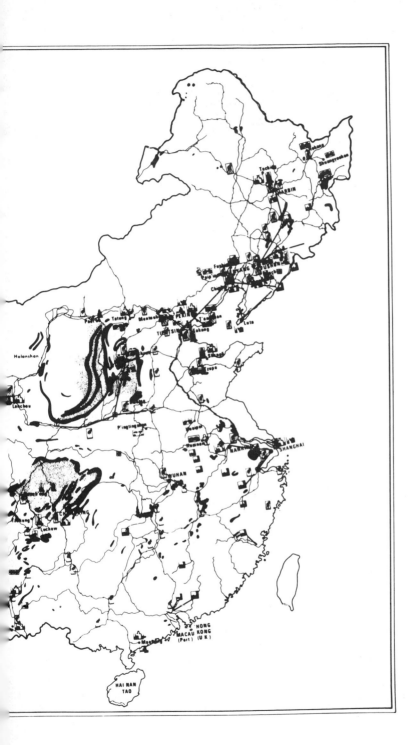

Map 9   Minerals and Metals in China

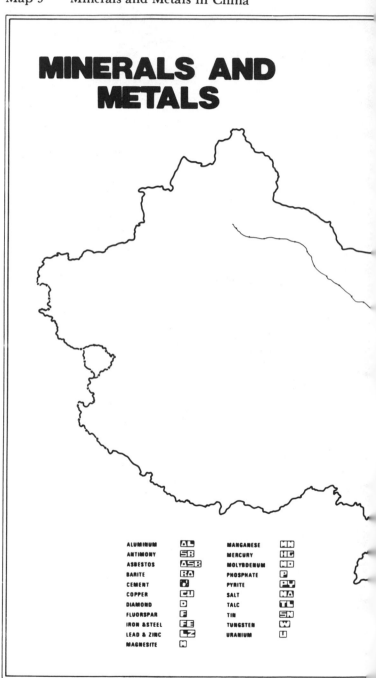

MINERALS AND METALS

ALUMINUM	AL	MANGANESE	MN	
ANTIMONY	SB	MERCURY	HG	
ASBESTOS	ASB	MOLYBDENUM	MO	
BARITE	BA	PHOSPHATE	P	
CEMENT	◻	PYRITE	PY	
COPPER	CU	SALT	NA	
DIAMOND	D	TALC	TL	
FLUORSPAR	F	TIN	SN	
IRON & STEEL	FE	TUNGSTEN	W	
LEAD & ZINC	LZ	URANIUM	U	
MAGNESITE	M			

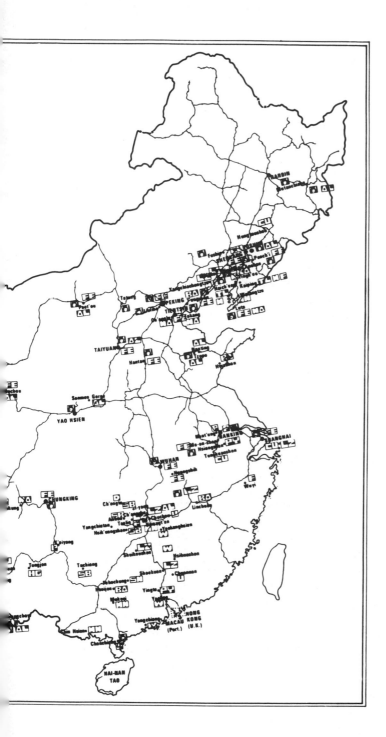

agriculture represents an area of scarcity in China's economy. Agricultural needs must be met internally, for China's huge food requirement precludes reliance on foreign trade for more than an insignificant share of national consumption. With the increasing pressures of population growth and development, agricultural costs have risen to secure increased crop yields and to modify poor land to make it fit for agriculture.

Between 1952 and 1976, grain and soybean output rose from 161 million tons to 285 million tons, representing a per capita increase from 283 to 300 kilograms. The current eight-year plan to 1985 has established an output goal of 400 million tons, which would raise per capita output to 372 kilograms. This target suggests planning for reserve production as well as raising living standards as incentives for modernizing production and to meet the needs of a growing nonfarm labor force. (A target for the year 2000 would probably involve no higher and possibly a lower per capita output. A 350 to 372 kilogram per capita output in the year 2000 would imply outputs of 465 to 494 million tons.)

Whether or not the 1985 target is met, it is clear that current economic planning places substantial emphasis on agricultural development. The question is, With what inputs and patterns of farm output? The experts that drew up the 1960-1968 farm development plan in the early 1960s ruled out expansion of farmland; the experience of the 1950s had shown that the land that could be reclaimed at reasonable cost was sufficient only to replace the farmland lost to roads, industrial sites, reservoirs, and other requirements of progress. The experts proposed to maximize the yields per hectare by combining modernizing industrial inputs with the labor-intensive practices of traditional agriculture. The program proposed substantial improvement in water management and great increases in fertilizer supply and mechanization, while reinvesting the growing rural labor force—and the labor economies through mechanization—in intensified cropping systems.

The program proposed initial concentration on the irrigated rice lands, which were more accessible than other crop lands and promised quick and initially large returns to modernizing inputs. In the later 1960s, the program would fan out to other farm areas capable of development, in step with a growing road infrastructure and an increased supply of inputs. At this time, a sharp drop in output returns compared to new inputs was projected, although output growth would be maintained by the rapidly rising scale of new inputs supplied. To qualify for intensive development, the various farm areas would have to establish conditions for "high, stable yields," for inputs could not be wasted on lands subject to frequent floods, droughts, or other disasters. It was noted that a significant portion of China's farmland had inherently low, unstable yields and could not be developed. Such land would eventually be retired from cultivation when conditions permitted but would be farmed while the need to maximize farm output existed.

Subsequent farm development appears to have followed this plan closely, with results much as predicted. Estimates of the supply of industrial inputs and of the equipment inventories on farms (as shown in Table 6.11) reveal a massive industrial support sufficient to materially change and improve the patterns of farming.

As planned, attention centered first on the 22 million hectares of irrigated rice lands, located largely in the south. Much of this land was located near major urban areas, with good local transport and access to surplus electric power, and it was feasible to quickly install electric-powered pumps to improve water management, to supply chemical fertilizer to farm areas, and to introduce fertilizer-responsive seeds. In 1957, official data showed that, with multicropping, 32 million hectares were planted with a yield of 2.7 tons per hectare and an output of 87 million tons. Although official data have not been published since the start of the 1960s, fragmentary press reports and statements of Chinese officials suggest that rice output had declined to about 76 million tons in the famine year of 1961 but had expanded rapidly to 99 million tons by 1965.[1] Rice output continued to expand, as modernization was extended to the whole of the irrigated rice lands and chemical fertilizer supplies became plentiful. A detailed press review reported that in 1976 36 million hectares of rice had been planted with a yield of 3.5 tons per hectare and an output of 126 million tons.[2]

These are very high yields and suggest China is rapidly approaching the economic limits of known rice-production technology. Two U.S. technical missions visiting China in 1974 could find little to recommend with respect to seed selection or water management to improve the state of the art.[3] Two countries with advanced rice technologies—Japan and Taiwan—have stabilized yields at their economic limits: Japan securing 5 tons per hectare with single crop rice and Taiwan 4 tons with double-crop rice. Since Taiwan's rice culture most closely resembles that of China, its rice yields are the better measure of China's achievement and of limits to further development. China's rice production appears to have entered a range of sharply diminishing returns to inputs, which will stabilize yields when China decides it can no longer afford the

Table 6.11 Industrial Inputs in Agriculture, 1953-1976

Aggregate Output or Supply in Period	Fertilizer Supply[a] (million tons)	Tractor Output (000)[b]	Output, Power Irrigation Equipment (million HP)	Output, Small Rural Plants[b]		
				Cement	Pig Iron	Coal
				(million tons)		
1953-57	1.4	n.a.	negl.	--	0.8	44
1958-60	2.0	34	4	6	29	n.a.
1961-65	6.3	88	4	13	5	n.a.
1966-70	16.3	219	n.a.	35	9	246
1971-75	29.5	647	26	100	43	517

Farm Inventories	Tractors (000)[c]	Powered Irrigation Equipment (million HP)	Rural Hydropower Plants (million KW)
1952	2	.1	negl.
1957	25	.6	negl.
1960	79	4.1	.5
1965	137[d]	8.5	.3
1970	320	16.9	.9
1975	972	43.0	3.0
1976	1,183		

[a] Chemical fertilizer output plus imports, in terms of nutrient content
(N, P_2O_5, K_2O).

[b] 1952-56.

[c] In terms of standard 15 HP units.

[d] Average of 1964 and 1966 estimates when 1965 estimate lacking.

Source: CIA, China: Economic Indicators, October 1977.

increasing costs of production increments. Even if it is assumed that this stabilized yield reaches 4.5 tons per hectare, it seems clear that rice production, which played a major role in meeting food needs in the period of "self-reliance," will make a much smaller contribution to the food needs of the year 2000.

Production of food grain crops, other than rice, defined here as wheat, coarse grains, tubers, and soybeans, has had a different history. About 75 million hectares are devoted to these crops, a figure arrived at by deducting from total crop land the irrigated rice lands and about 10 million hectares devoted to nonfood crops. In 1957, with multiple cropping (the growing of more than one crop per year), 108 million tons of foodgrains were obtained from 101 million hectares of foodgrain crops planted on 75 million hectares of land. This resulted in a crop-hectare yield of 1.1 tons (the yield of a single crop), or a hectare yield of 1.44 tons (the average output of a hectare of land from all crops). Much of the multiple-cropped acreage lies in the vast, flat North China Plain, 50 meters above sea level, which has fertile soils but low, highly variable, and maldistributed rainfall, and is drained by rivers choked with silt from the easily eroded and overcropped loess uplands where they originate. Each year large areas of the North China Plain are visited by drought and also by waterlogging after the summer rainy season, as well as by occasional floods as the rivers overrun their dikes.

The P.R.C. made major and costly development blunders in the North China Plain area during the exuberant "Great Leap Forward" of 1958-1960, promoting irrigation before solving the problems of siltation and drainage. The huge Sanmen Dam on the Yellow River, built to impound water for power and irrigation, was silted up and useless only a few years after construction, while the initial efforts at irrigation without proper drainage had salinized and reduced the productivity of large areas of crop land. Output of dry-land food grain crops dropped to 91 million tons in 1961, and by 1965 had only recovered to the 1957 level of output of 108 million tons.

From the mid-1960s to the early 1970s, however, the P.R.C. initiated major construction in the area to build a comprehensive drainage system, which together with local land leveling has substantially mitigated drainage and waterlogging problems. This effort was closely followed by a drive to construct tube wells, the number in operation increasing thirteen-fold to 1.3 million between 1965 and late 1974, when they were capable of irrigating 7.3 million hectares of farmland. The water supplied is sufficient to provide substantial protection against local drought and to permit timely planting independent of local rainfall, but not to permit shifts to modern, high yield crops. Peking plans a much greater extension of tube wells, with its surveys indicating that half the farmland in the major North China Plain provinces of Hopeh, Shantung, and Honan can be irrigated by wells. The ultimate irrigable acreage will depend on the rate of recharge of the underground water deposits.

These developments promoted a marked rise in dry-land food grain crops, which between 1965 and 1976 rose 47 percent to 159 million tons, with much of the increase occurring in the North China Plain. Both increased cropping and yields have played a role. Crop losses due to waterlogging and flooding have been considerably reduced, while winter wheat acreage has significantly increased as drainage reduced the land under water at fall planting. In addition, with the expanded rural labor force, multicropping has increased with the popularization of highly labor-intensive intercropping systems, in which a second crop is planted between the rows before the first crop is harvested. The widespread extent of intercropping is reflected by changes in soybean output. Soybeans, a low yield crop, were displaced to a large extent by high yield grain crops in the 1960s, but their output has more than doubled in the 1970s as an ideal food product for intercropping.

While the irrigated rice areas, amply supplied with the three basic ingredients of labor, water, and fertilizer, have been able to develop production toward their technical and economic limits, the dry-land crop areas have confronted water scarcities that constrain the elevation of crop yields. The potential for production growth in the dry-land areas is much greater than in the irrigated rice lands, but much of it will have to be realized through solving water supply problems if China is to meet its postulated food targets by the year 2000. If rice output is limited to 4.5 tons per crop hectare, or an increase from the 1976 output of 126 million tons to 162 million tons, then dry-land food crops must supply the balance and expand from 159 million tons in 1976 to between 303 and 332 million tons in the year 2000.

China will probably press its tube well program as far as it can, since, though not inexpensive, it is the most feasible alternative at present. But the supply of water from this source, though unknown, is almost surely insufficient to meet development needs through the remainder of the century. One may predict that at some time in the 1980s China will again try to impound run-off surface water for irrigation, this time ensuring an effective prerequisite soil conservation program to desilt the rivers. This program will be very expensive, not only because of the construction involved, but because of the necessity to retire from cultivation many millions of hectares of marginal farmlands and to relocate the rural populations involved. (In the mid-1950s when San-men Dam was being built, the Chinese announced a long-term program to retire one-third of China's farmland from cultivation as marginal, a large fraction of which was immediately concerned with soil conservation on the headwaters of the Yellow River. Although the dam was built on schedule, the subsequent drop in farm output and unforeseen problems of implementation resulted in only minor soil conservation achievements.) Even these two sources of water may not suffice, and it would not be surprising if before the end of the century China embarks on a still more expensive project of transporting surplus water from the Yangtze valley to the North China Plain. The transformation achieved and projected in China's farming that has been discussed above is summarized in Table 6.12.

The 1960-1980 program of self-sufficiency, in its farm aspects, carried the rationale of a need to slow industrialization and concentrate resources on agriculture for this period in order to secure an agricultural surplus as a prerequisite for future industrial growth. The

Table 6.12 Changes in Agricultural Land Use and Productivity,
1957, 1976, 2000

Food Grain Crops	Million Hectares	Output per hectare (tons)		
		1957	1976	2000
Irrigated rice land	22	4.0	5.7	7.4
Dry land grain crops				
(1) Marginal land	15	.67	.67	0.0
(2) Land capable of development	60	1.63	2.5	5.1-5.3
Nonfood crops	10	--	--	--
Total	107			
Kilograms grain per capita		305	300	350-372

1980-2000 period has been described as one of balanced growth that will bring China into the "front rank" of nations and will encompass the modernization of industry, agriculture, national defense, and science and technology. This policy description, though vague, carries the implication of a redeployment of the nation's resources and manpower.

Two conditions suggest that the rapid transfer of the labor force out of agriculture into nonfarm occupations, evident in the 1950s but subsequently slowed, may now be resumed to the end of the century. First, the changing structure of the population, as total population growth slows while the growth of the productive-aged population continues at a rapid rate for an extended period, will enable the farm surplus to support a greater share of nonfarm workers. Second, the extension and consolidation of the substantial beginnings toward farm mechanization and modernization should be reflected in more substantial growth in farm labor productivity and in an expanding farm surplus.

The farm program in the period of "self-sufficiency" relied importantly on shifts to more intensive cropping systems with heavy labor requirements. During 1960-1976, the farm labor force increased by nearly half to provide necessary labor inputs, with the cultivated land per farm worker dropping from a little over one-half hectare to a little over one-third hectare. This trend, were it continued, would seem undesirable and eventually self-defeating, while the level of mechanization and supply of industrial inputs to agriculture would appear to have reached a scale in recent years that would obviate the need for further large increases in farm labor.

Notes

1. In interviews, various officials placed food grain output at 162 million tons in 1961 and 200 million tons in 1965, while press reports stated that rice output had accounted for 60 percent of the total increase and a share of just under half of total grain output. *Jen-min jih-pao,* January 16 and February 6, 1966.

2. New China News Agency, Peking, September 29, 1977; Foreign Broadcast Information Service, September 29, 1977.

3. Dwight H. Perkins, "Constraints Influencing China's Agricultural Performance," in *China: A Reassessment of the Economy,* U.S. Congress Joint Economic Committee (Washington, D.C.: U.S. Government Printing Office, 1975).

7
Science and Technology Policy
Genevieve C. Dean

Politics and Science

Political changes in China have had a dramatic impact on science policy. Shortly after the fall of the "Gang of Four" following the death of Mao Tse-tung in September 1976, the official Chinese press carried the first signs of a new priority for science and technology. The pages of *People's Daily*, which had been filled with articles calling for near-total "self-reliance," now criticized views opposed to importing the advanced technologies needed to build "an independent, comprehensive modern industrial system." It attributed such views to the "Gang" (Mao's widow, Chiang Ch'ing, her radical cohorts on the Party Central Committee, and their followers). By the end of the year, the press was denouncing the Gang's policies for the obstructive and destructive effects they were said to have had on all aspects of China's scientific and technological development.

The campaign against the Gang and the ideas associated with them continued to gather momentum through the spring and summer of 1977. Acting on the mistaken belief that advanced technology was incompatible with Communist society, the Gang of Four, it was said, had emphasized "class struggle" and political and social change to the point of jeopardizing China's economic development and national defense. The situation was summarized by the new vice-president of the Academy of Sciences, Fang Yi (who was subsequently appointed minister in charge of the State Scientific and Technological Commission):

> Serious sabotage by the gang of four wrought havoc with China's science and education. Large numbers of universities, colleges and scientific

229

research institutes were disbanded. The gap between China's level of science and technology and the world's advanced levels has widened. Quite a number of key problems in science and technology in our national economy remain unsolved, and basic, theoretical research in particular has been virtually done away with. The quality of education has declined sharply. . . . Science and education are lagging so far behind that they are seriously hindering realization of the four modernizations [agriculture, industry, national defense, and science and technology].[1]

In the long-standing rivalry between Madame Mao's radicals and more "moderate" or "pragmatic" political figures—notably the late Premier Chou En-lai and Vice-Premier Teng Hsiao-p'ing—the radicals' intrusion into the realm of science and education seems to have been the provocation around which opposition finally crystallized. Science became an issue in this political conflict in about 1971, some five years before the Gang was toppled from power. The debate focused on institutional innovations introduced during the previous five years as part of the Great Proletarian Cultural Revolution. By 1972, the scientific community—through its spokesman, Chou P'ei-yuan, head of Peking University and of the Scientific and Technical Association of China—had convinced Premier Chou En-lai that some of these institutional experiments were having a negative effect on the long-term development of China's research capability. Their first concern was to resume basic research and to restore theoretical study to the curriculum for higher education. The "open-door" style of running research institutes, they argued, "sending out" scientific personnel and students for stints in factories or on agricultural communes and "inviting in" untrained peasants and industrial workers to research institutes and universities, was no conducive to basic research and theoretical work. Accordingly, Premier Chou had issued a directive calling for expansion of theoretical work in the natural sciences.

The radicals, however, regarded the "new-born" institutions of the Cultural Revolution as safeguards against elitism in science and education. By widening access to research facilities and advanced training, they sought to breach what they saw as the last stronghold of the "bourgeoisie" in China's socialist society. If this meant dispersing the institutes of the Academy of Sciences to the jurisdiction of various provincial authorities, dissolving the central government's science policy organs, dismantling the structure of research-supporting institutions (libraries, professional associations, scientific journals and publications), diverting scientists from research to manual labor and political study, depriving research units of adequate supplies and equipment, and diluting the academic training of students by injecting large doses of politics and factory or farm work into the curriculum, the radicals seem to have been prepared to make these sacrifices. They defended such "reforms" as enabling "politics" to be "put in command" of science and technology, thus ensuring that the scientists' knowledge and skills were applied in the interests of the laboring masses rather than being used "behind closed doors" to study problems of academic interest that were unrelated to immediate production needs.

The ideologues, headed by the Gang of Four, then struck back to defend the experiments of the Cultural Revolution. Their tactic was to launch an attack in the public press, which they partially controlled, accusing the intellectuals of seeking to restore the old social order that they had dominated. By historical analogy with the schools of Legalist and Confucian thought, the radicals associated progress in science and technology with social revolution and the assumption of political control by a new class. Thus they implied that reinstituting specialization of research "divorced from practice" would mark retrogression to a previous social order. They argued against the view that "bourgeois" scientists could contribute to socialist construction even as they were being gradually "remolded" under the "dictatorship of the proletariat." Instead, the radicals insisted, they must "consciously submit" to the philosophy of dialectical materialism before scientific and technological advance could occur.

The Fourth National People's Congress met at the end of 1974. In his address to the congress, Premier Chou announced the goals of achieving a "relatively comprehensive industrial and economic system" by 1980 and "comprehensive modernization" of agriculture, industry, national defense, and science and technology—the "four modernizations"—by the year 2000. Hua Kuo-feng, then vice-premier and later Mao's successor as Party chairman, reportedly was given responsibility for reactivating scientific research institutes and restoring theoretical work. In the summer of 1975, according to subsequent accounts, a symposium of scientific and technical personnel was convened under the aegis of Hua and with Mao's blessing.

Another champion of the scientists was Vice-Premier Teng Hsiao-p'ing, who had been dismissed during the Cultural Revolution but was reappointed in 1973. Teng's position was that political disruption of scientific research had slowed China's economic development and, if allowed to continue, would make it impossible to achieve the "four modernizations." Having effected key appointments in the Academy of Sciences, he commissioned a report on the status of scientific work in China, which was prepared by the academy and submitted to the State Council in September 1975.

This "Outline Report" was never published, but it is said to have been circulated without authorization by the Gang of Four, who instigated widespread criticism of it as evidence that the "'bourgeoisie" was attempting to regain political power by striking through the scientists. As pieced together from the published critiques, the Outline Report apparently recommended reinstituting professional administration of research institutes, with the Party secretary clearly subordinate to the institute director in scientific and technical matters. The Outline Report proposed that research be carried out by individuals or "small collectives," with the professional scientists the "core" of research groups, which would include workers and political cadres. It called for reinstatement of a system of promotion and of financial and material incentives for intellectuals. According to its critics, the Outline Report confirmed their view that the scientists had become advocates of the "theory of productive forces"; rejecting the view that class struggle was the "key link" in development, the Outline Report emphasized only the setbacks to the "production struggle" and to science and technology in China. The scientists were said to have espoused the view that class struggle had "died out" under the political dictatorship of the proletariat; that science and technology were part of the economic base of society, not the "superstructure," and therefore that dictatorship should not be exercised over science and technology; and that to do so was to implement the Party's policy on intellectuals incorrectly. Their report on the status of science, said the radicals, denied the positive accomplishments of the Cultural Revolution and instead asserted not only that there had been "no great achievements," but also that the "science and technology front" had been "a mess" since the Cultural Revolution.

The barrage of attacks against the scientists continued during the spring of 1976. In addition to criticizing the Outline Report, the radicals even managed to halt some research programs, according to charges later leveled against them, on such frivolous grounds as the claim that "the law of conservation of matter is conservative" or "the theory of relativity is a sham." While Hua Kuo-feng was acting on his brief to reintroduce academic freedom in the natural sciences, the Gang failed to distinguish between dissent on academic and political questions, "stopping academic exchange activities, stifling academic ideas, and sharply attacking those who held differing academic views" through their domination of professional journals as well as the mass media.

Following the Gang's ouster in October 1976, the new political leadership headed by Premier Hua Kuo-feng promptly and unequivocably gave top priority to economic modernization, rapid industrial development, and scientific research as a source of badly needed new technologies. Theoretical research, once castigated as being "divorced from practice," was acknowledged to be an essential part of the scientific endeavor, with an important bearing on future technological development.

As the direction of the new policy trends became clear, prominent scientists rallied to Hua's leadership. Concomitantly, in a campaign to restore the prestige of China's scientists and educators, Mao's writings of twenty years before were cited in support of the view that the majority of intellectuals in China had been "remolded," that they now accepted "dictatorship by the proletariat" and could be enlisted in the cause of "socialist construction." Measures to proletarianize science and technology were less urgent, in this view, and should be balanced with efforts to bring China's research capabilities and technology up to "advanced world levels." To reach state-of-the-art levels, China depended on academically trained scientists and engineers, irrespective of their class background. A proletarian outlook and ideology without professional qualifications, it was now recognized, were not enough to function at the frontiers of science and technology.

Months of mass rallies and public meetings convened throughout China to publicize the new commitment to scientific and technological development climaxed in August 1977 with the publication of a poem by Party Vice-Chairman and Minister of Defense Yeh Chien-ying:

> Scaling the heights of science
> Is like storming a fortified city;
> Victory belongs to those who advance,
> Defying difficulties.[2]

Election of a new Communist Party Central Committee in August 1977 indicated that the political situation had stabilized enough so that concrete steps could be taken toward fulfilling this commitment. Some ten months had elapsed since removal of the radicals from the Central Committee. During these months, as their followers were being ousted from local Party committees, provincial and local authorities signalled resolution of the political struggle in favor of Hua and the new central leadership by endorsing the new line on science. Criticizing the Gang of Four was called the "key link for promoting science and technology"; it might as well have been added that science and technology had become a "key link" in discrediting the Gang and their ideas. The new leadership based its claim to political legitimacy largely on the need to end policies that were said to obstruct scientific and technological development and undermine the country's economy and defense.

These political maneuvers prepared the way for a new science policy. In September, the Party leaders officially sanctioned measures that, in effect, would restore scientific institutions and structures of authority dismantled during the previous decade of radical reform. The urgency of such measures stemmed from the priority attached by these leaders to industrial development—a fundamental goal shared across the spectrum of political views in China, but less immediately pressing to the radicals than their social and ideological objectives. The new policy has to be viewed in the immediate political context, but it will also reflect previous experience in trying to make science contribute to the country's economic development and modernization. Restoration of earlier institutions may result in the revival of old problems.

As in many other countries, the problems in China seem to have had less to do with scientific research than with technological innovation—developing laboratory results into usable, economic technologies. After 1960, confronted with these shortcomings in the structures they had established in the 1950s, Chinese scientists and the political leadership at that time cooperated in trying to reform the original institutions and strengthen the links between research and production. Part of this effort was to adapt R&D institutions to changed economic conditions. In contrast to the previous decade, this was a period of retrenchment rather than expansion, of improving the operation of existing plant and equipment rather than of new construction. But research, engineering design, and education in China all were geared to rapid industrialization. Apart from adapting these institutions to new functions under different economic constraints, the new policy required complementary changes in economic planning and enterprise management.[3] When these were not implemented, the reform of R&D institutions was stalled.

The Cultural Revolution smashed through such obstacles after 1966, but in the end, nearly destroyed scientific research in China in trying to enhance engineering and technological innovation. Resumption of basic research, restoration of research institutions, and return of theoretical study to the curricula of schools and universities thus have symbolic importance to the political leaders seeking to discredit radical policies of the past decade. It is still not clear whether the new policy will aim at striking a balance between research and development by picking up the reforms of the early 1960s or whether, like the 1950s, it will focus exclusively on building up advanced research capabilities. In this respect, the past may be a guide to the future.

The Background:
Science, Technology, and Economic Development

The First Five-Year Plan (1953-1957)

The Chinese Communist leaders had come to power in 1949 committed to the goals of economic development and maintenance of the military security of their country. For both purposes they needed modern technology and more: the capability to sustain technological innovation; to adopt new, more efficient technologies in order to enlarge their production capacity (and their military capabilities); and, by continuously innovating, to remain at the forefront of "advanced world levels" in science and technology. With assistance from the Soviet Union and the Eastern European countries in the Soviet bloc, the Chinese leaders expected to establish a core sector of modern heavy industry that would eventually supply new technology in the form of modern machines and equipment to the rest of the economy. After this initial stage, however, technological advance was to continue "self-reliantly" (though this term was not used at the time); rather than importing new technologies, Chinese industry and agriculture and the military would increasingly look to domestic sources of innovation.

Though invention and innovation are inherently unpredictable, the most systematic source of new inventions and ideas for new technologies is scientific research. By rationalizing the organization of research facilities in China, and through centralized planning and support of research programs, the new Chinese leaders expected to make the most efficient use of scientific resources to generate the technologies specified in their economic and military plans. Accordingly, the Chinese Academy of Sciences was established by the new government within weeks of the founding of the People's Republic of China. Preeminent Chinese scientists were enrolled in the academy, which was to be a "center of excellence" in research. The academy was charged with responsibility for performing basic research, the creation of scientific knowledge on which the future development of new technologies would depend. Thus its work was intended to be relevant to the technological needs of a modern industrial economy that did not yet exist in China, but which would be constructed in accordance with a series of five-year plans for economic development.

While basic research and what is sometimes called "basic oriented research," which is not expected to have immediate applicability but is carried out with some future application in mind, were the function of the institutes of the Chinese Academy of Sciences, applied research and engineering design and development were assigned to institutes in the industrial ministries under the State Council of the national government. These institutes supplied technology—in the form of blueprints for factories and machines—for immediate application and innovation in state-owned enterprises. During the First Five-Year Plan, under the pressure of rapid construction and with ready access to Soviet and East European technology, the ministries' research and design institutes appear to have served primarily to channel imported technologies into the key projects in the five-year plan. Design consisted largely of copying imported blueprints with, at most, minimal adaptation to local production conditions. Projections of the economic and technical performance of new plant and equipment after they were in production had to be based on Soviet and European experience under quite different conditions. Unfortunately, design procedures in China were then bureaucratized and frozen into this mode.

The Great Leap Forward

The strategy underlying China's five-year plans[4] was to concentrate technological modernization initially in the heavy industrial sector of the economy, that is, first constructing the capacity to manufacture modern machinery and equipment. This meant that modernization of agriculture and consumer goods industries would have to be postponed; that, for the time being, growth in these sectors would come about only from more efficient use of existing means of production, rather than from investment in more productive technologies.

The limitations of this strategy were beginning to be felt even before the First Five-Year Plan was completed, and this was reflected in the greater attention paid to the nonpriority sectors in proposals for the Second Five-Year Plan. For example, the problem of generating enough capital to continue the program of industrial construction led to recommendations for building more small- and medium-scale enterprises, which cost less and could be put into production more quickly than the large plants that had been commanding most state investment.

The Second Five-Year Plan, however, was overtaken by the Great Leap Forward, which lasted from 1958 through 1960. The Great Leap was an attempt to continue to increase production in agriculture and light industry without diverting state investment to these sectors and without redirecting research and engineering resources to technological needs in this part of the economy. For this purpose, a "mass innovation campaign" was launched to promote the labor-intensive construction of facilities, like water control installations, to improve the productivity of agriculture, and even to resurrect traditional manufacturing techniques in order to increase the supply of tools and to mobilize scattered resources—the most notorious example being the "backyard steel furnaces." The mass innovation campaign was accompanied by exhortations to overcome a "superstitious" belief that only scientific "experts" could invent new technologies, to accept that the methods of production were best understood by those who labored and produced and, therefore, were best qualified to improve the means of production. The function of "science" was merely to summarize and find the general principles underlying this body of experience.

Because of the drama and sensation of the "mass innovation campaign," it is often overlooked that imports of modern technology for the priority heavy industries actually increased at the start of the Great Leap Forward. The urgency of expanding production with minimal investment in agriculture and light industry stemmed from the need to pay for these imports. The political momentum of the mass campaign, however, eventually carried it into the modern industries, where it was manifested in unauthorized modifications to equipment, operation of plant and machines at levels above the designed capacity, and "mass" construction of new facilities, sometimes without adequate design or materials, but certainly with an excess of enthusiasm on the part of workers and political cadres.

1961-1966

The experiences of the Great Leap Forward demonstrated the limitations of technical change and new construction carried out without adequate engineering development and testing. Attempts to expand local R&D facilities, both under government auspices at the provincial and municipal levels and in regional branches of the Academy of Sciences, tended to overextend China's still limited scientific resources. The early 1960s, therefore, saw a retrenchment to the centralized science system of the period before the Great Leap Forward. In the modern industries, technological management and control were restored to the enterprise managers and chief engineers, and "worker-innovations," now in the form of suggestions for technical improvements and adaptations, had to be submitted for review and testing by the technical department concerned before being adopted by an enterprise. Enterprises failing to show a profit were ordered closed down—which meant that many of the small enterprises and unauthorized facilities constructed during the Great Leap no longer counted in state economic plans, though some, at least, continued to exist and even to operate on the fringes of the state economy.

Three disastrous harvests, in 1959, 1960, and 1961, reduced China's capacity to continue new industrial construction and even necessitated imports of grain rather than capital goods. A major change in economic policy then ensued. Thereafter, industrial investment had to be funded mainly out of the profits of industry itself, while the surplus produced by agriculture would be reinvested in modernizing production in that sector. Taking "agriculture as the base," a larger part of industrial capacity than before would be diverted to manufacturing capital goods for agriculture and for agriculture-related industries.

Coinciding with the economic disaster that necessitated a cutback in China's imports of technology was the withdrawal of Soviet technical assistance in 1960. Soviet advisors are said to have left China abruptly, in some cases taking the blueprints for partly finished projects with them. For the next few years, therefore, comparatively little new construction was begun in China, while the designers' task was to attempt to duplicate the missing blueprints in order to complete the projects underway. The lesson of this experience for the Chinese was to maintain "self-reliance," for the flow of technology from external sources might be cut off at any time.

"Taking agriculture as the base and industry as the leading factor" meant a change in the kind of product to be made by heavy industry; the need was no longer entirely for the modern industrial machinery and equipment specified in national economic plans (and copiable from imported models), but for machines and tools adapted to local materials, to a lower level of industrial skills and experience in the work force, that would require less investment and would offer quick recovery of investment outlay. "Self-reliance" meant that new technologies would now have to come from domestic sources, that the R&D system would have to be reoriented toward the technological needs of the present rather than the future. But neither the research system in the Academy of Sciences and the universities, nor the industrial research and design facilities in the ministries had been set up to respond to technological "demand" from agriculture and small-scale industry. Under the first Five-Year Plan, the R&D establishment had been an instrument for introducing modern manufacturing technologies into the capital goods industries. Consequently, product design was relatively neglected; in the now heavily bureaucratized design institutes, there were no adequate procedures for investigating the conditions under which a piece of equipment would be used or where it would be manufactured, and little or no attempt to adapt a design to local requirements. As a result, it would later be claimed, the engineers kept on cranking out designs that were too expensive or too sophisticated for local governments and rural communes to build and operate.

Furthermore, the engineer's formal responsibility for his design ended when he handed over a set of blueprints to the enterprise. If the design could not be put into operation or if there were unforeseen problems with the product or process, the enterprise apparently was left with no effective recourse to the R&D establishment. Numerous cases of poor design were documented in the Chinese press during the 1960s. It was not surprising, therefore, to find a preference on the part of enterprise managers for plant and equipment that had been copied from foreign designs or, better still, for the imported machines themselves—quite the opposite of "self-reliance."

The economic crisis of the early 1960s made it more essential than ever to keep investment costs as low as possible and to improve the efficiency and productivity of existing plant and equipment, rather than building new facilities equipped with advanced technologies. Here again the R&D structures established during the 1950s were not appropriate for China's needs in the 1960s. Neither the industrial design institutes nor the research institutes of the Academy of Sciences were organized to devise the relatively minor technical improvements—"incremental innovations"—that can make the plant and equipment already in operation more productive. (As described further on, a system for contract research, negotiated between the research institute and the enterprise, was being developed in the 1960s. But the institute was required to show a profit on the research it undertook apart from its state-assigned projects, and the benefit to the enterprise of such minor improvements usually would not have justified a large enough fee to be "profitable" for the research institute.)

Such "incremental innovations" were made by the technicians in a factory or workshop, and even in the 1950s there already were widespread schemes to encourage "worker innovation." What was missing, however, was a system for "feeding back" information on such technical changes to the designers so that these improvements could be incorporated into subsequent models. Consequently, machines continued to be built and factories constructed according to the original designs, without the modifications and adaptations that had already been made on existing plant. Newly built facilities, therefore, could actually be less efficient than those already in operation. This left a margin of potential production capacity above the designed level, which the enterprise could realize by making technical improvements and "worker innovations." If such technical changes were not reported to the ministry in charge of that branch of industry, the additional capacity they created did not exist, as far as the state economic plan was concerned, and the quotas assigned to the enterprise continued to be based on the lower figures of the original design.

Whatever the problems the Chinese may have been having with their industrial technology, science flourished in the mid-1960s. It was during this period, between the Great Leap Forward and the Cultural Revolution, that Chinese scientists made some of their most impressive achievements in research and high technology, including the synthesis of crystalline insulin, proposal of the "straton theory" of elementary particles, theoretical work in mathematics and geophysics, test explosions of atomic and hydrogen bombs, and development of guided missiles. Work was in progress which, a few years later, would lead to such achievements as the launching and recovery of earth satellites. Progress in a number of technological fields was marked by trial-production of advanced prototypes, for example, a water-cooled turbogenerator, a 1 million ops computer, and digital-controlled machine tools. In 1964, an international symposium of scientists from developing countries was convened in Peking, followed two years later by an international physics colloquium. Enjoying the apparently unreserved support of the political leadership at that time, the scientists were relatively free from political interruption and control of their professional work. Articles signed by prominent scientists appeared regularly in the Chinese press, portraying the future in terms of scientific rationality and enhancement of "big science," which they said would lead inevitably to technological modernization.

Though many of the institutional innovations of the Great Leap were dismantled and the centralized organization of scientific facilities largely restored in the early 1960s, the need to adapt the original system to new circumstances was recognized. While the "professionalization" of science and technology was reasserted, it was also accepted that R&D now had to be linked more immediately and directly with production needs. A greater portion of professional science would have to be devoted to improving the technologies currently used by industry and agriculture; only in a few strategic areas could research continue on the advanced technologies China would need in the future for a modern, industrialized economy.

In short, the Chinese needed to strengthen precisely the weakest part of their science system, the structures for experimental development, engineering design, testing and trial-production, and "feedback" to the R&D establishment. This was to be accomplished by developing a network of institutionalized links among industrial enterprises, research institutes, and educational institutions. The intention seems to have been to create a system of contract research to cover R&D projects that were not prescribed in the central plans; to provide industry with access to research institutes for help with problems or with new ideas that had occurred in the production process. Such arrangements would also benefit the R&D and design institutes by giving them access to production facilities for pilot studies of new techniques or products under development in their laboratories. Thus the "three-in-one" concept of cooperation among a factory, a specific research unit, and a school, that was to be widely promoted in the Cultural Revolution, actually originated in the early 1960s and not, as later claimed, during the Cultural Revolution.

A major effort to revise engineering design procedures was announced at the end of 1964. The design function was redefined to extend the designer's role into the production stages. "Three-in-one" teams comprised of the designer, production workers, and factory managers were not only to insure that local production conditions and consumer requirements were reflected in the initial design, but also to keep the designer available for "troubleshooting" during the development and initial operation of the new facility. Any problems encountered in these stages could then be designed out of subsequent models. Thus consultation among the designer, manufacturer, and user of a product also had already been put forward as a means of strengthening the innovation process before the Cultural Revolution began.

The "three-in-one" combination was meant to be a bridge between specialized institutions to carry out essential stages of the innovation process that fell between them. It did not change the basic features of a science system that had been set up to implement long-range goals and was intentionally "divorced from" current production. Moreover, implementation of the "three-in-one" principle was often frustrated in practice for a number of specific reasons, including the respective financial obligations incurred by the participating institutions; the possibility of conflict between meeting output quotas and diverting production facilities to experimentation; entrenched methods and procedures, codified in rules and regulations difficult to change; and social structures that inhibited communication between shopfloor workers and professional engineers.

The Cultural Revolution (1966-1969)

The Cultural Revolution opened the way for the "three-in-one" combination to become more effective, chiefly by overriding or ignoring such obstacles. It did not create new institutions or new forms of organization for scientific activities (for example, the August 12, 1966, communiqué of the Party Central Committee launching the Cultural Revolution specifically exempted the scientific establishment from political interference) but, rather, changed the context in which the "three-in-one" functioned.

Like the Great Leap Forward, the Cultural Revolution was preceded by a debate over economic policy. One view held that the economy had recovered to a point where industrial construction once again could be accelerated. The other view was that priority should continue to be given to agriculture, that there was still considerable unused capacity in industry that should be mobilized before any more construction was undertaken. In this case, the fear was that a new industrial program at this time would require investment that the Chinese economy could not sustain without incurring external debt. The proponents of this view argued that existing plant and equipment could be made more productive—though not as productive as new, ultramodern technologies—and the extra surplus, or profit, that resulted could then be invested in new capital goods embodying modern, highly efficient technology. This was the prevailing view when the Cultural Revolution began in 1966.

The first problem was to inventory the existing capital stock in industrial enterprises, then to bring the enterprises' production quotas into line with their actual capacity and reallocate excess equipment, materials, and manpower. The design reform campaign served this purpose by encouraging the designers to investigate on-site conditions and, as much as possible, to include existing facilities in the blueprints for new projects.

Another drive for "worker innovations" was launched for the same purpose. Unlike the Great Leap Forward, this time worker innovation did not entail rejection of "science" or the professional engineer and the trained technician, who had a definite role on the "three-in-one" team. In the Cultural Revolution, "worker innovation" seemed to refer to any technical change not specifically assigned to the enterprise in the state plan; it might consist of completing an R&D project that had stalled or been abandoned, putting a disused piece of equipment into operation, or adopting a technical change that the management had previously refused to authorize. Such "worker innovation," it is important to note, was never expected to lead to technological breakthroughs but merely to the kind of technical improvements that would mobilize excess capacity and make current operations more efficient.

Even such technical improvements required more engineering skill and knowledge than production workers could be expected to acquire in the normal operation of their machines. For this reason, technical departments in many state enterprises began to be reorganized and members of the technical staff were "sent down" to work on the shop floor. Eventually the need for technicians to work on immediate production problems outweighed considerations of long-term technological advance, and research scientists and high-level engineers also were "sent down" to factories or agricultural communes to perform the kind of routine technical activities that would otherwise be carried out by technicians with very different training and experience. These problems lay behind the struggle over science policy in the mid-1970s.

1977: Emergence of a New Science Policy

On September 18, 1977, the newly elected Central Committee issued a "Circular on Holding a National Science Conference." Apart from announcing that such a conference would meet at an unspecified date the following spring, the science circular endorsed certain ad hoc developments that had been set in motion by the political currents of the spring and summer. The Central Committee asserted as official policy to be implemented prior to the national science conference:

> We must do a good job of consolidation without delay, quickly restore scientific research institutions that were disbanded as a result of interference and sabotage by the Gang of Four, and put in order those now in disorder.[5]

One effect of this directive was to confirm the trend toward transferring research institutes formerly under the Chinese Academy of Sciences, which had been reclassified as provincial institutes during the Cultural Revolution, back to the jurisdiction of the central academy. Thus the number of academy institutes, which had stood at some 120 ten years before, was only 37 in 1975 (and of these, half were jointly administered by the academy and local authorities); but in 1977, the number had already returned to more than 60. Another result was to clarify the status as research institutions of certain units that were "in disorder," i.e., units that had in effect become production facilities under the stricture of "linking research with production."

The science circular also directed that:

> All scientific research institutions must practice the system of directors' undertaking responsibility under the leadership of the Party committees.[6]

With this, the scientists finally succeeded in their effort, originally seen in the academy's 1975 Outline Report, to overturn one of the major institutions associated with the Cultural Revolution, the "revolutionary committee." Variously constituted of representatives of scientists, the Party committee, and workers, or of "young, middle-aged, and old" scientists, the revolutionary committee was intended to secure more effective representation of political views in decisions that had hitherto been left to the scientists. Such committees had become the administrative bodies of research institutes. The science circular restored this authority to the scientists by calling for restoration of the system under which institutes were headed by a director—appointed on the basis of his professional qualifications—and two deputy directors. Not long after the science circular was issued, the revolutionary committees were reportedly being phased out. By the end of 1977, seven new directors and twenty deputy directors, all of whom were qualified scientists, were appointed to head academy institutes.

Restoration of the directors' authority required complementary changes in the role of the Party committee in each institute.

> It is imperative to install as Party committee secretaries those cadres who understand the Party's policies and have enthusiasm for science, to select experts or near-experts to lead professional work, and to find diligent and hardworking cadres to take charge of the support work.[7]

The Party secretary was thus to defer to the director on professional and technical matters. Enjoined to respect the "special nature" of scientific work—that is, its "classlessness"—the Party committees were directed to subordinate their political functions to the institutes' primary role as scientific research units. The Party committee's main responsibility, in fact, was to create conditions conducive to scientific research.

The science circular specified other measures for restoring the institutes' research activities:

> Measures must be taken to transfer step by step to scientific or technical work those professionals who really know the work but are now in unrelated jobs. We must see to it that those scientists and technicians who have made achievements or have great talent must be assured proper working conditions and provided with necessary assistants. Titles for technical personnel should be restored, the system to assess technical proficiency should be established and technical posts must entail specific responsibility.[8]

The first of these instructions was a call for sorting out the employment of trained scientific manpower. A cardinal principle in the Cultural Revolution had been that science should break out of its academic ivory tower. Research personnel therefore had been required to work in factories or communes. Where this principle had been applied systematically and relatively rationally, a common practice had been to rotate one-third of the staff at a time out of an institute. Ideally, the scientists and technicians thus "sent down" were to apply their specialized knowledge to concrete problems they found at the production site. Upon returning to their institute, they would continue to do research on these problems. In practice, the intellectuals frequently had been assigned to menial jobs as a form of political reeducation, and some ended up spending long periods of time away from their research labs, employed in labor that made no use of their special training and skills.

All research had not ground to a halt, however, and one task after these practices were officially repudiated was to bring to light work that the scientists had managed to continue during the years of adversity. The science circular affirmed that research promising to be of scientific value would be supported with the necessary resources.

Abolition of academic titles during the Cultural Revolution meant that research personnel whose careers were then just starting were still in junior posts ten years later. According to the science circular, their qualifications were to be reassessed in view of their experience and achievements during that time, as were the credentials of still younger personnel whose education and professional training, curtailed by radical "reforms," did not equip them for research positions.

Furthermore, according to the science circular, "scientific research workers must be given no less than five-sixths of their work hours each week for professional work." At a stroke, the Central Committee thus disavowed what had been one of the radicals' fundamental beliefs, that scientific advance and technological progress would lead to "revision-ism" or "restoration of capitalism" unless made by "proletarian" scientists. Political activities aimed at imparting a proletarian "world outlook" to China's "bourgeois" scientists had been taking up as much as two-thirds of their time, according to critics of the Gang of Four and their ideas. Scientific theories and research had been reviewed for the taint of "metaphysical" and "idealistic" ideas—too often, apparently, with professionally unqualified political cadres deciding what was scientifically valid and what was not, and what could be published in scientific journals and taught in the schools and universities. The circular of September 18 declared science to be the preserve of specialists whose education, not their political outlook, determined their scientific capabilities. By this line of reasoning, it was not necessary to divert them from research in order to "remold" them into intellectuals who "served the proletariat." Rather, the more pressing problem, according to the science circular, was that "the number of scientists and technicians is still not large," and it was therefore imperative to maximize the research output of existing personnel.

These measures were already being enacted in some research institutes when the Central Committee issued its circular making them official policy for all scientific institutions. Grass-roots implementation of central policy was still not automatic, however, but depended on the situation in the individual institutes: the attitude of the Party committee secretary and the political acumen of the professional staff, as well as the balance of power between radicals and supporters of the new regime in the local Party and government organizations. Through the fall of 1977 and winter of 1978, as the political balance within local Party committees swung toward the new leadership, the provisions of the science circular were enforced. Where the political situation remained unresolved, resistance to the new policy continued to block implementa-tion of some of the circular's provisions, particularly the guarantee of five-sixths of the scientists' time for research.

Policymaking and Planning for Scientific Development

Apart from guidelines for local action to restore scientific institutions, the Central Committee's circular of September 18 also provided for resumption of science policymaking at the national level and for research planning at local and central levels.

The science circular officially reestablished the State Scientific and Technological Commission. This body had been the science policy-making organ of the State Council from 1958 until the Cultural Revolution, but it apparently had been abolished sometime after 1966. As central government structures began to be rebuilt in the early 1970s, a Science and Education Group seems to have briefly taken over the Commission's functions. This group, later described as a focal point of Gang of Four activities, disappeared, and the State Planning Commission appeared to inherit whatever science and technology planning functions remained in the central government. Reestablishment of the Scientific and Technological Commission in 1977 indicated both that the scope of these functions was expanding and that scientific research and long-range technological development policy had regained a status separate from (though coordinated with) economic planning. Indeed, the science circular declared that "no time should be lost in mapping out programs for the development of science and technology."

A process of "bottom up" planning was one aspect of this undertaking:

> All localities and departments should . . . draw up plans. . . . The State Planning Commission and the State Scientific and Technological Commission should coordinate and balance out the plans made by the various departments and localities and then work out a national program for the development of science and technology as a component part of the national economic plan.[9]

Local science plans would be oriented toward the short- and medium-term technological needs projected in economic development plans. Scientific advance and expansion of research capabilities per se, virtually neglected for ten years, would be planned at the national level. Centralized planning of scientific development and identification of research priorities got under way almost as soon as the Central Committee published its science circular.

In October, a planning conference attended by representatives of the Academy of Sciences, institutions of higher learning, and the scientific and technical departments of ministries and commissions under the State Council and those under provincial governments met to draft an "outline national program for developing the basic sciences." The long-term goal set in this draft plan was to reach "advanced world levels" in most of the basic scientific disciplines, identified as mathematics, physics, chemistry, astronomy, earth sciences, and biology, and to "rank among the leaders" in some branches of science by the end of the century. In effect, this plan revived China's program of theoretical research, which had been unsupported—indeed, was heavily criticized as having no economic value—since the start of the Cultural Revolution. Research in the basic sciences was now defined as "a continuous search for undiscovered natural phenomena" by experimentation, for the purpose of "understanding natural laws." To this end, the plan drafted in October specified that a "complete network" of modern laboratories "in a whole range of disciplines" should be established under the Academy of Sciences and in institutions of higher learning by 1985.

Following preparation of the "outline national program for the basic sciences," the Ministry of Education sponsored a conference in Peking to map out a similar program for applied science. Representatives of universities, colleges of science and engineering, and provincial education departments met to draft plans for the research to be carried out in institutions of higher learning. The outcome of their deliberations was a plan for the development of fourteen priority fields of applied science and technology: mechanical engineering, electrical engineering, civil engineering and architecture, water conservancy and hydraulic engineering, chemical engineering, radioelectronics, computer science, semiconductors, automation, mechanics, optics, environmental science, materials science, and engineering thermophysics. These applied sciences are to be distinguished from applied research: the plan drafted for these fourteen fields emphasized "long-term basic theoretical research" as the basis for the engineering disciplines.

This expansion of the universities' research role marked a departure from earlier patterns. Before the Cultural Revolution, most basic research had been conducted in the institutes of the Chinese Academy of Sciences. Since the Cultural Revolution, most research—especially in universities and colleges—had had to be closely related to specific practical applications. The new emphasis on university research was partly related to the training function. More important, unlike the specialized academy institutes, the university, as an institution in which work goes on in several disciplines, was seen to provide a unique opportunity for the cross-fertilization and mutual collaboration between specialists in different areas that, it was claimed, would lead to scientific advance and emergence of new fields of study.

As recommended in the Central Committee's science circular, the plans drafted for the basic and applied sciences focused on selected "points of emphasis." The strategy for scientific development adopted in these plans was to concentrate on making "breakthroughs" in particular fields of research, which were expected to trigger advance in related areas. By making suitable "overall arrangements," it was anticipated that the general level of science in China would rise in the wake of the first breakthroughs at critical points. This notion also underlay the draft Outline National Plan for the Development of Science and Technology 1978-1985, which was ultimately submitted to the National Science Conference in March 1978.

The National Science Plan for 1978-1985

The draft plan for scientific development listed eight such "comprehensive scientific and technical spheres." Concentrated effort in these areas was to "promote the high-speed development of science and technology as a whole and of the entire national economy," according to Minister of the Scientific and Technological Commission Fang Yi. The eight fields were agriculture, energy resources, materials, electronic computers, lasers, space science and technology, high energy physics, and genetic engineering. The draft plan covered research in a total of 27 "spheres" and specified 108 "key" projects, presumably in the eight priority areas. The draft was not published, but Fang's speech to the science conference indicated some of the items that would have priority in the national research program during the next eight years.

In *agriculture,* the goal continued to be mechanization and improvement of methods of intensive cultivation. Fang identified soil science, water control, and prevention of soil erosion and sandstorms as major research priorities. Both chemical fertilizers and biological nitrogen fixation were to be developed in order to raise agricultural productivity. Research leading to development of new seed strains and new crop varieties and continued work on pest control and prevention of plant diseases were other assignments handed to China's agricultural scientists.

Commenting on *energy,* Fang stated that "Every major breakthrough in science and technology concerning energy resources has led to a revolution in production techniques." He called for continuing China's program of exploration for oil and gas and for further development of "the theories of petroleum geology"; for "active research in basic theory, mining technology, technical equipment, and safety measures" related to mechanization of coal mining, and for research on coal gasification and liquefaction and on new uses of coal; for research on "key technical problems" involved in building large hydroelectric power stations and power grids and super-high voltage transmission lines; and for acceleration of China's research and development in atomic power and unconventional sources of energy.

Steel was given top priority in research on *materials*, with the focus on improving iron ore. According to Fang, other priorities in the metallurgical field were improvement of China's exploitation of its copper and aluminum resources, increasing production of titanium and vanadium, and improving techniques for refining certain nonferrous metals. Apart from developing specified "special purpose materials," the science plan called for "basic research on the science of materials, development of new experimental techniques and testing methods," and gradual development of a materials design capability.

Chinese scientists were already working on several of these problems, and their importance to China's economic development and technological modernization is obvious. The new science plan provided support for continuation and expansion of R&D in these areas after a decade in which basic research had been neglected.

Other parts of the science plan reflected the Chinese leadership's ambition to reach the forefronts of world science and technology. Here the object was not so much to find engineering solutions to immediate production problems as to develop scientific theory and create the research infrastructure for a modernized society and economy. Again, Chinese scientists had already scored achievements in most of these fields, but with support from the national government, this research could continue with the assurance of funds, equipment, and manpower.

Electronic computer science and technology were important, according to Fang Yi, because "The scientific and technical level, scope of production, and extent of application of computers has become a conspicuous hallmark of the level of modernization of a country." Computers were seen to have made a tremendous impact on research, production, and defense in the advanced industrial countries. The draft science plan therefore provided for basic research in computer science and related disciplines, applied mathematics, and work on peripheral equipment and software during the initial three years covered by the plan. This was to lead to a "comparatively advanced force in research in computer science" by 1985. A "fair-sized modern computer industry" would have developed by the same time. A first task was to "solve the scientific and technical problems in the industrial production of large-scale integrated circuits and to make a breakthrough in the technology of ultra-large scale IC's." Computer applications (at least in civilian industry), however, would still be limited to "a number of key enterprises."

Other fields were selected for special attention in the science plan because research in these areas was perceived to be advancing rapidly toward major discoveries—not just in China, but throughout the world. To establish itself as a significant scientific power, China would need to be in the phalanx of this advance. If this research was not immediately relevant or applicable to economic or defense needs, it was expected to have important fall-out for work in related scientific areas.

Laser science and technology, said Fang Yi, "is one of the most active branches of science and technology which began to develop in the 1960s. Its emergence, which marked a new stage in man's control and utilization of light waves, has effectively promoted the development of physics, chemistry, and biology." Work in laser physics, laser spectroscopy, and nonlinear optics during the first three years of the science plan would lay the basis for developing new types of laser devices, new wave-lengths, and new means of generating laser beams. The experimental applications Fang foresaw for this research included optical communications, isotope separation, and laser-induced nuclear fusion.

Similarly, *space science and technology,* according to Fang, "is bringing about tremendous changes in earth science, astronomy, and other disciplines." A program of research in "the basic theory of space science" and development of satellite exploration, skylabs, and space probes would find applications in meteorology, cartography, resource survey, environmental monitoring, and communications transmission and broadcasting.

High energy physics and genetic engineering apparently were selected as priority areas in the new science plan because they were considered especially dynamic fields of research. "At present," said Fang Yi, new discoveries are making high energy physics "one of the most active frontline branches of study in the development of natural science of our time." Construction of a high energy physics research center equipped with a proton accelerator of 30 to 50 billion electron volts was a "key project" for the coming five years; construction of a larger accelerator was planned for the following five-year period.

Genetic engineering was described by Fang as "fast developing and highly explorative." Having developed only in the past decade, this field had "a rather weak foundation" in China. As a tool for basic research in molecular biology, molecular genetics, and cell biology, it was to be strengthened by coordinating basic research in the relevant disciplines. Specific applications mentioned by Fang were pharmaceuticals and development of new nitrogen-fixing crops.

In focusing on specific scientific disciplines and fields, the planners did not intend that China should specialize in these areas alone. On the contrary, "in the next eight years, we must create a nationwide scientific and technological research system that covers all branches of study," Fang declared at the National Science Conference. Having identified the fields in which the planners felt China had special strength, Li Chang, a vice-president of the Academy of Sciences, predicted that China would soon reach "advanced world levels" in mathematics, theoretical physics, theoretical chemistry, and "other branches of science." The planners did not hesitate to direct that "particular attention" also be paid to "strengthening research in those disciplines where the work has been weak."

To realize the goal of "approaching or reaching advanced world levels" in the designated fields of science and technology, new research facilities were to be established and additional scientific manpower would be trained, according to Fang's report on the draft national science plan. The strategy again was to concentrate initially on building up certain key institutions. These were expected to produce the research breakthroughs and the corps of highly trained professionals that would sustain China's overall scientific and technological advance.

Accordingly, the plan for 1978-1985 provided for both "a number of up-to-date centers for scientific experiment" and a "nationwide system of scientific and technological research," in Fang's words. The "key scientific research institutions" would either be under the Academy of Sciences or in the State Council's departments and ministries or at the major universities and colleges; that is, they would be national institutions under the jurisdiction of the central government. The Academy of Sciences was to be the "comprehensive national center for research in natural science," with primary responsibility for basic research in China. It was to be the pacesetter, producing the breakthroughs that would "raise the standards" of all scientific work in

China. However, the academy's work would not be entirely theoretical. It was also directed to apply "new theories in the basic branches of science" to "vital areas of the national economy," and it would thus be responsible for the development of the most advanced technologies in China.

"A number of modernized scientific experiment bases," apparently separate from the research institutes, were also to be set up for work in high energy physics, heavy ion physics, controlled thermonuclear reaction, semiconductor science, solid state physics, molecular biology, and astrophysics under terms of the national science plan. Covering some of the eight priority "spheres" in the plan, these centers would facilitate interdisciplinary research as well as permit joint use of equipment in the most capital-intensive fields of research by scientists from different institutions.

The imposing task of planning, managing, and coordinating research in institutions under various branches of the central government was made even more daunting by the continued existence of a research network under provincial governments. The provincial research system had been augmented during the previous decade by transferring former academy institutes to the authorities where they were located physically. The new policy reversed this trend. However, local authorities were still expected to maintain research facilities.

Agricultural research institutions at the county level were confirmed in the science plan as the "nuclei" of networks of agro-technical experiment stations extending through rural communes, production brigades, and production teams. The plan also directed large enterprises to maintain research facilities and recommended that medium and small factories do so as well, pooling their resources where necessary.

It was not clear how these local institutions were to be coordinated with national research institutes. Institutions at an intermediate level— local branches of the Academy of Sciences and provincial science academies—were to be set up only "if it is at all possible . . . where they are needed," according to Fang Yi, though a number of provinces had already announced plans to reactivate their science academies.[10] In short, scientific advance in China would be concentrated in the key institutions at the national level.

Manpower and Education

Eight hundred thousand was the number of "professional research workers" targeted for 1985 in the national science plan. After years of egalitarianism in education, when expertise and professionalism were ideologically suspect, the task of training a "core force of scientific workers and top-notch scientists" required revamping the entire education system and reinstituting the notion of "key," or elite, universities.

The Cultural Revolution had closed the doors of institutions of higher learning. They reopened as essentially vocational institutions. Students were nominated by their work units for admission and were expected to acquire skills that would be applicable to their jobs. University faculty included "workers, peasants, and soldiers," who imparted both technical knowledge acquired on the job and the proletarian viewpoint. The radicals considered students in the key universities to be an "intellectual aristocracy," a bourgeois anomaly in China's socialist society, and had tried to bring elite institutions level with ordinary schools. They seem to have been rather successful in this, judging by the impressions of foreign visitors to Chinese universities in the mid-1970s. Once political change had led to changes in policy, the Gang of Four was castigated for having caused the "loss of an entire generation" of Chinese scientists by wrecking the higher education system in China.

By the end of 1977, the Chinese University of Science and Technology, the training arm of the Academy of Sciences, had been reconstituted, and the major universities had announced that they were resuming postgraduate education. Eighty-eight institutions were designated "key universities," to which students with the highest academic qualifications were admitted. Admission to higher education and to postgraduate research training programs was based on the results of competitive entrance examinations, held throughout China in December. Applicants' political credentials were secondary to their academic performance as criteria for admission, and the period of manual labor formerly prerequisite to university entrance was no longer required.

Outlook for the New Science Policy

The National Science Conference set the tone for China's new science policy. How long this policy will be in effect depends on politics and on whether the leaders responsible for the new policy remain in power; on the scientists and on whether they can meet the research goals and targets for scientific development and its military posture; and on whether the new policy does, in fact, deliver the "four modernizations."

It is possible to read nuances of disagreement in the speeches of individual political leaders at the National Science Conference. However, the leaders must hang together on their policy for scientific and technological development if they are not to hang separately, for, as a body, they base their claim to political legitimacy on the alleged failure of previous policies to result in such development. Their own tenure at the head of the Communist Party and the government of China may depend to a large extent on the success of the new policy for science and technology.

All indications are that the scientists welcome the new policies. Centralized planning and government control of research are not alien to Chinese scientists and are not regarded as, in principle, curtailing academic freedom. On the contrary, the stability provided by a national plan for science and the assurance of support for research that is included in the plan are associated with periods of rapid scientific development in China. Thus it is emphasized that the "main tasks" in the first plan for scientific and technological development, covering 1956-1967, were completed five years ahead of schedule—evidence of the beneficial effects of planning, rather than a reflection of inadequate planning methodologies. A second plan came into effect in 1963, its targets revised to reflect the loss of Soviet scientific and technical assistance in 1960. After 1966, there seems to have been no overall science plan in effect, except for a number of strategic or priority areas.

Scientists had a major role in drawing up the first plan (in consultation with the Soviet Academy of Sciences), and they seem to have had an equally important part in preparing the plan for 1978-1985. Not only did they participate directly in planning, but the strategy of scientific and technological development being implemented in the plan would have required the government planners to defer to the professionals' opinions on which were the most promising fields of research and what goals were within their capability to reach by 1985.

The Chinese scientists' concern to restore basic research and improve the training of the brightest students is understandable in view of what happened during the Cultural Revolution and later at the instigation of the political and ideological radicals. Equally understandable is the current concern of China's political leaders to modernize the country's economy and its military forces after ten years of technological stagnation. Against the background of recent experience, it is not surprising to find that concern for the links between research and production is almost entirely absent from public discussion in China of the new science policies and plans. But if anything is to be learned from China's earlier experience, it is that these links cannot be neglected. The science policy decisions made in 1977 and 1978 in what was still a highly charged political atmosphere will affect the development of science and technology in China, and it is not yet clear whether the outcome will be to restore the old system, accepting its costs as well as its benefits, or to tackle its shortcomings in new ways.

Notes

1. Fang Yi, report on science and education to the seventh session of the Standing Committee, Fourth National Committee, Chinese People's Political Consultative Conference, December 27, 1977. New China News Agency (NCNA) summary in English, Peking broadcast, December 29, 1977; text in Foreign Broadcast Information Service (FBIS), December 30, 1977, pp. E3-11 (this quote from page E4). The "four modernizations" are also sometimes referred to as agriculture, industry, and national defense science and technology.

2. Originally published in *People's Literature*, no. 9 (1977); republished in *People's Daily*, September 21, 1977.

3. Some sectors of the industrial system in China seem to have been much more innovative than others. See Hans Heymann, *China's Approach to Technology Acquisition* (Santa Monica, Calif.: RAND Corporation, 1975).

4. Although the P.R.C. is now in its fifth plan period, only the First Five-Year Plan has been published. Various preliminary outlines and discussions of the Second Five-Year Plan were made public.

5. Text of the Central Committee's Science Circular is translated in *Peking Review*, no. 40 (September 30, 1977), pp. 6-11 (this quote p. 9).

6. Ibid., p. 9.

7. Ibid., p. 9.

8. Ibid., p. 10.

9. Ibid., p. 10.

10. Fang Yi, report to the National Science Conference, March 18, 1978. NCNA abridgement in English, Peking broadcast, March 28, 1978; in FBIS, March 29, 1978, pp. E1-22 (this quote p. E15).

Bibliography

For extensive reference to further reading, see:

Annotated Bibliography on Science and Technology in China. U.S. House of Representatives, Committee on Science and Technology. Washington, D.C.: U.S. Government Printing Office, 1976.

Committee on Scholarly Communication with the People's Republic of China. *China Exchange Newsletter.* Washington, D.C.: 1973-present (bimonthly).

Dean, Genevieve C. *Science and Technology in the Development of Modern China, An Annotated Bibliography.* London: Mansell, 1974.

A thorough analysis of Chinese science policy and its social, political, and economic dimensions is found in:

Suttmeier, Richard P. *Research and Revolution: Science Policy and Societal Change in China.* Lexington, Mass.: D.C. Heath and Company, 1974.

A more recent perspective is provided in:

Science and Technology in the People's Republic of China. Paris: Organisation for Economic Co-operation and Development, 1977.

Periodic reviews of science policy appear in:

Fingar, Thomas and Genevieve Dean. *Developments in PRC Science and Technology Policy.* Stanford, Calif.: Stanford University, United States–China Relations Program (quarterly).

U.S. Congress, Joint Economic Committee. *An Economic Profile of Mainland China.* New York: Praeger, 1968 (Leo A. Orleans, "Research and Development in Communist China: Mood, Management and Measurement," pp. 549-578).

U.S. Congress, Joint Economic Committee. *People's Republic of China: An Economic Assessment.* Washington, D.C.: U.S. Government Printing Office, 1972 (Leo A. Orleans, "China's Science and Technology: Continuity and Innovation," pp. 185-219).

8
Social Affairs

Richard Curt Kraus

Both Chinese and Western analysts agree that tensions within the structure of pre-Liberation Chinese society contributed to the victory of the Communist Party in 1949, although there is sharp debate about the relative importance of such contradictions vis-à-vis other factors. Few, however, would dispute the assertion that tensions generated by the basic cleavages that divide the Chinese people provided at least the context, and perhaps the fuel, for the revolutionary struggle that led to the establishment of the People's Republic.

This chapter will review several of these contradictions a generation after Liberation in order to assess their role in helping China's leaders to achieve their stated goal of "continuing the revolution under the dictatorship of the proletariat." Seven contradictions will be considered here, by no means an exhaustive list: city and countryside, rich and poor, leaders and followers, Han and minority nationalities, male and female, old and young, and Chinese and foreign. To view Chinese society as a complex set of opposite tendencies is to emphasize the structural dimensions shared by China with other societies. To examine the ways in which these contradictions have been resolved is to draw attention to features that are more distinctively Chinese.

One of the most characteristic aspects of contemporary China is the attention paid to social tensions as forces that both propel and impede social change. The notion that the revolution should somehow have put an end to such tensions is repudiated in Peking as Soviet-style revisionism.

> Any kind of world, and of course class society in particular, teems with contradictions. Some say that there are contradictions to be "found" in socialist society, but I think this is a wrong way of putting it. The point is

not that there are contradictions to be found, but that it teems with contradictions (Mao, 1977, p. 516).

In accordance with Mao's assertion that socialist China "teems with contradictions," the Communist Party has assigned high priority to investigating and analyzing these tensions so as to fashion efficient policies for the revolutionary transformation of society. The purpose of this chapter is not to replicate these analyses (for which interested readers should consult the English-language weekly, *Peking Review*), but to examine some of the constraints that these contradictory relationships have placed upon the capacity of China's leaders to direct social change.

City and Countryside

The conventional wisdom about rural-urban relations in Third World nations is that millions of peasants migrate to squalid new shantytowns in a rapid and uncontrollable process of urbanization. That this phenomenon is highly visible in so much of Asia, Africa, and Latin America makes its absence in China particularly noteworthy. Although precise statistics are not available, the ratio of rural residents to city-dwellers in China is approximately eight to two. This is the same ratio that existed in 1949, despite an intervening three decades of intense economic construction.

The contradiction between city and countryside involves more than population balance. Industrialization also typically engenders a growing material and cultural gap between urban and rural areas; Marx's observation of this process in nineteenth-century Europe underlay his insistence that a Communist society would break down the urban-rural distinction. The Chinese have certainly not accomplished this, although they retain Marx's goal and have implemented some unorthodox measures in its pursuit. Although urban residents enjoy higher incomes, more sophisticated culture, and more elaborate social services than do rural Chinese, the political cultivation of rural interests has apparently prevented these gaps from increasing as they have in most Third World societies.

There has been a concentrated effort, especially since the middle 1960s, to improve the conditions of rural life. Special attention has been paid to the expansion of primary and secondary education in the countryside (Seybolt 1973), and to the introduction of new facilities and programs for health care (Sidel 1973). In the latter case, choices have been made to create more rural clinics (instead of urban medical centers), to train more paramedical personnel ("barefoot" doctors instead of highly educated M.D.'s), and to emphasize public health (preventive medicine instead of the treatment of comparatively exotic diseases). Nonetheless, urban services remain superior, although phenomena like the shortage of new investment in housing are indicative of the limits to the urban advantage.

More striking, perhaps, are measures to control the flow of population between city and countryside. The migration of peasants into urban areas had been regulated by the early 1960s, primarily through the strict use of ration cards for a few necessities (grain, cotton, cooking oil). Within a few years a massive program was instituted to resettle new graduates of urban high schools in agricultural areas (Bernstein 1977). Millions of persons have now been relocated in this "down to the villages" policy, often in distant provinces, but more commonly near their cities of origin. As a consequence of these policies, the urban population, depleted of many of its most fertile members, has become stable and a potential crisis of urban unemployment has been defused.

A second significant consequence of these policies has been to introduce into many of China's villages a group of sophisticated and ambitious young people who may add a new force for the transformation of the countryside. To be sure, the skills of these young urbanites are cultural, rather than agricultural, and many of them have great difficulty in adapting to strenuous peasant labor. There is little doubt that the program is unpopular with many of its participants, who often find themselves poorly integrated into village life. But China's leaders continue to support this program both because of demographic pressure in the cities, and in the hope that dissatisfaction will inspire the young people to work to improve the quality of rural life. Another benefit is that most older urban residents now have relatives or friends in the countryside and thus may identify more strongly than before with rural problems.

Yet another important aspect of rural-urban relations is the emphasis upon the construction of rural industries (Sigurdson 1977). Small in scale, these factories usually either manufacture products for agricultural use (machinery, cement, energy), or they turn agricultural produce into finished commodities (fruit preserves, vegetable oil, flour). They take advantage of the seasonality of the rural work force, often ceasing production during busy harvest periods. Although rural industrialization is viewed by China's leaders as an important step in narrowing the gap between city and village, it does not mean the end of state investment in large-scale urban industrial enterprises. In fact, many of the rural industries are constructed with minimal reliance upon state aid.

Self-reliance has been a key concept in China's rural strategy. Since 1964 the entire nation has been urged to study and emulate the experience of one model unit, the Tachai production brigade of Shansi. Tachai was an area of notorious poverty prior to Liberation, and although it remains poorly endowed in resources, the rise in its standard of living has been noteworthy. Tachai's success has been credited to the decentralization that accompanies self-reliance. Through disciplined political organization and determination, the peasants of Tachai were able to tap their meager resources and abundant enthusiasm to reconstruct their community, often moving whole hills to create new terraced fields. Tachai's former Party secretary, Ch'en Yung-kuei, has become a deputy prime minister, and thousands of visitors from the entire nation pass through the village in order to study its methods.

Similar celebrity is accorded China's national model industrial unit, the Tach'ing oil field and petrochemical complex in Manchuria. Again, an important aspect of the model is self-reliance, here manifest most vividly in the unit's near self-sufficiency in food production. The vast territory of an oil field makes this more practicable than it would be in an urban industrial setting, of course, but perhaps subtly underscores the primacy of agriculture over industry in China's economic priorities.

The decentralization of self-reliance bears an additional advantage beyond the mobilization of local resources; China's national transportation system is still relatively weak, and decentralized production reduces the burdens placed upon it.

The present rural bias in Chinese social policy has its immediate origins in the Great Leap Forward of 1958. Much maligned in the West as an utter failure, the significance of this campaign was not that it achieved its goals (which it did not), but that it marked the rejection of the Soviet model for industrialization, which had prevailed since Liberation; Soviet practice centered upon the creation of large, capital-intensive industries in urban areas, whence benefits were to trickle down eventually to the countryside. Mao and his associates in the Communist Party argued that the Soviet approach was inappropriate for Chinese conditions. They regarded it as excessively centralized (thus stifling local initiative and participation) and charged that it took resources for which there was more immediate need in agriculture. They may also have found it galling to rely upon a small army of Soviet technical experts in shaping China's future. The policies pursued since the middle of the 1960s, while certainly less flamboyant than the Great Leap Forward's heaven-storming attempt to transform China overnight, have more effectively pursued its themes. The Chinese leadership recognizes the centrality of agriculture to the entire economy, with the corollary that industry must be designed to serve agricultural needs. They also realize that China's shortage of capital is balanced by an abundance of labor, which can be mobilized to increase production through a combination of political appeals and decentralized, yet disciplined organization.

The roots of these policies toward city and countryside must also be traced to the character of the Chinese revolution. In the 1920s, the young intellectuals who led the Communist Party looked to the small urban proletariat as the motive force for the struggle against capitalists, landlords, and imperialists. But this urban strategy was quickly defeated, and the Party spent the years between 1927 and 1949 among the peasantry, first in Kiangsi, and then in North China, where thousands of new cadres of peasant origin were recruited. The cities that they entered at Liberation seemed like foreign territory to many of the cadres, as distinguished by foreign and capitalist influence as by proletarian purity. A certain ambiguity toward urban China has pervaded the attitudes of the revolutionary generation of Communist leaders, thus encouraging a willingness to experiment in radical ways with the conventional relationship between city and countryside.

Rich and Poor

Rich and poor may not be the best terms by which to characterize the relationship between privileged and disadvantaged economic groups in contemporary China. Although China is certainly a poor country, the extremes of wealth and poverty of the pre-Liberation era have been vastly reduced.

Restrictions upon individual wealth have been straightforward. Liberation was accompanied by a movement for land reform, a sometimes violent process that heightened consciousness of rural class relationships while it destroyed old wealth by confiscating and redistributing the property of landlords and rich peasants (Hinton 1968). The collectivization of agriculture in 1955-1956 assured that new fortunes could not be fashioned from the accumulation of land. Private property in the countryside has since been limited to such items as houses (for use, not speculation), trees, and small tools. Private capital in urban areas was severely limited with the socialization of most industry in 1956. Although individual capitalists were issued stock that continued to bear interest in the next decade, the autonomy of capitalist wealth was destroyed.

Restrictions upon poverty have been less direct, although they have been closely associated with the assault upon private property. The limitation of landlord and capitalist power removed a major impediment to the implementation of social reforms designed to broaden access to education and health care facilities. A gradual decrease in the cost of many consumer items along with a general avoidance of inflation in the economy have served the interests of the poor, as have the abolition of widespread prostitution, drug addiction, and gambling. An emphasis upon collective, rather than merely individual incentives in agriculture has helped the rural poor.

Although the tendency toward egalitarianism in the People's Republic is quite distinct in policies concerning private wealth and social welfare, it is less evident in the realm of personal income. Surprisingly large income differentials are justified on the grounds that unequal work should be rewarded by unequal pay. Thus a contradiction of interests between economically privileged and disadvantaged groups persists in China, albeit primarily within the narrow context of personal income.

Precise information about incomes is unavailable, but the general pattern of distribution is known (Whyte 1975). The highest incomes go to senior officials; the top hundred bureaucrats earn 400 jen-min-pi ($210) per month. Another few thousand officials earn 300 jen-min-pi, which is much greater than the 60 jen-min-pi that go to a typical industrial worker (Hoffman 1977). A 1977 wage increase for the lowest paid workers may diminish this gap, but possibly at the expense of adding to the approximately two-to-one ratio between all urban incomes and those received by peasants.

The Chinese bureaucracy is an elaborate civil service system, with formal salary steps (Barnett 1967). The system of salary grades was introduced in 1956, at the height of Soviet influence, and the great distance that separates Party and state leaders from petty officials has been a source of friction. Minor reforms have lowered the highest salaries, but no one has seriously attempted to replace this system with a more egalitarian one.

Industrial workers in state enterprises are also ranked according to a formal wage scale, although it has fewer gradations and smaller income differentials than the scale for bureaucrats. Somewhat higher wages exist for industrial technicians and engineers, although the cleavage that separates them from ordinary workers is not nearly so great as the internal rift that divides the workers into two categories, temporary and permanent. The tasks performed by "temporary" workers, whose transitory status is often only nominal, are similar to those of the permanent work force. Although the wages of temporary workers are comparable, they are not included in the system of welfare benefits (including pensions, sick leave, and health insurance) that protects their permanent co-workers (White 1976). The differential treatment accorded these two categories of workers has inspired political unrest, especially during the Cultural Revolution of 1965-1969. The explosiveness of the issue is contained, perhaps, by the fact that the living standard of temporary workers is generally quite superior to that of the peasants in the villages from which most of them have been drawn.

Peasant incomes are somewhat less formally stratified than those of urban cadres and workers. The income of peasant families combines a share of their production unit's collective harvest with private earnings from small gardens allocated to each family and from subsidiary economic activities, like the raising of pigs and the weaving of baskets (Parish 1975). Incomes vary according to such factors as strength and agricultural skills, which result in more work points and a larger share of the community harvest. But also critical is the ratio of able-bodied workers to nonworking dependents. A family with too many small children, or with aged parents, or in which the father or mother has been disabled is not apt to be able to afford such rural status symbols as bicycles, transistor radios, watches, and sewing machines.

Despite these bases for income differentiation, there is greater economic homogeneity within peasant communities than before Liberation. Rural policies of self-reliance, however, have the side effect of permitting increasing distinctions among production units: places with resources that can easily be mobilized have a clear advantage. Villages in areas that are richly endowed with water, for instance, can attain higher productivity through irrigation than can mountainous communities. And villages near major cities enjoy easy access to lucrative markets for their produce, often providing a standard of living comparable to that of urban workers.

Economic differences between such groups as officials, workers, and peasants and within each group are modest by comparison either with China before Liberation, or with most other Third World societies today, primarily because of the elimination of individual sources of wealth. But even the modest distinctions that remain can arouse envy and resentment and can inspire political activity to redress perceived inequities. One important mechanism for containing such tension is the institutionalized memory of past class position. Although individual wealth and poverty have been severely restricted, those who were formerly landowners, rich peasants, and capitalists continue to be stigmatized as corrupting influences. And former impoverished peasants today enjoy a high political status regardless of their actual economic situation. China's leaders have encouraged this historical consciousness as a means of protecting the gains of the revolution, although they are also aware of its value in confusing perceptions of more recent inequalities (Kraus 1977).

Leaders and Followers

Tension between persons with and without authority is common in any complex society. In the absence of private property, however, social distinctions based upon political power assume a specially prominent role. In part this is because of the weakness of alternative, market-based power centers in socialist society. The lack of private wealth also encourages a distribution of material comforts (housing, servants, use of automobiles) that honors bureaucratic position.

China is unique among socialist societies in the seriousness with which the contradiction between leaders and followers has been treated. While no one has argued that China can dispense with distinctions in authority, there is a widespread concern that these distinctions not become solidified into a new and exploitative class structure. There has been often bitter debate, however, about how best to treat this contradiction. Four trends may be distinguished in its resolution. First is a series of measures to disperse authority within society so as to blur the distinction between leaders and followers. At a minimum, officials are expected to heed what the Chinese call the "mass line," which refers to the solicitation of public opinion in both the formulation and implementation of policy. More ambitious are frequent campaigns to encourage the direct participation of workers and peasants in the management of their production units. Workers, managers, and technicians have been combined into administrative committees in

Chinese factories, while in the countryside peasants regularly elect their basic-level leadership.

A second approach to the tension between leaders and followers requires managers to experience the conditions under which their subordinates work. Its gentlest manifestation is the extended first-hand investigation of local conditions by high-level cadres, known as "squatting at point." More rigorous is the system of "May Seventh cadre schools"—farms established a decade ago by various bureaucratic units to which their personnel are sent regularly to experience physical labor (Chen 1973). These and other measures are intended to encourage humility toward the masses and to break down rigidly bureaucratic ways of solving practical problems. Rural cadres have been urged in recent years to adopt the model of Tachai, where from one hundred to three hundred days of physical labor (varying according to position) are required annually.

A third way of limiting bureaucratic abuse is to encourage criticism of its more serious manifestations. This can include the often mild regimen of mutual criticism and self-criticism that has been formalized within Chinese organizations (Whyte 1974). Such criticism also incorporates the more ambitious process of "open-door rectification," by which the shortcomings of Party members are discussed by non-Party citizens. Although many officials seek to limit this practice, they find it preferable to the most extreme institution for limiting their authority: cultural revolution.

Although it has been invoked only once in the history of the People's Republic, the Cultural Revolution of 1965-1969 was the most radical assault to date upon bureaucratic privilege and inertia. By mobilizing a coalition of students, activist workers, and junior officials, Mao Tse-tung and his allies in the Party leadership were able to remove large numbers of conservative officials from office, including the head of state, Liu Shao-ch'i. Although the Cultural Revolution was more complex than a mere bureaucratic reform, it did unleash a series of anti-bureaucratic policies. Many officials regard the Cultural Revolution as a period of harmful social disruption, an analysis that is increasingly common since the death of Mao Tse-tung in 1976. Although no leader in China has publicly rejected the legitimacy of the Cultural Revolution, nonetheless, any threat to revive this movement is not apt to be warmly received by most senior officials.

More palatable to these leaders is the fourth approach to the contradiction between the powerful and the weak: programs to rejuvenate the leadership continuously by encouraging upward mobility into its ranks from the lower strata of society. The leaders' memories of their own often humble origins has no doubt facilitated the cooption of thousands of model peasants, workers, and soldiers into leadership positions.

Considerably more controversial, however, have been educational reforms intended to prepare peasants and workers for leadership status. Cultural Revolution reforms in higher education were of two sorts. In one, new institutions were created that were directly attached to production units, with which they maintained close ties. The other reform was to abolish entrance examinations for higher education, substituting a requirement of two years of manual labor for eligibility for admission. Entrance examinations have now been restored because of a concern on the part of some about educational quality and also because of the interest of high officials in a system that stresses prior academic achievement for university admission. In a system emphasizing academic achievement, the children of officials are apt to be favored. Without personal wealth to pass on to their offspring, access to higher education has become a major device by which the powerful can assure their children a comfortable position in society.

There have been significant variations in the intensity with which China's leaders have attempted to resolve this contradiction, and it is difficult to measure the success of the programs implemented. One must balance the remarkably spartan life-style of most Chinese officials against the common observation of visitors to China that great deference is normally accorded persons of authority. This may indicate that Mao was correct in arguing that the battle against bureaucratic abuse must be constantly fought. But such victories as have been won (and one must count mere recognition of the contradiction as a major victory) have relied heavily upon the support of Mao and other radicals of the oldest generation of revolutionaries within the Chinese leadership. Other leaders have been less willing to oppose their own narrow class interests as bureaucrats, perhaps feeling that mass criticism is incompatible with the firm authority that may be necessary to make and execute policy in a rapidly changing society. After the death of Mao and the purge of his most radical associates, it remains to be seen whether the weak will be able to find new leaders willing to build their own power by attacking the bureaucracy.

Han Chinese and the Minority Nationalities

China is not an ethnically homogeneous society, although the dominant group of Han Chinese constitute 94 percent of the population. The remaining 6 percent are divided among at least fifty-four separate nationalities. There is enormous diversity among these minority nationalities, which range in size from the nearly 8 million Chuang of Kwangsi to the 600 Holchih of Heilungkiang, and vary in cultural sophistication from the large Korean minority in Kirin to the primitive Wa of Yunnan, who until recently believed "that their crops would not grow unless fertilized each year with a fresh Han head" (Dreyer 1976, p. 131).

For all of their mutual differences, three characteristics tend to place the minorities in opposition to the Han majority. First is the fact that this 6 percent of the population occupies between 50 and 60 percent of China's territory, with a much lower population density than the intensively settled Han regions. Although many minority areas are ruggedly mountainous (Tibet, Tsinghai) or desert (Sinkiang), other regions (Mongolia, Manchuria, and the southwestern provinces) are capable of sustaining large numbers of Han immigrants. In addition, these areas are often rich in natural resources, most of which have yet to be exploited.

Minority nationalities are also spread along China's borders. Indeed, none of the country's borders was heavily populated by Han Chinese prior to this century. This gives China's leaders a great strategic interest in the territories occupied by the minorities; concern for their loyalty is enhanced by the fact that several of these peoples are distributed on both sides of the borders with Burma, Outer Mongolia, and the Soviet Union.

Finally, memories of past relationships between Han and minorities are often tinged with bitterness. Manchus and Mongols have both conquered and ruled China in past dynasties, and Han contact with Tibetans and Muslims (Hui) has often been on the battlefield. Similarly, many of the more primitive groups of southwest China are mindful of the long process by which Han settlers have occupied rich agricultural land, forcing minority peoples to retreat to mountainous areas.

In past dynasties, the Han viewed minority nationalities as "barbarians," to be controlled through a combination of conquest and assimilation. Cultural arrogance pervaded imperial Chinese policies, although it did not aim at the physical destruction of minority peoples, which has been common in the West. One's status as a Han was essentially a matter of self-identification. Those barbarians who would acknowledge the brilliance of Han culture and would adopt Han ways could eventually gain acceptance into the majority. Although this policy forced the repudiation of minority cultures, it provided a source

Map 10   China's Minority Nationalities

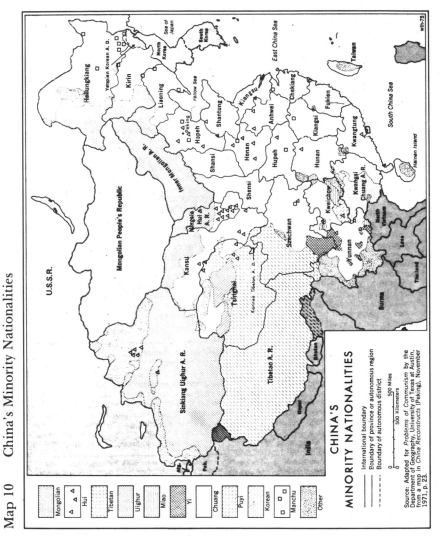

CHINA'S MINORITY NATIONALITIES

——— International boundary
——— Boundary of province or autonomous region
- - - Boundary of autonomous district

Source: Adapted for *Problems of Communism* by the
Department of Geography, University of Texas at Austin,
from a map in *China Reconstructs* (Peking), November
1971, p. 23.

Mongolian
Hui
Tibetan
Uighur
Miao
Yi
Chuang
Puyi
Korean
Manchu
Other

0   500 Miles
0   500 Kilometers

From *Problems of Communism*, Sept.–Oct. 1975: *Not* copyrighted.

of continuous regeneration for an expanding Han society.

China's present leaders have endeavored to deal with the traditional sources of tension between Han and minority nationalities by encouraging new attitudes by the Han majority. Because the contemptuous perception of the minorities as uncivilized wards of a greater Han culture is so deeply rooted, there has been a prolonged attack upon Han chauvinism. While this has not meant that minority interests typically prevail when they are in conflict with Han policies, it has assured that the minorities are at least treated seriously. Many reforms have been symbolic, like the restoration of the original Uighur name for Sinkiang's capital of Urumchi, in place of an earlier Han designation. New concern has been shown for the dietary habits of the large Muslim minority in Ningsia and Kansu, and occasions of national celebration are now regularly marked by the colorful costumes and music of the national minorities.

Accompanying these efforts to establish at least a formal equality among nationalities have been reforms in the autonomy enjoyed by the minorities to protect their language and culture. Five of China's provincial level units—Kwangsi, Tibet, Inner Mongolia, Sinkiang, and Ningsia—are known as "autonomous regions," and smaller units have been established within predominantly Han provinces to recognize the special characteristics of local minorities. The Communist Party certainly does not regard such autonomy as license to resist centrally determined policies, but it does serve as a mechanism by which local languages can be used in education and in the public media, and it is also a vehicle for the cultivation of minority officials and Communist Party members. At the same time, however, anti-Han chauvinism by minorities resentful of Han domination is vigorously criticized.

Despite policies of equal treatment for all ethnic groups, the long-term resolution of this contradiction seems to lie in assimilation. Extremely limited data make it difficult to assess the pace of this process, which has certainly varied among nationalities. The Mongols face strong pressures for assimilation because of the large-scale migration of Han Chinese into Inner Mongolia, where the majority of the populace is now Han. The Tibetans, however, have offered military resistance to the People's Liberation Army, and are poorly represented in Chinese society at large, a function of Tibet's geographical isolation and of its independent cultural tradition. Another extreme is represented by Kwangsi's Chuang population, which has long been sinicized in culture and language; one Chuang, Wei Kuo-ch'ing, enjoys the distinction of serving as Communist Party secretary for the predominantly Han province of Kwangtung. Indeed, at the very top of China's political system, two minority leaders serve as members or alternate members of the Political Bureau of the Party's Central Committee: Wei Kuo-ch'ing and Ulanfu (a Mongol). (A third, Saifudin, a Uighur, was recently removed from the leadership positions he had held for many years.) There are only twenty-six leaders at this high level, so minorities have been represented twice as strongly as their proportion of the national population should warrant. This does not, however, compensate for underrepresentation at middle and lower levels of authority in the political system.

The question of assimilation should perhaps be placed in a broader context. While population movements and the expansion of national communications and transportation facilities do increase pressure for the sinification of minority nationalities, these same trends strengthen the homogeneity of the Han majority as well. In the past, for instance, Han unity has rested upon a common written language, as the various dialects of the Chinese language are often mutually unintelligible. Vastly increased literacy since Liberation has incorporated many peasant villages more tightly into a national community, and the spread of Mandarin among younger Han Chinese of all native dialects has had a similar effect.

The relationship between Han and other nationalities is also heavily influenced by policies toward some of the other contradictions in Chinese society. One approach to the recruitment of minority cadres, for instance, has been to select persons who have been socially prominent in the past within their ethnic communities. When national policies toward class demand that leading roles be played by the lower strata, however, the authority of minority cadres from upper class backgrounds is undermined (Chang 1966). Similarly, when national policy supports decentralization most strongly, Han-minority friction is apt to be minimized by the encouragement of self-reliance for minority communities, while trends toward the reaffirmation of central power are likely to enlarge the scope of contact (and conflict) among ethnic groups.

Male and Female

China is a society in which millions of persons bear vivid memories (and frequently scars) of bound feet, female infanticide, concubinage, prostitution, and widespread female illiteracy. There is no doubt that enormous progress has been made since Liberation in redressing the past imbalance between the sexes in Chinese society. The 1950 Marriage Law, which for the first time established the legal rights of women to property ownership, divorce, and free choice in marriage, was especially significant in weakening some of the ancient institutional bases of male supremacy (Maijer 1971).

While changes in the position of women may be among the most radical innovations of the Chinese revolution, it is apparent that the pace of feminist advance has slowed since Liberation. One index of this is the extent of female representation at the upper levels of the Communist Party (Sheridan 1976). At present Ch'en Mu-hua is the only woman among the twenty-six full and alternate members of the Central Committee's Political Bureau. And the Ninth (1969), Tenth (1973), and Eleventh (1977) Central Committees had only 8.2 percent, 12.9 percent, and 8.8 percent female participation, respectively, among full and alternate members. To be sure, these rates of participation compare favorably to the 3.6 percent female membership in the 1975 U.S. Congress, or with the absence of women from the top leadership of the largest American corporations. Yet the efforts of the Chinese women's movement to deal with the contradiction between the sexes have not achieved equity.

Early successes in limiting the oppression of women were enhanced by a broad base of support for measures to undermine the traditional lineage system of rural China. Prior to Liberation, rural Chinese society was structured in large measure by powerful kinship groupings, organized around descent from a common male ancestor and maintained by filial attitudes and economic influences. Female activists demanded the Marriage Law of 1950 because it would extend dramatically the legal independence of Chinese women. Many male Party members sought this reform as a mechanism for weakening the social control exercised by leaders of large and powerful clans. Strong lineages tended to dampen class consciousness in the countryside by emphasizing the formal kinship bonds between poor peasants and landlords. The Marriage Law complemented land reform by attacking an important basis of the rural class system. But after this reform, the majority of male cadres accorded a lower priority to feminist goals than to other tasks faced by the new government. Breaking the legal bonds of female subservience was an easier task than smashing the social bonds that accompanied them (Davin 1976).

Changes in social structure, no matter how radical, cannot transform old attitudes overnight. The Confucian heritage of male domination has been deeply etched into the consciousness of Chinese of both sexes. Thus, even after legal reforms had been introduced, many men were unenthusiastic about helping women find employment outside the home, which could safeguard female independence. Although there was considerable regional variation in female participation in nondomestic labor, in most areas it was unusual for rural women to work in the fields. Although this had changed decisively within a decade of Liberation, urban women, who had a stronger tradition of nonhome employment, found that they could still be displaced from their jobs when male unemployment rose.

None of this is intended to imply that the politics of sex and of class are necessarily at odds. Indeed, as Chinese women have in the past been ill-served by the distribution of social benefits, attacks upon inequality of all sorts are likely to be especially helpful to women (Andors 1976). Reforms in rural education and health care, for instance, have probably had a greater impact upon the lives of women than of men, who formerly received disproportionate shares of what limited services were available. But the continuing role of the family as a production unit in the countryside (Parish 1975; Salaff 1972) may be an obstacle to linking class and feminist interests more tightly. For within the rural family, women still defer to men in the making of decisions, and continuous administrative pressures for increased production tend to reinforce the family's solidarity. An additional impediment to change is the lack of adequate pension schemes for rural Chinese; China is too poor to establish a national social security system, which means that families continue to provide old-age support as they have for centuries. This is of course an inducement for rural women to bear large numbers of children, which tends further to hamper their independent economic role.

The participation of women in rural leadership positions has been harmed by a strong tradition of females moving away from their native villages when they marry. Local Party leaders are often unwilling to recommend promising young women for educational opportunities or for Party membership because this investment will be lost when the women marry and move away. A trend toward more frequent intravillage marriage may reduce this problem, but the Party has been unwilling to support a deeper change by encouraging new husbands to take up residence in the villages of their wives.

Policies of self-reliance by rural communities may inadvertently discourage faster progress in sexual equality. Although it is clear that central leaders have a firm commitment to this goal, local adherence to this public ideology often slackens in the absence of a strong hand at the center to force compliance. A perennial problem, for instance, has been the undervaluation of work points earned by women performing the same tasks as men.

Central authorities attempt to counter the lack of enthusiasm for equal treatment by local male cadres through the propagation of model women workers in the national media. Although the constant exposure of men to women in roles traditionally occupied by males is no doubt helpful, there are few contrary examples of men in roles associated with women, like child care or cooking. The Party has attempted to deal with these two particular issues by encouraging the creation of public facilities, located outside the home. Urban day-care facilities have been successful in allowing mothers of young children to participate in production. But an analogous plan to create public dining halls in rural areas, enthusiastically advocated by Mao, was never popular. The public canteens that were established in 1958 were soon abandoned amid complaints that home cooking was more enjoyable. Mao never went a step further to suggest that men might share the heavy burden of preparing meals (rural China lacks not only frozen foods, but running water).

Old and Young

The association of youth with revolution, and of age with conservatism is common enough in even highly stable societies that the prominence of these couplings in revolutionary China should not be surprising. While revolution cannot be reduced to generational conflict, the struggle of children against parents has been significantly interwoven with the broad pattern of social change in China at least since the May Fourth Movement of 1919, which began as a protest against Versailles Treaty provisions regarding Chinese territory. Then, young radicals berated their elders for insisting upon such Confucian values as filiality and the veneration of authority. Half a century later, young radicals again attacked filiality and the veneration of authority in the Cultural Revolution and in the ensuing campaign against the doctrines of Confucius. The social context had changed, but the issues and even the terminology were remarkably similar. This should remind us that the contradiction of old and young insistently recreates itself with each generation. That the older generation of Chinese is today dominated by former young revolutionaries adds special interest to the policies they have selected for the resolution of this contradiction.

Central to this relationship have been the methods advocated by the older generation to socialize the young (Kessen 1975; Raddock 1977). The desire to bequeath radical values to a generation of "revolutionary successors" has conflicted with the need to prepare young people for roles as productive citizens in a well-ordered society. The choice is not starkly put between either teaching the young to make revolution or training them in the skills necessary for operating an increasingly complex society. In fact, China's leaders share a consensus that the young should be both "red and expert": politically conscious, yet technically competent. Controversy has arisen over the proper mix of redness and expertise.

This controversy has been felt in the institutions through which China's young people are socialized. One set of political organizations, including the Communist Youth League and the Young Pioneers, has attempted to teach youth to cherish the values of the revolution. Educational institutions have repeated this task but have also emphasized career training. In many cases, the two missions have been compatible, as in the common practice of incorporating physical labor into the school curriculum. But some leaders, led until his death by Mao Tse-tung, have feared that the disciplined atmosphere of these institutions has encouraged an attitude of "studying in order to become an official." Fearing the conservative impact of China's formal institutions for the socialization of youth, Maoists in the Cultural Revolution supported the closing of universities and high schools, and freeing young people to learn revolution by the personal experience of political struggle as Red Guards against conservative officials.

The enthusiastic response of many young people to this Maoist appeal was colored by demographic and occupational concerns as well as by feelings of political conviction. Although the Chinese economy had grown considerably between Liberation and the beginning of the Cultural Revolution, the number of new jobs created could not easily keep pace with a growing population of young people. The establishment of domestic peace after Liberation had encouraged a baby boom, whose products were anxious about their futures in the Cultural Revolution period. Similarly, junior officials found their career ambitions frustrated by the longevity of the founding generation of Communist leaders. The revolutionaries who had established the People's Republic in 1949 still dominated its bureaucratic positions almost two decades later. Both students and younger officials had very personal reasons, then, to support a massive shake-up of China's administration.

Young people of worker and peasant origin were especially concerned that children of officials enjoyed definite advantages in the contest for desirable positions. These anxieties were perhaps allayed somewhat by the abolition in the Cultural Revolution of special preparatory schools that had catered to children of leading bureaucrats. The introduction of the requirement for two years of physical labor prior to university admission was similarly intended to equalize opportunity for advanced training and desirable jobs. The "down to the villages" program was also a response to severe competition for jobs, in addition to its function as a system for steeling the younger generation under the guidance of the peasantry.

Many of these reforms have been resisted. A major scandal of 1974, for instance, concerned a leading military official in Fukien Province, who used his influence to circumvent the new procedures for university admission to get his son in through the "back door." Since the death of Mao in 1976, several of the more radical innovations in education have been restricted. An even clearer change has taken place in the idealized relationship between the generations that is now propagated in the national media. The radical leaders now under attack are accused of arguing that China's officials become more conservative with age. While this was certainly an impolitic analysis, it is not an unreasonable one for any society. The rebellion of youth is always sustained by its relative rootlessness, which bestows upon young people a degree of flexibility often denied their elders in treating the status quo. The restriction of private property in socialist China may have increased this potential for youthful rebellion by severing a crucial link—the inheritance system—by which older generations have often imposed their values upon the young. Against the generational conflict of the past decade a new order is now being advocated. Instead of campaigns to resist authority by daring to "go against the tide," readers of the Chinese press now learn of efforts to restore classroom discipline and the authority of teachers, and of the need to respect the elder generation of veteran revolutionaries. There is some irony that this change in official attitudes toward intergenerational relations was made possible only by the death of the revolutionary octogenarian, Mao Tse-tung.

Chinese and Foreign

Chinese leaders have regarded the pursuit of greater domestic social equality as intimately bound up with a struggle against foreign domination. The militant nationalism of the Chinese revolution is in large measure the heritage of a century in which imperialist powers plundered China's resources and killed its people. Japan, Britain, Germany, France, and Russia all seized Chinese territory, either placing it directly under colonial administration or establishing exclusive zones of commercial exploitation. Chinese resistance was easily suppressed through the technical superiority of Western and Japanese arms and organization. Some scholars argue that the Chinese revolution owes its success primarily to popular support for the Communist struggle against the Japanese invasion of the 1930s. Communist leaders, however, regarded imperialism as a doubly menacing force: imperialist exploitation buttressed the more reactionary elements of China's social structure, thereby intensifying the revolutionary struggle.

When Mao proclaimed in 1949 that "the Chinese people have stood up," he revealed the pride of the successful revolutionaries at limiting foreign influence in Chinese affairs. But while Western missionaries, soldiers, and businessmen were soon sent home, and capitalist methods of social organization were quickly discredited, Soviet influence rose rapidly. This was partially a reaction to the embargo on trade with China led by the United States, but it also reflected the new government's desire to learn from its "elder brother in socialism."

Although the elder brother had not been particularly supportive of the Chinese Communist Party during its long struggle for power, and although it demanded an old tsarist naval base in Manchuria and mineral rights in Sinkiang, China's industrialization effort in the early 1950s proceeded under the tutelage of thousands of Soviet experts. But Chinese leaders soon concluded that the Soviet model was excessively centralized and too urban in its orientation to meet China's needs. When an indigenous strategy for industrialization was implemented in the Great Leap Forward, Soviet outrage over this and other Chinese "heresies" in the realm of foreign policy was so great that all technical and economic assistance was suddenly withdrawn in 1960. Even blueprints for unfinished industrial plants were taken back to the Soviet

Union, leaving bitter feelings among the Chinese and a new sense of double isolation from both the capitalist powers and from a Soviet bloc accused of revisionism.

China now has diplomatic and trade relations with the vast majority of the world's nations, but its painful past experience has encouraged policies designed to minimize dependence upon external powers. This has not meant a rejection of all sophisticated technology of foreign origin. Rather it indicates a restoration of Ch'ing dynasty efforts to find a formula by which foreign things can be borrowed selectively to serve China (Oksenberg and Goldstein 1974). This has often resulted in dichotomous policies, simultaneously attempting to equal international standards in advanced technology and to cultivate native Chinese traditions and skills. In military affairs, for example, extensive resources were assembled for an independent research program to construct atomic weapons, thereby attaining high world standards in military deterrence. At the same time, however, the People's Liberation Army (PLA) based much of its program upon the glorification of the simple traditions of guerrilla struggle, emphasizing an infantry-oriented military force with high political consciousness and low investment in expensive and sophisticated technology. Even the current campaign for military modernization seems unlikely to forsake the effort to combine foreign and advanced elements with native and simple ones.

Health care programs offer another example of the policy of national self-reliance (Horn 1969). Two schools of medicine coexisted in China prior to Liberation. "Western" medicine, introduced by medical missionaries and foreign foundations, gained adherents in areas under greatest foreign influence. As Western medicine became more popular, it increasingly competed with "Chinese" medicine, a miscellany of ancient practices, including acupuncture and herbal remedies, which emphasized holistic treatments of the body rather than surgical intervention to cure diseased parts. Since Liberation there have been efforts to fashion an amalgam of the two schools, often against the resistance of the higher-status Western-style physicians. This policy was dictated in part by nationalistic pride in China's indigenous medicine, but also by the need to rapidly expand the provision of health care to China's peasant majority. The creation of Western-style hospitals throughout the countryside was impractical because of China's poverty, whereas each village already contained a certain level of expertise in traditional medical practices. Institutional reforms forced the cooperation of the two schools by simultaneously sending Western physicians to rural areas and sponsoring new paramedical roles (the "barefoot doctors"). Medical research has similarly attempted to integrate the two schools. While China has shown great pride in the synthesis of insulin, an accomplishment that received much attention from foreign medical researchers, significant effort has also been devoted to discovering new uses for traditional techniques, like the use of acupuncture in anesthesia.

There is serious disagreement within China about the proper balance between native and foreign influences. While no one argues against the ideal of self-reliance, this phrase is variously interpreted; scientists and managers of capital-intensive industries have tended to adopt a less restrictive conception than have personnel in areas where foreign inputs are less obviously useful. When the boundaries of self-reliance have been drawn narrowly, special political pressure has been felt by personnel with foreign training (most of the senior generation of Chinese scientists, for instance) and by those residents of large cities who have a fondness for Debussy or Hong Kong hairstyles.

Even those who argue most strenuously for broader contacts with other societies, however, have tended to favor those interactions that will enable China to strengthen its self-reliance in the long range. Thus the commodities imported from the United States after the limited restoration of relations during the Nixon administration have included jet aircraft for the improvement of domestic transportation and chemical fertilizer plants to permit both higher agricultural productivity and the avoidance of large-scale fertilizer imports in the future.

Conclusion

This survey has introduced some central issues as the core of certain basic contradictory relationships within Chinese society. How does the present resolution of these relationships affect the prospects for continuing the revolution that led to the establishment of the People's Republic? Three broad generalizations seem appropriate.

1. Because no permanent resolution of any of these social tensions is possible, they will remain a dynamic source for continuing change in social life. Each of the seven relationships discussed here is a polarity, rather than a continuum along which one can locate a policy that will forever satisfy China's national needs. Instead, the contradictions are subject to shifting, temporary resolutions as new policies are introduced

to deal with the competing demands of Han and minorities, city and countryside, or old and young. Additional volatility is introduced into Chinese society by the fact that policies intended to influence one relationship often spill over to affect another. Thus the decentralization that accompanies rural policies may delay the attainment of feminist goals by minimizing central pressures within rural communities. Or the restrictions upon private property that have characterized Chinese policies toward the relationship between rich and poor may also weaken the power of older Chinese to influence the behavior of the young, inasmuch as inheritance has long been a mechanism by which parents have influenced their offspring. The fact that a generation of Chinese has been educated to analyze society as a system of contradictory relationships may in itself provide a pressure for continuing change. Consciousness of one's social position is the most obvious prerequisite for the pursuit of group interests. Some high officials may conclude that their own interests are best served by discouraging popular attention to changes in the structure of Chinese society, as this might allow them greater latitude to determine policies without constant need to mediate the claims of particular segments of society. It is to avoid such a development that the Party's official newspaper, *People's Daily*, has urged: "Major issues must be constantly discussed so that everyone pays heed to them. It is very dangerous to become engrossed in minor matters and not discuss major issues, for this inevitably leads to revisionism."

2. Against continuing pressure for change is the fact that individuals are commonly affected by more than one of the cleavages that divide Chinese from one another. To the extent that these contradictions cut across each other, consciousness of social position is obscured and motivation to demand a clear alteration in the policies governing any single relationship is diminished. A person who is advantaged in economic terms but disadvantaged by age or ethnic status is likely to have rather complex attitudes toward which social changes are most desirable. Pressure for radical social change is enhanced when social cleavages are cumulative, rather than cross-cutting, as when youth, political weakness, and anxiety about economic position converged among many supporters of the Cultural Revolution.

3. The greatest impediment to continuing the revolution is probably to be found in the past successes of revolutionary change. The government that came to power in 1949 has vigorously instituted programs to ameliorate the most grievous inequalities within each of the

contradictions discussed in this chapter. While tensions remain within each of these relationships, they are not sufficiently potent to support serious counterrevolutionary activity that might endanger Communist authority. At the same time, the relative mildness of these tensions, when compared to those found in Chinese society prior to Liberation, makes it difficult for the Communist Party to sustain the revolutionary momentum that brought it to power. Worker and peasant annoyance at bureaucratic privilege and abuse, for instance, is no substitute for the deeper class feelings provoked by past exploitation by capitalists and landlords.

The successful transformation of important aspects of China's social structure has made it increasingly difficult to replicate the Party's pre-Liberation formula for revolution. During the long years of struggle against the Kuomintang and the Japanese, the Communists learned to mobilize supporters by uniting large coalitions against privileged, but socially isolated, minorities. But the Party's policies since 1949 have eroded the extremes within each of these contradictions, rendering identification of targets for revolutionary action extremely problematic in many cases. The narrowing of income inequalities in the countryside, for instance, coupled with the abolition of private land holdings, has produced a relative homogeneity in material life which undermines appeals for revolutionary social change.

None of these comments is intended to imply that the Communist Party has become a conservative, anti-revolutionary force within Chinese society. To the contrary, the Party's continued dedication to systematic and penetrating social change is noteworthy. But "revolution" in Chinese political discussion has increasingly come to signify either the protection of the social benefits won since 1949, or the continued implementation of reforms to resolve China's social problems. Only in the Cultural Revolution has "revolution" been used to denote the forceful seizure of power from those who were held to be preventing further reforms. After a generation of intensive efforts at revolutionary change, it is perhaps not surprising to discover that the People's Republic of China's social structure has been so altered that there is less cause for revolution, although still much cause for reform.

References

Andors, Phyllis. 1976. "Politics of Chinese Development: The Case of Women, 1960-1966." *Signs* 2 (Autumn):89-119.

Barnett, A. Doak. 1967. *Cadres, Bureaucracy, and Political Power in Communist China.* New York: Columbia University Press.

Bernstein, Thomas P. 1977. *Up to the Mountains and Down to the Villages: The Transfer of Youth from Urban to Rural China.* New Haven, Conn.: Yale University Press.

Chang, Tse-i. 1966. *The Party and the Nationality Question in China.* Translated by George Moseley. Cambridge, Mass.: M.I.T. Press.

Chen, Jack. 1973. *A Year in Upper Felicity.* New York: Macmillan.

Davin, Delia. 1976. *Woman-Work. Women and the Party in Revolutionary China.* London: Oxford University Press.

Dreyer, June Teufel. 1976. *China's Forty Millions. Minority Nationalities and National Integration in the People's Republic of China.* Cambridge, Mass.: Harvard University Press.

Hinton, William. 1968. *Fanshen. A Documentary of Revolution in a Chinese Village.* New York: Vintage Books.

Hoffman, Charles. 1977. "Worker Participation in Chinese Factories." *Modern China* 3 (July):291-320.

Horn, Joshua. 1969. *Away with All Pests.* New York: Monthly Review Press.

Kessen, William. 1975. *Childhood in China.* New Haven, Conn.: Yale University Press.

Kraus, Richard Curt. 1977. "Class Conflict and the Vocabulary of Social Analysis in China." *China Quarterly* 69 (March):54-74.

Mao Tse-tung. 1977. *Selected Works.* Volume 5. Peking: Foreign Languages Press.

Maijer, M. J. 1971. *Marriage Law and Policy in the Chinese People's Republic.* Hong Kong: Hong Kong University Press.

Oksenberg, Michel, and Steven Goldstein. 1974. "The Chinese Political Spectrum." *Problems of Communism* 23 (March-April):1-13.

Parish, William L. 1975. "Socialism and the Chinese Peasant Family." *Journal of Asian Studies* 34 (May):613-630.

Raddock, David M. 1977. *Political Behavior of Adolescents in China.* Tucson: University of Arizona Press.

Salaff, Janet W. 1972. "Institutionalized Motivation for Fertility Limitation in China." *Population Studies* 26 (July):233-262.

Seybolt, Peter J. 1973. *Revolutionary Education in China.* White Plains, N.Y.: International Arts and Sciences Press.

Sheridan, Mary. 1976. "Young Women Leaders in China." *Signs* 2 (Autumn):59-88.

Sidel, Victor W., and Ruth Sidel. 1973. *Serve the People.* Boston: Beacon Press.

Sigurdson, Jon. 1977. *Rural Industrialization in China.* Cambridge, Mass.: Harvard University Press.

White, Lynn T., III. 1976. "Workers' Politics in Shanghai." *Journal of Asian Studies* 36 (November):99-116.

Whyte, Martin King. 1974. *Small Groups and Political Rituals in China.* Berkeley: University of California Press.

———. 1975. "Inequality and Stratification in China." *China Quarterly* 64 (December):684-711.

9

Education and Culture

Ralph C. Croizier

One element of continuity between Communist and Confucian China is the close link between education and "culture" (i.e., literature and the arts). In traditional China this came from the Confucian emphasis on moral cultivation as the basic purpose and ultimate justification for both formal education and artistic expression. The content of that morality has changed in the People's Republic of China, but the underlying presupposition that learning and culture serve a socially useful purpose remains.

Of course, there are differences in the degree to which an officially approved morality pervades all education and cultural life. Not just the pervasiveness of Communist ideology, but also the imperatives of modernization in a twentieth-century nation, impel the state to control the lives of its citizens in ways unimaginable to the most morally sincere and imperially autocratic Confucian monarch. The drastic reduction of the private sphere is one of the basic changes brought by the Chinese revolution, and it has affected both the form and spirit of all cultural and intellectual expression. In that sense the Communists are choosing, or perhaps subconsciously following, only one side of a poised dichotomy between private and public, personal and social morality in traditional China. The difference can be as great as that between the serenity of a traditional scholar's painting of bamboo and the exuberance of a Maoist propaganda poster. But there is enough similarity of underlying purpose behind education and culture to make Communist China as different from contemporary socialist and nonsocialist nations as it is from its Confucian past. This essay will examine those similarities, and differences, in education and the most important of the arts.

Before looking at specific developments in each of those spheres, it is necessary to point out that cultural and educational policy has not been

static in the People's Republic and that in the aftermath of Mao's death
and the fall of the "Gang of Four" these areas especially are in great flux.
This requires a somewhat historical approach, examining the dynamics
of change over the last three decades in order to understand the present
situation and possible future trends. Any confidence about analyzing
such trends, however, must be tempered by the realization that
educational and cultural policy in the People's Republic has not
progressed in an uninterrupted straight line. Rather, there have been
drastic swings or zigzags in the line. These have been in large
part reflections of political struggles within the Communist Party and
shifts in general Party line. But they also stem from uncertainties about
how in these important areas the Chinese people can realize the long-
range goals of the revolution and, even more important, resolve tensions
between different goals.

Western analysts are fond of using the Chinese Communist term "red
and expert" to express these tensions. In Chinese usage the two are
supposed to go together and reinforce each other. "Redness," proper
ideology and commitment to building the new society, makes sure that
technical expertise or cultural knowledge is devoted to the right ends
and motivates the individual to acquire that expertise. Yet in many areas
"red and expert" has seemed more contradictory than complementary.
Nowhere has this been more obvious than in education where questions
of relative emphasis on political-moral indoctrination versus academic
content, or on egalitarian leveling versus high standards, have acquired
explosive significance. It can also be found, somewhat modified, in the
arts where at times Mao's injunction that all art and literature must serve
the masses makes popularization the overwhelming objective, but at
other times his simultaneous injunction that this work should have a
high artistic content brings effusive praise and patronage for China's
most famous artists.

It will be worthwhile keeping this "red"–"expert" dichotomy in mind
for each area in education and culture, but there are other equally useful
terms or concepts for analyzing the tensions in these fields. One could
even take the Cultural Revolution's celebrated struggle between the
socialist road of Chairman Mao and the capitalist road of the much
maligned Liu Shao-ch'i as expressing something similar to "red and
expert." The former puts emphasis on equality, moral-ideological zeal,
and political training in education; the latter stresses high academic
standards, formal study, and technical expertise. In culture the former
lends itself to art both for and by the masses with emphasis on amateur

actors, peasant painters, and worker poets; the latter has regard for a more sophisticated and varied art appealing to and satisfying the intellectual elite, which is deemed necessary to build a modern socialist state and economy.

Yet not everything in China's intellectual or cultural life can be explained in terms of "socialist-roaders" and "capitalist-roaders." Perhaps it is more meaningful to see a continuing tension between the goals of China's two simultaneous but distinct revolutions—the national revolution for achieving China's independence, unity, and modernization, and the socialist revolution for achieving a collectivist economy, an egalitarian social order, and a new socialist morality. The telescoping of these two revolutions, which Marx saw as two chronologically distinct stages, has created more than theoretical problems. It means that the impulse to realize ultimate social and moral goals has frequently clashed with the stubborn realities of an underdeveloped economy, a poorly educated population, and strong surviving personal values from the old society. Moreover, impatience to achieve these goals can conflict with imperatives of the national revolution such as national unity and rapid scientific-economic modernization. The Great Leap Forward in 1958 and the Red Guard stage of the Cultural Revolution in 1966-1967 are the most obvious examples. Thus the swings between egalitarianism and educational elitism, between total politicization and preserving national cultural traditions in the arts can also be seen as a product of the competing demands of these two revolutions and differences between the political leaders who incline to one or the other.

The arts, and in fact the whole cultural sphere, manifest one more tension or contradiction. Again it can be found in a catch phrase or slogan: "national in form, socialist in content." In practice, this slogan too hides more problems than it solves. For instance, national form, which appeals to patriotism and is readily recognizable by the masses, has not always easily accommodated socialist political content. It has not been easy to pour the new wine of socialist content into the very old bottles of Chinese culture without either spoiling the wine or shattering the bottles. New socialist art forms frequently lose most of their national flavor, and with it risk losing their national appeal; old national art forms often have little socialist content and pose the danger of reinforcing traditional values that the revolution wants to change. Given enough time the dilemma is not unresolvable, but the leaders of the new China have been impatient and in the last three decades they have not yet resolved this contradiction. By their own admission they have not yet created an art that is simultaneously popular and aesthetically powerful, distinctively Chinese, and unmistakably socialist. So long as so many contradictions remain—whether we call them red versus expert, socialist versus capitalist roaders, the socialist versus the national revolution, political content versus national form—no such art is likely to emerge. Nor is there likely to be much stability in either educational or cultural policy.

Education

There is an old Chinese proverb (very Confucian in its emphasis on the long-range importance of education) to the effect that if you are planning for one year you plant grain, if you are planning for ten years you plant trees, but if you are planning for 1,000 years you "plant" (i.e., educate and morally nurture) men. The leaders of the new China are planning, and planting, for the long run.

Certainly education, particularly mass literacy and high-level scientific training, is a top priority for any modernizing nation. This is particularly true for Communist countries with their ambitious plans for rapid economic development and social transformation. But in China the extremely high value traditionally placed on learning, reinforced by the continued belief in its socially moral function, attaches even more importance to education. The formal education system must also be seen as part of the overall emphasis that Chinese Communism puts on transforming human consciousness as the prerequisite for transforming material conditions. Whether this strong "subjective" strain in Chinese Marxism (as opposed to economic determinism) comes from traditionally Chinese assumptions about man and society, as argued brilliantly and persuasively in Donald Munro's book, *The Concept of Man in Contemporary China,* or from the challenge of making revolution in an economically backward country, it has put an enormous burden on the educational system. The schools are expected to teach the academic or technical skills necessary for building a modern economy, while at the same time inculcating in the young the moral values appropriate to the new socialist society. Academic training and childhood socialization are not tasks unique to the Chinese school system. But the Chinese have put more demands and higher expectations on their schools to do this than most other societies.

This has led to extreme swings in educational policy as the tensions between red and expert, and between socialist and national revolution have worked themselves out. It will be necessary to follow the sometimes erratic course of educational policy over the last three decades before attempting even a tentative assessment of how well the Chinese educational system has performed its twin tasks of national and social transformation.

The Soviet Experiment

When the Chinese Communists came into power in 1949 they inherited more immediate legacies from the recent past than the general traditional assumptions about education discussed above. On the one hand, there was the educational system built up by their Nationalist predecessors, which, despite the damage inflicted by foreign invasion and civil war, had some notable if limited achievements. On the other hand, there was the Communists' own experience with mass education among the peasants and with ideological reeducation of intellectuals who had joined the Party during the Yenan years. Both were relevant to their early attempts to build a new national system of education; neither was adequate for the scope of their ambitions and the complexity of the problems they faced.

The Nationalists had attempted to build a mass education system, but limitations of time, money, and degree of control over the countryside had severely circumscribed the efforts of Nanking's educational planners. At the lower levels most of their plans remained on paper, especially outside the major cities. At the upper level China had some outstanding universities and specialized institutes, like the Peking Union Medical College, but the number of university-trained specialists was woefully inadequate for China's enormous needs, especially in scientific-technical fields. Clearly mass education had to be given a high priority by any new government in China; but the Communists wanted to do more than extend formal schooling to a larger proportion of the population. They also wanted to remake the moral or ideological content of education in accord with the values of the new society. Their experience in the Yenan period (1935-1945), incorporating a strong political content and an emphasis on down-to-earth practicality that aligned formal education with the daily lives of the masses, was relevant. They also learned how to bring basic education to the peasants without an expensive educational infrastructure. Still, what was adequate for the guerrilla war period was not adequate for the period of national reconstruction. Even though political organization and ideological zeal could go a long way toward solving material shortages in popularizing education, they could not implement the high levels of formal academic training necessary to provide the large core of educated personnel required by China's rapid economic modernization. For that, expertise of a different kind, and a different model for education, seemed necessary.

A foreign model was nothing new for China's educational planners. From the late nineteenth century on, Western missionary schools had been pioneers in bringing new education to China and under both the Republican and Nationalist governments foreign experience (American, European, and Japanese) had been eagerly sought. After the revolution of 1949 these foreign models were rejected and surviving foreign-run schools were nationalized. The sole remaining foreign model, in education as in everything else, was the Soviet Union.

In some ways the Soviet model did not sit well on China from the start. It had brought mass education to the U.S.S.R. and had trained the technocratic elite for Stalin's forced-draft industrialization. But since the abandonment of experiments in "progressive" and collectivist education in the late 1920s, it had emphasized formal academic training and individual intellectual achievement more than Communist social goals. In that sense, it was more suited to China's national revolution than to its socialist revolution. It also, ironically, reinforced the elitist Mandarin tendency in Chinese educational thought, which the Communist revolution was supposed to destroy, while ignoring the deep-rooted Chinese feeling that education should also be social and moral in its purposes. Finally, the Soviet emphasis on high-quality urban institutions was no better suited to the needs of China's much more numerous and much poorer rural masses than the strongly rejected plans of Western educators.

So long as the Sino-Soviet alliance remained intact and Russian influence predominated in most economic, military, and scientific affairs, the Chinese education system bore a strong Soviet imprint. Even after the Sino-Soviet split this influence remained because the new system was producing some of the results needed for building the nation economically and militarily. Yet, even at the height of the Russian influence, there were countervailing currents stemming from national pride, China's unique needs and possibilities, and the Chinese Communists' own experiences and outlook. Thus, tensions remained in the Chinese educational world throughout "the Soviet experiment" of the 1950s and would lead to drastically new departures in the next decade.

Up until 1966, however, the main outline of the Chinese educational system resembled that of the Soviet Union more than any other. To begin with, it was sharply pyramidal in structure with only a tiny percentage of those in elementary school continuing on to university or other postsecondary education. If figures given on the tenth anniversary of the People's Republic are reliable, as of 1958 elementary school enrollments (the first six years of formal schooling), were 86.4 million, secondary school enrollments (three years junior secondary, and three years senior), 10 million, and higher education (universities and post-secondary technical schools), 660,000.[1] In other words, there were 131 elementary school students for each university student or, perhaps more relevant, less than 1 out of 15 high school students could expect to go on to university.

The reasons for this pattern are obvious. Basic education, no matter how limited, had to be provided to a vast, poor population among whom estimates of illiteracy ran as high as 85 percent before 1949. Given shortages of trained teachers, financial exigencies, and emphasis on maintaining standards at the higher levels, it was difficult to expand higher education as quickly as primary schooling. It was also hard to absorb huge numbers of highly educated young people into the labor force at work suitable to their training unless industrial growth was very rapid. After 1958 there were problems in the economy, so both the funds for expanding higher education and the demand for its graduates dwindled. Under such circumstances it was logical to continue building a broad base while concentrating more on quality at the top.

The emphasis on "quality"—high academic standards, individual intellectual achievement, strict discipline, authority of the teachers, competitive entrance examinations at higher levels—fit in well with the Soviet example. From all accounts, Chinese secondary schools and higher institutions were well run, although not very innovative in teaching methods. Chinese students studied hard and learned a lot, although imagination and creativity were not encouraged, and teachers tended to retain the authority given them by Chinese tradition and Soviet example.

One way of reconciling the elitism inherent in this pyramidal structure with the egalitarian values of the revolution was to create part-time schools for those already in the work force. Particularly during the Great Leap Forward in 1958 the number of schools of various kinds was greatly enlarged. They included factory-organized schools to raise workers' technical and general educational level, correspondence programs, rural elementary and secondary schools for peasants, and vocational training institutions, somewhat similar to the Soviet polytechnical schools, which served high school graduates who had not got into universities. By 1960 there were allegedly 25 million students in such schools. This was in addition to the vast numbers reached by mass movements like the basic literacy campaigns.

These statistics, impressive even if the figures are inflated, can be misleading if they are interpreted to mean that scarce educational resources were being spread evenly. One of the advantages of the part-time schools was that they were relatively inexpensive to run and did not remove students from productive labor. Ideological considerations about combining labor with study aside, this was not an inconsiderable factor. Most lower-level and part-time schools could be run on the principle of maximal local self-reliance while the Ministry of Education (at times there was also a separate Ministry of Higher Education) concentrated funds and attention on the higher levels and on certain key schools. Chou En-lai himself defended an elite school system for the most able students by telling the National People's Congress in April 1959: "We must devote more energy to perfecting a number of 'key' schools. We will then be able to train specialist personnel of higher quality for the state and bring about a rapid rise in our country's scientific and cultural level."[2]

The system was democratic in form—based on intellectual ability and accomplishment—but not very egalitarian in practice. The poorer sections of the population, especially the peasants, found access to the higher rungs of the educational ladder rather difficult. Apart from surviving fees and other costs to the parents, differences in cultural background and quality of available elementary schools between city and countryside and between upper and lower classes made equal educational opportunity more a myth than a reality. There were also allegedly many outright abuses by those in power, like favoring their own children for admission to the best schools. Yet it was more than the abuses that denied the egalitarian goals of the revolution. In its emphasis on quality, the very system itself favored inequality. Designed to draw a highly trained elite from a mass base, an elite that would spearhead scientific and cultural development, the new education system echoed the philosophy of Soviet education and more distantly, the idea behind the imperial civil service examinations of China's own past.

These tendencies did not go unchallenged. Among the top Party leadership, Mao was probably the most disturbed by the social, ideological, and political implications of such a policy. But when his more mass-based, voluntaristic effort at rapid social and economic transformation in the Great Leap Forward broke down after 1958, it could only reinforce the elitist tendencies in educational policy. With economic planners and technocrats back in ascendancy by the early 1960s the "specialist personnel of high quality" that Chou En-lai had called for seemed all the more precious. Ma Yin-ch'u, the feisty and outspoken president of National Peking University, put the purpose of universities even more bluntly: ". . . to train advanced technical personnel and principal cadres for national construction."[3] Apparently the Sino-Soviet split had not changed the basic technocratic and elitist character of Chinese educational policy. It would take an internal political upheaval to do that.

Educational Reforms of the Cultural Revolution

The role of students (the "Red Guards") in the Cultural Revolution is well known. Starting at the universities but spreading down to high schools and even elementary schools, they provided the shock troops with which Mao attacked the "capitalist roaders" within the Party who were allegedly betraying the ideals of socialism. Their motives for flocking so enthusiastically to Mao's banner may have come from youthful idealism, Mao's charismatic leadership, or general dissatisfaction with the established Party leadership. But they also came from causes within the educational system. The severely competitive nature of the system and the high attrition rate at each level certainly must have ranked high among them. Yet it was not those who had failed in the entrance-examination rat-race but those who had done best—students at the elite institutions of Tsinghua and Peking National universities—who started the Red Guard movement. From the content of their charges against school and Party administrators it seems that they took the Maoist ideals of an egalitarian, selfless, and ideologically purified society very seriously. The emphasis on academic knowledge and grades over political ideology and moral character, the "elitist" admissions policies that favored those with the best educational opportunities over workers and peasants, the sin of "bourgeois careerism" as the goal of higher education , the separation of students from the laboring masses— all of these were condemned and those who had implemented such policies were driven out of power and subjected to ruthless verbal criticism, or sometimes even worse.

"The revolution within the revolution" may have been called a Cultural Revolution because it was supposed to eradicate surviving bourgeois influences within the cultural superstructure. It could just as accurately have been called an educational revolution because its purpose was to reeducate people to appreciate the superiority of collectivist, egalitarian, socialist virtues. The cultural and educational spheres were seen as indissolubly linked—in fact, almost identical. Education's prime purpose was to inculcate new values; all cultural creations should express and teach those values. Morality and social purpose are again the connecting links.

As a "revolution," albeit one called for from above, the Cultural Revolution had its destructive side, smashing the existing educational system so that something better could be built on its ruins. It is clear from Mao's later directives in the Cultural Revolution that the destruction went on longer and perhaps farther than he had originally desired. Schools were closed for almost two years from summer 1966 to 1968. And only when leadership of the Cultural Revolution was taken away from student Red Guards and given to army-backed Mao Tsetung Thought propaganda teams could any semblance of order be restored in the schools. Even then it seems that academic education restarted very slowly, as it was easier to denounce the bourgeois line in education than to fill in the details of the new socialist line. Nevertheless, by the early 1970s universities were beginning to enroll new students, secondary and elementary schools were fully reopened, and the major reforms of the Cultural Revolution in education were becoming clear.

At the beginning of the Cultural Revolution in August 1966, a Central Committee directive called for "education serving proletarian politics and education combined with productive labor." This emphasis on politics and productive labor would be at the core of the new system with the central purpose of education redefined from training "advanced technical personnel and principal cadres for national construction" to instilling in youth the moral values that would make both national and socialist construction possible. It was to be value-oriented education first, academic or technical education second.

The values to be incorporated in the new system can be summed up as equality, practicality, and morality. Equality meant no intellectual elite, separated from the masses, that enjoyed material and status privileges. Practicality meant linking formal education with productive labor, especially manual labor, both as a means of eliminating status differences and developing a practical work ethic suitable for economic construction in a backward country. Along with this went a depreciation of theory and abstract knowledge divorced from practical problems of production. The old Mencian dictum about those who worked with their minds ruling over those who worked with their hands was to be eliminated by the creation of a "proletarian intelligentsia" who worked with both. Thus practicality was intimately related to the stress on equality. It also was part of the new socialist morality. The common terms for this morality were "class consciousness," "ideology," or even "politics," but they amounted to a moral code emphasizing personal selflessness (especially denial of bourgeois careerism through education) and a missionary-like zeal for realizing the new social order through political activism. The new educated youth was to have dirt on its hands but no dirty bourgeois ideas in its mind. Education would make a new socialist man, not a new ruling elite.

The concrete reforms to realize these principles took some time to implement. First, the discredited Party authorities and educational administrators had to be replaced, initially by rampaging Red Guards who swept away the old system but proved incapable of creating any new order. That order was established after 1968 when Mao Tsetung Thought propaganda teams took over administration of all schools. They were to implement the "working class leadership" in education that Mao had called for in his August 1968 directive on education. In fact, they had a large component of People's Liberation Army (PLA) cadres, although they also introduced worker and peasant activists into the running of schools.

The impact of these reforms was probably greatest at the university level. The entire system of admissions was changed to open up the universities to workers, peasants, and PLA veterans. This meant scrapping the competitive entrance examinations. Instead, university students would be taken, not fresh out of high school, but through recommendation from basic production units. All would have had at least two years working in a factory or in commerce before being eligible for this recommendation, which would be based on their political attitude and integration with the masses (i.e., their moral qualities) more than on their intellectual abilities. Naturally, this created a different student body at the universities: older with direct experience in production labor, more heavily drawn from worker and peasant class backgrounds, not so well prepared academically but more active politically.

It also led to drastic changes in the content of university education. Courses were shortened: the former four- or five-year program was reduced to two or three years. Cultural subjects like history or literature were reduced and heavily politicized. Scientific and technical subjects like chemistry or engineering were simplified and made more practical. Examinations and grades were downplayed or completely eliminated. Students would not "flunk out" for academic reasons. Individual competitiveness was discouraged. And, in accordance with the principle of combining study and labor, a good deal of time was spent in productive labor either in workshops attached to the universities, in factories and farms during breaks in the school year, or as part of the regular course work. It was also expected that most of the students recommended for university education by specific production units would return to those units after graduation, thus giving the factories and communes a direct interest in higher education and breaking down the separation between schools and society. University students were constantly urged not to forget their class background and duty to serve the masses; they were to become not intellectuals but educated workers or peasants.

The changes in the high schools were only slightly less drastic. Entrance exams were abolished to open them to workers and peasants. The elite residential high schools, which had enrolled many children from the Party and technocratic elite, were converted into community schools, thus democratizing the composition of the student body at this level too. Workers were admitted to the administration of the schools through the Mao Tsetung Thought propaganda teams and the "revolutionary committees" that succeeded them. Workers and peasants also did part of the teaching, particularly of practical labor courses and of ideological courses teaching about the class struggle and "the bitterness" of the old society. There was, in fact, the same stress on moral-political values and on practical labor-related education as found at the universities, with a consequent deemphasis on formal academic subjects and academic discipline. Examinations, grades, and individual competition were particularly discouraged. The curriculum was simplified, politicized, and shortened. Junior and senior high school became a four-year program (two and two) instead of the former three years each.

These general reforms also applied to the much more numerous primary schools. Emphasis was to be placed on all-around development, not just academics. As the original Party directive on educational reforms of August 1966 said, students should "develop morally, intellectually, and physically." The order is not accidental. Moral, or political, development was to have priority. At this level, too, education was to be spread more widely with greater stress on the countryside. It was to be more decentralized both in control of curriculum and in greater reliance on local financing. It was also shorter (five years instead of six) and more practical in its content.

Thus the entire regular school system was restructured in accord with the ideals of the Cultural Revolution. These reforms also tended to blur the distinction between full-time and part-time education, as both types of schools now featured close integration of labor with study. One of the notable innovations of the Cultural Revolution was the creation of part-time institutions of higher learning attached to productive units. Perhaps most important were the "July 21 workers universities," the prototype of which was set up by the Shanghai Machine Tools Plant in 1968. Its students were workers averaging twelve years of labor experience and junior-high-level schooling who took a two-and-a-half year program while continuing to work in the factory. The content was technically oriented so as to create educated worker-technicians. Similar institutions in the countryside were called "May Seventh Universities" (not to be confused with the May Seventh schools for reeducation of political cadres). Their function and management are not so clear. Apparently they, too, were designed to produce technicians without separating them from productive labor and their local unit. Although most of these would not be recognized as "universities" in the usual sense, this was also true of much of the work at the regular institutions of higher education after 1966. The Cultural Revolution's massive effort at social engineering through education had a marked leveling effect on the whole educational system.

One more education-related policy with enormous social and political consequences should be mentioned. That is the "rustication of educated youth," the relocation of urban high-school graduates in the countryside. It was an economic, social, and political policy but it attempted to serve educational purposes as well. Primarily, it promoted (or forced) the integration of students with the masses that was a cornerstone of Cultural Revolution educational policy. It also addressed the problem of vocational placement for the large number of urban high-school graduates who could not easily be absorbed into the urban sector of the economy. Such students could hope to be recommended by their commune to go on to university after proving themselves in rural labor, but statistically the chances for this were rather small. "Rustication" *(hsia-hsiang,* "down to the villages"—not to be confused with the often punitive *hsia-fang,* "down to a local place," assigned to cadres and intellectuals) has been a basic policy and a basic fact of life for China's high-school students. It is estimated that since 1969 perhaps 20 million youth have participated in this program.

The Cultural Revolution, therefore, completely restructured the educational system and the lives of Chinese students. The changes made for a much tighter system politically, with massive infusions of the "thought of Mao Tse-tung," but a much looser one administratively, with more room for pedagogical experimentation and adaptation to local conditions. The Ministry of Education had ceased to function after 1966 and was replaced by a looser group on education in the Party's Central Committee. Ideological control, not bureaucratic regulation, was their main concern. After 1968, China's schools were more integrated with society, and both schools and society were saturated with political-moral education. Heroic efforts had been made to overcome the perceived problems of elitism, impracticality, and indifference to politics. But swinging so far to one side of the "red and expert" dichotomy did not solve all the problems inherent in the tension between them.

Struggles over the Cultural Revolution's "New Born Things" in Education

Problems showed up in several different areas but the common denominator was that the nation's needs for educated manpower for scientific and economic development were not being met. The emphasis on social goals in education (the socialist revolution) was interfering with the attainment of economic goals (the national revolution). For example, the new enrollment policies in the universities brought more students from the right class backgrounds and presumably proper political ideology but many of them were not prepared, or perhaps not intellectually able, to do university-level work. Moreover, the two-year gap between high-school graduation and university entrance led to serious memory losses, especially in scientific subjects and foreign languages. Much of the work at universities had to be remedial or review of forgotten high-school subject matter. Educators and economic planners were concerned at the drop in the level of academic work at the universities and by the amount of intellectual talent discarded by the stress on social and political values in the selection system.

The Cultural Revolution's assault on "bourgeois intellectuals" also made it difficult to restore academic discipline and the authority of the teachers. That this had a serious effect on teachers' morale is shown by the widespread saying, "To be a teacher is dangerous and has no future." By the early 1970s, numerous admonitions had appeared in the press about restoring respect for study and for teachers. Apparently these problems of lower standards, lack of academic motivation, poor teachers' morale, and lax student discipline were most severe at the universities, which by the mid-1970s had not reached their pre–Cultural Revolution levels of enrollment and were much inferior in terms of academic content.

In 1975 the new minister of education, Chou Jung-hsin, made a series of scathing off-the-record comments on the quality of education in the universities, which were publicized after his dismissal in 1976. He attacked the neglect of standards and poor preparation of entrants, called for more respect for intellectuals and intellectual work, and insisted on more attention to scientific theory. His dismal picture of higher education was summed up in one line: "In the universities now: no more culture, no more theory, no more scientific research."[4] This bleak picture was perhaps exaggerated, but it is confirmed by the impressions of many Western visitors in these years (including the author) and it reflected the concern of the Party moderates that China's national development was being impeded by unrealistic social experiments in education.

However, it was difficult to reverse the course of educational policy so long as Mao was alive and the Cultural Revolution radicals, his wife Chiang Ch'ing prominent among them, were still powerful in cultural, educational, and especially mass media fields. At the first post–Cultural Revolution National Conference on Education in 1971, the radicals had pushed through their "two assessments" of the state of education. According to the first, during the seventeen years up to 1966, "in the main" education had not followed Mao's line. The second was that the majority of teachers were "bourgeois intellectuals" who required correction and could not lead education work. For the next five years there was a tug and pull quality in Chinese education, as in Chinese politics in general, with the moderate administrators quietly trying to undo or modify what they regarded as the excesses of the Cultural Revolution and the radicals noisily defending its "new born things."

Thus, when by 1973 universities were using examinations to test the qualifications of recommended applicants, the radicals built up the protest of a student-worker who refused to take the exams into a nationwide publicity campaign against restoring bourgeois academic standards for university admission. Later in the year they launched another campaign based on a letter from a fifth-grade Peking student complaining against the authoritarian manner of his teacher. With the media and politically powerful leaders inveighing against "the absolute authority of the teacher," it was difficult to restore normal discipline and academic standards in the schools.

The battle in the educational field reached its peak two years later after Teng Hsiao-p'ing, with Chou En-lai's blessing, tried to push a national plan for scientific-technological development that would have required a change of educational policy. With Chou En-lai on his deathbed, and Mao apparently unwilling to enter the controversy, by December 1975 the radicals had launched a vigorous counterattack against this "right deviationist wind." In education they defended recruitment of workers and peasants into universities, running "open-to-society" schools that combined labor and study, and the principle of working class leadership with laymen guiding specialists in scientific fields. Soon afterwards Minister of Education Chou Jung-hsin was purged; he was followed shortly afterwards by Teng Hsiao-p'ing. The Cultural Revolution's "new born things" in education were safe for the moment.

After the Gang of Four: Reverse Course in Education

That moment did not last long. When Mao died in September 1976 and his successor, Hua Kuo-feng, struck quickly to eliminate the radicals, not only was political protection removed for the Cultural Revolution's educational reforms, but everything associated with the now infamous Gang of Four was suspect. Yet it was not simple to undo all that had happened in education since 1966. Since the new rulers were eager to cloak themselves in Mao's mantle and in the educational reforms that had been closely associated with the venerated late chairman, they had to proceed with some caution. The Cultural Revolution itself could not be denounced, only the perversions of it by the Gang of Four.

As early as December 1976, the Gang was accused of lowering educational standards and of denigrating the authority of the teacher as part of their plot to keep the proletariat ignorant in order to facilitate usurpation of supreme political power. Their egalitarian and popularizing educational policies had been one more instance of "waving the red flag to oppose the red flag." With this trick exposed, academic standards could be raised and discipline tightened.

Nevertheless, it was only after Teng Hsiao-p'ing's full rehabilitation in July 1977 that the tempo picked up in criticizing existing educational practices and in blaming all shortcomings on the Gang of Four. In August, a major article in the leading theoretical journal, *Red Flag*, called for measures exactly opposite to those advocated in the same journal a year earlier. More stress on theory, higher academic standards, and the need for experts—these were the new watchwords in education. If they sounded like the pre-1966 policies of the discredited capitalist road, no one in China commented on the similarity. Instead, throughout the rest of 1977 the chorus swelled on how students must study hard, teachers and intellectuals should be respected, scientific research should be stimulated, and intellectual talent should be sought out and cultivated.

Teng Hsiao-p'ing, now firmly ensconced as China's number two man with prime responsibility for technological and industrial development, "confided" in an interview with Han Su-yin, published in *Der Spiegel*, that education had lagged badly in the last decade especially in scientific research and theory. The emphasis would now be on raising quality in education and training scientific personnel. For this he expected the length of schooling to be increased to five years in high school and four, or "if need be more," in universities. Postgraduate education would also be stressed.

Recent events have confirmed his prediction. Most notably, the university enrollment system has been drastically overhauled with recommendations from the masses apparently becoming little more than a formality and high-school education the prerequisite for taking competitive entrance examinations. In late 1977, a special nationwide exam was announced open to all those whose educational careers had been interrupted by the tumult of the previous ten years. Moreover, 20 to 30 percent of the entering university class would be selected directly from high school without a prerequisite of two years of manual labor. Coupled with praise for hard study and intellectual achievement, this seemed to confirm that the educational pendulum had swung back to its pre-1966 position.

Such a verdict may be premature. The tensions in China between red and expert, and socialist and national revolutions, have not been resolved. It is doubtful that Hua Kuo-feng, or even Teng Hsiao-p'ing, wants to breed a new class of mandarins in China's universities. They have not repudiated the principle of combining academic study with productive labor and political-moral training, although they have shifted the emphasis. They continue to talk about measures to encourage a higher proportion of worker-peasant children in higher education. Part-time and work-study schools are still being promoted.

It is still too early to tell how much of this is verbal deference to Mao's ghost and how many of the reforms of the Cultural Revolution will really stick. The history of education in China has taken too many sharp turns before to make it certain how far the present course will go. China may be in for a long period of educational, as well as political, stability, but most foreign observers thought the same thing in the early 1960s.

Culture

Chinese emperors were both patrons of culture and guardians of its moral effects. The classical poet and omnipresent calligrapher Mao Tse-tung continued and expanded upon this role. Perhaps more meaningful, the entire mandarinate of imperial China simultaneously possessed political and cultural authority and saw the two as inextricably linked. Here, too, the Chinese Communist Party has inherited Chinese habits as well as Stalinist ideas about controlling the arts and literature. The causal importance that Chinese Communism attaches to the cultural superstructure may reflect more than a quirk of Mao's interpretation of Marxism or the exigencies of the Party's twentieth-century historical circumstances. Traditional Confucian assumptions are not necessarily incompatible with a militant anti-Confucianism.

In the People's Republic all pronouncements on cultural policy refer back to Mao Tse-tung's "Talks at the Yenan Forum on Art and Literature" in 1942. There, speaking to writers and artists who had come to serve in the liberated areas during the anti-Japanese war, he laid down the general guidelines for Party cultural policy. In main outline they were clear enough and have remained constant, but they were given in very different circumstances than would prevail after 1949 and were vague enough to permit quite different interpretations. Therefore, it is not surprising that there have been swings in Party cultural policy comparable to those in education. It might not be quite so easy to summarize them under a convenient phrase like "red and expert," but similar tensions have been at work. Still, the tensions and fluctuations of line should not obscure several overall trends in artistic, cultural, and intellectual life, which go back to 1949 or, for the Communist Party, to 1942.

The first general trend is politicization. Mao claimed in the Yenan talks that all art serves a class interest. Whether that should be exclusively the proletariat (the socialist revolution) or all progressive classes (in the national revolution or "New Democracy" that Mao originally called for) has indeed fluctuated. But the principle of art serving politics has remained and with it a strong emphasis on the didactic function of all artistic and intellectual expression. At its most extreme, the arts are "gears and wheels of the revolution"; literature is "a powerful weapon for class struggle"; and history is "a tool for exposing feudal and bourgeois oppression."

The second trend is popularization. This includes mass participation in the creation and performance of culture, not just its consumption: thirty million amateur actors since the Cultural Revolution; 300 million poems collected in farms and factories during the Great Leap Forward; 3,000 peasant-painters in one rural district. In culture, as in politics, no one should remain passive. Besides popular participation, the arts should also be designed to appeal to the tastes of the broad masses. Therefore, ever since the Yenan talks, professional writers and artists have been urged to aim at a mass audience—"the workers, peasants, and People's Liberation Army fighters"—not just at a handful of bourgeois intellectuals and aesthetes. Mass culture for the masses required a certain leveling out, a "vulgarization" to use a pejorative term. It does not particularly encourage diversity or creativity, although Party cultural authorities continually urge artists to be creative, because the artist must appeal to established popular tastes. Politicization and popularization may therefore lead to a certain uniformity and dullness in artistic and cultural production; this was one of the complaints, even in China, about the culture of the Cultural Revolution period.

In culture, as in education, the road toward politicization, popularization, and possibly standardization, has not been straight or smooth. An overview of cultural trends since 1949 will show the main turns and bumps.

National Tradition and Socialist Transformation in Culture, 1949-1965

In the first few years after 1949 the Chinese cultural, artistic, and intellectual world was saturated with Soviet borrowings. This was part of the general campaign to remold the thinking of non-Communist intellectuals by weaning them away from the "bourgeois culture" of the capitalist West and the "feudal culture" of the national past. Kuo Mo-jo, Mao's favorite spokesman on such matters, exhorted his fellow intellectuals at the First National Conference of Writers and Artists: "We must sweep away the remaining forces of the old semi-colonial and

semi-feudal literature and arts . . . and finally adopt the precious forms
of expression of Soviet Russia, the land of socialism."[5]

But these "precious forms" were not always well suited to Chinese
popular tastes and the heavy dependence on a foreign model was not
palatable to Chinese nationalism. By 1953 official attitudes toward
national tradition were changing and the call was for a carefully
discriminating inheritance of the cultural legacy in order to build a new
culture "national in form, and socialist in content." Another slogan
from Mao Tse-tung, "weed through the old to let the new emerge,"
expressed this renewed interest in indigenous sources for a new Chinese
culture and a desire for a distinctively Chinese style. Ever since Mao's
essay "On New Democracy" in 1940, Party policy had encouraged
developing popular, "democratic," folk culture. Only the rotten, elitist,
upper-class feudal culture should be discarded. Thus there was no
ideological problem in praising folk dances, peasant New Year's
pictures, or popular paper-cuts as "people's culture." But when by the
mid-1950s traditional theater, literati ink painting, and classical poetry
began to be included in the popular, democratic culture, other criteria
like "realistic," "patriotic," and "progressive" had to be introduced to
justify this reappraisal of traditional arts and artists. Behind the
broadened definition of what could be preserved may have been a
pragmatic realization that popularization of culture required forms that
appealed to the Chinese people; there also seems to have been not just a
little national pride in Chinese cultural achievements, a pride
manifested both within and outside the Communist Party.

The renaissance of traditional culture reached its peak in the
political liberation of the Hundred Flowers Movement in 1956-1957.
Mao, of course, intended the liberalization to appeal to intellectuals and
to elicit their enthusiasm for building socialism. Culturally, it produced
both an upsurge of activity in traditional art forms and renewed interest
in non-Soviet forms of Western culture. Intellectually, it stimulated
interest in China's past and criticism of many features in the present.
The Party reacted by launching an "antirightist movement," which
uprooted all nonsocialist flowers and froze any more blooming.

Hard on the heels of this backlash against cultural and intellectual
liberalization came the ideological fervor of the Great Leap Forward,
which, in its zeal for laying the social and economic foundations for
communism, had little time or patience for cultural frills. Insofar as the

Great Leap Forward had a cultural policy, it was cultural populism with a vengeance—art of, by, and for the people. This was not Soviet-inspired, but it was also not very favorable to any expressions of high culture.

As the Great Leap spirit waned amid economic difficulties and political bickering, intellectuals ("the experts") were once again in demand and the Party leadership, dominated more by Liu Shao-ch'i's pragmatism than Mao's idealism, cautiously revised the Hundred Flowers Movement. This may be seen as a tactical concession to revive the support of disillusioned intellectuals or even as a means of diverting popular attention from the economic failures of the Great Leap. In any event, the early 1960s saw a less vigorous but still considerable blooming. Unlike 1956, the inspiration was overwhelmingly traditional Chinese culture. Traditional-style artists and actors were highly publicized; dying art forms, ranging from K'un Chu opera to jade carving, were painstakingly revived and praised. China's historical and philosophical legacy, recovering from the Great Leap Forward injunction "More present, less past," attracted more and more attention from Party and non-Party intellectuals.

The study of the past, and its implications for the present, eventually got China's whole intellectual and cultural world into serious political trouble and led directly to the Cultural Revolution. When scholars like Liu Chieh, Feng Yu-lan, and Wu Han were not only praising Confucius for his historical role but also claiming that Confucian virtues transcended class lines, the implications were clear for contemporary society and the new socialist morality that was supposed to accompany it. When Wu Han and others carried historical analogy to the point of thinly veiled attacks on Mao's leadership, traditional culture and its values seemed all the more menacing. And, finally, when P'eng Chen and other top Party bureaucrats blocked Chiang Ch'ing's efforts to sweep traditional plays off the stage in favor of new revolutionary dramas, Mao saw the danger of a nonsocialist superstructure subverting the socialist base of the People's Republic. In brief, traditional values carried by the old cultural forms began to appear subversive to Mao's new social order and his rule.

In the Great Proletarian Cultural Revolution, Mao not only struck against his political enemies and their cultural spokesmen, but also against traditional culture, those "ghosts, monsters, and demons" that had risen from the grave of the old society to subvert Mao's new kingdom of socialist virtue. The Cultural Revolution was one long exercise in exorcism.

The Proletarian Culture of the Cultural Revolution

The destructive aspects of the Cultural Revolution were apparent first: attacks on "bourgeois intellectuals" and revisionists, purges of the Party and government cultural apparatus, and the suspension of all normal cultural and intellectual life as schools and museums closed. Simultaneously, journals ceased publication and no books were printed except Mao Tsetung Thought. Lenin had said that the proletariat would take over the high culture of the bourgeoisie; Mao had previously called for a critical inheritance of China's cultural legacy. It now seemed that a truly proletarian culture would have to be built on a tabula rasa. Rampaging Red Guards smashed recently restored historical monuments in their zeal to destroy the "four olds" (old habits, old thoughts, old values, and old things), thus cutting China off from its cultural roots. New revolutionary cultural spokesmen inveighed against bourgeois foreign cultural influences, which by now meant revisionist Soviet art as much as decadent capitalist art. The formerly flourishing cultural diplomacy was suspended. Even hitherto approved "realist" and progressive foreign authors, including Lenin's favorite, the nineteenth-century Russian populist Chernyshevsky, were condemned. The denunciation of former cultural czar Chou Yang for praising such foreign writers sounded a note of militant cultural chauvinism:

> Is there any trace of the Chinese national pride in him? Not the least. His was the manner of a vassal begging from the Western bourgeoisie. . . . He saw only the bourgeoisie of the West, and not the proletariat of the East.[6]

But where was the new culture of the proletariat? In its fear of the bourgeois ideological contamination, the Cultural Revolution's radicalism manifested a puritanical fervor inimical to any cultural variety or creativity. For example, the editor of a leading Shanghai newspaper warned students not to read "old" (pre–Cultural Revolution) novels: "The heaps of mildewed bad books are rows of cannon balls with which the bourgeoisie attacks the proletariat."[7] The cultural field was conceived of as a battleground between the bourgeoisie and the proletariat, between the revisionism of the discredited "capitalist-roaders" and Mao's socialist morality. For a time it seemed as if the assault on old and foreign art forms would leave this battlefield a desert with nothing but posters for art, slogans for literature, and Mao Tsetung Thought propaganda ·for entertainment.

The spirit of the new age was expressed in a September 16, 1969, article in what had been the leading intellectual newspaper, *Kuang-ming jih pao*, signed only as "Criticism Group of a Certain PLA Armored Unit." These cultural critics saw culture in these terms:

> It is the job of proletarian literature and art to sing heartily about our great leader Chairman Mao and the invincible thought of Mao Tse-tung, fervently create the heroic image of workers, peasants, and soldiers, sing about their great achievements, expose the weakness and ugly character of U.S. imperialism, Soviet modern revisionism, and all reactionaries and their inevitable doom, and make literature and art an effective weapon for uniting and educating the people and hitting and destroying the enemy with one heart and one purpose.

But, for all their politicization and popularization of culture, the ideologues behind the Cultural Revolution had more in mind than just destruction. They wanted to build a new "proletarian culture" aimed directly at the masses and inculcating in them the political values of socialism and the thought of Mao Tse-tung.

The theater, where some of the earlier skirmishes of the Cultural Revolution had been fought over the creation of model revolutionary plays, was the main testing ground for the new proletarian culture. There are several reasons for this. Mao's wife Chiang Ch'ing's own experience in the theater world, and the scores she had to settle with major figures there, may have been one factor. But there was also the important role that theater, especially traditional opera, played in China. No other nation, except possibly Italy, is so permeated with enthusiasm and appreciation for the theater. As far back as the Yenan period the Communist Party had realized the importance of the stage for reaching illiterate and semiliterate masses. Then, simple skits and spoken drama had been the most prevalent way for getting their political messages across. In the Cultural Revolution, Chiang Ch'ing proposed to take over the higher levels of theatrical art, the traditional opera, for her new revolutionary art.

The first versions of the model revolutionary plays had been performed at the Shanghai festival for revolutionary plays in 1964 under the auspices of Chiang Ch'ing and the PLA. They had been thought too crudely propagandistic by some of the former Party leaders, but after the apocalypse of 1966-1968 the plays were rewritten to heighten the political content even further and to stress the revolutionary heroism of the main character. The plots for each of the six model revolutionary operas showed how far they had departed from the tradition-dominated subject matter of conventional Peking Opera and the numerous regional variants. *Taking Tiger Mountain by Strategy* featured the exploits of the PLA in subduing a "Chiang Kai-shek bandit gang" in the last days of the civil war (see Photograph 1). *Shachiapang* dealt with anti-Japanese guerrillas in World War II; *The Red Lantern* (perhaps Chiang Ch'ing's favorite) told of three generations of a heroic railroad worker's family resisting the Japanese invaders and their Chinese lackeys. *Raid on the White Tiger Regiment* was set in the Korean War, *On the Docks* featured production struggles at home, and *Ode to Dragon River* showed class struggle in the communes. All possessed very edifying themes in accord with the new political line for the arts, and all were very melodramatic in accord with Chiang Ch'ing's dictum about emphasizing the "three prominences": "prominence to positive characters among all characters, prominence to heroic characters among positive characters, and prominence to the main heroic character among heroic characters." There should be no room for "middle characters," dramatic subtlety, or moral ambiguity. Foreign observers have compared the new plays to Victorian melodrama, or even medieval morality plays, in their predictable triumph of good over evil and their obvious moral message. Moreover, these model plays, with the doctrine of the three prominences and the rejection of narrow realism in favor of "heroes larger than life," were taken as the correct guide for other art forms like literature, film, and painting. Politicization was the keynote for all the arts; Chiang Ch'ing's model plays would show the way.

Yet there was a significant difference from the other extreme periods of politicization, the early 1950s and the Great Leap Forward. In the first, a foreign model, Soviet culture, had been upheld; in the second, folk art had been the approved cultural form. This time, selected parts of the old high culture would be taken over for the use of the revolution. The emphasis was still on national form with the main acting conventions, singing style, and music for the new plays retained from the old opera. Admittedly, Chiang Ch'ing introduced Western elements as well, like realistic stage settings and piano accompaniment, but Peking opera was to remain Chinese in style and to be a model for other art forms in this respect. The emphasis on national style even affected the other "model" stage productions, which used imported Western forms. Thus, the two famous revolutionary ballets *Red Detachment of Women* and *The White*

Photograph 1   Scene from model revolutionary Peking Opera, *Taking Tiger Mountain by Strategy*. The disguised PLA hero uses traditional acrobatic Chinese stage techniques to symbolize riding a horse, but the naturalistic stage backdrop is a Cultural Revolution innovation.

Haired Girl (a remake of an earlier modern Peking opera) adopted many
stage conventions and singing styles from Chinese opera. "Critical
inheritance of the cultural legacy" was now interpreted to sanction free
borrowing and integration with selected Western stylistic elements, a
complete change in subject matter, but also insistence on retaining a
strong national identity. It was by far the most ambitious attempt to
produce an art and culture that would satisfy all the competing demands
for mass appeal, national flavor, socialist content, and ideological
purity. Like the drastic reforms in education, the total transformation of
culture was running into problems by the early 1970s.

The Anti-Confucius Campaign and Beating Back the Right Deviationist Wind, 1973-1976

By the spring of 1973 there was a noticeable relaxation in the cultural
sphere. A few books on subjects other than contemporary political
struggles were beginning to appear; famous old artists were being
commissioned to do traditional-style paintings for public buildings;
and there was some tentative discussion about bringing back more of the
traditional theater. A *People's Daily* article on April 28 discreetly
suggested that more attention might be paid to artistic form. After all,
citing the ever-relevant and ever-malleable Yenan talks as authority,
"No matter what the progress politically, art products that lack artistic
character are ineffective."

With PLA tutelage for the arts shaken by the recent perfidy of its
commander, Lin Piao, and with Chou En-lai's bureaucrats slowly
reemerging to restore order and promote production, the political
ground seemed prepared for at least a partial pullback from the Cultural
Revolution's extreme politicization of the arts. There were no new
hundred flowers in sight, but a few timorous artistic sprouts were
pushing forth.

These flowers budded but did not bloom, for in the next few months a
new cold front descended on the cultural field. It came from the radicals'
fear that the main reforms of the Cultural Revolution and their own
political position were in danger. Their control of the mass media gave
them the opportunity to launch another public campaign in favor of the
Cultural Revolution's policies; the weight they attached to the arts as
molders of political opinion and social values made sure the cultural
front would be the spearhead of their counterattack. But the particular
form this offensive took, a mass campaign to jointly criticize Lin Piao
and Confucius, showed how strong the traditional habit of using the
past to teach present political lessons remained with the Chinese left-
wing as well as with "rightists." Wu Han and others had helped

provoke the Cultural Revolution by dredging up historical parallels to criticize Mao in the early 1960s. Ten years later Mao's leftist defenders would turn again to history to discredit their contemporary opponents.

This time, however, the manipulation of the past was even trickier. The "Anti-Lin, Anti-Confucius Campaign" had to be a two-edged sword explicitly disassociating the leftists from the memory of the erstwhile leftist, now renegade, Lin Piao, and implicitly criticizing the moderates who would turn the clock back to before the Cultural Revolution. The precarious balance of power within the civil and military bureaucracies made it impolitic to make that criticism too direct, but the radicals had confidence that manipulation of mass opinion would make their cause prevail. Whether or not this was a conspiratorial plot to seize power, as alleged after their fall, it was a deliberate attempt to use history and culture as a weapon in a bitter political struggle that was itself partly being fought over cultural issues.

In any event, the form it took was hardly conspiratorial in the conventional sense. Instead of secret back-room dealings between elites, this was a mass publicity campaign calling on the whole nation to study history in order to criticize Lin Piao and Confucius. It started with a standard Russian and Chinese interpretation of Marxist historical theory that posited an inevitable development from slavery to feudalism to capitalism. This sequence was valid for China as well as for all other societies. In a series of popular and pseudo-scholarly articles Confucius was held to be the arch-villain who had tried to check this progressive sequence by restoring the power of the declining slave-owner class and opposing the emergence of feudalism, which was represented by the "progressive" Legalist school of philosophy and their political exemplar, the unifier of ancient China, Ch'in Shih Huang-ti. Subsequent Confucian philosophers' attempts to turn back the clock and restore the pre-Ch'in slave-owner society, and the efforts of Legalist statesmen to thwart these reactionary designs, were then held to be the central theme for the next 2,000 years of Chinese history.

The connection with Lin Piao was twofold. First, he was said to have been a closet Confucianist who had kept quotations from Confucius hidden in his bedroom. Second, and more important for the current struggle, he had been a restorationist who like Confucius had wanted to turn the clock back. Of course, he had tried to mask his reactionary designs by passing as an ultraleftist but now he was exposed. History, and the enlightened masses, guided by the thought of Chairman Mao, would expose all other restorationists who plotted to undo progressive revolutions like the Cultural Revolution. History and philosophy were hailed as weapons of class struggle. The masses were urged (and compelled?) to join in a nationwide study movement and to write their own criticism of Lin Piao and Confucius. Probably never before had so much been written by so many about ancient history. It was Carl Becker's "everyman his own historian" come to life, but every man followed the same historical line. This was no hundred flowers blooming and contending.

The general tightening up on the ideological front extended across the arts. In theater, one of the second generation of revolutionary operas, *Three Trips to Peach Mountain,* was found to have contained concealed praise for Lin Shao-ch'i and his discredited "capitalist road," and a vigorous publicity campaign was launched to denounce it; Chiang Ch'ing and her cultural watchdogs quashed this and several other plays and films for alleged ideological distortions. Simultaneously, the model operas were adapted to local theatrical styles in order to increase their appeal in various regions of China, and filmed versions of the original Peking Opera productions were widely shown throughout the country. Although they had virtually monopolized the stage for seven years, there were no complaints about the constant reruns of these new theatrical classics. The newer revolutionary operas being produced by 1973 did not challenge their preeminence or deviate from their heavily political format.

In other areas, after a brief appreciation of Western classical music during the Philadelphia Symphony's visit to Peking, internal ideological demands took precedence over external diplomatic relations and a press campaign attacked the fallacy of such music without class character. While foreign music was being rejected for its bourgeois class character, Chinese-style painting was criticized for lacking socialist character and the famous artists who were starting to paint for public consumption again in 1973 were told to create their art to suit the new age or stop painting. To drive home the lesson about what was not acceptable for the new proletarian culture, and probably also to embarrass Chou En-lai, who had supported many of these veteran artists, Chiang Ch'ing arranged exhibitions of "black art" where, as in the anti-Confucius campaign, the masses were urged to become masters of the new culture by criticizing the offending paintings (see Photograph 2). The artists did not seem to benefit much from such criticism or the public humiliation that went with it. Most of them proved unable or unwilling to apply Chiang Ch'ing's theory of the three prominences to their work and dropped out of sight. The graphic arts were dominated

Photograph 2　Li K'o-jan, *Landscape*, 1973. This is an example of the allegedly pessimistic "black art" condemned by Chiang Ch'ing.

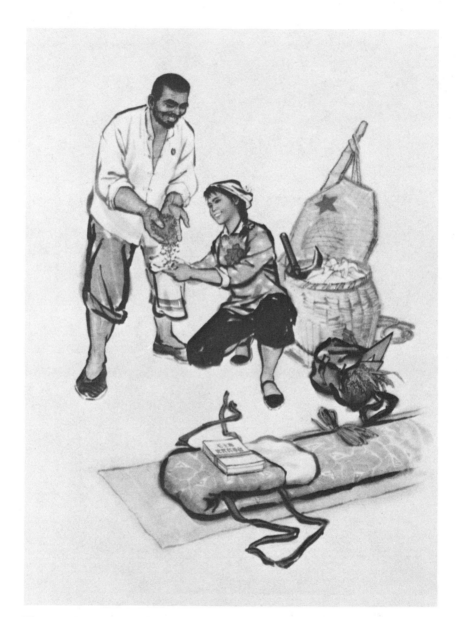

Photograph 3   Wen Cheng-ch'eng, *Going to University*, 1972. This is the kind of "Chinese-style painting" favored by the Cultural Revolution radicals. It still uses Chinese inks and retains some traditional brush techniques but obviously has little in common with traditional painting in style or subject matter.

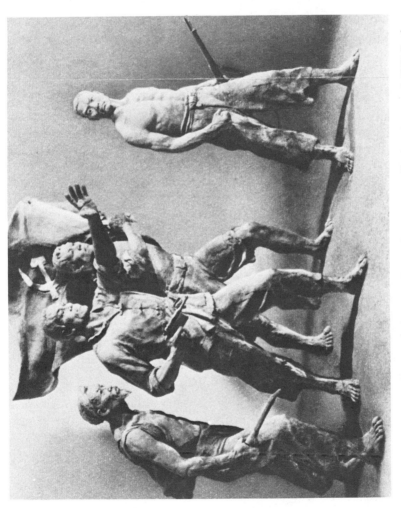

Photograph 4   Life-sized clay sculptured figures from *Rent Collection Courtyard*, 1967. In the final scene oppressed peasants overthrow their feudal masters. By Cultural Revolution standards all art had to have a positive message.

by stereotyped portraits of model workers and peasants, PLA woodcuts, and amateur peasant paintings (see Photograph 3). This simplified and didactic approach to art was also followed in sculpture, where the Cultural Revolution's revolutionary tableau of life-size clay sculptures with glass eyes, *Rent Collection Courtyard*, was emulated in a series of new groups with titles like *Wrath of the Serfs* and *Song of the Tachai Spirit* (see Photograph 4).

Finally, in literature, the new generation of writers emerging after almost all previously established authors had dropped from sight in the Cultural Revolution was seriously enjoined to eschew "bourgeois naturalism" or "critical realism" and take the model revolutionary operas as their models. In all its forms art was to be "higher, more typical, and more intense than real life" so as to be able to move the hearts and souls of the revolutionary masses. "Revolutionary romanticism"—showing the masses heroic exemplars rather than real people—clearly predominated over "socialist realism." Direct political relevance to current political issues and struggles was also predominant.

By the end of 1975 the cultural counteroffensive had prepared the way for a direct attack on "the right deviationist wind" and its alleged progenitor, Teng Hsiao-p'ing. Right up to Mao's death in September 1976, the arts carried the burden of a vitriolic attack on Teng and other, yet-to-be-rooted-out, hidden revisionists. According to subsequent revelations, Chiang Ch'ing and her cohorts in the Gang of Four were preparing a new series of revolutionary operas all on the current theme of resisting capitalist roaders. But in October Hua Kuo-feng and his associates proved that control over the propaganda and cultural media are only a means to power, not power itself. Overnight the radicals, now condemned as a "Gang of Four," fell and the organs of propaganda were turned against them.

After the Gang of Four: A New Hundred Flowers?

Within two months of the fall of the Gang of Four a *People's Daily* headline hailed a "New Spring in Proletarian Literature and Art." Over a year later, it is still unclear how much the climate has changed.

Almost immediately a number of works that had been banned or suppressed by the Gang were revived with great fanfare. Among the earliest was a Hunan opera and film, *Song of the Gardener*, that praised obedient, hard-working students and solicitous but firm teachers. Chiang Ch'ing had considered it an affront to her campaign against the absolute authority of the teachers. The new line in education and art made it a national hit.

With the revived plays and films went a revival of traditional art forms, like landscape painting, and some cultural opening to the outside world symbolized by the commemoration in Peking of Beethoven's 150th anniversary. Republication of long out-of-print literary and historical works also showed that respect for the "cultural legacy" was once again reviving, and there was even a hint of a more cosmopolitan cultural spirit in the air (see Photograph 5).

Veteran writers and artists who had not been heard of since 1966 suddenly reappeared to join the chorus of condemnation for the purged radicals and to promise new work by themselves. The denunciation of recent cultural autocracy was accompanied by promise of more variety and more freedom for artists and intellectuals. For instance, in discussing the Gang of Four's perverted version of ancient history, the critic Chou Wen observed that dating the transition from slave owning to feudal society was "an academic question [where] differing opinions are free to contend."[8] Even more hopeful for those who read political-cultural essays, on January 29, 1977, the *People's Daily* called for an end to stereotyped forms of writing.

The other side of this cultural liberalization has been the continuing campaign to use artists and intellectuals to discredit their former political masters: Chiang Ch'ing and her cohorts. Thus the litany of rehabilitated artists ran from indignation at the way they were treated by the Gang to joyful gratitude toward Chairman Hua and the new leadership. The Gang of Four are repeatedly denounced for perverting the arts, culture, and history to promote their own evil political ambitions. But the most serious of their crimes seems to have been their attempted illegal usurpation of power, not their corruption of the arts; the idea of art serving immediate political causes or factions, not just general ideological principles, does not seem to be questioned.

It is also worth noting that the Gang is not being condemned for leftist excesses, foisting too much politics on the arts, but for an "ultraright line." Like Lin Piao they only pretended to be leftists but secretly wanted to restore bourgeois control by stultifying the intelligence of the masses. A critical outside observer might agree that a lot of the Cultural Revolution's artistic offerings were pretty stultifying, but the new cultural authorities were not rejecting those literary and art works so much as denying the Gang of Four any credit for them. Thus it was explained in a straight-faced manner that Chiang Ch'ing had had nothing to do with creating the revolutionary model plays. It had all been done under the guidance of Chairman Mao's thought and Premier Chou's tender solicitude. Chiang Ch'ing was an "ignoramus" and a

Photograph 5   Mao Tse-tung's Mausoleum in T'ien An Men Square, Peking, 1977. Solid and dignified, drawing more on Western neoclassical than Chinese architectural tradition, it stands at the center of Peking.

"pickpocket" who took credit for other people's accomplishments.

In other words, the fall of the Gang of Four has not removed the arts from the political battlefield. The plays, films, and works of art featured in 1977 went back before the Cultural Revolution to prove that China's socialist art and literature were not all created during Chiang Ch'ing's ascendancy, but the main creations of the Cultural Revolution period have not been rejected either. Moreover, most of the revived or newly produced works have made direct political points, either discrediting the Gang (for example, the latest hit play of 1977 was a ballet on Yang K'ai-hui, Mao's first wife), or stressing the historic role of deceased Party leaders, particularly Chou En-lai, but also figures denounced in the Cultural Revolution like Ch'en Yi and Ho Lung. There has also been no lack of fulsome praise for the new leaders. At a PLA theatrical festival in October 1977, 5,600 performers hailed the rule of Hua Kuo-feng. The festivities included

> scenes in which Uighur dancers offer him sweet milk tea, Tibetan peasants, singing his praises, offer him barley wine at harvest time, armymen pledge to be his good fighters and youngsters embroider a silk banner to demonstrate their good will to the new leader.[9]

The scene bears a striking resemblance to innumerable pictures of Mao in the late 1960s, or to Stalin in the late 1940s.

The new official position on the arts was spelled out in an authoritative article by the "Theoretical Group of the Ministry of Culture," which appeared in *Red Flag* in June 1977. The title, "Advance Triumphantly, Holding Aloft the Great Banner of the Thought of Chairman Mao on Literature and Art," was in the best polemical style of the Cultural Revolution, but the article itself was much more moderate in balancing insistence that art serve politics with admonitions to raise the quality and variety of artistic production. Political orthodoxy was reaffirmed by citing Mao's injunction from the Yenan talks that all art should be for the workers, peasants, and soldiers. But close behind that came a reminder of his 1956 call to "let a hundred flowers bloom" in order to justify more freedom for artists and writers. The tension between these two Maoist legacies—"the worker-peasant-soldier orientation" and "let a hundred flowers bloom"—is central to China's cultural and artistic life today. Again, in principle the two are complementary but often in practice one principle has been used to sanction orthodoxy and vulgarization of art, while the other has been used to justify diversity and liberalization.

Even more so than in education, the future seems uncertain on the cultural front. The present trend is obviously toward liberalization, often more in practice than in theory. At the Chinese New Year celebrations in Peking in February 1978, two very significant new flowers blossomed amid a carefully cultivated garden of more standard varieties: Dvořák's "New World Symphony" was performed, proving that classical Western music and culture were once more respectable; and for the first time in ten years excerpts from prerevolutionary Peking Operas were staged. But two flowers do not make a spring and certain legacies from the Cultural Revolution remain strong. They are manifested in specific forms like revolutionized opera or politicized Chinese ink paintings, and also in the continued didacticism that pervades most, though no longer all, artistic efforts. But there are powerful forces behind the liberalization too. Though the most obvious is the political backlash against the Gang of Four's cultural despotism, the general policy of calling for more technical and intellectual expertise may be more fundamental in creating an atmosphere and a clientele for more sophisticated art. Such factors were important for "the thaw" in the Soviet Union after Stalin. They may lead to more of a thaw in China, too, but the Soviet example also suggests that there may be limitations on how far these imperatives behind scientific and economic development will carry liberalization in the cultural sphere.

Chinese Culture, Past and Future

At present, then, the Chinese cultural world seems poised between conflicting forces. There are strong pressures for relaxation, partly as a revulsion against the "cultural autocracy" of the Gang of Four, partly as an appeal to once-again-valued intellectuals, partly as an end to the intellectual isolation that China's present leaders realize has cost it dearly in terms of scientific development. And finally, by no means least, there is the continued pride in China's past cultural achievements, which will not let the traditional culture be swept away as so much feudal garbage. But there still are the fears that too much cultural liberalization will weaken the didactic role of the arts in promoting socialist values and publicizing current political causes. Foreign bourgeois cultural influences are still suspect; traditional culture still must have its feudal values sanitized in order to serve the present. And, most important, the Party continues its close supervision over intellectual life and all the arts. The rehabilitation of figures like the former chief cultural commissioner, Chou Yang, may symbolize complete rejection of the Gang of Four's cultural politics, but it does not augur well for freedom in the arts. No stable balance has been found between these tensions during the last thirty years. It is doubtful that one will be achieved soon.

Yet certain factors seem clear. No real revival of past culture is possible: this is a new society, with new demands on the arts and a different social basis from that of the old China. Through cultural nationalism, the past will continue to pull on the present but there will be no reversion. One of the beneficial effects of the Cultural Revolution may have been its smashing of an incipient national museum culture by insisting on changes in national forms to create a present-day culture. Traditional Peking Opera or Ming-style paintings might satisfy the need for cultural continuity, but they were not creating a new culture.

What then about China's openness to modern foreign cultural influences? The question of how much foreign culture to borrow without losing a sense of one's own cultural identity has been an issue for Chinese intellectuals since the last century. The People's Republic's efforts to wall out undesirable influences have not solved it. One might expect that the current trend toward a diplomatic and economic opening to the West could carry some cultural by-products. It is difficult to foresee how significant these might be and, in any case, they will probably be adapted to Chinese forms and needs. The days of wholesale cultural importation from the West are long over, and neither Communist orthodoxy nor national pride will permit their revival. Nevertheless, it is unlikely that China will continue to be as impervious to outside influences as it has been for the last decade.

It is also unlikely that intellectual and artistic expression will remain in such a tight political straitjacket. In the recent relaxation, signs of an unofficial art and literature somewhat like that of the Soviet Union have appeared. Manuscripts of "underground novels" circulate among students and intellectuals; apolitical traditional-style paintings are passed from hand to hand. Some of this may be protest art, but much of it is probably more to satisfy educated persons' demand for more variety and less political stereotyping. This tendency is likely to manifest itself in official art as well. Thus, although politicization and popularization will remain dominant features in China's cultural works, there may be considerably more room for diversity and perhaps even for creativity. On the latter aspect, the vastly expanded popular base for the arts created by popular educational and cultural policies may produce both more demand for culture (entertainment as well as education) and, given a loosening of political controls, the emergence of more creative artistic talent. Mass education and economic progress have created a much broader base for a real "hundred flowers" blooming than existed in 1956, but the political climate may be the crucial determinant for how many blooms actually appear.

In culture more than most areas, then, there are more questions than answers. In no way should post-Mao China be seen in terms of traditional China but, as suggested earlier, some habits and cultural patterns from the past do persist. Mao's own fondness for combining poetry and historical allusions with current politics is well known. Less well known is that his iconoclastic wife Chiang Ch'ing took the pen-name "Lang Yeh T'ai" for a poem she published in 1974. The name referred to a terrace built in her home county of Chucheng, Shantung Province, by the first unifier of China, Ch'in Shih Huang-ti. Subsequent denunciations of Chiang Ch'ing claimed that this pointed historical reference indicated her ambition to emulate the first emperor in taking supreme political power. Whether such accusations are literally true or not, the episode reveals how China's political leaders still think in terms of historical references and poetical expression of inner feelings. Where else would rulers and their politically ambitious consorts choose poetry to express political plans or ambitions? Where else would such poems be taken so seriously? Because of conscious cultural nationalism and unconscious habits from the past, culturally China is still China. Neither the recent Cultural Revolution nor any reruns of it in the future are likely to change that.

Notes

1. *Wei-ta shih-nien* [Ten Great Years], Peking, 1959, p. 170.

2. Quoted in Robert Taylor, *Education and University Enrollment Policies in China, 1949-1971* (Canberra: Australian National University Press, 1973), p. 14.

3. Quoted in R. F. Price, *Education in China* (London: Routledge, 1970), p. 142.

4. Quoted in John Gardiner, "Chou Jung-hsin and Chinese Education," *Current Scene* 15, nos. 11-12 (November-December 1977):12.

5. Quoted in Mei Hsu, *New Art in China* (Hong Kong: no

publisher, no date), p. 12.

6. Shanghai Writing Group for Revolutionary Mass Criticism, "Advertising Bourgeois Art and Literature Means Restoration of Capitalism," *Red Flag*, no. 4 (March 31, 1970), in *Survey of China Mainland Magazines*, no. 680, pp. 84-85.

7. Editorial note, *Shanghai wen hui pao*, in *Survey of China Mainland Press*, no. 4135 (February 15, 1968), p. 11.

8. Chou Wen, "Distorting Ancient History to Serve Present Needs," *Peking Review*, no. 44 (October 28, 1977), p. 21.

9. "Army Theatrical Festival in Peking," *Peking Review*, no. 43 (October 21, 1977), p. 30.

Selected Further Readings

Journals Useful for Education and Culture

Asian Survey (Berkeley, Calif.)
Bulletin of Concerned Asian Scholars (San Francisco)
China Pictorial (Peking)
China Quarterly (London)
China Reconstructs (Peking)
Chinese Studies in Education (White Plains, N.Y.)
Chinese Studies in History (White Plains, N.Y.)
Chinese Studies in Philosophy (White Plains, N.Y.)
Chinese Literature (Peking)
Current Scene (Hong Kong)
Journal of Asian Studies (Ann Arbor, Mich.)

Education

Barendsen, Robert Dale. *The Educational Revolution in China.* Washington, D.C.: HEW, 1974.
Ch'en, Hsi-en. *The Maoist Educational Revolution.* New York: Praeger, 1974.
Fraser, Stewart E., and Kuang-liang Hsu. *Chinese Education and Society: A Bibliographic Guide.* White Plains, N.Y.: International Arts and Sciences Press, 1972.
Fraser, Stewart E., ed. *Education and Communism in China, An Anthology of Commentary and Documents.* London: Pall Mall Press, 1971.
Hu, C. T., ed. *Aspects of Chinese Education.* New York: Columbia

University Press, 1969.

Hu, Shi-ming, and Eli Seifman. *Toward a New World Outlook, A Documentary History of Education in the PRC, 1949-76*. New York: AMS Press, 1976.

Munro, Donald J. *The Concept of Man in Contemporary China*. Ann Arbor: University of Michigan Press, 1977.

Price, R. F. *Education in Communist China*. London: Routledge and Kegan Paul, 1970.

Seybolt, Peter J. *Revolutionary Education in China, Documents and Commentary*. White Plains, N.Y.: IASP, 1973.

Taylor, Robert. *Education and University Enrollment Policies in China*. Canberra: Australian National University Press, 1973.

Culture

Croizier, Ralph C. *China's Cultural Legacy and Communism*. New York: Praeger, 1970.

Feuerwerker, Albert, ed. *History in Communist China*. Cambridge, Mass.: M.I.T. Press, 1968.

Goldman, Merle. *Literary Dissent in Communist China*. Cambridge, Mass.: Harvard University Press, 1967.

Hajek, Lubor. *Contemporary Chinese Painting*. London: Spring Books, 1961.

Hsu, Kai-yu. *The Chinese Literary Scene*. New York: Random House, 1975.

Huang, Joe C. *Heroes and Villains in Communist China, The Contemporary Chinese Novel as a Reflection of Life*. New York: Pica Press, 1973.

Jenner, W. J. F. *Modern Chinese Stories*. London: Oxford University Press, 1970.

Leys, Simon (pseud.). *Chinese Shadows*. New York: Viking Press, 1977.

Mackerras, Colin. *Amateur Theatre in China, 1949-1966*. Canberra: Australian National University Press, Contemporary China Papers no. 5, 1973.

———. *The Chinese Theatre in Modern Times*. London: Thames and Hudson, 1975.

Mitchell, John D., ed. *The Red Pear Garden: Three Great Dramas of Revolutionary China*. Boston: Godine, 1973.

Scott, A. C. *Literature and the Arts in Twentieth Century China*. New York: Doubleday Anchor, 1965.

Snow, Lois Wheeler. *China on Stage*. New York: Random House, 1972.

Sullivan, Michael. *Chinese Art in the Twentieth Century*. Berkeley: University of California Press, 1959.

Witke, Roxanne. *Comrade Chiang Ch'ing*. Boston-Toronto: Little, Brown and Co., 1977.

10
Military Affairs

A. M. Fraser

It is clearly not possible to recount, or even to name, all of the events and conditions that have affected military affairs in the People's Republic of China. This chapter therefore focuses on a selection of representative events, physical and conceptual, that have shaped the conduct of affairs and the development of the People's Liberation Army (PLA), a term used to designate all of China's armed forces.

Military Doctrine

Ideology has always played a large part in the formulation of policy and in the conduct of the PLA. In Communist China the putative fount of correct thought has been Mao Tse-tung. There have been debates and opposition; Mao did not always prevail in the short run, but in the end almost every principle and practice was given authority by association with Mao's name. Ideological rectitude has been a major criterion in the rating of units and in the assessment of men.

The "line" has been altered and history revised whenever it was necessary. A most transparent shift, for example, was evident in a series of articles that appeared in the *Peking Review* in 1974 and 1975. These statements discussed the major campaigns in the closing phases of the Civil War in the north. They held that Lin Piao, once designated as Mao's chosen successor, but now dead and disgraced, far from being the architect and commander of successful efforts, was the captive of bad doctrine and personal weakness—it was Chairman Mao who had developed the tactics and made the plans that won. As exemplified by the case of Lin Piao, no military leader in the P.R.C. can count himself safe from grave accusations of ideological inadequacy by one side or another in national debates, and such charges may concern events that took place any number of years ago.

In the early days there was a "now or never" imperative in Communist military thinking. Mao's early military writings pointed to the need to expand areas of red influence and to consolidate smaller areas into larger ones. In one essay he urged his followers to "adopt the policy of advancing in a series of waves to expand the area under the independent regime, and oppose the policy of expansion by adventurist advance." Continuously aware of the contradiction between the need to press the revolution immediately and of the Communists' comparative physical inferiority, he counseled prudent action that would neither waste nor scatter resources. The need for continuous action in one form or another pressed hard on the resources of the Red Army. As a result, policies of careful conservation of supplies and equipment and of positive efforts to capture weapons from the other side developed. There was strong encouragement for self-sufficiency in the production of subsistence and matériel. The "base areas" controlled by the Communists served to enlist broad support and made the pacification of the countryside by Kuomintang forces or the Japanese more difficult.

The doctrine of "people's war" embodies ideological and social precepts and strategic and tactical concepts. Governed by the objective facts of his position, Mao was obliged to produce a doctrine that was ideologically sound and persuasive, and that minimized the massive military disabilities of the revolutionary forces and made the most of their assets. The product was people's war.[1] The people's war approach to national military strategy may be seen as a formula. The inputs include a number of factors: men, arms, geography, physical resources, endurance, and dedication. The values of the several components will add up to success if the inputs are correct. In the case of the Chinese revolution, the total input had to include a large measure of manpower and esprit to offset weaknesses in material resources. It should be cautioned that the emphasis on man and esprit does not equate with the simplistic concept of "Mongol hordes" or with the myth that the P.R.C. is not aware of the power of modern weapons. Even so, in a defense of the national territory, the active commitment of the mass of the people can make the task of the invader much more difficult. A night filled with hostile activists is not restful. The reality of the force of this style of warfare is reflected in a negative way in the comments of some of the PLA prisoners taken in Korea; they complained about the absence of the "sea of people" that they were accustomed to operating in on home territory.

The people's war formula is flexible. In practice, *people's war* means exactly what the user of the term intends it to mean. In 1977, one year after Mao's death, officials were telling visitors that the concept was still viable. Within the P.R.C., the debate over how to implement the idea under conditions of modern warfare is still very much alive. The now discredited "Gang of Four," a faction of radicals who rose to prominence in the Cultural Revolution of 1966-1969, is identified with an ideological rigidity that impeded progress toward military moderni- zation. While making the necessary gestures toward the concept of people's war, the current leadership is pressing forward with the nuclear weapons program, the race for better air defense, and other force improvement actions.

In the professional military sphere, Mao showed fine appreciation for the functions of time and space. He projected the course of the Civil War against the Nationalist regime (1927-1949) through the several phases necessary for final victory. Although he reiterated the "men over weapons" idea, his writings show a sophisticated understanding of the need to reorganize and equip his forces before final victory would be possible. He taught the tactics and strategy of "protracted war," which would keep his cause alive while gathering strength for the future. He urged his people to "despise the enemy strategically and respect him tactically."

Mao was more than a sloganeer: he can claim a place among the great strategists. His objective view of his own situation and the proper use of his resources were reinforced by his ability to articulate a doctrine that fitted the style and tradition of his people. His major directives on the substance of military affairs show his talent for seeing into the heart of a problem. His *Selected Military Writings* should be explored to gain some feeling for his grasp of military matters. In this work may be found the rationales of progression from guerrilla warfare through mobile operations to major positional combat. Mao's "Ten Principles of Operation" (found in "The Present Situation and Our Tasks") may sound unusual to Western ears, but his formulations of universals like the principles of the objective, mass, surprise, and concentration are presented in ways that any professional soldier would be comfortable with. A comparison with the U.S. "Nine Principles of War" produces many similarities.

It is in its unflagging insistence on the role of politics that the Chinese military differs. The PLA emphasizes that the political stance and conviction of an army is sometimes more important than its weapons;

that for a country defending against an invader or engaging in a revolutionary action, a politically aware people is a basic necessity for existence; and that the political will of an opponent is as important a target as any of its forces. The Chinese Communist forces have always been involved in intensive political and ideological activity. Zeal, loyalty, and self-sacrifice are regarded as the highest expressions of soldierly virtue.

Evolution of the Chinese Red Army

During the revolutionary and anti-Japanese war periods, military affairs and all other functions were so interwoven that they must be seen as one. It is useful, however, to review these periods briefly to demonstrate how the stream of events affected the military establishment.

Military Campaigns

The 1927 Communist-led uprisings at Nanchang, Changsha, and Canton marked a clean break between Communists and Nationalists that had been some time in the making. Previously, the Communists had propagandized and operated within the general structure of the Nationalist army. Their participation in command and in the operation of such important agencies as the Whampoa Military Academy and their service in regular operating forces, while Chiang Kai-shek pursued his aim of unifying the nation, did not satisfy the Communist demand for political power. Mutual distrust and political enmity made a break between the two groups inevitable.

The uprisings were not military successes, and after very short periods the revolting units withdrew into several small base areas and began efforts to consolidate their holdings and further their cause. The principal enclave, the Kiangsi soviet in the Chingkangshang area, was the center, with Mao the political leader and Chu Teh the military commander. The pioneering spirit was reinforced by the need to defend against powerful Nationalist efforts to destroy the movement. In late 1930, Chiang's forces began the "bandit extermination" campaigns against the Communists. In the first four of these, attempts were made to effect deep penetrations by separate columns. This tactic played into the Communist ability to conduct guerrilla warfare from friendly bases and to interrupt almost at will the attacker's lines of communication. Chiang probably finally heeded his German advisors and began broad front encirclement, consolidating territory as he went, steadily pressing the Red forces into smaller and less useful areas. The change in tactics overcame Mao's earlier advantages, and perceiving that the Communists would have to evacuate the soviet in order to escape this heavy and consistent pressure, it was decided that a refuge should be sought in the forbidding northwest. During this period, a showdown conference brought key control of the Party to Mao, and the Long March began under Mao's direction in October 1934 in several columns. Some 100,000 people began the journey headed for Shensi Province; one year later, 6,000 miles from the starting point and at a strength of some 16,000, the main column reached Yenan, and an equal number arrived somewhat farther to the west. Moving at the impressive rate of more than sixteen miles per day, the Communist forces had traversed mountains, rivers, and gorges and had fought off attacks by unfriendly aborigines and Nationalist ground and air forces. They had performed some notable river crossings and maintained themselves despite their heavy losses. The leadership learned—if it needed to—just how durable the Chinese peasant soldier could be. The Long March may be seen as a military operation led by political persons, during which the Red Army gained much experience in living and operating in difficulty and in fighting mobile engagements.

Military affairs became even more important when Japan opened its major attack on China in 1937. Nationalists and Communists found their opposition to one another somewhat tempered by a common need to deal with the invader. Observers have argued that both sides hoarded their resources against the time when Japan would be defeated by the Allies and the Chinese could resume their basic contest. Each side maneuvered politically in trying to shape a united front that would best work to its advantage. The Communists sought, largely in vain, to share the military aid coming from the United States. In their base areas, the Communist leaders faced many of the problems of nationhood long before actually taking power. Some of the principals, particularly Chou En-lai, accumulated extensive experience in negotiations at the highest level. The Communists also gained some fighting experience, particularly in the north. The Battle of P'inghsingkuan in 1937 and the "Hundred Regiments" campaign of 1940 added to their experience and knowledge but did little to affect the outcome of the war with Japan.

Although the United States continued to promote accommodation between the Communists and Nationalists, all efforts at conciliation failed. The issue in the Chinese Civil War was finally settled on the battlefield in the north: here, between 1945 and 1949, were fought the great battles. The battles in North China and Manchuria set the tone: Liaohsi-Shenyang, Huai Hai, and Peking-Tientsin. Large forces were involved in these battles; for example, the Communist troops at Huai Hai numbered half a million. The peasants of the countryside gave some substance to the claim that this was a people's war, but these great encounters were finally settled by regular-type formations armed with the best weapons that could be obtained.

In October 1949, the Communists had a tough, experienced army with all ranks trained in their jobs. Even so, its equipment was, by the standards of other nations, second-rate. Organization was complex and inefficient; air and naval units were, for any real purpose, nonexistent. However, of transcendent importance, the PLA held a body of doctrinal and tactical precepts that had met the ultimate test—and won.

There were remnants of military business to be cleaned up after victory on the mainland had been achieved. In October 1949, an amphibious assault on the main island in the Quemoy group in the Taiwan Strait foundered on a heavily defended beach. Estimates of Communist casualties ran as high as 20,000, but half that figure is perhaps more accurate. The assault failed because Communist troops apparently did not understand the techniques of such operations and had failed to muster the necessary resources. However, the Nationalist position on Hainan Island off Kwangtung Province was taken in a second attempt in April 1950.

When the P.R.C. was established on October 1, 1949, Tibet was not under its control, although the Chinese claim to some form of suzerainty over Tibet had long persisted. In 1950 Peking decided to enforce its claim. A force of some six or seven divisions began the wearisome work of getting to Tibet over rough, roadless country. The initial entry was easy enough, but "General Winter" and savage tribesmen made the establishment of control costly and time-consuming. The Tibetans were less than enthusiastic about the Chinese plan to change their lives, and their feelings erupted into open rebellion in 1956. Fighting was widespread and intense, and the rebels enjoyed some success. Over time the PLA sequestered the opposition and, using modern air and ground weapons and perhaps 250,000 troops, broke the back of the resistance. The operation was a costly one and the problems of operating among an unfriendly populace were trying. The experience in high altitude and cold weather operations broadened the army professionally and proved useful in 1959 when opposition again flared. Even in 1978, Tibet remained far from pacified.

Ideological Campaigns

In the early days, Party and army were almost completely one, but the growth and complexity of new problems soon began to require some separation of function and, in time, style and goals. Since the PLA was clearly the irreplaceable instrument of power and control, measures had to be taken to ensure that revolutionary spirit and ideological dedication were maintained. Over time there have been a number of campaigns and programs aimed at this effort.

The tradition of the soldier's profession has not always been a particularly honorable one in China. One of Mao's first tasks was to give his armed forces standards of conduct and codes governing relations with civilians that clearly marked the Red Army as different from earlier troops. Some early precepts for conduct evolved and grew until, in 1947, there was a formal and structured statement: the "Three Main Rules of Discipline and the Eight Points for Attention." This code laid down some very simple rules for soldiers in the conduct of their duties and in their relationships with the people. Over the years these precepts have been enriched by further guidance: the "four good and five good" standards for units, the "eight characters," the "four firsts," and many others.[2] The troops are from time to time exhorted to emulate a model soldier who has performed an outstanding feat, usually but not always at the cost of his life. Such practices provide easily transmitted and remembered rules for ideological stance, performance of duty, and personal relations.

One of the most significant slogans of recent history is associated with the Great Proletarian Cultural Revolution: the "three supports and two militaries." This slogan urged the PLA to support industry, agriculture, and the Left, and to exercise military control and give military training. In effect the PLA was being called to oversee the affairs of the nation.

In political affairs the operative slogan often appears after the event. After Lin Piao disappeared in 1971, the "criticize Lin, criticize Confucius" campaign set out to demonstrate that these unlikely partners were equally guilty of betraying the nation's ideals. From the military point of view, it is significant that the attacks on Lin represented him as a military incompetent whose ideas about the conduct of the great campaigns in the Civil War were completely in error. Earlier, during the Cultural Revolution, President Liu Shao-ch'i and his associates were denounced on the grounds that they had been seduced away from the path of true communism by the temptations of the "capitalist road." In 1977-1978, the "Gang of Four" was the target of criticism, slogans, and invective for, among other sins, tampering with the PLA.

The Military Since 1949: Foreign and Domestic Roles

Since 1949, the PLA has had to perform as a national army. Military affairs, previously centered on revolutionary war and fighting the Japanese invader, entered the larger system wherein military posture affects foreign policy. The wars and battles in which the PLA has been involved since 1949 make possible an examination of the essence of the army's experience and an estimate of what the lessons learned have meant in Chinese military thinking and doctrine.

External Operations

The Korean War (1950-1953). The initial North Korean crossing of the 38th parallel into South Korea on June 25, 1950, led President Truman to interpose the Seventh Fleet in the Taiwan Strait, foreclosing what had appeared to be Chinese Communist preparations for an invasion of Taiwan. There is some doubt about Peking's reasons for entering this war in October. Its entry may have been primarily a response to a political threat to the government that, it must be remembered, had been formally established less than one year before. It is equally plausible that Peking could not tolerate the possibility that the United Nations might come to the Yalu River and threaten Manchuria. Whatever the reason, Chinese "volunteer" forces were on hand in strength by November 1950. U.N. forces were pushed back to the 38th parallel, and the war settled into a relatively static and sometimes locally violent situation. An armistice was finally signed on July 27, 1953. Where "victory" ultimately rested is hard to determine, but Peking boasts that its troops repelled an effort to destroy the Communist state of North Korea. The degree of PLA involvement is reflected in the numbers present: at one time there were 750,000 Chinese troops in Korea; casualties were more than half a million. A number of the "volunteers" were officers and men with recent combat experience, but here for the first time they confronted the realities of modern firepower and enemy control of the air. The PLA was armed and resupplied for Korea by the Soviet Union, and for some time this massive accession of new equipment sustained it. The problems of logistical support of large forces were only partially solved, however, and the lack of tactical and logistical mobility played a part in the limited nature of some attacks.

This was true even though it has been pointed out that Chinese forces could operate on daily consumption tonnages that were hopelessly inadequate by American standards.

The Taiwan Strait (1954, 1958, and 1962). It is questionable whether the first two Chinese Communist attacks on the smaller Nationalist-held islands in the Strait of Taiwan were truly preludes to an attempted invasion of the large island. The actions were directed at destruction and intimidation of island garrisons and coercion of the Taipei leadership, mainly through heavy bombardment by shore batteries. There was some air action in the 1958 fighting, and the PLA air force met the Sidewinder air-to-air missile and, by inference, modern technology. The large amounts of ammunition expended apparently did not overtax the Chinese Communist supply system. An unwelcome military result for the Communists was the post-1954 strengthening of the island garrisons by the Nationalist authorities. The 1958 attack produced a large flow of new equipment from the American military aid program. Politically, the 1958 incident provided a test of the reality of the Soviet commitment, which, in comparison to the U.S. support of its Taiwanese ally, left Peking disappointed.

In mid-1962, trouble again seemed imminent in the strait. The P.R.C., reacting to Nationalist actions that it thought presaged a major assault on the mainland, began moving forces into the threatened coastal area and, over a period of about one month, brought in about 100,000 troops. The situation dissolved into vagueness and nothing further happened. The P.R.C. did register a significant political gain when President Kennedy gave assurance that the United States would not support an assault from Taiwan.

India (1962). The clash with India in 1962, which almost had the appearance of a chastisement of the Indian army, strengthened the Chinese position in several disputed border areas, including one very important part of the Aksai Chin in the northwest frontier area, where the Chinese had built a tactically important road connecting Sinkiang and Tibet. As a military operation the venture was carefully planned and its execution was briskly professional. After forcing a sharp salient into the Indian position in the northeast, P.R.C. forces voluntarily halted and indicated a willingness to discuss the matter. This action had wide political effect, but it should not be forgotten that further advance would have been difficult to support in winter and would have exposed a rather tenuous line of communications. The Chinese store of high altitude experience was increased and the PLA's view of its effectiveness was reinforced. In the war over the establishment of Bangladesh in late 1971, it is noteworthy that Peking maintained an alert posture on the Indian border and gave material and political support to Pakistan but avoided any overt act that might have produced significant responses from either India or the Soviet Union.

The Sino-Soviet border (1969-1978). The Sino-Soviet border situation obscures and overrides any other military consideration. In 1978, it was still tense, and any lessening of intensity seemed unlikely. Military actions on a small scale have tested both sides but larger encounters have been carefully avoided. The Ussuri River incident of March 2, 1969, apparently initiated the chain of events that produced a situation in which China now faces a modern Soviet force said to number perhaps 1 million and armed with the most advanced conventional and nuclear weapons.

China's first reaction in 1969 was to move some troop units toward the northern borders, to increase its preparations for war, and to encourage the digging of tunnels as population shelters. (The figures and area locations shown in the "deployments" column of Table 10.1 on page 352 show the Chinese posture in 1977-1978 and suggest a steady progress toward reasonable goals.) The increase in total armored divisions between 1972-1973 and 1977-1978 is noteworthy. Peking has also increased the regional and militia presence in key areas. In places, Chinese main force troops are held some distance from the border and the space is filled with second-line elements. This application of people's war would force the Soviet invader to deploy too early and confront him with the tiresome problems of guerrilla warfare and sabotage. It is generally believed that the P.R.C.'s modest arsenal of nuclear weapons is deployed to strike targets in both Asian and metropolitan Russia. Statements from both sides about the menace and aims of the other vary in their degree of alarm, but each consistently describes the other as aggressive and unstable. During 1977, the Chinese relaxed the polemical content of their statements at times, probably to suit audience and immediate purpose. Whatever the polemics may be at any given time, it is true that no major escalation had taken place in the nine years after the Ussuri River encounter, and a nervous stability obtains. For both sides the maintenance of large forces deployed forward may have some cost, but neither seems to be too concerned about this. Peking insists to the nations of Western Europe that it is Europe that is in real peril and that Soviet actions illustrate an ancient Chinese injunction: "Make a noise in the east and strike in the west." It is

NATO that should be concerned. One perhaps unforeseen result of the Russian threat is the encouragement and support now going to the PLA leaders who seek modernization of China's armed forces.

The Paracel Islands (1974). The P.R.C. has claimed the Spratly and Paracel islands in the South China Sea for some time, rejecting the claims of Vietnam and others. In January 1974, the PLA launched a small amphibious operation to seize the closer islands, the Paracels. The action included land, sea, and air elements and, from the few accounts available, was well executed. Overall command rested in the Canton Military Region headquarters with the navy in charge on the scene. Fighting was apparently neither severe nor long-lasting. The force captured some forty-eight South Vietnamese soldiers and one American advisor. No similar operation to take the Spratlys would be advisable until air support of greater range becomes available. Professionally, the PLA showed the ability to plan and conduct, albeit on a very small scale, a combined-arms operation.

Air and naval actions. The air and naval forces of the PLA have a lesser history of experience. The 1958 encounters over the Strait of Taiwan, some experience in the Paracels, and frequent redeployments in response to actions from Taiwan and the Soviet Union are the only seasoning the PLA air force (PLAAF) has had since Korea. The PLA navy (PLAN) has had some raiding and patrol experience and occasional short actions with Taiwan forces, but no sustained and large-scale tests of efficiency. There was an incident near Quemoy in 1965 in which several PLAN vessels "ambushed" and damaged some small Nationalist vessels.

Internal Events

In addition to external operations, a number of internal events have contributed to the shaping and style of the PLA.

The Great Leap Forward (1958-1960). The Great Leap Forward was Mao's attempt to hasten the advent of true communism by increasing production in all areas and promoting communal social organization. Troops were ordered to work two months each year in support of the Great Leap. The general effect on the military was one of disenchantment with this heavy diversion of military energy. Nevertheless, much prominence continues to be given to PLA support of farming, large-scale construction and conservation, and service in disasters or emergencies. There are recurring campaigns encouraging mutual help and affection between the troops and the people.

The Cultural Revolution (1965-1969). The experience of the Great Proletarian Cultural Revolution was uniquely complicated, even for a highly politicized army. The position and performance of the PLA in this movement suggest that the P.R.C. is, in its own particular way, a military dictatorship. The formal Party manifesto of August 8, 1966, proclaiming the Cultural Revolution said very little about the PLA, and this tended to isolate and insulate the armed forces from the massive actions that were ordered for other organs. By January 1967, this policy had been completely reversed. The army was ordered by Mao to move beyond its earlier public security role into active support of the Left in the spreading contest. The "support the Left" injunction was variously interpreted, however. Events seem to suggest that there was a built-in bias toward more conservative positions in much of the PLA. There were some significant encounters, and in places the rebelling youth stole weapons from the PLA. With a few important exceptions the units participating in the action were regional rather than strategic forces. Air, naval, and airborne units effectively supported the central authority in a serious incident at Wuhan in July 1967 when local leaders detained emissaries from Peking. To some degree, the PLA has seemed able to pick its allies. On balance the leading soldiers have seemed more comfortable with conservative elements, although political opportunism has produced considerable flexibility in some. There was some disaffection over the part played by Chiang Ch'ing, Mao's wife, who, with her officially sanctioned Cultural Revolution Small Group, set out to prescribe and regulate the role of the PLA and thus to control its actions. While she did have formidable power, its exercise alienated some military figures not ready to accept her leadership.

As the Cultural Revolution slowed and halted, there emerged new governing structures in the form of revolutionary committees, which took control at all levels. In almost every case these committees were dominated and run by military men. Whatever the original intent, the Cultural Revolution produced a situation in which the control and influence of the military was greater than before. Some of the duties incident to taking charge of the administrative apparatus of the country were not particularly welcome, but some PLA leaders did enjoy the "taste of honey" that comes from political power. This is not to suggest that the military sought to use its new position to replace the Party, but it is clear that the PLA gained much greater influence within the Party than it had had before. The Cultural Revolution witnessed an event of considerable importance: the national army had been used as an instrument of coercion against a sizable portion of the people in the political encounter.

Maintaining internal order (1975-1976). The effectiveness of the army in maintaining or restoring tranquility has been demonstrated in more recent incidents, like the restoration of order in Hangchow, Wenchow, and Chinhua. In these places there were serious clashes between rival militia units. The militia had been officially disbanded in March 1975, but fighting continued until July when Teng Hsiao-p'ing ordered in regular army units to disarm the dissidents and to maintain production in the local factories. During the T'ien An Men disturbance in April 1976, regular units were brought into Peking from some distance away to calm rioters protesting what they regarded as disrespect to the memory of the recently deceased Premier Chou En-lai. These units surrounded the area but never became directly involved. A European journalist present at the time thought that the PLA units had exercised a significant calming effect.

The T'angshan earthquake (1976). The massive earthquake in T'angshan on July 28, 1976, brought out an unspecified number of army units. It was reported that the soldiers performed with great effect and devotion to the teachings of Chairman Mao. While doing dangerous work and giving aid to the stricken, soldiers reportedly found time to put up posters and remind one another of revolutionary slogans.

Organization, Command, and Control

The structure of the Chinese Communist armed forces is a product of its own experience, tempered by residual Soviet influences and perhaps even a few traces of German influence. Figure 10.1 shows the general shape and flow of the system of Chinese military organization, but it must be cautioned that specific knowledge of actual performance is scarce.

Control over military affairs rests in the Party. The military element within the Party is the Central Military Commission (CMC) of the Party Central Committee. The chairman of the Chinese Communist Party is the commander of the armed forces and chairman of the CMC. The latter post seems to be the one where effective action is taken. On the government side, the senior agency is the Ministry of National Defense. The National Defense Scientific and Technological Commission reports to the CMC. In turn, the CMC is in direct control of three lines of authority: the political apparatus of the Party (General Political

Figure 10.1   Military-Political Relationships in the P.R.C.

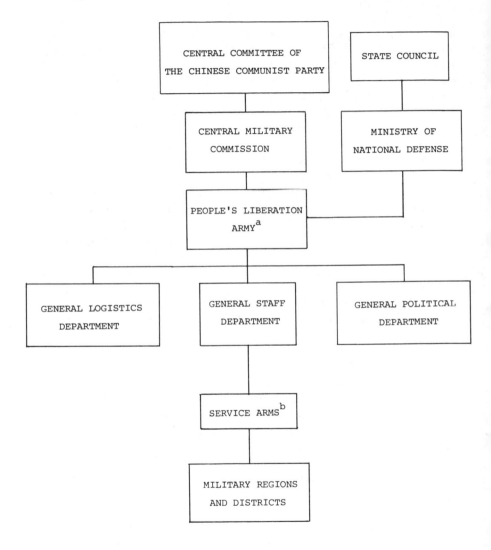

a.   The actual command over main
     force units in the regions
     flows from the CMC, with the
     several staff departments as
     conduits and staff supervisors.

b.   See text for list of service
     arms.

Department), the military command hierarchy (General Staff Department), and the administrative and supply channel (General Logistics Department). The eleven military regions exercise these functions over the forces within their borders with one major exception: the main force ground units come under the operational control of the CMC and thus of the Party Central Committee. This control is exercised with due awareness of the situation within the region and the influence of the commander there, but regional commanders have only limited control over the use and movement of main force units.

The air, ground, and sea services provide the operating units of the PLA. Air and sea forces are described as "service arms" and appear at the same level as the armored corps, artillery corps, engineer corps, railway engineer corps, capital construction engineer corps, and the second artillery corps. This last agency is fairly new and obviously is involved in nuclear weapons matters. It is not yet clear how authority and function are divided between this agency and the complex of planners and operators who would be necessarily involved in a national program.

In addition to the main force units there are less well equipped regional forces, production-construction units, border defense and internal security elements, and, as noted elsewhere, several varieties of militia. As a general rule these second-line troops answer to the regional commander.

The overall processes by which military establishments allocate resources and produce tangible results can, in functional terms, be compared. There must be a central policy-making authority to establish basic strategies and set the major lines to follow toward national goals. Within such a framework there must operate mechanisms for planning, programming, and budgeting. In the P.R.C. the necessary actions are obviously taken but there is little direct and detailed knowledge of the process. Several studies offer plausible explanations of how the system works, but in the public literature there is no organized study of the system that follows some action in specific terms, differentiating between actors and reactors or locating the issues and pressures that have gone into a major decision. Before Mao's death it was easy—and in most cases, reasonable—to attribute final decisions to him. In the absence of information, it is possible only to produce assumptions based on what is known about structures and people. It is important to remember that there is no open parliamentary process in the P.R.C. Further, senior officials often serve on more than one of the important agencies and it is thus difficult to locate the actual body in which a critical decision was taken. While Figure 10.1 may hint at procedures and flows, there is no definition of the pressure points and loci of interests in the system. However, it does certify that the Party does indeed control the gun.

The Navy

To take the smaller services first, the navy is focused completely on close-in defensive operations from three mainland bases. The continued production of submarines that are vulnerable to modern antisubmarine warfare measures is puzzling. The submarine force has not exercised at sea for long periods or at great distances and it may be that coastal defense and (under proper conditions) a blockade of Taiwan are the total missions of these vessels. Other weapons—destroyers, escorts, and large numbers of good patrol boats—reinforce the inshore defense concept. The amphibious vessels now on hand are old and inadequate in number for any sizable assault; few are being built.

The Air Force

The air force is the most serious victim of obsolete weapons. How well or how long it could survive against the sort of attack that either the Soviet Union or the United States could mount is a nagging problem for the Chinese. The P.R.C.'s most pressing requirement in military modernization is that of upgrading its air defense system—aircraft, surface-to-air systems, radar, and communications. The offensive capabilities of the air arm are limited by the number of aircraft that can survive and reach significant targets. The nuclear missile array is perhaps minimally effective as a deterrent and little else.

The Army

The army is China's strongest military service. As noted above, it is composed of main and regional forces. The main force units comprise some forty corps (sometimes known as armies), each normally consisting of three divisions and other support units, plus armor, artillery, railway divisions, and specialized regiments. The primary mission of the main forces is national defense, although main force units did take sustained action during the massive disturbances of the Cultural Revolution and more recent civil disturbances.

The regional forces are under the command of military regions and districts, and their armament and duties reflect two considerations: first, they supply visible evidence of coercive power across the nation; second, if an invader is to be engaged by people's war tactics, these forces are the replacements, the saboteurs, the guerrillas, and the "sea of people" that engulf the enemy. This concept has been the object of ridicule in the Soviet press. In the summer of 1969, several articles warned the Chinese that the experience gained in fighting the Japanese would be of little use in a war with modern weapons. There was no mention of the Korean experience, nor of that of Vietnam.

As an effective fighting force, the ground forces can be given only "fair" marks. The movement toward generational upgrading has been hesitant and modest. Even so, sheer numbers and the ability of the Chinese soldier to operate and endure would make battle costly to an opponent.

Paramilitary Units

Communist militia units were formed as early as 1928. Various types of units did intelligence work in the enemy's rear, ran small attacks on isolated targets, and performed sabotage, particularly on roads and railways. The years since Kiangsi have seen many changes in organization, missions, and political roles, with recurring emphasis on the maintenance of civil order. The actual numbers of militia forces have varied with many differing understandings of what the word means. At times in the past, it has been claimed that there were more than 200 million people in a universal militia. When the crude figure is broken down by function, a more plausible count emerges. Of an estimated current strength of 100 million, three-quarters, or 75 million, have no duties and get no training. Of the remainder there may be as many as 10 million militia members equipped with weapons and trained by the PLA, with duties focused on border security but also including some public safety tasks. All militia men are, of course, in the general manpower pool.

The political uses of the militia are very important in the Chinese setting. The Gang of Four organized its own "urban militia" in Shanghai for its partisan purposes. Militia units have been used in the past to locate and punish wrongdoing, particularly political misdeeds, and to enforce compliance with such programs as the "down to the countryside" undertaking, in which many urban youths have been sent to work in agriculture or public works. In addition to the militia, there are lightly armed production-construction units that do substantial work in remote and politically sensitive areas like Sinkiang Province. Beyond directly military forces, there is a pervasive public security apparatus that operates under entirely different authority and need not be discussed here.

The Maoist strategic doctrine is comfortable with the militia concept, which embodies people's war in its purest sense. There have been aberrations in the behavior and loyalty of these forces, but they often manage to finish on the side of whatever political orthodoxy prevails. There is the continuing problem of attempts to form competing units. As noted earlier, such elements clashed violently in Hangchow and other places in the 1970s, and the regular army had to intervene. As recently as January 1977, radicals were accused of trying to subordinate the public security organization to the militia, which they had tried to develop as a fighting force.

The effectiveness of the militia in wartime has been questioned. Lin Piao was censured for, among his many other sins, referring to the militia as "cannon fodder." During Teng Hsiao-p'ing's most recent period out of favor, he was accused of having opposed the militia in politics and of having wanted to abolish it. It was said that he particularly disliked the Shanghai type of "worker-militia" that took part in class struggle. The militia's future is a matter of surmise, but it does meet certain requirements of the P.R.C. and will no doubt survive in some form.

Military Regions

In 1971, the number of military regions—the great command and control entities—was reduced from thirteen to eleven. The Tibet region was absorbed by Chengtu Military Region, except for a section of western Tibet that has become part of the Sinkiang region, and what had been the Inner Mongolia region was divided among Shengyang, Peking, and Lanchow military regions. There were political overtones in these transactions, particularly in the case of Tibet, but sound military considerations were also involved. In each case, the change gave major tactical integrity of command throughout the depth of each region. Previously, responsibility for dealing with an attacker would have been passed from front to rear across boundaries that were perpendicular to the most likely routes of advance into Chinese territory.

The Climate of Modernization

Chinese Communist operational experiences have been valuable. The considerable group that experienced the realities of modern war as troop leaders or staff officers in forward units in Korea, as a general proposition, are likely to support modernization. Experience in smaller operations, like the border war with India and the seizure of the Paracels,

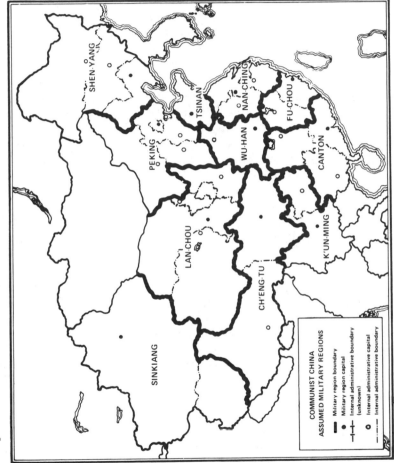

Map 11   Communist China's Assumed Military Regions

have further taught the virtues of military professionalism. A number of deployments in response to a perceived threat have been useful staff and command exercises. The Soviet situation involves almost all military people in one way or another. Forward units face demanding tasks of organizing the ground, planning defensive reactions, training troops and militia, and maintaining vigilance and morale in a relatively static situation. These problems in different forms beset all of the PLA— ground, naval, and air, and forward and rear units.

The original fighting men of the Chinese Communist Party were a mixed group of defectors from the national army, poor peasants, and urban workers—described by Mao as lumpenproletariat. They were armed with what they had been able to bring with them when they joined the Communists and with what they were able to capture as the war went on. They fought, in Mao's words, with millet and rifles. After the 1927 uprisings and the establishment of the Kiangsi soviet, resupply and expansion of the Red Army depended mainly on the machine guns, mortars, and rifles captured from the Nationalists. Later, the anti-Japanese fighting yielded some captured weapons; a few primitive Chinese arsenals contributed as well. At the end of World War II, the Soviet army saw to it that the Communists got the opportunity to harvest the store of Japanese matériel in Manchuria. It has been estimated that during the 1945-1949 period the Red Army gained more than 54,000 artillery pieces, 319,000 machine guns, 1,000 tanks and armored cars, 20,000 motor vehicles, and great quantities of other equipment. The haul included some 189 aircraft. A good portion of all this was U.S. equipment that had been supplied to the Nationalist army. At the end of the period of revolutionary war and upon the proclamation of the People's Republic, the PLA was awkwardly large, battle-trained, and equipped with a mixture of armaments that would tax any logistics system.

Chinese entry into the Korean War began a rationalization of PLA organization and equipment that affected all service branches. With strong Russian tutelage and material support, the army was reorganized and fitted out with Soviet weapons. World War II models in most categories were still far from outdated, and PLA ground forces were reequipped with standardized artillery, transport, and smaller weapons of several kinds. In effect, the PLA became the complete client, and in some cases, a scale model of the Soviet armed forces.

The air force also benefitted from the crisis. By June 1952, Peking had built an air force that boasted more than 1,800 aircraft, including 1,000 jet fighters and 100 IL-28 bombers. The ground environment was updated with Soviet radars, communications, and antiaircraft artillery. At about that time, General Vandenberg said, "Almost overnight Communist China has become one of the major air powers of the world." This estimate was true in terms of numbers, but the PLA air force was never able to control the air beyond a relatively small space in the northwest of the Korean peninsula. Communist losses in air-to-air fighting were some 976 aircraft, as compared to 139 in U.N. air units.

Throughout its history, China has shown only sporadic interest and modest investment in naval forces. There was little naval action in the Korean War, except for some rather effective mining in coastal waters, probably done by Chinese under Russian supervision, using Russian mines.

The end of the Korean War found the PLA in excellent shape but completely dependent on an ally for maintenance. For a time, the PLA was a reasonably modern force but while the superpowers were producing more modern equipment, the PLA languished in the posture of the early 1950s.

The Sino-Soviet split and the withdrawal of Soviet technicians and support in the early 1960s left the PLA armed forces in serious condition. Although home manufacture of arms and parts had begun, the P.R.C. was in no way self-sufficient and, moreover, found itself compelled to continue to produce and maintain Korean-generation weaponry. Settling for some time on the idea that the better is the enemy of the good, and keeping faith in the mystique of people's war, the Peking leadership has made the best of an essentially bad situation. Outdated technology and plant have continued to produce copies of obsolete models. Even critical items like radar and surface-to-air missiles are the Russian versions of two decades ago. Thus, the principal problem facing the Chinese high command is the establishment of priorities for improvement in forces that have been frozen for some time in an outdated position. The new attention being given to science and technology and the professed interest in buying articles like French antitank missiles may mark the first stirrings of a new direction.

The navy also has problems of obsolescence. Since the Korean War, it has developed a small but apparently competent coastal defense force and a sizable submarine force, based almost entirely on two types of Soviet boats of the period just after World War II. Except for some recent development of hydrofoil patrol boats and a new class of destroyers (LUTA)—purely indigenous efforts—its designs are those of Soviet models. The OSA and KOMAR patrol boats represent a ship-to-ship missile capability that is, however, becoming obsolete.

For the PLA air force, the loss of Soviet aid led to problems of reduced training and flying time and what was perceived as a general reduction in combat effectiveness. This problem now seems to have been resolved. China has recently even been able to furnish spares for Russian-built aircraft in Egyptian hands and has for some time been a major supplier of aircraft to Pakistan, including MiG-19s.

Nuclear Weapons and Missile Development

China became a nuclear power despite the loss of Soviet aid, exploding its first nuclear device on October 14, 1964. This was an "atomic"-type bomb of about 20 kilotons yield and was apparently fired as a tower shot from the Lop Nor establishment in Sinkiang. The twenty-fourth test took place on December 14, 1978. This, too, was an open air shot in the 20-kiloton range. There have been tower firings, aircraft drops (using the TU-16), and at least four underground tests. The Chinese army newspaper reported that "China . . . launched guided missiles with nuclear warheads." Dates were not given, but the story was published in an issue that appeared in September 1977 on the first anniversary of Mao's death. Test yields have run from less than 20 kilotons to 4 megatons, showing mastery of hydrogen weapons techniques. At least one shot was a failure and has never been mentioned by the Chinese.

Chinese rhetoric on nuclear warfare has followed a set pattern. Peking usually claims that it is working to break the superpower monopoly of nuclear weapons in the interest of the Third World and in the service of peace. "No first use" is emphasized, and a willingness to discuss total nuclear prohibition is asserted. In 1971 Peking vigorously rejected a Soviet proposal for a five-power nuclear conference, saying that all nations should be present.

Chinese nuclear weapons of 1978 did not meet the standards of other powers. Peking's dependence on liquid fuels would be dangerous in wartime. Although it was reported that work on solid fuels was being done, there was not any open evidence of their use in 1978. The hardening of launch sites was not complete. The advent of a true intercontinental missile has been anticipated for some time. Secretary of Defense McNamara said in the late 1960s that the P.R.C. should have a modest ICBM operational capability by the mid-1970s. There have been some collateral indications: reports of an instrumented ship for down-range observations and tracking stations in Zanzibar and the north slope of the Himalayas, but no full-range test has been fired. There is evidence of a "reduced-range" weapon with about a 3,500-mile reach that could strike many targets in metropolitan Russia.

The apparent neglect of the ICBM program may be due to any of several reasons. The immediacy of the threat from the Soviets may have so dominated Peking's thinking that a decision was taken to concentrate on developing the ability to retaliate in that quarter. The pinch on available resources may have forced a choice to achieve the easier goal first. It is possible that the development of the Ming and Han classes of submarines indicates a desire to move to a modest seaborne nuclear capability, although a realistic program would be time-consuming and costly.

China had launched eight satellites by 1978. The first firing took place on November 1, 1969, and the most recent on December 7, 1976. The vehicles are closely related to the nuclear weapons program as well as to scientific and communications tasks. Rockets are in service for a 600- to 800-mile MRBM, a 1,500- to 1,800-mile IRBM, and for the longer-range weapon mentioned earlier. In 1975, there were hints that China had achieved a soft landing return of a space capsule, but no particulars of weight or content were given. It was also suggested that this firing was a "spy-in-the-sky" device to look at a Soviet nuclear test facility.

The PLA's Self-Image

Despite China's weaknesses relative to the Soviet Union and the United States and its continuing problems of obsolescence in armaments, the PLA is taught to hold a high opinion of itself. It is repeatedly told that it is a victorious army, able to defeat menacing enemies and powerful weapons because of its skill, courage, and purity of motivation. A 1973 instructional document, "Education for Companies," emphasizes the lessons of Vietnam: a weaker nation, armed with ideological correctness, can win over a stronger one. The great celebrations of the PLA's part in national life continue to extol its support of the dictatorship of the proletariat and its allegiance to the Party. An example was the major speech of Yeh Chien-ying, then defense minister, on the fiftieth anniversary of the founding of the PLA (August 1, 1977). In summarizing Peking's view of military history, he stressed the traditional place of the armed forces in the continuing revolution, but he also appealed to the soldiers' self-view by paying more attention to their professional concerns. Quoting Party Chairman Hua

Kuo-feng's call to "accelerate the revolutionization and modernization of the PLA," Yeh explained that these two tasks were linked and described the actions necessary to develop a modern army. The same theme was strongly reemphasized in the National Day celebrations two months later. While the recurring emphasis on the need for major force improvement may reflect the views of the new central authorities, it is probably also meant to signal to career military men that their professional concerns are in no way incompatible with their prescribed roles as workers, teachers, and fighters.

Current Troop Levels, Deployment, and Training

There is no problem in bringing forward each year the half-million young men required to maintain the PLA. Military duty offers advantages over other careers to many, and the uniform is respected. Officers and NCOs seem to be genuinely sensitive to morale and motivation problems. The army is never represented as being superior to the populace at large, but it is regarded as the principal model of correct behavior and an important teacher of the masses.

Current trends in Peking's military posture are shown in Table 10.1, which is derived from the authoritative *Military Balance*, published annually by the International Institute for Strategic Studies. This table compares the 1972-1973 and 1977-1978 levels of equipment and troop deployments in the PLA. Even this consistent, conservative, and reliable study must be regarded as an estimate, however, for no figures concerning the P.R.C. can be completely trusted.

The problems of military training are intertwined with the problems of political training and action. This issue over the years has been the center of serious internal differences. So far as military work is concerned, the emphasis for a long time was on small unit training and the techniques of close engagement. The need for more sophisticated preparations has long been advocated by military leaders like Lo Jui-ch'ing and Yang Ch'eng-wu, both of whom are prominent as deputy chiefs of staff in the new leadership. The PLA is currently expanding training in the larger aspects of war after a long period of neglect, while probably looking nervously at the northern borders. In July 1976 there was a week-long, tri-service exercise opposite Taiwan. Attack aircraft bombed and strafed in support of parachute troops, and the entire force was protected by interceptor aircraft. Although the chairman of the U.S. Joint Chiefs of Staff described the exercise as "elementary by U.S. standards," he noted that "it did show increased sophistication in the use of tactical air power by the P.R.C."

The Military Budget

American intelligence officials and other observers have been able to learn much concerning the substance of the P.R.C.'s military spending. The Chinese are generally given credit for substantial and continuous economic growth. Estimates of gross national product in 1973 were in the neighborhood of $170 billion. The current figure is around $300 billion, and prices have remained stable in the interim. Military expenditures are believed to amount to 8 to 10 percent of GNP or some $30 billion—about one-quarter of the money spent on the military by the United States. It must be warned, however, that the whole process of calculating Chinese costs is liable to sizable error since the pricing methods and practices used are necessarily adaptations of American theory and practice. It is probably more useful to think about the P.R.C. in terms of visible output.

The U.S. Congress was told in 1974 by CIA officials that there had been a downturn in P.R.C. military spending. A sharp decrease was variously attributed to changes in strategic thinking, economic constraints, or realization that further spending on obsolete systems was not productive. The director of the CIA, in testimony before a congressional committee in June 1977, said that total Chinese military expenditures grew very rapidly in the late 1960s, peaked in 1971, fell substantially in 1972, and have remained at roughly the 1969 level since.

Whoever makes the decisions in Peking is confronted with a massive series of problems. There are factions and special interests to be placated, and the establishment of production priorities must take these pressures into account. At the same time, choices for investment must lead to weapons and systems that meet the most pressing needs of the current military situation. The magnitude of the requirements for modernizing strategic defensive forces will require some difficult decisions about the distribution of industry's output among competing claimants. Finally, there is the discouraging fact that no effort within reach of the P.R.C. economic or social, can significantly reduce the gap between the PLA and the military arrays of the United States or the Soviet Union—the superpowers continue to develop and produce the most modern and deadly hardware.

Despite the economic constraints on its military budget, Peking has provided military aid for various purposes. The size and presence of the P.R.C. particularly affect its Asian neighbors. Chinese technicians and advisors assist in friendly countries; when Peking feels it useful,

Table 10.1

PLA Force Levels and Deployment, 1972-1973 and 1977-1978

	1972-1973	1977-1978
Total regular forces	2,880,000	3,950,000
Strategic (main) forces	15-20 IRBM 20-30 MRBM Up to 100 TU-16	30-40 CSS-2 30-40 CSS-1 About 80 TU-16
Army: Force levels		
Infantry divisions	120	121
Armored divisions	5	12
Airborne divisions	2	3
Artillery divisions	About 20	40 (including antiaircraft artillery)
Railway and combat engineer divisions	None	15
Independent regiments	Unknown	150
Regional (local) forces		
Infantry divisions	Unknown	70
Independent regiments	Unknown	130
Artillery: guns, rocket launchers, mortars	Unknown	20,000
Tanks	Unknown	10,000[a]
Armored personnel carriers	Unknown	3,500
Army: Deployment, by divisions		
North and Northeast	40	55 main forces 25 local forces
East and Southeast	25	28 main forces 18 local forces
South Central Central	20	15 main forces 11 local forces
West and Southwest	30	18 main forces 8 local forces
Mid-West North and Northwest	15	20 main forces 8 local forces

[a] The chairman of the U.S. Joint Chiefs of Staff has said that the PLA does **not** yet have the most modern antitank weapons but does possess large numbers of older types, including the RPG-7.

Table 10.1 (continued)

	1972-1973	1977-1978
Navy:		
Total strength	150,000	300,000
Submarines		
"G" class	1	1
Fleet types (including coastal and training)	22	66 (36 "R" class 21 "W" class 2 "Ming" class attack 1 "Han" class nuclear-powered, under test)
Destroyers	4	6 LUTA class 4 SU GORKY class
Destroyer escorts	9	12
Patrol escorts	14	16
Other craft	15 missile patrol boats 220 motor torpedo boats (including hydrofoils) 320 motor gunboats Some landing ships and craft	90 OSA and 70 KOMAR missile patrol boats with STYX missiles 100 hydrofoil patrol boats 400 motor gunboats Misc. coastal and amphibious
Naval Air:	100 IL-28 Substantial numbers of MiG-15 and MiG-17	130 IL-28 (torpedo), TU-16, TU-2 About 500 fighters including MiG-17, MiG-19, F-6, some F-9 50 helicopters
Air Force:		
Total strength	180,000	400,000
TU-16	About 100	About 80
IL-28	200	400
TU-2	100	100
MiG-15 and MiG-17	1,700	
MiG-15 and F-9		About 600
MiG-19	Up to 1,000	
MiG-17 and MiG-19		About 4,000
MiG-21	75	120
F-9	About 200	Some
Transport aircraft	400	450
Helicopters	300	350
SAM-2 sites	Up to 50	About 100
Antiaircraft guns	Unknown	10,000

however, it can also give support to a friendly country's dissidents or, as it has done toward Thailand or Laos, it can deploy its forces in a menacing way. Peking has been very active in assisting road-building efforts in nearby countries, and it is easy to see the military value in most of these projects.

During the Vietnam war, the P.R.C. provided military aid to the ultimate value of almost $1 billion. No combat forces on the Korean model appeared, but there were several PLA railway construction divisions in the rear areas, performing very effectively tasks of railroad construction, repair, and maintenance, protected by PLA antiaircraft troops. At times Chinese voices were heard in air-to-air and air-to-ground communications, but the air presence was modest and avoided conflict with U.S. forces. Within China, close attention was given to strayed American airplanes; several military aircraft and reconnaissance drones were shot down. The praise and publicity given these events suggested awareness of the acute overall weaknesses in the air defense system.

In addition to Vietnam and Pakistan (mentioned earlier), Peking has been involved in several undertakings in the Middle East and Africa, where it has played the military assistance game as a lesser competitor. The $400 million railway in Tanzania and Zambia was a major program, which was reinforced by training and weapons, including aircraft and tanks, for Tanzania. For some time Peking maintained a mission in Zaire to train Angolan partisans but was finally "priced out of the market" by the superpowers. Recently, the P.R.C. has been able to pick up some benefits from the split between Egypt and the Soviet Union. Much general support and some weapons have been given various rebel groups, including some in friendly nations. Literally tens of thousands of AK-47 rifles of Chinese manufacture are scattered throughout Asia.

Party-Army Relations

The Chinese officer at the middle level or above is the product of some very special internal and external influences that have shaped his attitude toward military-political relationships in Chinese society. The "Long March generation," in which there was no sharp differentiation between military and political leaders (the same men playing both roles simultaneously or successively), is slowly disappearing, although it is still represented at the top by major figures like Yeh Chien-ying and the recently rehabilitated Lo Jui-ch'ing and Yang Ch'eng-wu. The rising men in the military system are legitimate inheritors, but theirs is a different history, one in which professional experience, motivations, and goals have become increasingly important.

The catalogue of PLA experience in both internal and external undertakings implies the presence of a struggle for the mind of the military leadership. The basic experience of combat service or of realistic preparation for it direct thought toward professional military goals. Thus, even under the Chinese Communist system of personal relationships within the forces and between soldier and civilian, the soldier is bound to develop attitudes and standards that set him apart to some degree. In addition, at the very highest levels of command experience there is some encouragement to think in terms of the power with which military force endows its holder. The synthesis of these sometimes contradictory political and military realities produces the attitudes and desires that condition relations between politician and soldier. Current evidence suggests that the new leaders in Peking are acting positively to ensure the political fealty of the forces and, at the same time, giving sympathetic attention to the problems of modernizing the nation's defenses. Political activity has not diminished within the PLA, but the focus of interest is shifting for some: responsibility for the defense of the nation has become a powerful influence on the thinking of many soldiers.

There is a fundamental contradiction between the basic slogans "Power grows out of the barrel of the gun" and "the Party commands the gun and the gun must never command the Party." They seem to suggest, when compared, that those who command the power to assert the realities of control must be conditioned to accept the use of that power by a separate hierarchy, which also defines the correct political line. This was not a problem in the early days when, for all practical purposes, the Party and army were one. The political leaders exhorted the people to learn from the PLA. The army was, as is often the case in revolutionary situations, the best structured and most efficient element in the new system. Then, for the first few years of national existence, the P.R.C. and the PLA were occupied with the Korean conflict. At home military officials were called to operate the military administrative committees, which, until 1954, governed the six major regions that were established. Although military men were prominent in this arrangement, the basic integrity of the Party-army relationship was maintained. A physical base in the military is essential in Chinese politics, and the political importance of the army has never been denied, although the control and content of its program and the balance between military and political training have been debated. For most of its life, the PLA has been praised for its devotion to correct political orientation. It has not always been easy, however, to locate and follow the correct line. As a statement in the communiqué of the Third Plenary Session of the Tenth Central Committee (July 21, 1977) said, "The struggle between our Party and the Wang-Chang-Chiang-Yao anti-Party clique [the Gang of Four] is the eleventh major struggle between the two lines in the history of our Party." A *Peking Review* article of August 12, 1977, noted that the PLA had taken an active part in the struggle against cliques that had preceded the Gang of Four. In 1955, for example, it was reported that regional Party leaders Kao Kang and Jao Shu-shih had been removed from office on the grounds that they had been dealing privately with the Russians in a plot to establish an "independent kingdom" in the northwest.

In September 1959, Mao dismissed Minister of Defense P'eng Teh-huai. P'eng, who had commanded the "volunteers" in Korea, had become minister of defense in September 1954 and had quickly set about moving the PLA toward the more professionally oriented model of the Soviet army. Special schools were established, and ranks were restored: officers began receiving perquisites of rank and wore better quality uniforms (this system of rank was discarded in 1965 in a massive return to egalitarianism). Tension between Mao and P'eng originally arose from their differing views on modernization; even though Mao gave a little, particularly on nuclear weapons, their differences persisted. P'eng and his professionally minded associates were greatly disturbed by the effect of the Great Leap Forward on the army. P'eng's opposition became so strong that Mao finally relieved him. He was placed by Lin Piao, and thus began another major era in China's military affairs.

Further perils in the climate of high command may be seen in the career of Lo Jui-ch'ing, who came in under Lin Piao as chief of staff, serving from 1959 to 1966. Lo's paper of May 10, 1965, "Commemorate the Victory Over German Fascism! Carry the Struggle Against U.S. Imperialism Through to the End!," if read as a military document is a strong plea for intensive modernization of the PLA. The document was larded with praise of Chairman Mao and people's war, but a contradiction emerged in Lo's opposition to some of Mao's strategic and economic policies. Lo was removed from office, but reappeared in 1975.

The major story is, of course, that of Lin Piao, who served as minister of defense from 1959 to 1971. He combined great military influence with a singularly sharp perception of the political climate. His statement of

September 7, 1965, "Long Live the Victory of the People's War," was, in effect, a rebuttal of Lo. It was a testament to the power of people's war and an affirmation of the omniscience of the chairman. He produced the "Little Red Book" of selections from Mao's thought and made it the staple of the army's political indoctrination. At the Ninth Party Congress in April 1960, Lin was officially anointed as Mao's closest supporter and chosen successor. According to official accounts, somewhere the spur of ambition overcame caution and Lin was exposed in a massive plot to replace Mao. It is said that he tried to flee the country and died in a plane crash in Mongolia in September 1974. Also disappearing at the same time but never formally accounted for were the chief of staff of the PLA, the commander of the air force, the political commissar of the navy, and the director of the General Logistics Department. Since his death, Lin has been held as the model of disloyalty, political error, and professional incompetence.

The subsurface tension between military and political forces was further illustrated by the events of late December 1973. With only five days of advance notice, eight of the eleven powerful military region commanders were transferred, exchanging posts in several cases. It was reported that each was permitted to take along a personal staff of only five. Significantly, in their new commands they did not receive the Party posts that they had held in their old assignments. Whether they had been suspected of active opposition to the central authority or were simply seen as becoming too strongly entrenched in their localities is not clear.

The importance of military support for those with political ambitions is demonstrated by Chiang Ch'ing's efforts to establish control over the PLA by use of her Cultural Revolution Small Group. Her attempt, as part of the Gang of Four, to establish the Gang as Mao's successors, ended with arrests in the month following Mao's death in September 1976.

Generally it may be said that the central authority has been able to deal with senior military commanders in the field, though at some cost in concessions and change. Military interests hold a share of the power, but they do not form a solid front and may be played off against each other. There are, for example, loyalty groupings within the PLA, which have been attributed to a number of influences. For example, associations with a particular field army have established close bonds and effective working associations within the officer corps. This interpretation is particularly supported by the personnel manipulations involving officers who served with Lin Piao in the Fourth Field Army. Other career affiliations with a service branch or a certain region, or from military education experiences, have also had some weight. The establishment of "teams" around a particular leader or institution is a common attribute of military systems, one that is by no means peculiar to Communist China. Given the basis for such rivalries, the unique element in the Chinese situation is the dominant part that political rectitude has played. It has not always been easy to identify and follow the correct line of the moment, and there has also been some peril in attempts to interpret official policy or the utterances of the chairman in terms favorable to one's enterprises.

Although the central authorities have been able to dominate the military, the Teng Hsiao-p'ing affair demonstrates that the army can swing its support in an opportunistic way. In April 1976, when Teng was dismissed as vice premier by the Central Committee, the participation of army men in the rejoicing was prominently noted. One account said that all eleven of the powerful regional commanders had endorsed the resolution turning Teng out of office. At the end of July 1977, the army newspaper joined other major journals in celebrating Teng's restoration to office. The inference may be drawn that PLA behavior cannot be predicted solely on the basis of an identified political stance. While the army does not constitute a "gun for hire" in political quarrels, it has been able to change allegiances when the climate has changed. The military hierarchy as such cannot define the primary national issues, but it can give powerful support to one side or another in accordance with its perceptions. In the most recent internal struggle, the animosity that senior officers felt toward being directed by a woman, particularly one like Chiang Ch'ing, was definitely a factor in the downfall of the Gang of Four.

In sum, the PLA has been consciously apolitical only during the mid-1950s when the attempt was being made to build a professional force. Today there is, as noted earlier, an apparent attempt to identify the functions of the military with the other affairs of nation. One example of the style now prevailing is the condemnation of the Gang of Four for its opposition, on ideological grounds, to plans for modernization of the PLA.

The constant pressure along the northern borders (and, in theory at least, from Taiwan and India) helps to dampen other concerns or dissatisfactions. Somewhere in the strategic system there is probably also some memory of the destructive power of U.S. air and naval strength evident in the Vietnam war. It is not difficult to indoctrinate the PLA with a sense of important mission or to claim, on behalf of defense, a good share of plant and budget. The rising generation in the army is exposed to the compulsions of professionalism and does not necessarily march to the drum of earlier leaders. The need for better equipment and trained people has been recognized by recent increases in interest in science and technology and in the return to more rigorous educational standards and procedures. National authorities still have before them the task of dealing with competition for inadequate resources between military and civilian bidders. The balance achieved will be important in shaping the attitudes toward political authority obtaining in the officer corps.

External Pressures on China's Military Posture

In a world dominated by two superpowers, China's global aspirations, whatever they may be, are closely contained by physical realities. The conduct of the nation's military affairs is shaped by pressures from outside the P.R.C. and by internal considerations that are uniquely Chinese.

Threats and Dangers in Asia

Aside from the Soviet Union, no Asian nation is immediately menacing to the P.R.C. U.S. policy guarantees that there is no prospect of an attack from Taiwan; in this sense, the task of "liberating" that island by force of arms can be postponed indefinitely. Japan has foresworn military action as an instrument of national policy. The nations of Southeast and South Asia are not capable of major efforts against China. The competition between the Soviet Union and the United States for world hegemony will, in Peking's propaganda, eventually produce World War III. The threat from the U.S.S.R. is now the chief concern, with the American menace far less imminent. The U.S. is still perceived to some extent as an imperialist monster, but new Sino-American relations and the visible withdrawal of American forces from forward positions in Asia makes American aggression unlikely. The reduction of the U.S. presence, together with the search for détente, has in fact led Peking to warn that too many concessions to the Soviet Union might encourage Moscow to engage in dangerous adventures. Japan is advised that, for the time being, maintenance of its security treaty with the United States is desirable. The U.S.S.R. is clearly *the* object of concern.

If the prospects and outcomes of full-scale war between the P.R.C. and the U.S.S.R. could be calculated on the basis of simple firepower comparisons, the Chinese case would be hopeless. A disarming nuclear strike against Peking's modest force, followed by an offer to discuss a settlement, would jeopardize the P.R.C.'s hard-won industrial base should Peking not respond. Surely, the condition that inhibits such Soviet action is the uncertainty over collateral results. There is no way to predict the reactions of the United States and other powers or to ensure that the action would not spill over into other settings. It can only be deduced that the need to punish China is not so great as to require this level of action.

It is theoretically possible to suggest that the Soviet Union might turn to the more conventional mode of ground warfare. The "Education for Companies" said in 1973:

> Militarily, Soviet revisionism is stationing 64-67 army divisions along the several thousand kilometer border between China and the Soviet Union and between China and Mongolia. . . . The troops at the border possess 15,000 tanks . . . several thousand aircraft and [have] built several dozen missile bases in the border area, therefore, posturing for a large-scale war against China. It is actively making battlefield preparations.[3]

This statement probably exaggerates the danger, but Moscow has indeed directed major resources toward its borders with China.

Against such an array China can field the forces described in Table 10.1. Space and distance problems and a relative lack of tactical mobility would be surmounted by the deployment in depth of defensive forces and the techniques of people's war. Recent visitors to China have theorized that the best option for a Soviet attack would be some sort of "blitzkrieg" to take and hold Sinkiang. The terrain, the opposing strengths, and the fact that the native populace in the province is not primarily Han Chinese and might welcome some sort of autonomy would all seem to favor such an action, but the idea leaves unanswered questions about the utility of holding that particular territory and the forms that Chinese retaliation might take. The Trans-Siberian railway and such important centers as Khabarovsk and Vladivostok are tempting targets and their loss or serious damage would greatly harm the Russian position in the east. The Chinese have often warned potential foes "you fight your way, we will fight in ours." Moscow has done much to enhance the PLA's sense of mission and of its usefulness in time of danger, by eliminating any sense of boredom or unimportance among the Chinese armed forces.

Political and International Considerations

Empirically, it may be said that the military structure evolved through the experience and mental conditioning of the PLA has been successful in withstanding external pressures and in maintaining the security of nation and Party. Military affairs are, however, only one part of the national process. Political considerations in international relations exert their own sorts of influence on policies and strategies. The P.R.C.'s environment is *total* and military responses must be planned with this in mind.

The current military task is two-fold. First, it is necessary to maintain the threshhold-raising/deterrent quality of the armed forces as a credible component of the national foreign policy strategy. Second, exterior actions like the takeover of the Paracel Islands must be carefully orchestrated with current considerations to avoid the provocation of some other power. To Peking's exterior audience the impression must be that of vigilance and readiness to act, without suggesting that forces are being prepared for massive undertakings abroad. The nation's total economic situation and the complex problems related to weapons development and production reinforce the strategic concept of defense of the homeland on interior lines as the principal response to external threats. This policy has, of course, been the topic of intense debate within the Chinese leadership at times, but it has never deteriorated, even in the Cultural Revolution, to the point where an outside power was tempted to intervene.

Preparing To Fight the External Threat

It has been shown that the Chinese nuclear weapons program appears to reach for a modest capability either to strike Soviet targets in retaliatory action or to take hostage some of the territory of the United States' allies in Asia. The leisurely progress toward intercontinental nuclear forces and the slow growth in the numbers of lesser weapons available to the PLA suggest strong reliance on a deterrence strategy as an umbrella under which large-scale preparations for, and conduct of, conventional action can proceed. A hypothetical list of force-improvement weapons and systems that would fit this mode would include:[4]

1. Improved air defense missiles and aircraft.
2. Improved radar and other ground-air defense equipment.
3. New families of small antitank and antiaircraft weapons.
4. A modern main battle tank (in the defensive posture, this item would be of less importance than modern antitank defenses).
5. Improved tactical and logistics system mobility (this would require a coordinated program of rail, road, and air transport upgrading).
6. Continuous improvement in artillery, mortars, and small arms is desirable, but the current families are demonstrably effective. The number of larger artillery pieces should be increased to something closer to the "per division" level of other armies.
7. Finally, given the role of nuclear weapons in this concept, the reach should be for greater security of launch sites, mobility of weapons, and solid fuels.

The naval contribution to defending against exterior threat is implicit in current force structure and projected plans. China actually has little experience of modern naval warfare, but the extensive use of patrol vessels for close-in defense, stiffened by a modest number of larger vessels, is a reasonable reply to the second-level danger of Soviet sea action. The significant number of submarines could establish some blockades in narrow waters but, as has been said previously, their survivability in the modern antisubmarine environment is doubtful.

People's war must keep a prominent position for several reasons. First, the prospect of having to deal with guerrilla activities adds a significant dimension to the problems of a would-be invader. Further, people's war is a proven device for rallying and directing the masses, who are, and will remain for some time to come, a major asset. Finally, however much Mao's dogma may be ignored or perverted in practice, it will be politic to invoke it in support of national undertakings. Programs for dispersion of industry or obedience to the injunction to "dig tunnels deep and store grain everywhere" are sound defensive measures, made stronger by their origin with the chairman.

It is apparent that the military strategy operating within P.R.C. foreign policy is static, with very little consideration for long-range operational capabilities. Tactically, of course, the ability to counterattack or preempt in a threatening situation along the line of contact is present. Although it is too early in the life of the new leadership in Peking to permit assessment of its strategic view, there is little chance that there will soon be substantial change in its military reaction to pressures from outside China.

The Internal Climate

The various external pressures on China's military posture are accompanied by a number of internal constraints and considerations.

Military Budgets

Earlier considerations of budget matters in the P.R.C. suggested the need for very careful management of the allocation of resources among the several areas of needed modernization. In June 1977 rallies in Peking appealed for modern weapons, but counteractivity also stressed the "men over weapons" concept. The most important evocation of authority in the arms debate was probably the resurrection of Mao's 1956 statement, "On the Ten Major Relationships." The *Peking Review* of January 1, 1977, presented the full text, edited slightly over time, without comment or introduction. In this talk Mao had called for the reduction of military and administrative spending from 30 percent to 20 percent of the state budget. The general thrust of Mao's remarks was toward reduction in immediate spending in these categories in order to invest savings in building more factories and turning out more machines. This concept was widely discussed in public press and radio during 1977. A number of outside economists have said that this path would be the most efficient for China. During the 1970s, the late Lin Piao has been criticized for pressing too hard for immediate large-scale weapons production and thus depriving the industrial base of needed investment.

Several conferences have been devoted to specific problems of defense, and Hua Kuo-feng has met with the conferees. Little of substance from these meetings has emerged but the fact that they were all held in January 1977 and that Hua met with them strongly suggests that efforts are being made to see the budget problem in the round.

The normal function of the budget in allocating resources is complicated by an overall shortage of specific inputs. The P.R.C. has had serious problems in making high-quality special steels for military applications. The general shortage of plant and trained workers makes competition among programs very keen. Higher level scientific and engineering people are spread thin and the impact of the Cultural Revolution on the education and training of the next generation has been severe. China's general poverty and backwardness are the targets of a massive struggle, but the lack of resources in so many categories will condition military thinking for some time to come.

Modernization

There has been some interest in modernizing the PLA ever since the Korean War. The program now operating began to take shape not with the death of Mao, but with the passing of Lin Piao. The Spey engine deal was initiated while Mao was still alive.[5] Discussions have been held with authorities in several nations concerning such equipment as the Harrier aircraft, helicopter and transport aircraft, antitank weapons and improved surface-to-air missiles, and a wide range of electronic items, including computers, with military applications.

It will be useful to follow the modernization process in China. Not only will programs be shaped by strategic perceptions, but sponsors will have to compete with other requirements that support the other elements of Chou En-lai's four modernizations in industry, agriculture, and science and technology. It may thus be difficult at times to tell whether a new or improved weapons system reflects a defense perception or an economic compromise.

Leadership

The new Hua Kuo-feng–Teng Hsiao-p'ing leadership has been certified by the Fifth National People's Congress, which met from February 26 to March 5, 1978. The military policies and background of the new men require some examination.

Hua Kuo-feng, as the designated successor to Mao and titular commander of the armed forces, has put forward his plan for the army of the future. It is to be smaller and streamlined with more modern weapons and equipment. Discipline is to be tougher and the lines of command centralized. Hua, whose background in Party and security work seems unlikely to have produced such a statement, probably got substantial advice and encouragement from Teng.

Teng Hsiao-p'ing is the real moving force in military affairs. His curious personal history includes military service as commander and as political commissar. He has served as Party secretary and once represented Mao in a most important meeting with Khrushchev in Moscow. Throughout his career, in or out of favor, he has been hardheaded and contentious and has often dared to directly contradict Mao. His more recent history testifies to a great talent for survival. He was purged by the radicals in the Cultural Revolution but returned to office in 1973, apparently sponsored by Chou En-lai. He was purged again in April 1976 by the Gang of Four and reappeared in July 1977. This last return was formally approved by a "Resolution on Restoring Teng Hsiao-p'ing to His Posts," passed at the Third Plenary Session of the Tenth Central Committee in its meeting of July 16-21, 1977. The offices listed were "member of the CPC Central Committee, member of the Political Bureau of the Central Committee and of its Standing Committee, vice-chairman of the CPC Central Committee, vice-chairman of the [Central] Military Commission of the CPC Central Committee, vice-premier of the State Council, and chief of the General Staff of the Chinese People's Liberation Army." It is clear that Teng has a seat in every major body with control over military affairs. His strategic views have not been published in detail, but he has expressed antagonism to the Soviet Union and has asserted that reconciliation with Moscow would not occur in this generation.

The people involved with Teng have, in terms of their past activities, some sympathy for military force improvement. The venerable Yeh Chien-ying has been replaced as minister of defense by a man with a long history of association with Teng, Hsu Hsiang-ch'ien. Yeh has been given the largely ceremonial post of chairman of the Standing Committee of the National People's Congress, but his heavy involvement in military affairs from the Long March onward and his powerful advocacy of military modernization are not forgotten.

As noted earlier, Lo Jui-ch'ing, who as chief of staff of the PLA was purged in the Cultural Revolution, and Yang Ch'eng-wu, who as acting chief of staff later suffered the same fate, have both reappeared as deputy chiefs of staff. Both officers have good credentials as professional military men who understand the roles of weapons in war. Yang led the delegation that visited France in September 1977 and it was he who told high French officials that China was interested in modern antitank weapons. To take the important post of director of the General Political Department, Teng has brought forward Wei Kuo-ch'ing, who had sheltered and protected Teng after his purge in the Cultural Revolution. The ubiquitous Hsu Shih-yu, experienced in command of both the Nanking and Canton military regions, at one time seemed destined for high national office but the congress did not elevate him. Neither did Wu Teh, the mayor of Peking, nor Ch'en Hsi-lien, commander of the Peking Military Region, prosper. In general the men dealing most directly with military affairs have extensive records of high-level service and open identification with efforts to improve the combat efficiency of the PLA. Individual fortunes will rise and fall, but do not necessarily signify major policy changes within the new leadership.

Political Pressures in Military Affairs

The history of military involvement in the internal affairs of Communist China makes clear the importance of the PLA in the governing structure. The relationship between Party and army continues to be celebrated, and early actions in military affairs taken by the new leadership suggest the Party's firm hold over the PLA. The armed forces are well represented in the higher Party councils, and there appears to be a reasonable consensus over goals.

The new leadership has shown itself fully aware of the PLA's role in blocking any internal opposition in China. The location and eradication of threats to Maoist ideology and to the Communist Party will continue to be a primary duty of the army and a major factor in the development of the forces of the future, although the demands for more sophisticated military training will divert some of the energies of the troops. There is evidence that the need for some elasticity in army-Party relations is clearly understood.

There will no doubt be disagreement over the pace and content of improvement programs, but this condition is rarely absent in military systems. Military region commanders will continue to enjoy considerable prestige and power, and some effort will be made to keep them satisfied. The forceful personality of Teng Hsiao-p'ing and the sophistication of his close military associates will probably reduce somewhat the power of regional officials.

Regular troops may again be summoned to intervene in essentially political events like the T'ien An Men disturbance and the Hangchow troubles. In a larger sense, the PLA will remain the tutor, friend, and helper of the people. The shift toward more time for military training and preparations, and away from political and civic action may generate some Party-army differences, but dominant trends will overcome those who would advert to earlier policies.

There is always some danger, however remote, of a worsening of relations between the PLA and the people. The need to enforce order and conformity among the people could create psychic conflicts in the PLA in regard to its mission to "serve the people" and to unite the army with the workers and peasants. Flagrant display of the perquisites of rank—use of automobiles, better clothing, access to special facilities—is an irritant to those who witness displays of privilege. At least one air force unit has made public self-criticism for its bourgeois practice of indulging in sumptuous banquets. In a larger sense, the PLA could, unless skillfully managed, take on some of the characteristics of conventional national armies. Secular pride and spirit, hazardous service, the special character of military discipline, and a sense of civilian ingratitude or neglect of the PLA could have a substantial impact on national life.

The Shadow of Mao Tse-tung

Events since Mao's death have shown that those who follow the chairman must work in his shadow. The process seems more an exercise in semantics and exegesis than a rigorous adherence to a previously established and sanctified line. The five volumes of the *Selected Works of Mao Tse-tung* (and much other material) can, properly quoted, support almost any proposal or line of action.

The amenability of Mao's thought to service in a cause is impressively illustrated by an article on "Integration of 'Millet Plus Rifles' With Modernization—The Crimes of the Gang of Four in Undermining Modernization of National Defense," prepared by the theoretical group of the National Defense Scientific and Technological Commission and broadcast on January 20, 1978. In this article some of Mao's instructions and other writings are marshaled to demonstrate that Mao did indeed see the need for incremental progress from simple weapons and equipment to more sophisticated and effective systems, and from conventional to nuclear weapons as well. The Gang of Four is shown to be wickedly disloyal for its attacks on military modernization as the chairman saw it.

The document discussed the proceedings of an enlarged meeting of the Central Military Commission in 1975 where, "adhering to Chairman Mao's instruction on army consolidation and preparedness for war," a number of important decisions on military affairs were taken. The paper manages to show the deepest deference to people's war while defining extensive policies and goals for modernization. It can be expected that the scriptural authority of Mao will be invoked for almost any significant undertaking for some years to come.

Trends for the Future

Ignoring the perils of prophecy, there are some significant trends in Chinese military affairs. The authority of Mao remains, but it has been transfigured into a body of scripture, to be interpreted by those who now control the country.

The new men in charge have some history of close association with the PLA and of support for modernization. They are giving active direction to the formulation of force improvement plans. The taboos against seeking military material abroad are relaxing, producing selective shopping lists. The virtues of self-reliance will not prevent some business transactions with more advanced powers. It is apparent, however, that the Chinese are not rushing into the market and buying indiscriminately.

The suggestion that the United States might supply some types of military equipment and technology has been discussed with only moderate enthusiasm on both sides. High-technology material that could improve functions like air and sea defense has been mentioned, but neither side has acted at a very high level and no movement is apparent. In at least one case—the Spey engine deal—Washington looked the other way and did not invoke COCOM.[6] However, this method of procurement is too expensive to become widespread. The pace of modernization will be set by the imminence of a major threat to China's security and the availability of money and means of production. Any sudden shift in the direction, size, or imminence of an external threat would create alarm, thereby affecting the content and course of modernization programs. The P.R.C. has, after all, a command economy and much can be forced from it on demand.

To conclude, within the central bodies of the Chinese government and Party there will naturally be debates over military behavior, programs, and goals. The problem lies in managing the tensions. The intermingling of military and political elements produces conflict, but it also makes for effective synthesis and cooperation. There are no voices now being raised against the attempt to make China into a major industrial power by the year 2000. Today's powerholders may over time be replaced, but the prospects for a new Cultural Revolution are receding. Finally, there seems to be a decreasing danger of an all-out strike on the P.R.C. by the Soviet Union. The reasons against such an action become more compelling as time passes—the best time for a Russian attack was yesterday.

Notes

1. This chapter is concerned only with the military concept of people's war as an internal and war-fighting doctrine. For an

examination of its history in political affairs in other places, see Johnson (1973).

2. "Three Main Rules and Eight Points for Attention" laid down rules of behavior toward civilians and their property. The "four good" and "five good" precepts enjoined correct ideology and effective work and training. The "eight characters" form four terms: unity, promptness, dignity, and liveliness. The "four firsts" set priorities, giving eminence to man himself, political work, ideological work, and living ideas (as compared to things found in books).

3. *Chinese Communist Internal Politics and Foreign Policy: Reviews on Reference Materials Concerning Education on Situation Issued by the Kunming Military Region* (Taipei: Institute of International Relations, 1974), p. 12.

4. It is interesting that the items in this list, developed by hypothetical considerations, correspond closely to a similar list derived from reports of interests shown by Chinese officials in conversations with foreign contacts. See the discussion above relating to the climate of modernization.

5. This transaction was announced by Rolls Royce in December 1975. It was the subject of widespread discussion because of its size and content. The Rolls Royce company contracted to supply some sixty whole engines of fighter plane quality, to build a plant for the Chinese, and to furnish advisory and training personnel for twenty years. Total cost was said to be $160 million. Even more importantly, this transaction represented the first large Chinese purchase of modern military material from a Western power.

6. The Coordinating Committee on Export Controls (COCOM) was established by agreement between the United States and its major allies to extend multilateral controls over exports of selected commodities and technology to the Sino-Soviet bloc.

Bibliography

Cheng, J. Chester, ed. *The Politics of the Chinese Red Army: A Translation of the Bulletin of Activities of the People's Liberation Army*. Stanford, Calif.: Hoover Institution, 1966.

Clough, Ralph N., A. Doak Barnett, Morton H. Halperin, and Jerome H. Kahan. *The United States, China and Arms Control*. Washington, D.C.: Brookings Institution, 1975.

Fraser, Angus M. *The People's Liberation Army: Communist China's*

Armed Forces. New York: Crane, Russak, 1973.

Garthoff, Raymond L., ed. *Sino-Soviet Military Relations.* New York: Praeger, 1966.

Gittings, John. *The Role of the Chinese Army.* London and New York: Oxford University Press, 1967.

Griffith, Samuel B., II. *The Chinese People's Liberation Army.* New York: McGraw-Hill, 1967.

————. *Peking and People's War.* New York: Praeger, 1966.

Hsieh, Alice Langley. *Communist China's Strategy in the Nuclear Era.* Englewood Cliffs, N.J.: Prentice-Hall, 1962.

Johnson, Chalmers. *Autopsy on People's War.* Berkeley, Calif.: University of California Press, 1973.

Mao Tse-tung. *Selected Military Writings.* Peking: Foreign Languages Press, 1966.

The Military Balance. London: International Institute for Strategic Studies, annual.

Nelsen, Harvey W. *The Chinese Military System: An Organizational Study of the Chinese People's Liberation Army.* Boulder, Colo.: Westview Press, 1977.

Whitson, William W., ed. *The Military and Political Power in China in the 1970s.* New York: Praeger, 1972.

Whitson, William W., and Chen-hsia Huang. *The Chinese High Command: A History of Communist Military Politics.* New York: Praeger, 1972.

11
Foreign Relations

King C. Chen

The development of China's foreign relations since 1949 can best be understood in the light of Peking's foreign policy objectives. This chapter will therefore adopt a China-centered and historical approach to the topic.

Objectives of Chinese Foreign Policy

Succinctly, the foreign policy of the People's Republic of China (P.R.C.) can be defined to have short-, middle-, and long-range objectives. Its short-range objectives are to maintain national security, achieve unification, promote international relations and cooperation, increase national power, and enhance national prestige and influence. The most essential among these are unification and security (territorial and national), as Peking clearly announced in 1949.

While several middle- and short-range objectives overlap, like national power, national prestige, and influence, one significant middle-range goal is the establishment of leadership in Asia. In view of China's geographical location, its long history, and the characteristics that its population shares with other Asians, this objective appears reasonably realistic and attainable. Such leadership would not seek to restore the traditional system of tributary relations with weaker states. Nevertheless, Peking undoubtedly has acted out of its desire to establish its leadership in modern Asia.

The long-range objectives, apart from the continuing promotion of power, prestige, and influence, are aimed at world leadership. Peking has performed for years, both in words and in deeds, inside and outside the United Nations, as a leader of the Third World. The P.R.C. has also struggled strenuously against Soviet "revisionism" in order to assert its coleadership of the Communist world. Its recent campaign against the hegemony of the superpowers indicates the beginning of Peking's struggle for leadership on a global scale.

Whether or not China can achieve its objectives depends mainly on its capabilities and the international environment. A review of Peking's foreign relations since 1949 will show not only the country's successes and failures but its capabilities and the international environment it works with as well.

"Lean-to-One-Side" and the Korean War, 1949-1953

The first phase of Chinese Communist foreign policy occurred in a context of recovery from the Civil War of 1946-1949 and the War of Resistance Against Japan of 1937-1945. The new government needed to consolidate its power and to restore the economy, and its foreign relations were meant to serve these purposes.

"Lean-to-One-Side"

On June 30, 1949, three months prior to the establishment of the People's Republic of China in Peking, Mao Tse-tung announced that Chinese Communist foreign policy would "lean to one side"—to the Soviet side. One day after the Peking government was established on October 1, 1949, the Soviet Union recognized it. This action was followed by the Communist countries in Eastern Europe and Northeast Asia. Despite his past disagreements with and even distrust of the Soviet leaders, Mao Tse-tung went to Moscow on December 16, 1949—his first visit—to negotiate with Stalin. He stayed there for nine weeks (until February 17, 1950). As a result, the Sino-Soviet Treaty of Friendship, Alliance, and Mutual Assistance was concluded. The treaty reinforced the "lean-to-one-side" policy.

The 1950 treaty, inheriting both the obligations and the rights outlined in the Sino-Soviet Treaty of August 1945, included the following important provisions: (1) a thirty-year military alliance directed against Japan and the other states allied with it (implying the United States); (2) joint Sino-Soviet administration of the Chinese Eastern Railway in Manchuria; (3) joint use of the naval base at Port Arthur until the conclusion of a peace treaty with Japan or at the end of 1952; (4) Chinese administration of the international trading port of Dairen; (5) a Sino-Soviet guarantee of the independence of the Mongolian People's Republic (Outer Mongolia); and (6) a Soviet economic credit of $300 million to cover a five-year period (1950-1954).

The alliance was extended by other economic agreements on minerals, civil aviation, petroleum, and shipbuilding. But no specific military agreement was made known.

Other diplomatic channels were rapidly opened. From December 1949 to June 1950, the P.R.C. exchanged recognitions with five Asian nations (Burma, Pakistan, Ceylon, India, and Afghanistan) and with seven European countries (the United Kingdom, the Netherlands, Switzerland, Norway, Sweden, Denmark, and Iceland). In addition, Peking, preceding the Soviet Union by thirteen days, granted recognition to the Democratic Republic of Vietnam (North Vietnam) on January 18, 1950.

Intervention in the Korean War

The existence of divided Asian states (Vietnam and Korea) was, and is still in the case of Korea, a destabilizing element in the postwar world that has thus far resulted in two major wars.

On June 25, 1950, the North Koreans invaded South Korea. They won an initial victory by taking Seoul and pushing the South Korean army to the Pusan area until the Inchon landing by United Nations forces in mid-September halted the North Korean drive and then pushed back their invading troops. Little more than one month later, the U.N. forces reached the Sino-Korean border area.

Several factors had contributed to the outbreak of the war: the South Korean army was weak compared to the much stronger North Korean troops; U.S. exclusion of South Korea from its defense perimeter in the Far East; greatly reduced U.S. forces in Korea and Japan; and a disarmed Japan. On top of these, a well-devised invasion plan had apparently been developed by Stalin and Kim Il-sung. Although there is no evidence to substantiate Mao's role in the decision to invade, he and his associates had undoubtedly been informed of the war prior to the advent of the conflict. One of the solid indications of this was the movement of Lin Piao's and Ch'en Yi's armies from south and southeast China to Manchuria, which began in May 1950, more than one month before the war broke out.

In mid-October, as the U.N. troops neared the Sino-Korean border, Peking secretly sent a good number of "volunteers" into Korea. On October 26, the "volunteers" began to attack South Korean units and U.N. forces near the Yalu river. In less than two months, the Chinese pushed the U.N. forces back below the 38th parallel. Seoul was recaptured by the Communist forces in early January 1951. In mid-January, the U.N. forces counterattacked and pushed the Communists back to the north of the 38th parallel. On February 1, 1951, as the

Chinese and U.N. forces seesawed around the 38th parallel areas, the U.N. General Assembly passed a resolution condemning the P.R.C. as an aggressor; and in May, the U.N. recommended that its members place an embargo on the shipment of strategic commodities to China.

Why did Mao, instead of consolidating his year-old government, attack the U.N. troops, most of whom came from the most powerful nation on earth? There are several explanations: the need to safeguard national security, especially in Manchuria; Stalin's pressure (as Mao stated in 1956); the desire to prevent the U.N. forces from overrunning North Korea and reunifying it with the South; and promotion of China's influence and leadership in Asia.

From early 1951 to March 1953, war as well as peace talks dragged on without any significant progress. The United States through the intermediary of the Indian government, threatened Peking with the possible extension of the war to mainland China and with the use of nuclear weapons. More important, Stalin's death on March 5, 1953, brought internal issues to the fore in the Soviet Union. On March 30, four days after his return from Stalin's funeral and consultations with the new Soviet leaders in Moscow, Premier Chou En-lai proposed an immediate resumption of armistice negotiations. Both Kim Il-sung and Molotov endorsed his move on April 1, and negotiations resumed at Panmunjom only five days later. On July 27, an armistice agreement ended the Korean conflict. For Peking, the war had an embarrassing aftermath when 14,207 Chinese prisoners of war, out of a total of 22,500 Chinese and North Korean POWs, refused to return to Communism and chose to go to Taiwan in late January 1954.

The intervention as a whole produced both gains and losses for Peking. On the credit side of the ledger, the war had enhanced internal unity; it had restored China's traditional relationship with Korea; Peking had demonstrated its determination and ability (for the first time in a century) to play a leading role in opposing Western "imperialism" in Asia; and it had received massive military aid from Moscow. On the debit side, tens of thousands of lives were lost (including that of Mao's son); Taiwan was placed under the protection of the U.S. Seventh Fleet; and economic development was delayed for at least three years.

Hostility toward the United States

During this "lean-to-one-side" period, the United States was depicted by Peking as the "number one enemy" of the Chinese people and Washington's attitude toward Peking was also hostile. This development was unfortunate and perhaps unavoidable.

On October 24, 1949, the Chinese put Angus Ward, American consul-general in Mukden, and four other diplomats under house arrest on spy charges. The State Department described the incident as a "direct violation of the basic concept of international relations." Quietly, however, the State Department was sponsoring discussions on the possibility of recognizing the Peking regime. On January 10, 1950, the U.N. Security Council debated the issue of Chinese representation, but a resolution calling for Peking's admission was defeated on January 13. On the following day, the Chinese police in Peking invaded and seized the American consular building there. Secretary of State Dean Acheson declared that the United States would certainly "not recognize Peking in such circumstances" and would oppose the seating of the Peking regime in the United Nations. Less than six months later, the Korean War broke out, with China and the United States soon fighting on opposite sides.

Other U.S. moves related to the war had a substantial impact on Sino-American relations. The P.R.C. regarded American actions toward Taiwan as a hostile intervention in the continuing Chinese civil war. One such move was the protection of Taiwan by the U.S. Seventh Fleet. In addition, the United States initiated military aid to the island as a result of the Korean War. Moreover, China charged that the United States dominated the United Nations. Although the United States invited a Chinese delegation in August 1950 (headed by Wu Hsiu-ch'üan) to testify on "the United States invasion of Taiwan," nothing concrete resulted from the visit. Nevertheless, during the Korean War, President Truman turned down Taiwan's request for military participation in the war under the U.N. flag. In 1951, when a peace treaty with Japan was signed in San Francisco by forty-eight states led by the United States, both the Taipei and Peking regimes were excluded. In 1952, Taiwan separately concluded a peace treaty with Japan; Peking did not sign a similar treaty with Japan until August 1978.

Peaceful Coexistence, 1953-1959

The ending of the Korean War meant the conclusion of a period of conflict and the beginning of an era of conciliation. In this new era, both the Soviet Union and the P.R.C. practiced almost simultaneous policies of peaceful coexistence. Internationally, these policies created a thaw between East and West.

Economic Development and Soviet Aid

Right after the Korean War, Peking turned its efforts to its First Five-Year Plan. The Korean intervention had given Peking a degree of bargaining power for Soviet aid, and the death of Stalin had left Mao one of the world's most senior Communist leaders. Peking's influence on the course of Sino-Soviet relations increased considerably, and there were a number of important developments relating to the alliance of the two countries.

In September 1953, two months after the Korean armistice, Peking obtained Moscow's aid for the construction or renovation of 141 industrial enterprises. On February 14, 1954, when the Chinese embassy in Moscow gave a reception in honor of the fourth anniversary of the signing of the 1950 treaty, almost the entire Soviet Party leadership attended. The visit to Peking by Khrushchev, Bulganin, Mikoyan, and others in September-October 1954 was truly important because it was the first visit by any top Soviet leaders after 1949. The Russians reached several agreements with Mao. First, Soviet troops would be completely withdrawn from Port Arthur in May 1955 (the 1952 withdrawal schedule had been delayed because of the Korean War); second, the Soviet Union would help China construct an additional fifteen industrial projects ($230 million worth of credit); third, the four existing Sino-Soviet joint-stock companies (minerals, petroleum, civil aviation, and shipbuilding) would be transferred to exclusive Chinese control in 1955; and fourth, the Soviet Union and China would cooperate on projects and exchanges in the fields of science and technology. It was significant that these agreements were carried out in full and on schedule. Soviet aid substantially promoted Sino-Soviet friendship.

The Impact of De-Stalinization

Peking's response to Khrushchev's denunciation of Stalin in February 1956 at the Twentieth Congress of the Soviet Communist Party was both mixed and slow in coming. In April, a lengthy statement in *People's Daily (Jen-min jih-pao)* endorsed the criticism of Stalin's "cult of the individual" and agreed that Stalin should not have expelled Yugoslavia from the Cominform, but it praised Stalin's contributions to the world Communist movement. (Peking's final evaluation of Stalin's record, according to Mao in 1956, was one of 70 percent achievement and 30 percent errors.) By delivering such a conditional endorsement (which was apparently solicited by Moscow) two days prior to Mikoyan's visit to China on April 7, 1956, Peking was able to request a new Soviet loan to assist fifty-five more industrial projects.

The impact of de-Stalinization was broad and profound. The Hungarian revolt in November 1956 provoked a criticism of Stalinism by Tito that China strongly disagreed with. Accordingly, Sino-Yugoslav relationships deteriorated until the 1970s. The Eighth Congress of the CPC in September 1956 elected, for the first time, four vice-chairmen under Mao—a move calculated to avoid any charges that the "cult of the individual" was practiced in China. In early 1957, under the impact of the Hungarian revolution, Mao initiated the Hundred Flowers Movement permitting criticism of the Chinese Communist regime. It was short-lived, however.

In July 1958, a Middle East crisis broke out in which the governments of Lebanon and Jordan requested the landing of American and British troops, respectively, in their countries to avoid any Iraqi-style coup influenced by Egypt. The Soviet Union, a strong supporter of Egypt, denounced the American and British move as a new act of imperialism and demanded an immediate withdrawal of the two Western nations' troops from the Middle East. For a time, the area faced a threat of a major war with possible involvement of the United States and the Soviet Union. Khrushchev flew to Peking for support. Mao exercised his leverage by exacting new Soviet aid from Khrushchev for another forty-seven industrial enterprises. In February 1959, when Premier Chou En-lai went to Moscow, he was able to obtain another credit for thirty-one more industrial projects.

Despite all these efforts and new credits from Moscow, an undercurrent of Sino-Soviet disagreement was growing. As Peking revealed in 1963, it had all originated with de-Stalinization.

The Geneva Conference

Although the Peking government in 1950-1954 had given enormous amounts of material and personnel assistance to the Viet Minh (the Vietnam Independence League led by Ho Chi Minh), which was fighting against French colonialism for Vietnam's independence, China did not fight a second Korean War in Indochina as many observers had feared it might. The two most convincing among several important reasons for its abstention were the fighting ability of the Viet Minh, which eliminated the need for Chinese "volunteers," and the absence of any threat to Chinese security by the war.

The eight years of the Indochina War (1946-1954) ended with a conference at Geneva. The conference (April 26–July 20, 1954) had two issues on the agenda: Korea and Indochina. The Korean issue reached a deadlock and was dropped on June 15. Discussion of the Indochina issue began on May 8 with nine participants: France, Britain, the United States, the Soviet Union, the P.R.C., the Viet Minh, South Vietnam,

Cambodia, and Laos. The Viet Minh victory over the French force at Dien Bien Phu on May 7 (the United States had declined a French request to intervene because of the lack of support for such a move from the U.S. Congress and the Allies) gave added bargaining power to the Viet Minh delegation. At this juncture, the Eisenhower administration decided to assist South Vietnam to remain non-Communist. Meanwhile, the United States was taking the lead to establish the Southeast Asia Treaty Organization (S.E.A.T.O.) to defend the region from Communist aggression or subversion.

At first, the conference made no progress. Many conferees became impatient. On June 10, Anthony Eden, British chief delegate to and a co-chairman of the conference, warned the participants that if the conference was unable to make progress in a short period of time, he might call for adjournment of the meeting. On June 15, the discussion on Korea was suspended. The participants then sensed the seriousness of Eden's warning and the danger of a breakdown in the meeting. On the morning of June 16, Chou En-lai visited Anthony Eden. He told the British foreign secretary that he would try to settle some problems of the conference in order to keep the meeting going. Eden had a "strong impression that Chou wanted a settlement." At the restricted session in the afternoon, Chou made a formal proposal for the withdrawl of the Viet Minh forces from Laos and Cambodia. This had been a thorny problem for the conference. On the following day, Pham Van Dong, the Viet Minh chief delegate, agreed to withdraw the Viet Minh forces from Laos and Cambodia if there were still "some troops" there. Shortly thereafter, the meetings recessed for further consultations. On June 23, Chou met Mendès-France (the new French premier) at Bern, Switzerland. They agreed upon a political settlement in Indochina in addition to an armistice. On July 3-5, Chou met Ho Chi Minh on the Sino-Vietnamese border, presumably to persuade Ho to agree to the same political settlement. Moreover, Chou proposed India, Poland, and Canada as the members of the ICC (International Commission for Supervision and Control). The components of the ICC had been another thorny issue for more than two months. But Chou's proposal was accepted unanimously. "From that moment," as Eden commented, "the tangled ends of the negotiations began to sort themselves out." The conference concluded on July 20. It registered the end of French colonialism in Indochina, agreed to a cease-fire throughout Indochina, and promised a unified Vietnam by national elections two years after the armistice. As a result of its performance at Geneva, China's international status was enhanced considerably.

The Bandung Spirit and Peaceful Coexistence

When the Geneva conference held a recess between June 21 and July 9, 1954, the chief delegates returned home for consultation. Chou En-lai visited India on his way to Peking and concluded with Nehru the well-known Five Principles of Peaceful Coexistence: (1) mutual respect to each other's territorial integrity and sovereignty, (2) nonaggression, (3) noninterference in each other's internal affairs, (4) equality and mutual benefit, and (5) peaceful coexistence. These principles were also endorsed by U Nu (premier of Burma) and Ho Chi Minh. They became a landmark of the era of peaceful coexistence and had a far-reaching impact on Chinese foreign policy.

The Asian-African Conference (April 18-24, 1955) at Bandung, Indonesia, was another significant development in this era. It was attended by twenty-nine Asian-African countries, which included two Communist nations (China and North Vietnam), twelve neutral countries, and fifteen anti-Communist states. The original purposes of the conference were to promote goodwill and to review the position of Asia and Africa in the world. As the meeting went on, however, the participants engaged in political quarrels.

Fully realizing the conflicting viewpoints and the general anti-Communist and even anti-Chinese atmosphere at the conference—the anti-Chinese sentiment was caused mainly by Peking's support for insurgency and its manipulation of overseas Chinese in some nations of the area—Chou En-lai, Chinese chief delegate, put on an impressive performance. He first appeared to be a quiet listener. Later, when the anti-Communist and neutral nations quarreled over their conflicting political stands, Chou came out to mediate and urged them to seek the "common ground" of anticolonialism. He also announced China's willingness to negotiate with the United States on Taiwan. His eloquent and moderate attitude convinced many of the delegates that he was a reasonable and sincere man of goodwill, pursuing a peaceful policy. As the conference concluded, Chou had undoubtedly helped create the so-called Bandung spirit, which was generally defined to mean peace, goodwill, conciliation, unity of Asian-African nations, and anti-colonialism. In the four post-Bandung years (1955-1959), China received diplomatic recognition from nine Asian-African nations. It also began to enter a new world: Africa.

The grand tour of eight Asian nations by Chou En-lai in 1956-1957 was an extension of Peking's policy of peaceful coexistence. This was the most extensive visit to Asia ever made by a Chinese premier; well received, Chou strengthened China's relations with these nations. More significant was the new flow of thousands of Asian visitors to Peking in this era (1954-1959). It was a period of diplomatic growth in which Peking began to rebuild its traditional leadership in Asia.

Beginning of the Warsaw Talks

Peking and Washington had had few contacts immediately after the Korean War. But in December 1954 Washington and Taipei signed the Taiwan-U.S. Mutual Defense Treaty to protect Taiwan. It formalized the Taiwan issue as the hard-core problem between the United States and the P.R.C.

At the beginning of 1955, Dag Hammarskjöld, secretary-general of the United Nations, visited Peking to seek the release of six U.S. prisoners of war from Korea and to discuss the Taiwan Strait issue. He reached no agreement with the Chinese leaders on the Taiwan Strait issue, but Peking did release the six POWs later in the year. This development was followed by the beginning of ambassadorial talks at Geneva between China and the United States.

The crisis arising from China's intensive bombardment of Quemoy and Matsu in August-October 1958 (the two island groups are as close as six miles to mainland China but about 125 miles from Taiwan) provided Chou En-lai with an opportunity to offer peace talks with the United States on Taiwan. Washington welcomed the offer, but no immediate negotiations took place to ease the crisis. After Secretary of State John Foster Dulles flew to Taiwan in late October and pressured Chiang Kai-shek, president of the Republic of China on Taiwan, to renounce military force as a means to recover mainland China, the crisis subsided. Peking and Washington then returned to their distant relationship, except for the Warsaw talks, which served as a limited line of communication between the two capitals.

Competition and the Sino-Soviet Dispute, 1959-1965

The Chinese First Five-Year Plan (1953-1957) progressed smoothly with Soviet assistance. Its outcome was impressive. The combined agricultural-industrial output increased by 60.8 percent, and the GNP rose at an annual rate of about 8 percent (Japan's output in the 1950-1956 period grew 8.6 percent). The achievements of the plan as a whole exceeded its objectives. A debate broke out, however, over economic development methods: fast (by Mao) versus slow (by Ch'en Yun). This two-line struggle, as President Liu Shao-ch'i reported to the Party on May 5, 1958, was finally and fully decided in 1957 in favor of Mao's fast method when the rectification campaign and the antirightest struggle (to counteract the Hundred Flowers Movement) were launched.

As Peking's domestic policy underwent radical transformation from right to left, its impact on foreign relations was significant. In resistance to the accelerated steps toward communization and unification, a revolt broke out in Tibet in 1959; this rebellion, in turn, helped to bring on the Sino-Indian border conflicts of 1959 and 1962. Meanwhile, China's fast, radical method for nation-building annoyed Khrushchev. Coupled with Peking's reactions to de-Stalinization, the Great Leap Forward for economic development in 1958 generated a Chinese campaign against Soviet "revisionism" and led to the "earth-shaking" Sino-Soviet dispute.

Sino-Indian Border Conflicts

The Tibetan revolt in October 1959 was suppressed by Chinese military force. The Dalai Lama, most of his ministers, and many followers fled to India (in all some 80,000 Tibetans were refugees in India, Nepal, Bhutan, and Sikkim by 1978). The Indian government granted them political asylum and made the incident known to the world. As the Chinese border guards stopped the fleeing Tibetans and secured the border, they came into conflict with Indian border policemen in late October in the Ladakh area, about 370 miles north of New Delhi, and twelve Indian policemen were killed.

The conflict alarmed Asia. To demonstrate that the P.R.C. could and would reach agreements by negotiations with neighbors on border issues, Peking concluded in 1960-1962 friendship and border treaties with Burma, Nepal, Pakistan, Afghanistan, and Outer Mongolia. China, which was denounced by Premier Nehru of India as a country that "cared least for peace," was refused a similar accommodation with New Delhi. The Indians bitterly accused China of illegally building a highway through the disputed Aksai Chin area, a stretched-out region from Ladakh to Tibet, and actively prepared for self-defense. By September 1962, India had built forty-three outposts and proudly accepted Soviet military aid (jet fighters) in addition to that of Britain and the United States. One month later, a new war broke out; this time the Indians were reported to have initiated it. After one month of fighting (October-November), India suffered a greater defeat than in 1959. The Chinese advanced deep into Indian territory, both in Ladakh and in the Northeast Frontier Agency. Peking then announced a unilateral cease-fire and withdrew its troops to the original area in dispute.

Six Afro-Asian nations (Burma, Cambodia, Ghana, Ceylon, Indonesia, and the U.A.R.) held a conference for mediation at Colombo, Ceylon, in December 1962. Peking rejected their proposal in January 1963, and the Sino-Indian border dispute has remained unsettled ever since.

Laos and Vietnam

Events in Laos and Vietnam also reflected the difficulties in maintaining the principles of peaceful coexistence.

In 1958-1960, while the United States offered military and economic aid to the non-Communist government in Laos, Hanoi and Peking gave the same assistance to the Communist Pathet Lao (Land of the Lao). In 1960-1961, Soviet arms for both the Laotian government and the Pathet Lao flew in via China and Vietnam. By early 1961, the Soviet Union had become very influential in Laos. The Laotian crisis then came to a head when the combined forces of the Pathet Lao and North Vietnam overran the highlands of eastern Laos.

As the Sino-Soviet relationship deteriorated and U.S. influence persisted in Laos, the Soviet Union found it necessary to agree to a conference on peace and neutrality in Laos so as to check Peking and Washington there. A lengthy Geneva conference was held from May 1961 to June 1962. In early May 1962, a Pathet Lao victory prompted the United States to dispatch 4,000 combat troops to Thailand to reassure the nervous Thai government. Swiftly, an agreement on Laotian neutrality and the withdrawal of foreign troops was reached. Ironically, although the American forces withdrew on schedule, the Chinese and the North Vietnamese military-economic personnel stayed on.

In South Vietnam, U.S. military and economic aid in 1955-1959 had significantly strengthened the Ngo Dinh Diem government. The Diem regime's military campaign had almost "destroyed" the South Vietnamese Communists and revolutionaries who were members or followers of the Viet Minh (later the Vietnam Workers' Party) but after the 1954 Geneva conference the Party leadership in Hanoi ordered them to stay underground in the South to engage in "political struggle" rather than "armed struggle." The years 1958-1959 were "the darkest period" of the South Vietnamese revolution. Hanoi finally approved in January 1959 the repeatedly requested "armed struggle" for the South. It was not until December 1963, however, when the precarious post-Diem military junta in Saigon refused to negotiate with Hanoi, that the Hanoi leadership decided to adopt an offensive strategy for the South. It began to offer massive military aid to the Viet Cong, the Vietnamese Communists in the South.

China, having suffered from economic setbacks in 1959-1960, displayed a cautious attitude toward Vietnam. Publicly supporting the revolt in the South, Peking did not immediately follow Hanoi's example by intensifying its commitment. In fact, until the Gulf of Tonkin incident in August 1964, Peking had now and again urged the parties concerned to convene a new Geneva conference on South Vietnam. In the Gulf of Tonkin incident, American naval vessels were reportedly attacked by Hanoi's patrol boats, provoking the U.S. Congress to pass the Gulf of Tonkin Resolution, which authorized the American president to use military force in Vietnam.

The Sino-Soviet Dispute

After 1959, several major issues aggravated the Sino-Soviet dispute; by 1965, even more issues were involved, and the polemics had reached a point of no return. Apart from the problems discussed earlier (de-Stalinization, Yugoslavia, and so on), the major issues raised between 1959 and 1965 are succinctly enumerated below:

1. *The secret atomic agreement.* In October 1957, Peking had concluded with Moscow a secret atomic agreement whereby Moscow would help China develop its nuclear capability. Concerned that a nuclear China might be too powerful and too free to be kept aligned, Khrushchev asked for control over China's nuclear delivery system. Mao refused it. Khrushchev then discarded the agreement in June 1959, thus acting to prevent China from becoming a modern military power.

2. *Imperialism, war, and peace.* Peking resented Khrushchev's visit to the United States in September 1959 to promote his peaceful coexistence policy. In order to explain his détente diplomacy, Khrushchev rushed to Peking on October 1—one day after his return from the United States—for the tenth anniversary of the founding of the P.R.C. It was of no avail, however. On April 16, 1960, *Red Flag (Hung Ch'i,* the Chinese Party's theoretical journal) published a 15,000-word article entitled "Long Live Leninism" in honor of Lenin's ninetieth birthday. It openly challenged Soviet ideological leadership and stressed Lenin's belief that war was

"an inevitable outcome" of the imperialist system. With an eye on Khrushchev's upcoming participation in a summer conference in Paris, the article warned that "Marxism-Leninism absolutely must not sink into the mire of bourgeois pacificism." One month later, the U-2 affair of May 1960, in which the Soviets shot down an American military intelligence plane over their territory, aborted the summit conference. The incident seemed to "justify" Peking's hard line on imperialism.

3. *Withdrawal of Soviet economic assistance.* The Third Congress of the Rumanian Communist Party in late June 1960 unexpectedly witnessed an open confrontation between Khrushchev and P'eng Chen, Chinese chief delegate. Peking later charged that the confrontation was an "all-out and converging attack" by the Soviet Union on the CPC. In anger, Khrushchev ordered in July 1960 the withdrawal of the entire Soviet economic and technical mission.

4. *The 1960 Moscow conference.* After long and hard debates, the Moscow conference of eighty-one Communist parties in November 1960 produced a compromise statement. The major propositions contained in the document included the upholding of the Soviet leadership; the acknowledgment of China's influence on the peoples in Asia, Africa, and Latin America; the condemnation of Yugoslav revisionism; the encouragement of national liberation wars; the avoidability of world war; and peaceful coexistence among socialist and non-imperialist capitalist countries. The negotiation of such a statement also registered Moscow's loss of its monolithic authority over the world Communist movement.

5. *The Albanian issue.* The Albanian Communist Party disapproved of Khrushchev's de-Stalinization campaign because Enver Hoxha (Party chief) owed his power to Stalin and because Albania was worried that Khrushchev's resumption of his friendship with Tito might bring Albania back under Yugoslav control. But tiny, poor Albania found an ally in China. At the 1960 Moscow conference, Hoxha revealed that Khrushchev had lobbied for Albania's support against China. At the Twenty-second Congress of the Soviet Party in October 1961, Khrushchev openly criticized Albania and Stalin, but China unrestrainedly defended Albania and finally, in strong disagreement, walked out of the conference and went home. Khrushchev then attacked the CPC for its support of Albania against the U.S.S.R.

6. *Indian border conflicts and the Cuban missile crisis.* After the Sino-Indian border conflicts discussed above, Peking repeatedly accused Moscow in November-December 1962 of helping the Indian "reaction-

ary group" with military weapons and of collaborating with British and
U.S. imperialists against China. As Khrushchev withdrew the missiles
from Cuba in late October 1962, Peking denounced him for perpetrating
"another Munich" and betraying the Cuban people. Khrushchev
replied sharply to the Chinese attacks, and the polemics escalated.

7. *Sino-Soviet ideological meeting.* After repeated appeals by several
small Communist parties (the parties of Indonesia, Vietnam, New
Zealand, Britain, and Sweden), Peking and Moscow held a two-week
meeting in Moscow in July 1963 on their ideological differences. It
ended in failure and was followed by a full year (July 1963–July 1964) of
escalated polemics. The intensity of the dispute reached a new high.

8. *Partial nuclear test ban treaty.* On July 30, 1963, a partial nuclear
test ban treaty was signed by the Soviet Union, the United States, and
Britain. Peking made violent attacks on the Soviet Union for allying
with imperialism against China and deceiving the people of the world.
For propaganda effect, Chou En-lai proposed on the next day to the
governments of the world the convening of a world conference on
complete nuclear disarmament (he received only a few favorable
responses from small Communist nations).

9. *Border territories.* The Sino-Soviet territorial issue did not come up
until the dispute had been brought into the open. China voiced
complaints against Russian and Soviet acquisition of Chinese
borderlands in the past, totaling approximately 500,000 square miles,
through the "unequal" treaties of Aigun (1858), Peking (1860), and St.
Petersburg and others (1861-1894). The Sino-Soviet treaties of 1945 and
1950, reversing the provisions of the 1924 treaty, had severed Outer
Mongolia from China. Speaking with some bitterness to a delegation of
the Japanese Socialist Party in July 1964, Mao argued in favor of new
Sino-Soviet discussions on the status of Outer Mongolia and advocated
the return of the Kurile Islands to Japan.

Khrushchev fell from power on October 15, 1964. When the
preparatory meeting for a proposed international Communist conference was held on March 5, 1965, after several postponements, of those
invited, nineteen Communist parties attended and seven (China, North
Vietnam, North Korea, Japan, Indonesia, Albania, and Rumania)
declined to attend. Mao and other Chinese radicals began to refer to
Brezhnev and Kosygin as "Khrushchev revisionists."

China and the Third World

Although China is a Third World country, Africa and Latin America are relatively new to China. Peking's relations with these two continents did not begin until the mid-1950s. The Bandung conference of 1955 set the stage for Peking's approach to them, and the African independence movement welcomed China with open arms.

Seeking to promote friendship with Africa, Chou En-lai restated in 1964 China's "five principles" of international relations. They were, in terms of Africa, (1) support for the national independence of the African states; (2) support for their policy of peace, neutrality, and nonalignment; (3) support for the desire of African states to achieve unity and solidarity; (4) support for the settlement of their disputes through peaceful consultation; and (5) respect for African sovereignty and opposition to encroachment and interference. In offering economic aid to Africa, China also advocated eight principles, emphasizing equality and mutual benefit, economic cooperation, respect for recipients' independence, assistance with no conditions attached, low interest loans, and self-reliance. The Africans were impressed by this approach. From 1960 to 1965, China gained fifteen nations' recognition and it offered approximately $296 million worth of economic aid. In addition, Chou En-lai's "safari" to eleven nations in 1964 and 1965 promoted China's image and influence in Africa.

The activities of leftist "people's organizations" were also developing rapidly. The "Afro-Asian People's Solidarity Committee" (1957), an influential offshoot of the Bandung conference, sponsored three successive meetings in Guinea (April 1960), in Tanganyika (February 1963), and in Ghana (May 1965). The delegations of nations and regions grew from thirty-seven to seventy-two.

On the other side of the coin, Peking's support for local revolutionary activities in several African nations met with little success. Its engagement took two basic forms: training and weapon supplies. In the years 1960-1965, Peking had trained several hundred leftist Africans from the Congo (now Zaire), Cameroon, Ghana, Guinea, South Africa, Mozambique, and Tanzania. The main training center was the military academy in Nanking. The Chinese embassy in Bujumbura, Burundi, and the Obenemase training camp near Konogo, Ghana, also served as temporary training centers before 1966. In supplying weapons, Peking's heaviest involvement was in the Congo rebellion of 1963-1964. Chinese military materials were shipped through Tanzania to Bujumbura and then across the Ruzizi River to the rebels in the eastern Congo, headed by Gaston Soumialot, Christophe Gbenye, and Pierre Mulele. The Chinese embassy in Bujumbura served virtually as the center to direct the shipments and advise the rebels, who also had a liaison office in the same city. At a critical point in late 1964, Peking pledged "all possible measures" to help the Congolese rebels. The turning point was the suppression of the rebels by white mercenaries in late 1964, followed by Burundi's suspension of Chinese diplomatic ties in January 1965. At the training center in Ghana, Peking also supplied weapons for instruction and for equipping graduated cadres. Such activities were stopped after the military coup in February 1966 that overthrew Nkrumah.

The Soviet Union wanted to participate in the Afro-Asian conference scheduled to meet in June 1965 in Algiers as the successor to the Bandung conference of 1955, but China opposed Soviet participation. Several nations, like India and the U.A.R., preferred to postpone the conference rather than yield to Chinese demands. In October 1965, one month prior to the rescheduled conference, China realized that its support had declined and proposed an indefinite postponement of the conference. Thus, a second Bandung conference was never held. In one decade (1955-1965), China's triumph at Bandung had almost completely faded away.

In October 1965, on the heels of the postponement (and later cancellation) of the Afro-Asian conference, China suffered a setback in Indonesia. The failure of the September 30 coup staged by the Indonesian Communist Party (PKI) in cooperation with elements of the air force resulted in the slaughter of the Communists and the destruction of the PKI. It eventually ruined Sukarno's presidency. China had been informed of the coup plan and had delivered to the PKI a large portion of a promised shipment of 100,000 small arms without the knowledge of Indonesian army authorities. Many Indonesians blamed China for its involvement. Diplomatic relations were broken in 1967, and there was much violence against Chinese residents in Indonesia.

In Latin America, where Peking had no diplomatic relations except with Cuba, cultural exchanges were important. Peking's approach was to use New China News Agency correspondents and friendship societies between China and Latin American countries to engage in "people's diplomacy." Peking sent numerous delegations, ranging from trade missions to acrobatic teams. A great number of Latin Americans were invited to China, including former government officials, legislators, Communist Party leaders, workers, intellectuals, newsmen, artists, and students. Some of them were received by Mao Tse-tung and were particularly impressed because, as one of them said, they "had never had the honor of being received even by the most obscure member of the Central Committee" in Moscow.

The Cultural Revolution and Foreign Relations, 1965-1970

The Great Proletarian Cultural Revolution, which began in November 1965, caused great chaos in China after the Red Guards were mobilized in mid-1966. In retrospect, we can see more clearly that the Cultural Revolution, in addition to several other known motivations, was a radical movement directed not only against the old, capitalist, revisionist "poisons" as Mao had originally planned, but also against almost all Party veterans, civilian or military. Its final goal was seizure of power by the radicals or the so-called Cultural Revolution faction, including the group now known as the "Gang of Four." Although partially and temporarily successful due to Mao's support, its impact was so devastating that it "wasted us ten years," as Foreign Minister Huang Hua said in July 1977, in economic development and caused serious diplomatic setbacks.

Peking seemed to have perceived in 1965-1966 that a Sino-American war over Vietnam was unlikely to break out although the Vietnam war was escalating fiercely and the Chinese leaders were publicly and positively supporting Hanoi. As the Cultural Revolution ran apace, Peking and Washington seemed to have reached a tacit "no-war" understanding (to be discussed later), which served as a foundation for a future improvement in their relationship. On the other hand, the Sino-Soviet relationship deteriorated dramatically during this period.

A Policy for the Vietnam War

After the passage of the Gulf of Tonkin resolution in August 1964, Peking, in addition to dropping its long-standing proposal for a new Geneva conference, changed its line so as to support Hanoi's offensive strategy. It immediately sent a squadron of MiG-15 and MiG-17 jets to North Vietnam. But it took Peking about fifteen months (August 1964–November 1965) to define a policy for the Vietnam war. The main reasons were internal debates over the escalating U.S. intervention and the resumption of Soviet interest in the war after Khrushchev's downfall.

For simplicity, the main points of Peking's policy may be enumerated as follows:

1. *Increase in military and economic aid and encouragement of self-*

reliant people's war. The dispatch of a squadron of MiG jets in August-September 1964 was accompanied by the construction of new airfields in Yunnan and Kwangsi provinces in China as an air sanctuary for Hanoi. After the American bombing of the North began in February 1965, Mao decided not to meet the U.S. air force in kind. Instead, he sent to Vietnam some 50,000 "engineer-soldiers" to repair the damage to bridges, roads, and railways caused by U.S. air raids. Meanwhile, Peking increased its military and economic aid to both Hanoi and the Vietcong. More important, it encouraged them to fight their own people's war as Lin Piao's article of September 1965, "Long Live the Victory of the People's War!," had indicated.

2. *No Sino-American war over Vietnam.* The traditional saying, "we will not attack unless we are attacked" *(jen pu fan-wo, wo pu fan-jen),* described Peking's attitude toward the United States on Vietnam. It developed consistently into a "no-war-with-the-U.S." policy throughout the war. Ch'en Yi (July 1964), Mao Tse-tung (January 1965), Lin Piao (September 1965), and Chou En-lai (April 1966) all made similar statements that China would not "take the initiative to provoke" a war with the United States. The message was clear. Reciprocally, the United States informed China at the Warsaw talks in March 1966 that it had no intention of invading China.

3. *Rejection of the Soviet proposal for "united action."* As a result of Kosygin's visit to Hanoi in February 1965, Moscow adopted new measures for Vietnam, including the important "united action" proposal to Peking. The Soviets proposed (1) transit rights for Soviet military weapons to Hanoi through China by rail; (2) the use of airfields in Yunnan and Kwangsi and the right to station 500 men there; (3) an air corridor over China; (4) rights of passage for 4,000 Soviet military personnel through China to Vietnam; and (5) trilateral talks among Moscow, Peking, and Hanoi on the war. Hanoi eagerly endorsed the proposal, but China, except for the rail transit agreement that was concluded with the Soviet Union after some difficulties, formally rejected it in November 1965. Obviously, Peking was concerned that Moscow might skillfully use "united action" to achieve not only a stronger Soviet role in Indochina but a Sino-Soviet rapprochement and a Soviet military presence in China, both of which would mean the failure of Mao's anti-Soviet policy and would threaten Chinese national security.

4. *No peace talks on Vietnam.* After August 1964, Peking actively disapproved of any peace negotiations on the war. As long as it did not

become directly involved in the war as it had been earlier in Korea, Peking saw advantages in the continuation of the Vietnam war: it served to undermine a possible Soviet-American détente; it presented a model for wars of national liberation in the Third World; it aroused anti-American sentiment in China and around the world; and it promoted the antiwar movement and other domestic problems in the United States. Mao believed, as he told Edgar Snow in January 1965, that the United States would lose its interest in Vietnam after a short period of time and would eventually withdraw. Peking therefore rejected any peace talks proposal on the ground that "conditions for negotiations" were "not yet ripe" and advised the Vietnamese to fight until final victory.

5. *Two conditions for intervention.* As of early 1966, when the tumultuous Cultural Revolution had just begun, China's policy toward Vietnam and the pattern of its involvement in the war had been established. It must be made clear that Peking had never ruled out the possibility of a Korea-type intervention. As reported by Anna Louise Strong and stated by Teng Hsiao-p'ing in 1966, the P.R.C. would intervene in the war under either of two conditions: the invasion of North Vietnam by American ground forces, and the destruction or overthrow of the Hanoi government by combined U.S.-Saigon military forces. It could be assured that under either condition, North Vietnam would have been forced to invite China to intervene.

Diplomatic Setbacks

As discussed earlier, Peking met with diplomatic setbacks in 1964-1965 in the Congo (Zaire), Burundi, and Indonesia, and in the abortive Asian-African conference in Algeria. The great convulsion of the Cultural Revolution aggravated these setbacks.

Less than a year after the Red Guards were mobilized, all forty-five Chinese ambassadors, except Huang Hua (foreign minister since late 1976) in Cairo, were recalled for reeducation (Huang Hua was later recalled in July 1969). Chargés d'affaires were left in control of other embassies, and diplomatic activities were kept unprecedentedly low. The Red Guards verbally attacked senior diplomats and the Foreign Ministry. Such criticisms reached a climax in late spring 1967 when Ch'en Yi was forced to "confess" his errors. In August of the same year a revolt was staged in the ministry when radicals led by Yao Teng-shan, who had formerly served in Indonesia, "seized power" in the ministry, with Yao acting as foreign minister, for four days (August 19-22).

Moreover, the Red Guards turned violently against the Soviet Union (see below), foreigners, and foreign missions in Peking. For instance, in mid-June 1967, Red Guards physically attacked Indian diplomats in Peking. A few days later, the Indians, in retaliation, staged an anti-Chinese demonstration in New Delhi and attacked Chinese embassy officials there. On June 29, Maoist demonstrations in Rangoon ignited serious anti-Chinese riots in the city, which resulted in the suspension of Chinese economic aid to Burma. On August 22 of the same year, Red Guards set fire to the British mission in Peking. Donald Hopson, the British chargé d'affaires, and several of his staff were beaten when they rushed out of the building. A few days later, the personnel in the Chinese mission in London touched off a fight with British police. Three Chinese, three policemen, and one photographer were hospitalized. The convulsion and rivalry among the Red Guard factions even interrupted the arms shipment from Russia to Vietnam via China. Antiforeign and anti-"imperialist" sentiments ran high.

Exchanges of delegations between China and foreign countries dropped from 1,322 in 1965 to 66 in 1969. During the same period, there were five suspensions of diplomatic relations (Dahomey, 1966; the Central African Republic, 1966; Ghana, 1966; Indonesia, 1967; and Tunisia, 1967) as against two recognitions (Mauritius and South Yemen, both in 1968). In sum, the Cultural Revolution created a situation in which China experienced a period of contraction in its foreign relations. As China turned inward, most nations adopted a "wait-and-see" policy in dealing with Peking.

The Sino-Soviet Border Conflicts

During the same period, the Sino-Soviet dispute escalated (to culminate in the border conflicts on the Ussuri River in March 1969). Early in August 1966, thousands of Red Guards, to whom Soviet "revisionism" was anathema, demonstrated in Peking's streets near the Soviet embassy. *Pravda* (September 16) denounced them bitterly. In October Moscow expelled fifty-five Chinese students in reprisal. In late November, *Pravda* called for Mao's overthrow, repeating this summons several times in 1967. In retaliation, Chinese troops joined the Red Guards in late January 1967 in staging a semi-siege of the Soviet embassy that lasted nineteen days. In return, the Soviets surrounded the Chinese embassy in Moscow in early February; bothered by the Chinese chanting Maoist slogans in front of them, the Soviets touched off a fight with the embassy personnel, and then invaded the Chinese mission and beat several Chinese aides. The Red Guards in Peking immediately harassed Soviet dependents and made them bow to Mao's portrait when they evacuated from the capital. The emotional, vicious interactions seemed to continue endlessly.

The real Chinese concern over the Soviet invasion of Czechoslovakia in August 1968 was not Soviet aggressive behavior there, which Peking criticized as "social imperialism"; rather it was the possibility of a similar Soviet move against China. On March 2, 1969, Lin Piao, it is believed, provoked a conflict with the Soviet force over the disputed Chenpao (Damansky) Island in the Ussuri River. His motivation was apparently to promote his own indispensability as the successor to Mao in the face of a seemingly mounting Soviet "threat" to China. This "indispensability" was "proved" by the April 1969 CPC Party congress at which he was elected the "successor" to Mao against other power groups, particularly the rapidly growing radicals.

In the March 2 conflict, the Chinese gained the upper hand. Unprecedented publicity was given to the incident by both the Chinese and Soviets, and the sentiment of nationalism ran high on both sides. In retaliation, the Soviets sent a full battalion of troops to strike at the Chinese on the same island on March 15. This time the Chinese suffered heavy casualties. Observers wondered whether a large-scale Sino-Soviet war was imminent.

Kosygin visited Peking on September 1, 1969, after attending Ho Chi Minh's funeral in Hanoi. Chou En-lai met him at the airport. Rumania was credited by Communist diplomats in Eastern Europe with helping to arrange the visit. Kosygin reportedly made a conciliatory proposal for improving relations in three areas: state-to-state relations, border talks, and ideological discussions. Excluding the area of ideological dispute (Party-to-Party relations), which may continue for "9,000 years" as Mao said to Edgar Snow on December 18, 1970, relations in the other two areas registered some minor improvements in 1969-1970.

On October 8, 1969, Peking announced its agreement with Moscow to resume the border talks in Peking that had been broken off in 1964. Ten days later, a Soviet delegation led by Vasily V. Kuznetsov, first deputy foreign minister, flew to Peking for negotiations. But after two months of talks, no progress had been made. Thereafter negotiations as well as mutual accusations went off and on. In November 1970, nonetheless, the two nations exchanged new ambassadors after four years of no ambassadorial relations, and signed a trade agreement in Peking. In late December of the same year, they signed an annual accord on water navigation along the Amur, Ussuri, Argun, and Sungacha rivers and Lake Khanka. However, Party-to-Party relations remained strained.

Peking and Washington: An Undercurrent of Conciliation

By the end of 1966, the United States seemed to have developed a consensus in favor of continued containment of China without isolation. As the Cultural Revolution and the Vietnam war ran apace, it became abundantly clear in 1966-1967 that neither turbulent China nor the war-burdened United States had any intention at all of starting or risking a war against the other. In October 1967, Richard Nixon expressed the view in *Foreign Affairs* that the restoration of domestic tranquility could be achieved only by defusing the Vietnam war, and that China should have its position in the world community.

Whereas the U.S. peace offer to North Vietnam in April 1968 showed Washington's intention of deescalating the war, the Czechoslovakia invasion in August of the same year displayed Moscow's willingness to employ force against a Communist ally. In a surprise shift, on November 26, 1968, Peking proposed that an ambassadorial meeting be held in Warsaw with the new Nixon administration on February 20, 1969, for the purpose of concluding an agreement based on the five principles of peaceful coexistence. The proposed meeting was canceled by Peking on February 19, 1969, on the ground that the United States had granted political asylum to a Chinese diplomat, Liao Ho-shu, who had defected in the Netherlands. Yet Peking's intention was significant.

To move toward conciliation with Peking, Nixon took the initiative. According to the accounts of several White House aides including H. R. Haldeman (in his book, *The Ends of Power*), Nixon put out a feeler via Secretary of State William Rogers, who visited the home of President Yahya Khan of Pakistan in Lahore on May 24, 1969; Rogers expressed Nixon's interest in meeting the top leaders of the People's Republic of China. In June, the United States began to withdraw troops from Vietnam. One month later, it acted to relax curbs on travel to and trade with China. On August 1, Nixon repeated his China signal to Yahya Khan in Lahore when he visited there, and flashed it again through President Nicolae Ceausescu of Rumania the next day in Bucharest. In January 1970, the Warsaw talks resumed after almost two years of suspension; a second meeting was held in February. Such moves signaled China's favorable response to Nixon.

The Cambodia incursion by American and South Vietnamese forces in May 1970 interrupted the Warsaw dialogue, but two weeks before the

United States completed its withdrawal from Cambodia, Chou En-lai told Eastern European diplomats in Peking that China expected the Warsaw talks to be resumed soon. In early July, Secretary of State Rogers appealed to China from Tokyo for a settlement in Vietnam. In the same month, China released the Most Reverend James Edward Walsh (an American) after a twelve-year imprisonment. But there was still no definite response from Peking to Nixon's meeting proposal. On October 2, 1970, when Nixon met again with President Yahya Khan in the White House, he knew the Pakistani president was to visit Peking in three weeks. He asked Yahya Khan to transmit a message directly to Chou En-lai: Would the Chinese welcome Nixon's visit to China?

One day in mid-November, Chou En-lai, after a discussion of Nixon's message with Mao Tse-tung, gave the visiting Yahya Khan in Peking a reply: "We welcome the proposal from Washington for face-to-face discussions." And on December 18, 1970, Mao told Edgar Snow that he would welcome Nixon's visit to China. On March 15, 1971, the United States lifted its ban on travel by Americans to China. Three weeks later (April 7), Mao reversed Chou En-lai's earlier refusal to grant a visa to the U.S. table-tennis team then in Japan, so that they could visit China. The undercurrent of conciliation had grown from a stage of uncertainty into an incipient rapprochement.

Foreign Relations since the Sino-American Rapprochement

The Sino-American rapprochement was a major strategic move by Mao and Chou. It turned the United States from an "enemy" into a potential friend, played off the United States against the Soviet Union, eliminated one powerful source of support for the creation of a "two-Chinas" situation, and shifted Japan's and the United States' diplomatic relations from Taiwan to Peking. Making use of the contradictions among the major international actors, it was a master stroke of the Mao-Chou foreign policy.

Rapprochement and the Expansion of Diplomatic Relations

From the visit of the U.S. table-tennis team in April 1971 to Henry Kissinger's first visit to Peking in early July, an atmosphere of conciliation developed gradually but steadily. Peking endorsed for the first time the peace proposal of the South Vietnam National Liberation Front in early July; American visitors began to flow into China; Nixon ordered a further easing of the trade embargo against China; and

American troop withdrawal from Vietnam began to speed up.

It is unnecessary to dwell upon Nixon's first visit to China and the Shanghai communiqué of February 1972. There were, however, three features of major importance in the communiqué. First, the United States announced that it would withdraw its remaining military personnel from Taiwan "as the tension in the area diminishes"; second, the United States stated that it did not "challenge" the view that Taiwan is a part of China; but third, the two sides were not able to agree upon how to "settle" the Taiwan issue. Whereas the United States reaffirmed its interest in a "peaceful settlement" of the matter, the P.R.C. insisted that the "liberation of Taiwan" was China's internal affair and one in which no other country had the right to interfere.

Meanwhile, Peking's international position was improving significantly in other respects. Canada recognized Peking in mid-October 1970 after twenty months of negotiations. The Canadian government "noted" the Peking government's claim to the Nationalist-ruled Taiwan as an "integral part" of the territory of the P.R.C. but took no position on the issue because the Canadian government "does not consider it appropriate either to endorse or to challenge the Chinese government's position on the status of Taiwan." This "formula" was adopted by Italy, Chile, Austria, Turkey, Belgium, and other countries when they recognized Peking in 1970-1971. This recognition trend spread to the United Nations. After a week-long heated debate in late October 1971 on Peking's admission to the United Nations, the General Assembly finally voted on October 25 to seat the P.R.C. in lieu of the Republic of China (Taiwan). The wave of recognition continued to surge as one nation after another either granted recognition to or resumed diplomatic relations with the P.R.C. government. As of the end of 1978, Peking had established diplomatic ties with 115 nations whereas Taiwan kept relations with only twenty-two.

There was another significant development. Partly as a result of reaching a rapprochement with both China and the Soviet Union in 1972, the United States was able to conclude a peace agreement with North Vietnam in January 1973. Although the agreement was violated in 1975 by the Communists, the war ended without seriously disrupting the trend toward détente.

Peking, Tokyo, and Moscow

Realizing the great political and economic significance of Japan to China, Peking has applied the strategy of polarization to Japan in a most effective way. Prior to the rapprochement, the Peking leaders had bitterly accused Japan of striving for a revival of Japan's wartime militarism directed against China. When Japan recognized Peking in September 1972, Mao unexpectedly but benignly declined to accept Premier Tanaka's apologies for Japan's military aggression in China during World War II. As Mao explained, if it had not been for Japan's aggression, the CPC might not have had the chance to seize power from the Kuomintang in 1949. To polarize the situation further, Peking has also tried to draw Japan closer to China as a means of coping with the Soviet Union.

Both Moscow and Peking are desirous of a peace treaty with Tokyo. The Soviet treaty has been stalled by a territorial issue. Japan requested that Russia return all of the four northern islands (Iturup, Kunashir, Shikotan, and the Habomai group) in exchange for a peace treaty. The Soviet Union has agreed to return no more than two and in reality seems unwilling to return any. Furthermore, Moscow objects strongly to the Chinese demand for the inclusion in Peking's proposed treaty of an "antihegemony" clause, which Moscow believes is directed against the Soviet Union. Although such a clause had been written in the joint Chou-Tanaka communiqué of September 29, 1972, when Japan recognized China, Japan had been reluctant for years to agree to it in a formal treaty until August 1978.

In a change of tactics, Moscow proposed in late 1972 a joint Soviet-Japanese development project in Siberia. The Siberia project, of which developing oil was the main item, would have had Japan invest more than $6 million in Siberia over a period of twenty years. In return, Japan was to get annual shipments of 40 million tons of petroleum, 5.5 million tons of coal, 18.4 billion cubic meters of timber, and 10 billion cubic meters of natural gas. But the Soviets later reduced their offer from 40 million tons of oil to 25 million and made a new request that Japan construct a 2,000-mile railroad along the Chinese border to ship the oil from Tyumen to a port near Khabarovsk; the Soviets also created other difficulties. Above all, the strategic significance of such a railway alarmed the politically sensitive Japanese, and they became reluctant.

From the outset of the Soviet-Japanese negotiations on the Siberia project, Peking had endeavored to torpedo it. In the spring of 1973, Peking began to lead Japan away from the project by offering the Japanese 1 million tons of oil per year. In 1974 Peking increased the oil offer by 4 million, and in 1975 to 8 million. Moreover, Peking lowered its oil price from $12.80 to $12.10 a barrel (Indonesian oil cost to Japan: $12.60 a barrel). Furthermore, Peking endorsed Japan's request for the Soviet return of the four northern islands. As China's oil offer and territorial support continued, Japan saw no urgent need for the joint development in Siberia. Thus, the Siberia project was shelved, at least temporarily.

A significant amount of Sino-Japanese trade, especially the export of Japanese technology to China, has been for years a Japanese economic dream—in early 1978, Japan may have seen the beginning of its realization. On February 16, China and Japan, after almost a year of negotiations, signed a $20 billion trade agreement in Peking for a period of eight years effective immediately. The pact specified that Japan would sell $8 billion in plants and technology to China in the first five (1978-1982) of the eight years; in return, over the same period, China would sell to Japan a total of 47.1 million tons of oil, up to 5.3 million tons of coking coal, and up to 3.9 million tons of other coals. Sales volumes for the final three years (1983-1985) will be negotiated after 1981. This agreement represented the most dramatic improvement in Sino-Japanese economic and political relations since September 1972. Officials in Tokyo regarded the deal as the beginning of a "new era" between the two countries. Undoubtedly, the agreement was concluded on the basis of mutual needs and mutual benefit. Yet it has also overshadowed the shelved Soviet Siberia project. As the event developed, Japanese opposition to the proposed "anti-hegemony" treaty with China gradually faded away, whereas there was no prospect of an early conclusion of a Soviet-Japanese peace treaty.

Moreover, the Peking government, for the purpose of securing an early conclusion of the "anti-hegemony" treaty, deliberately eased unexpected Sino-Japanese tension that arose over an incident on April 14, 1978, involving the disputed Senkaku Islands (Tiao Yu Tai, 215 miles southwest of Okinawa). On that date thirty-eight Chinese fishing boats (some armed with machine guns) came into conflict with Japanese aircraft. Peking described the presence of the Chinese fishing boats as "accidental," "neither intentional nor deliberate." It did not reiterate its previous claims to the islands (Peking had issued a formal statement of its claims on October 31, 1971). The Chinese tactic, apparently, was to push aside the Senkaku issue before the conclusion of the treaty, although it will almost certainly raise the issue again now that the treaty has been signed.

Peking's "Anti-Hegemony" Campaign

Since the Sino-American rapprochement, Peking's foreign policy has increasingly taken on a global dimension. The P.R.C. has sided more closely than ever with the Third World and even the Second World in opposition to the "hegemonism" of the two superpowers: the United States and the Soviet Union. Antihegemony policy was embodied in the Party constitution of 1973 and 1977. To advance this policy, Mao Tse-tung developed his "three-worlds" concept in February 1974. According to Mao, the United States and the Soviet Union form the First World; Asia (except Japan), Africa, and Latin America belong to the Third World; and the countries between the First and Third worlds, including Canada, Japan, and those in Europe, belong to the Second World. To reinforce its opposition to the superpowers' "hegemonism," Peking campaigns for an international united front of cooperation between the Second and the Third worlds.

China defines "superpowers" by their military, political, and economic power as well as their aggressive ambition and imperialist policy. As Teng Hsiao-p'ing stated at the United Nations in April 1974, a superpower is an "imperialist country" that subjects other countries to its aggression and interference, and strives for "world hegemony." The United States, Peking asserts, has conducted numerous imperialist acts, but its counterrevolutionary global strategy has met repeated setbacks, and its aggressive power is weakening. The Soviet Union, on the other hand, because of its "social-imperialist" nature, is more adventurist and deceptive than the United States and is "the most dangerous source of war" today. For the Chinese, the Czechoslovak invasion, the Ussuri "aggression," and the Angola intervention all exemplified Soviet "imperialist" behavior in both socialist and nonsocialist countries.

According to Peking, the superpowers contend fiercely with each other for control of the world while colluding temporarily and opportunistically for a détente. Peking insists that this "détente" is a fraud: this is proved by the endless Soviet-American competition all over the world and by the increasing arms race in sophisticated weapons. The P.R.C. states that the contention between the superpowers is bound to lead to world war some day.

Moreover, Peking has charged that the superpowers have over-exploited the natural resources of the world, particularly in the Third World countries. The energy crunch in 1973-1974 and the ensuing international economic crisis were inevitable results of this exploitation and the superpowers' struggle for hegemony (*Red Flag*, February 1975). To oppose such imperialist actions, Peking advocates the protection of the Third World's natural resources and rights and its economic independence. In the past few years, therefore, Peking has endorsed every move relating to Third World control over Third World resources, like the Declaration on the Establishment of a New International Economic Order adopted by the United States (1974); the Dakar (Senegal) Conference on Raw Materials, the Ministerial Meeting of the "Group of Seventy-seven" in Algeria, the First OPEC Summit Conference in Algeria, the Ayacucho Declaration of eight South American countries, the Lomé (Togo) convention (all in 1975); the meeting of the "Group of Twenty-four" in Jamaica, meetings of the Twenty-two-nation Group of Latin American and Caribbean Sugar Exporting Countries (all in 1976); the International Economic Cooperation Conference ("North-South dialogue") in Paris, and the Second Summit Conference of the Association of Southeast Asia Nations (ASEAN) (both in 1977); and so on. In this campaign, Peking's real target, naturally, was and still is the Soviet Union, whose exploitation it regards as much worse than that of the United States.

Meanwhile, Peking has begun to develop a policy of active cooperation with the Second World. It supports a strong N.A.T.O., praises the independent policy of France against the Soviet Union, dispatches military delegations to visit France and Rumania, is willing to learn from the Yugoslav worker management system, and invited Tito to visit China because he has practiced an independent line against the Soviet Union. In addition, the strategic goal of China's $20 billion trade agreement with Japan in February 1978, as discussed earlier, is to pull Japan away from the Soviet Union.

In sum, Peking's international campaign against the hegemony of the two superpowers, particularly the Soviet Union, is buttressed by its policy of cooperating with the Second and Third worlds. Under such a policy, Peking's ties with the Second and Third worlds have been considerably strengthened.

Policy Directions after Mao

A year and a half after Mao's death, the Hua Kuo-feng leadership had purged the ultraradical Gang of Four, rehabilitated Teng Hsiao-p'ing, and convened the Eleventh Party Congress (August 1977) and the Fifth National People's Congress (February-March 1978). As of late 1978, Mao's successors had seemed to have tidied up a Party and government leadership that had been weakened by deaths and purges over the previous few years and to have rehabilitated civilian and military veterans, revitalized the intellectuals' role in the nation, and set an ambitious modernization program in motion. In which directions will the post-Mao foreign policy move? An answer to this question can be approached through an examination of the following issues.

Modernization

The Hua leadership is committed to rapid modernization in an effort to turn China into a "powerful, modern socialist country by the year 2000." This commitment was laid down by Chou En-lai at the Fourth National People's Congress in January 1975 and reiterated by Hua Kuo-feng and Teng Hsiao-p'ing in 1977 and 1978.

The post-Mao modernization program includes four fields: agriculture, industry, national defense, and science and technology. With almost all scientists and technocrats being rehabilitated, the tempo of modernization is expected to gain momentum. Such a drive will inevitably adopt the policy of offering material incentives; Peking moved in this direction with its October 1977 announcement of a wage increase for workers. There is also likely to be a limited relaxation of life as the regime moves somewhat away from the rigidity of ideology under Mao and imports more advanced foreign technologies. In his speech in February 1978 at the Fifth National People's Congress, Hua Kuo-feng expressed China's commitment to promote foreign trade in a big way. By this time, China had begun to import technology and military equipment from Japan and various European countries. Here we see the close link between Peking's modernization program and its cooperation with the Second World for the promotion of its "antihegemony" policy.

Sino-American Relations

Before the United States recognized China on January 1, 1979, Peking had repeatedly expressed its desire for the establishment of full diplomatic relations with Washington. The Chinese had also insisted consistently on its three conditions for normalizing the relationship: withdrawal of U.S. troops from Taiwan, severance of U.S. diplomatic ties with Taiwan, and abrogation of the United States–Taiwan Mutual Defense Treaty. As the Carter administration accepted these conditions, the United States established formal diplomatic ties with Peking and severed the governmental relationship with Taiwan. Sino-American relations thus entered a new era.

In this era, one can envision an increasing Sino-American political cooperation for peace and stability in Asia and in the world, intensive

Chinese absorption of American science and technology, and a rapid growth of trade and cultural exchanges. While the governmental relations between Washington and Peking progress, the nongovernmental ties between the United States and Taiwan will also continue to develop.

The Second World

Undoubtedly, Peking will strengthen its relations with Canada, Japan, and the European countries, including Yugoslavia. A better relationship with Second World countries is designed both to meet China's modernization needs and to advance its international "anti-hegemony" strategy. In this context, the improvement of Peking's relations with these countries will not only include economic and technological areas, but political and cultural areas as well.

The Albanian Labor Party has been critical of developments in China. An article in the Party organ *Zeri I Popullit* in July 1977 criticized China's "three-world" theory and its policy of cooperating with the Second and Third worlds against the superpowers. The source of this minor disagreement, according to Foreign Minister Huang Hua, was Albania's opposition to the Sino-American rapprochement, aggravated by China's cooperation with Yugoslavia, an old adversary of Albania. Peking has decided to hold off any rebuttal of Albania's criticism so as to minimize this dispute. It is fair to observe, therefore, that Peking will make similar efforts to bring under control any minor differences with Second World countries that may occur in the near future. As Huang Hua pointed out in July 1977, China's policy, its struggle against the Soviet superpower, is to try to reach major agreements with Second World countries while allowing minor differences to exist (*Ch'iu ta-t'ung, ts'un hsiao-i*).

Policy toward the Soviet Union

While Mao Tse-tung's radical policy and revolutionary romanticism were distant from Chou En-lai's moderate approach and pragmatism, there was no substantial difference in their policy toward the Soviet Union. The Hua Kuo-feng leadership has inherited the Mao-Chou Soviet policy, and anti-Soviet sentiment continues to prevail in China. Although the two nations' state-to-state relations, including their border talks, have improved somewhat, the ideological polemics will definitely go on. The Sino-American rapprochement has provided

China with more leverage to deal with the Soviet Union. The rapprochement may also be one of the factors that Teng Hsiao-p'ing had in mind when he told some German visitors on September 25, 1977, that there was no chance for Chinese-Soviet relations to warm up again for a generation or more.

Barring unforeseen circumstances, a Sino-Soviet war is an unlikely possibility in the near future, although minor border conflicts may continue to occur. A limited rapprochement at some time in the future is not impossible, because China's economic policy is now ironically moving in a direction similar to that of the "capitalist" and "revisionist" Soviet Union. For the time being, however, the "no war, no détente" situation will drag on until the interests of the two nations conflict or converge more sharply than they do at the present time.

The Third World

China will continue to claim that it sides with the Third World, despite the fact that it has not been fully accepted as a Third World nation itself, as it has claimed to be. In Asia, Peking is unlikely to engage in serious dispute or conflict with North Korea or Vietnam, although Sino-Vietnamese border clashes were reported and the status of Vietnamese residents of Chinese ancestry was a source of tension in 1978.

The Cambodian-Vietnamese border war that began in mid-1977 may be seen as a nationalist (territorial) as well as a Communist conflict. The Cambodian Liberation Army, after its 1975 victory, had purged its Vietnamese-trained components, which were supported by the Soviet Union, while keeping the Chinese-trained and locally organized components. In anger, the Vietnamese started the skirmishes in the disputed border area. China's policy, according to Huang Hua, is to support "the stand of Cambodia" and to serve as a mediator in calling for negotiations. The purpose of the unusual visit of Teng Ying-ch'ao (widow of Chou En-lai) to Cambodia in January 1978 clearly was to prevent the stronger Vietnam from defeating the weaker Cambodia so as to curtail the expansion of the Soviet influence in the area. Meanwhile, China was reported to have informed the Cambodian leaders that it would not fight against Vietnam for Cambodia. In January 1979, the Vietnamese forces and Cambodian rebels defeated the Cambodian government—only two months after the signing of the Soviet-Vietnamese Treaty. China did not militarily come to Cambodia's rescue. This event, a setback for Peking, is another indication that China at present is very unlikely to engage in an armed conflict in Asia.

The predominant position of the United States in Latin America leaves limited room for China to maneuver there. Peking's policy in this region will be generally guided by its relations with Washington. It seems certain, however, that trade, cultural, and political exchanges will be steadily promoted now that the U.S. has recognized China.

Africa is another battleground in the contest between Peking and Moscow. From Angola to Ethiopia, the P.R.C. has paid unusual attention to Soviet activities. The overriding theme is antihegemony and antiexploitation. Since the end of the Cultural Revolution, Peking has resumed an active policy of cultural exchange with and economic aid to selected African countries. Peking's concern at being outmatched by the Soviet Union will probably lead to a continuing high level of Chinese activities in Africa.

Conclusion

In seeking a way to project the future of the P.R.C.'s foreign policy, one must rely mainly on conclusions drawn from its past record. For this purpose, several significant conclusions can be drawn from the foregoing survey.

First of all, the P.R.C. in the past thirty years has made impressive progress toward achieving its foreign policy objectives. It has been most successful with respect to its short-range objectives of security, unification (except for Taiwan), power, and influence; somewhat less successful with respect to its middle-range objective of becoming an Asian leader; and least successful in its long-range goal of becoming a world power. For reasons of both physical limitations and politics, it is credible at present that China, as Mao pledged, is not going to become a superpower. If China's objective of "world" leadership is out of reach in the near future, its only attainable goal is to be an influential "Third World" leader through essentially peaceful and cooperative approaches. Any resort to violent means may well boomerang against China.

Second, the fluctuations of the P.R.C.'s policy have brought about several changes in the country's image. Beginning with the Korean War, China has gone through phases of appearing as an "aggressor" in Korea, a "sponsor" of peaceful coexistence policy at Bandung, again an "aggressor" on the Indian border, an "ungrateful ally" of the Soviet Union, and a "weapons supplier" to revolutionaries in a number of Third World countries. Such role changes have been more a reflection of China's national interests than of Communist ideology. The tactics of alternating zigzags, straightforward advance, and retreat were usually designed to facilitate the execution of policy. In operation, China's policy has appeared sometimes peaceful, sometimes violent.

Third, after the long, tumultuous struggle of the Cultural Revolution, harmony (peace, unity, and relaxation) seems to be a vital interest of the Chinese society and people. This contradictory but complementary relationship between harmony and struggle is a social norm in China. Originally evolved from the philosophy of *yin* and *yang*, it coincides with the theory of contradiction that Mao employed so often to interpret society and revolution in China. The developments of 1977-1978 seem to have substantiated this observation.

Fourth, Peking's foreign policy has shown a pattern of alternating expansion and contradiction that corresponds rather closely to the graph of the nation's growth under the imperial dynasties. When China is unified and strong it expands its influence, power, and even territory; when disintegrated and weak, it contracts and retreats. The development of such a pattern is determined as much by the internal situation as by foreign influence. From diplomatic growth in the peaceful coexistence era and again during the détente period, to the diplomatic setbacks of the Cultural Revolution, the P.R.C. has followed this course to a considerable degree.

In light of developments since 1949, it is beyond doubt that the P.R.C. will continue to strive for its long-range objective of becoming a world power. To this end, Hua Kuo-feng is holding high "the great banner of Chairman Mao" while actually carrying out the domestic and foreign policies of Chou En-lai. On the other hand, it will not be surprising if China, en route to such a goal, once again follows a cyclical course of alternating advance and retreat. In the immediate future China's modernization drive and its anti-Soviet campaign will dominate its efforts to promote a policy of peaceful coexistence toward the United States and the Second and Third worlds.

Selected Bibliography

Barnett, A. Doak. *Communist China and Asia: Challenge to American Policy*. New York: Harper & Brothers, 1960.

———., ed. *Communist Strategies in Asia: A Comparative Analysis of Governments and Parties*. New York: Praeger Publishers, 1963.

———. *China Policy: Old Problems and New Challenge*. Washington,

D.C.: Brookings Institution, 1977.

———. *China and the Major Powers in East Asia*. Washington, D. C.: Brookings Institution, 1977.

Chen, King C. *Vietnam and China, 1938-1954*. Princeton, N.J.: Princeton University Press, 1969.

Chiu, Hungdah, ed. *China and the Question of Taiwan: Documents and Analysis*. New York: Praeger Publishers, 1973.

Cohen, Jerome Alan, and Chiu, Hungdah. *People's China and International Law*. 2 vols. Princeton, N.J.: Princteon University Press, 1974.

Copper, John F. *China's Foreign Aid: An Instrument of Peking's Foreign Policy*. Lexington, Mass.: D. C. Heath, 1976.

Fitzgerald, Stephen. *China and the Overseas Chinese: A Study of Peking's Changing Policy*. Cambridge, Mass.: Cambridge University Press, 1972.

Gittings, John. *Survey of the Sino-Soviet Dispute*. London: Oxford University Press, 1968.

Griffith, William E. *Albania and the Sino-Soviet Rift*. Cambridge, Mass.: MIT Press, 1963.

———. *The Sino-Soviet Rift*. Cambridge, Mass.: MIT Press, 1964.

———. *Sino-Soviet Relations, 1964-1965*. Cambridge, Mass.: MIT Press, 1967.

Gurtov, Melvin. *China and Southeast Asia—The Politics of Survival*. Lexington, Mass.: D. C. Heath, 1971.

Halpern, A. M., ed. *Policies Toward China: Views from Six Continents*. New York: McGraw-Hill, 1965.

Hinton, Harold C. *Communist China in World Politics*. Boston: Houghton Mifflin, 1966.

———. *China's Turbulent Quest: An Analysis of China's Foreign Relations Since 1945*. New York: Macmillan, 1970.

———. *Peking-Washington: Chinese Foreign Policy and the United States*. Beverly Hills, Calif.: Sage Publications, 1976.

Hsiao, Gene T., ed. *Sino-American Détente and Its Policy Implications*. New York: Praeger Publishers, 1974.

Hsiung, James C. *Law and Policy in China's Foreign Relations*. New York: Columbia University Press, 1972.

Hsueh, Chun-tu, ed. *Dimensions of China's Foreign Relations*. New York: Praeger Publishers, 1977.

Jo, Yung-Hwan, ed. *Taiwan's Future?* Tempe: Center for Asian Studies, Arizona State University, 1974.

Johnson, Cecil. *Communist China and Latin America, 1959-1967.* New York: Columbia University Press, 1970.

Lall, Arthur. *How Communist China Negotiates.* New York: Columbia University Press, 1968.

Larkin, Bruce D. *China and Africa, 1949-1970.* Berkeley and Los Angeles: University of California Press, 1971.

Lovelace, Daniel D. *China and "People's War" in Thailand, 1964-1969.* Research Monograph no. 8. Berkeley: University of California, Center for Chinese Studies, 1971.

Maxwell, Neville. *India's China War.* New York: Pantheon Books, 1970.

Mozingo, David P. *Chinese Policy Toward Indonesia, 1949-1967.* Ithaca, N.Y.: Cornell University Press, 1976.

Passin, Herbert. *China's Cultural Diplomacy.* New York: Praeger Publishers, 1962.

Robinson, Thomas W. "The Sino-Soviet Border Dispute." *The American Political Science Review* (December 1972), pp. 1175-1202.

Scalapino, Robert A. "China and the Balance of Power." *Foreign Affairs* (January 1974), pp. 349-385.

Simmonds, J. D. *China's World: The Foreign Policy of a Developing State.* New York: Columbia University Press, 1970.

Simmons, Robert. *The Strained Alliance: Peking, P'yongyang, Moscow, and the Politics of the Korean War.* New York: The Free Press, 1975.

Taylor, Jay. *China and Southeast Asia: Peking's Relations with Revolutionary Movements.* New York: Praeger Publishers, 1976.

Tsou, Tang, ed. *China in Crisis.* China's Policies in Asia and America's Alternatives, vol. 2. Chicago: The University of Chicago Press, 1968.

Tsou, Tang, and Halperin, Morton H. "Mao Tse-tung's Revolutionary Strategy and Peking's International Behavior." *The American Political Science Review* (March 1965), pp. 80-99.

Van Ness, Peter. *Revolution and Chinese Foreign Policy: Peking's Support for Wars of National Liberation.* Berkeley and Los Angeles: University of California Press, 1970.

Whiting, Allen S. *China Crosses the Yalu: The Decision to Enter the Korean War.* New York: Macmillan, 1960.

———. *The Chinese Calculus of Deterrence: India and Indochina.* Ann Arbor: University of Michigan Press, 1975.

Williams, Jack F., ed. *The Taiwan Issue.* East Lansing: Asian Studies

Center, Michigan State University, 1976.

Wu, Yuan-li. *The Strategic Land Ridge: Peking's Relations with Thailand, Malaysia, Singapore, and Indonesia.* Stanford, Calif.: Hoover Institution Press, 1975.

Yu, George T. *China's African Policy: A Study of Tanzania.* New York: Praeger Publishers, 1975.

Zagoria, Donald S. *The Sino-Soviet Conflict, 1956-1961.* Princeton, N.J.: Princeton University Press, 1962.

———. *Vietnam Triangle.* New York: Pegasus, 1967.

Appendix: Economic Data

The statistical tables in this appendix are reprinted from various unclassified studies published by the Central Intelligence Agency of the United States. The following abbreviations are used in these tables:

b/d	barrels per day
bil	billion
dwt	deadweight ton
hp	horsepower
kg	kilogram
km	kilometer
kW	kilowatt
kWh	kilowatt-hour
LSD	light ship displacement
m	meter
m³	cubic meter
mil	million
th	thousand
. . .	Indicates no estimate is available

Table A.1   People's Republic of China: Economic Profile

	Unit of Measure [1]	1960	1965	1970	1971	1972	1973	1974	1975	1976
Aggregative data										
Gross national product [2]	Billion 1976 US $ ...	133.8	164.9	231.0	246.9	258.4	291.6	302.5	323.2	323.7
Index of industrial production [3]	1970=100	57	63	100	110	122	138	144	159	159
Total population (midyear)	Million	682.1	750.4	840.1	859.9	879.5	898.7	917.3	934.6	950.7
Fuels and power										
Primary energy (crude oil equivalent) [4]	Million b/d	3.3	2.8	4.3	4.8	5.2	5.6	6.0	6.7	7.2
Electric power (gross)	Billion kWh	47	42	72	86	93	101	109	121	N.A.
Hard coal [5]	Million mt	280	220	310	335	357	377	389	427	444
Crude oil	Million b/d	0.1	0.2	0.6	0.7	0.9	1.1	1.3	1.5	1.7
Metals										
Crude steel	Million mt	18.7	12.5	17.8	21.0	23.0	25.5	23.8	26.0	23.0
Pig iron	Million mt	27.5	13.8	22.0	27.1	30.4	33.7	31.4	33.8	N.A.
Iron ore	Million mt	100.0	38.3	72.3	91.1	103.4	107.2	99.9	109.0	N.A.
Tungsten ore (60 percent WO_3)	Thousand mt	29.4	17.1	11.5	16.3	16.6	18.7	17.1	14.9	N.A.
Primary aluminum	Thousand mt	80	140	180	192	238	286	316	357	N.A.
Agriculture										
Grain [6]	Million mt	156.0	194.0	243.0	246.0	240.0	266.0	275.0	284	285
Ginned cotton	Million mt	0.9	1.6	2.0	2.2	2.1	2.5	2.5	2.4	2.4
Manufactured items										
Mineral fertilizer (nutrients)	Million mt	0.5	1.5	2.8	3.3	3.9	4.9	5.0	5.5	N.A.
Cotton fabrics	Billion lm	4.9	6.4	7.5	7.2	7.3	7.6	7.6	7.6	N.A.
Cement	Million mt	12.0	16.3	26.6	31.0	38.1	41.0	37.3	47.1	49.3
Tractors	Thousand	9.9	9.6	29.2	43.8	47.9	57.5	50.0	58.3	53.6
Trucks	Thousand	15	30	70	86	100	110	121	133	146
Transportation and trade										
Railroad freight traffic	Billion mtkm	228.0	213.0	298.0	352.0	373.0	403.0	420.0	458.0	N.A.
Imports (c.i.f.)	Billion US $	2.0	1.8	2.2	2.3	2.8	5.1	7.4	7.4	6.0
Exports (f.o.b.)	Billion US $	2.0	2.0	2.0	2.4	3.1	5.0	6.6	7.0	6.9

[1] Abbreviations for units of measure are as follows: metric tons, mt; kilowatt-hours, kWh; barrels per day, b/d; linear meters, lm; and metric ton-kilometers, mtkm.

[2] Converted at US purchasing power equivalents.

[3] Estimates of this office computed by applying value-added weights to data for commodity production. The data are fragmentary and uncertain; therefore, the index should be regarded as providing only a tentative indication of the general level and trend in production.

[4] Data are for coal, crude oil, natural gas, and hydroelectric and nuclear electric power expressed in terms of crude oil equivalent, and exclude minor fuels such as peat, shale, and fuelwood. Data were converted from hard coal equivalents into barrels per day of crude oil equivalent by multiplying by the coefficient 0.014.

[5] Including a negligible amount of brown coal.

[6] Data are for barley, corn, oats, rice, rye, and wheat, and also include kaoliang, broad beans, and field peas. Tubers are included on a grain equivalent basis of 4 metric tons of tubers to 1 metric ton of grain.

Table A.2 China: Selected Economic Indicators

	1952	1957	1965	1970	1971	1972	1973	1974	1975	1976
GNP (bil 1976 US $)	87	122	165	231	247	258	292	302	323	324
Population, midyear (mil persons)	570	640	750	840	860	880	899	917	935	951
Per capita GNP (1976 US $)	153	190	220	275	287	294	325	330	346	340
Agricultural production index (1957 = 100)	83	100	104	127	130	126	142	146	148	148
Total grain (mil metric tons)	161	191	194	243	246	240	266	275	284	285
Cotton (mil metric tons)	1.3	1.6	1.9	2.0	2.2	2.1	2.5	2.5	2.3	2.3
Hogs (mil head)	58	115	168	226	251	261	...	261	...	280
Industrial production index (1957 = 100)	48	100	199	316	349	385	436	455	502	502
Producer goods index (1957 = 100)	39	100	211	350	407	452	513	536	602	...
Machinery index (1957 = 100)	33	100	257	586	711	795	930	992	1,156	...
Electric generators (mil kW)	Negl	0.3	0.8	...	3.0	3.5	4.0	4.6	5.5	...
Machine tools (th units)	13.7	28.3	45.0	70.0	75.0	75.0	80.0	80.0	90.0	...
Tractors (th 15-hp units)	0	0	23.9	79.0	114.6	136.0	166.0	150.0	180.0	190.9
Trucks (th units)	0	7.5	30.0	70.0	86.0	100.0	110.0	121.0	133.0	...
Locomotives (units)	20	167	50	435	455	475	495	505	530	...
Freight cars (th units)	5.8	7.3	6.6	12.0	14.0	15.0	16.0	16.8	18.5	...
Merchant ships (th metric tons)	6.1	46.4	50.6	121.5	148.0	164.6	209.4	288.4	313.6	318.8
Other producer goods index (1957 = 100)	41	100	200	294	336	371	415	429	472	...
Electric power (bil kWh)	7.3	19.3	42.0	72.0	86.0	93.0	101.0	108.0	121.0	...
Coal (mil metric tons)	66.5	130.7	220.0	310.0	335.0	356.0	377.0	389.0	427.0	448.0
Crude oil (mil metric tons)	0.4	1.5	11.0	28.2	36.7	43.1	54.8	65.8	74.3	83.6
Crude steel (mil metric tons)	1.3	5.4	12.5	17.8	21.0	23.0	25.5	23.8	26.0	23.0
Chemical fertilizer (mil metric tons)	0.2	0.8	7.6	14.0	16.8	19.8	24.8	24.9	27.9	...
Cement (mil metric tons)	2.9	6.9	16.3	26.6	31.0	38.1	41.0	37.3	47.1	49.3
Timber (mil m³)	11.2	27.9	27.2	29.9	30.7	33.2	34.2	35.2	36.2	...
Paper (mil metric tons)	0.6	1.2	3.6	5.0	5.1	5.6	6.0	6.5	6.9	...
Consumer goods index (1957 = 100)	60	100	183	272	272	295	334	347	368	...
Cotton cloth (bil linear meters)	3.8	5.0	6.4	7.5	7.2	7.3	7.6	7.6	7.6	...
Wool cloth (mil linear meters)	4.2	18.2	...	...	...	...	...	65.2	...	...
Processed sugar (mil metric tons)	0.5	0.9	1.5	1.8	1.9	1.9	2.2	2.2	2.3	...
Bicycles (mil units)	0.1	0.8	1.8	3.6	4.0	4.3	4.9	5.2	5.5	...
Foreign trade (bil current US $)	1.9	3.0	3.8	4.3	4.7	5.9	10.1	14.0	14.4	12.9
Exports, f.o.b.	0.9	1.6	2.0	2.0	2.4	3.1	5.0	6.6	7.0	6.9
Imports, c.i.f.	1.0	1.4	1.8	2.2	2.3	2.8	5.1	7.4	7.4	6.0

Table A.3a   China: Indicators of Aggregate Performance

	Gross National Product (Bil 1976 US $)	Index: 1957 = 100	
		Agricultural Production	Industrial Production
1949	51	54	20
1950	63	64	27
1951	74	71	38
1952	87	83	48
1953	93	83	61
1954	97	84	70
1955	106	94	73
1956	115	97	88
1957	122	100	100
1958	145	108	142
1959	138	84	173
1960	134	74	181
1961	106	79	105
1962	118	89	111
1963	132	96	134
1964	149	103	161
1965	165	104	199
1966	185	113	232
1967	178	118	202
1968	179	110	221
1969	199	113	266
1970	231	127	316
1971	247	130	349
1972	258	126	385
1973	292	142	436
1974	302	146	455
1975	323	148	502
1976	324	148	502

Average Annual Rates of Growth [1] (Percent)

	1949	1952	1957	1965	1970	1975
Gross National Product						
1952	19					
1957	12	7				
1965	8	5	4			
1970	7	6	5	7		
1975	7	6	6	7	7	
1976	7	6	5	6	6	Negl
Agricultural Production						
1952	15					
1957	8	4				
1965	4	2	Negl			
1970	4	2	2	4		
1975	4	3	2	4	3	
1976	4	2	3	3	3	0
Industrial Production						
1952	34					
1957	22	16				
1965	15	12	9			
1970	14	11	9	10		
1975	13	11	9	10	10	
1976	13	10	9	9	8	0

[1] The years across are base years; the years down are end-of-period years.

Table A.3b   China: Indicators of Aggregate Performance

	Index: 1957 = 100		Foreign Trade (Bil Current US $)	
	Construction Activity	Modern Transport Performance	Exports, f.o.b.	Imports, c.i.f.
1949	13	16	0.4	0.4
1950	21	27	0.6	0.6
1951	32	31	0.8	1.1
1952	41	39	0.9	1.0
1953	53	49	1.0	1.3
1954	72	62	1.1	1.3
1955	73	65	1.4	1.7
1956	110	87	1.6	1.5
1957	100	100	1.6	1.4
1958	149	148	1.9	1.8
1959	173	201	2.2	2.1
1960	161	196	2.0	2.0
1961	102	132	1.5	1.5
1962	92	136	1.5	1.2
1963	116	148	1.6	1.2
1964	140	156	1.8	1.5
1965	182	172	2.0	1.8
1966	197	192	2.2	2.0
1967	157	161	1.9	2.0
1968	202	170	1.9	1.8
1969	230	203	2.0	1.8
1970	266	245	2.0	2.2
1971	300	286	2.4	2.3
1972	351	302	3.1	2.8
1973	369	326	5.0	5.1
1974	335	340	6.6	7.4
1975	404	372	7.0	7.4
1976	...	...	6.9	6.0

Average Annual Rates of Growth (Percent)

	1949	1952	1957	1965	1970	1975
Construction Activity						
1952	47					
1957	29	20				
1965	18	12	8			
1970	15	11	8	8		
1975	14	10	8	8	9	
Modern Transport Performance						
1952	35					
1957	26	21				
1965	16	12	7			
1970	14	11	7	7		
1975	13	10	8	8	9	
Foreign Trade: Exports						
1952	31					
1957	19	12				
1965	11	6	3			
1970	8	5	2	0		
1975	12	9	9	13	28	
1976	11	9	8	12	23	-1
Foreign Trade: Imports						
1952	36					
1957	17	7				
1965	10	5	3			
1970	8	4	4	4		
1975	12	9	10	15	27	
1976	11	8	8	12	18	-19

[1] The years across are base years; the years down are end-of-period years.

Table A.4   China: Population by Province

Th Persons as of 1 July 1977

	1953	1958	1965	1970	1975	1976
Total	582,603	654,727	750,394	840,148	934,626	950,744
Northeast						
Liaoning	22,269	26,638	32,403	37,811	43,504	44,474
Kirin ...., ...	12,609	14,396	17,177	19,786	22,532	23,000
Heilungkiang	12,681	16,220	21,320	26,104	31,141	32,000
North						
Hopeh	33,181	36,599	41,428	47,304	54,032	55,193
Shansi	14,314	16,128	18,349	20,432	22,626	23,000
Inner Mongolia	3,532	4,478	5,778	6,998	8,281	8,500
Peking	4,591	6,193	7,730	8,277	8,460	8,490
Tientsin	4,622	5,416	6,386	6,846	7,180	7,226
Shantung	50,134	55,989	63,257	70,076	77,253	78,478
East						
Kiangsu	38,329	42,759	48,523	54,195	60,403	61,504
Anhwei	30,663	33,833	37,442	40,828	44,392	45,000
Chekiang	22,866	25,536	28,918	32,090	35,430	36,000
Kiangsi	16,773	18,868	22,271	25,465	28,826	29,400
Fukien	13,143	14,873	17,823	20,590	23,503	24,000
Shanghai	8,808	9,888	10,966	11,712	12,260	12,312
Central-South						
Honan	43,911	48,795	54,829	60,491	66,451	67,468
Hupeh	27,790	31,102	35,221	39,086	43,155	43,848
Hunan	33,227	36,526	40,563	44,351	48,338	49,018
Kwangtung	34,770	37,233	42,684	47,798	53,182	54,100
Kwangsi	19,561	21,660	24,776	27,698	30,775	31,300
Southwest						
Szechwan	65,685	72,827	81,634	89,898	98,596	100,080
Kweichow	15,037	17,060	19,302	21,407	23,622	24,000
Yunnan	17,473	19,312	22,120	24,754	27,527	28,000
Tibet	1,274	1,342	1,458	1,566	1,680	1,700
Northwest						
Shensi	15,881	18,318	20,800	23,130	25,582	26,000
Kansu	11,291	13,005	15,200	17,258	19,425	19,795
Tsinghai	1,677	2,093	2,664	3,199	3,762	3,858
Sinkiang	4,874	5,744	7,119	8,410	9,768	10,000
Ninghsia	1,637	1,896	2,253	2,588	2,940	3,000

These estimates were prepared by the US Department of Commerce, Bureau of Economic Analysis, Foreign Demographic Analysis Division. All figures reflect post-1971 boundaries and are thus comparable.

Table A.5   China: Estimated and Projected
Population and Vital Rates

| | | Th Persons as of 1 July 1977 | | | | | |
| | | Distribution Among Main Age Groups | | | Vital Rates per Th Persons | | |
	Population	Under 15	15-64	65 and Over	Natural Increase	Births	Deaths
1949	537,918	200,105	322,751	15,062	12.0	45.4	33.4
1950	547,364	205,809	326,229	15,326	13.5	45.4	31.9
1951	558,096	211,518	330,393	16,185	15.1	45.3	30.2
1952	569,904	218,273	335,104	16,527	18.0	45.2	27.2
1953	582,603	225,237	340,102	17,264	22.5	45.0	22.5
1954	596,064	232,571	345,559	17,934	23.1	44.1	21.0
1955	610,201	240,344	351,185	18,672	23.8	43.1	19.4
1956	625,004	248,608	356,940	19,456	24.2	42.6	18.5
1957	640,024	256,961	362,799	20,264	23.3	41.3	18.0
1958	654,727	264,902	368,747	21,078	22.1	40.2	18.1
1959	668,930	272,385	374,679	21,866	20.8	40.1	19.3
1960	682,091	279,088	380,427	22,576	18.2	39.9	21.7
1961	693,624	284,439	386,003	23,182	15.4	39.1	23.7
1962	705,486	289,460	392,192	23,834	18.5	37.7	19.2
1963	719,301	295,219	399,458	24,624	20.3	37.6	17.4
1964	734,359	301,061	407,812	25,486	21.2	37.2	16.0
1965	750,394	306,725	417,258	26,411	22.0	36.5	14.4
1966	766,946	312,174	427,403	27,369	21.6	36.2	14.6
1967	784,017	317,451	438,222	28,344	22.4	36.2	13.8
1968	801,983	322,723	449,907	29,353	22.9	36.3	13.4
1969	820,733	328,124	462,221	30,388	23.3	36.3	12.9
1970	840,148	333,851	474,837	31,460	23.4	35.7	12.3
1971	859,927	339,626	487,741	32,560	23.1	34.9	11.8
1972	879,520	345,184	500,654	33,682	22.0	33.5	11.6
1973	898,695	350,551	513,305	34,839	21.2	32.0	10.8
1974	917,256	355,291	525,933	36,032	19.7	30.0	10.2
1975	934,626	358,735	538,642	37,249	17.8	27.6	9.8
1976	950,744	360,794	551,453	38,497	16.4	25.5	9.1
1977	965,937	361,569	564,586	39,782	15.3	24.1	8.8
1978	980,417	360,967	578,361	41,089	14.4	23.0	8.6
1979	994,332	359,136	592,782	42,414	13.7	22.1	8.4
1980	1,007,858	356,497	607,601	43,760	13.3	21.5	8.2
1985	1,075,999	335,887	689,213	50,899	13.2	21.1	7.9
1990	1,151,665	320,873	771,480	59,312	14.0	21.9	7.9
1995	1,237,029	340,759	827,122	69,148	14.5	22.7	8.1
2000	1,328,645	375,343	872,993	80,309	13.7	22.0	8.3

These estimates were prepared by the US Department of Commerce, Bureau of Economic Analysis, Foreign Demographic Analysis Division.

Table A.6 China: Estimated Population, by Age and Sex

	Th Persons			Percent Distribution			Males per Hundred Females
	Total	Males	Females	Total	Males	Females	
All ages	965,937	485,579	480,358	100	100	100	101.1
0-4	121,548	61,760	59,788	12.58	12.72	12.45	103.3
5-9	128,075	64,906	63,169	13.26	13.37	13.15	102.7
10-14	111,946	56,624	55,322	11.59	11.66	11.52	102.4
15-19	99,458	50,116	49,342	10.30	10.32	10.27	101.6
20-24	95,500	48,152	47,348	9.89	9.92	9.86	101.7
25-29	77,307	39,165	38,142	8.00	8.07	7.94	102.7
30-34	60,203	30,821	29,382	6.23	6.35	6.12	104.9
35-39	52,718	27,013	25,705	5.46	5.56	5.35	105.1
40-44	49,246	25,126	24,120	5.10	5.17	5.02	104.2
45-49	42,683	21,373	21,310	4.42	4.40	4.44	100.3
50-54	35,536	17,473	18,063	3.68	3.60	3.76	96.7
55-59	28,888	13,862	15,026	2.99	2.85	3.13	92.3
60-64	23,047	10,940	12,107	2.39	2.25	2.52	90.4
65-69	17,507	8,239	9,268	1.81	1.70	1.93	88.9
70-74	11,928	5,496	6,432	1.23	1.13	1.34	85.4
75 and over	10,347	4,513	5,834	1.07	0.93	1.21	77.4

These estimates were prepared by the US Department of Commerce, Bureau of Economic Analysis, Foreign Demographic Analysis Division.

Table A.7 China: Selected Inputs to the Agricultural Sector

		Supply of Chemical Fertilizers [1] (Th Metric Tons)			
		Production			
	Total	Nitrogen	Phosphorous	Potassium	Imports
1949	5	5	0	0	0
1950	34	14	0	0	20
1951	67	27	0	0	40
1952	79	39	0	0	40
1953	133	53	0	0	80
1954	205	69	0	0	136
1955	243	84	1	0	158
1956	401	117	14	0	270
1957	429	137	22	0	270
1958	626	202	64	0	360
1959	639	275	94	0	270
1960	710	345	150	0	215
1961	589	280	84	0	225
1962	788	444	104	0	240
1963	1,297	542	215	0	540
1964	1,485	712	416	0	357
1965	2,120	902	578	0	640
1966	2,604	1,046	800	36	722
1967	2,763	883	658	68	1,154
1968	3,128	1,040	761	92	1,235
1969	3,558	1,180	963	100	1,315
1970	4,266	1,562	1,103	116	1,485
1971	4,820	1,900	1,300	140	1,480
1972	5,494	2,345	1,447	152	1,550
1973	6,435	2,930	1,819	168	1,518
1974	6,093	3,162	1,611	180	1,140
1975	6,701	3,543	1,806	200	1,152
1976	...	...	...	...	983

[1] Actual weight of primary nutrient content. For domestic production figures in terms of standard weights, see table A.17d.

Table A.8　China: Production of Major Agricultural Commodities

Mil Metric Tons

	Grain [1]	Cotton	Raw Sugar
1949	111	0.4	0.198
1950	130	0.7	...
1951	141	1.0	...
1952	161	1.3	0.531
1953	164	1.2	...
1954	166	1.1	...
1955	180	1.5	...
1956	188	1.5	...
1957	191	1.6	0.832
1958	206	1.7	...
1959	171	1.2	...
1960	156	0.9	...
1961	168	0.8	...
1962	180	1.0	...
1963	190	1.2	...
1964	194	1.7	...
1965	194	1.9	1.4
1966	215	1.8	1.4
1967	225	1.9	1.6
1968	210	1.8	1.4
1969	215	1.8	1.4
1970	243	2.0	1.6
1971	246	2.2	1.4
1972	240	2.1	1.6
1973	266	2.5	1.9
1974	275	2.5	1.8
1975	284	2.3	...
1976	285	2.3	...

[1] Grain includes soybeans and converts potatoes to a grain equivalency by taking one-fifth of their actual weight.

Table A.9　China: Consumption of Primary Energy

	Total	Industry and Construction	Agriculture	Transport	Residential/ Commercial
		Mil Metric Tons of Coal Equivalent [1]			
1952	42	11	Negl	5	26
1957	97	36	1	9	51
1965	185	89	6	14	76
1970	278	159	12	16	91
1974	380	235	24	19	102
1975	421	260	27	21	113
1976	497	307	32	25	133
		Percent			
1952	100	26	Negl	12	62
1957	100	37	1	9	53
1965	100	48	3	8	41
1970	100	57	4	6	33
1974	100	62	6	5	27
1975	100	62	6	5	27
1976	100	62	6	5	27

[1] The coal equivalent employed has a calorific value of 7,000 kilocalories per kilogram.

Table A.10a China: Crude Oil Production

Mil Metric Tons

	National	Ta-ch'ing	Sheng-li	Ta-kang	Yu-men	K'o-la-ma-i
1949	0.121				...	
1950	0.200				...	
1951	0.305				...	
1952	0.436				0.143	
1953	0.622				0.198	
1954	0.789				(0.239)[2]	
1955	0.966				0.414	
1956	1.163				0.533	
1957	1.458				0.755	0.05[3]
1958	2.264				1.002	0.25
1959	3.7				1.337	(0.239)
1960	5.1	0.792[3]			1.700	(0.226)
1961	5.186	(1.022)			1.600	(0.214)
1962	5.746	(2.726)	0.046[3]		(1.303)	0.201
1963	6.360	4.427	(0.321)		(1.006)	(0.307)
1964	8.653	(5.765)	0.596		(0.709)	(0.416)
1965	10.961	7.106	0.735		0.412	0.523
1966	14.074	8.776	2.0		(0.414)	(0.473)
1967	13.9	(9.045)	(2.625)	0.20[3]	(0.416)	(0.423)
1968	15.2	9.297	(3.250)	(0.34)	(0.417)	(0.373)
1969	20.377	12.830	(3.875)	0.48	0.419	0.323
1970	28.211	17.666	4.5	0.96	0.490	0.384
1971	36.700	22.136	6.5	(1.64)	0.544	0.503
1972	43.065	25.550	8.45	(2.33)	0.620	0.604
1973	54.804	28.298	9.50	3.00	0.676	0.725
1974	65.765	34.608	11.02	3.74	0.710	1.036
1975	74.261	40.072	14.90	4.34	0.785[4]	1.065[4]
1976	83.608	43.093	...	...	...	...
Total	**503.994**	**273.209**	**63.318**	**17.030**	**16.842**	**8.335**

[2] Parentheses indicate linear interpolation.
[3] First year of production.
[4] Regression analysis, 1969-74.

Table A.10b China: Crude Oil Production

Mil Metric Tons

	Tsaidam[1]	Fu-yu[2]	P'an-shan[2]	Ch'ien-chiang[2]	Residual[3]
1949					
1950					
1951					
1952					
1953					
1954					
1955					
1956					
1957					
1958	0.03[4]				
1959	(0.044)[5]				
1960	(0.058)				
1961	(0.072)				
1962	(0.085)				
1963	(0.099)				
1964	(0.113)				
1965	0.127.				
1966	(0.135)				
1967	(0.144)				
1968	(0.152)				
1060	0.160				
1970	0.165	(1.15)	0.14	(1.15)	1.606
1971	0.180	1.44	0.74	(2.21)	0.807
1972	0.320	2.58	1.57	3.28	−2.239
1973	0.442	2.83	(2.20)	3.63	3.503
1974	0.530	3.08	2.83	3.97	4.241
1975	0.582[4]	3.25	4.05	4.10	1.117
1976	...				...
Total	**3.438**	**14.330**	**11.530**	**18.340**	

[1] Consists of three separate fields.
[2] Likely upper limits of crude oil production, with parentheses indicating interpolation or extrapolation.
[3] The residual is a true error term and may be either positive or negative. It also contains small amounts of shale oil not accounted for elsewhere.
[4] First year of production.
[5] Parentheses indicate linear interpolation.
[6] Regression analysis, 1969-74.

Table A.11   Production of Minerals and Metals [1]

Th Metric Tons

		Iron Ore [2]				Metal-lurgical Coke [5]	Refined Copper [6]	Primary Aluminum	Primary Tin Metal [7]
	Total	Large Mines	Small Mines	Tungsten Ore [3]	Bauxite [4]				
1957	17,670	14,140	3,530	. . .	. . .	. . .	. . .	. . .	. . .
1965	38,300	. . .	. . .	17	1,120	10,100	200	140	12
1970	72,300	54,200	18,100	12	1,500	16,200	290	188	10
1971	91,100	65,800	25,300	16	1,500	20,100	290	192	13
1972	103,400	. . .	. . .	17	1,900	22,400	290	238	13
1973	107,200	. . .	. . .	19	2,300	24,300	290	286	15
1974	99,900	. . .	. . .	17	2,500	22,600	300	316	15
1975	109,000	. . .	. . .	15	2,800	24,300	300	357	18
1976	. . .	. . .	. . .	14	. . .	. . .	. . .	. . .	. . .

[1] See table A.1 for information on pig iron and steel production.

[2] Gross weight of ores in the state in which they leave mines.

[3] Estimated tonnage of tungsten concentrates, 60-percent tungsten trioxide (WO_3) basis.

[4] Data are for aluminous shales and clays used for the manufacture of aluminum and exclude exported shales and those used for refractories, abrasives, and cement.

[5] Oven and beehive coke, excluding breeze coke.

[6] Primary and secondary refined copper produced from domestic and imported ores and scrap.

[7] Excluding tin derived from scrap or detinning.

Table A.12   China: Inventories of Transportation Equipment

	Mainline Locomotives [1] (Th Units)				Freight Cars [1] (Th Units)	Merchant [1] Ships		Trucks [1] (Th Units)
	Total	Diesel	Steam	Electric		Units	Th dwt	
1952	3.3	0	3.3	0	58	101	270	42
1957	3.7	0	3.7	0	86	93	302	63
1965	5.4	0	5.4	0	143	174	933	230
1970	6.4	0.7	5.7	0	175	269	1,944	434
1971	6.7	0.9	5.8	0	185	305	2,290	506
1972	7.1	1.1	5.9	0.1	197	329	2,657	590
1973	7.5	1.4	6.0	0.1	209	368	3,291	677
1974	7.9	1.7	6.1	0.1	222	430	4,592	793
1975	8.3	2.0	6.2	0.1	237	495	6,082	914
1976	. . .	. . .	. . .	. . .	. . .	556	7,081	. . .

[1] For data on domestic production of these types of equipment, see table A.16b.

Table A.13   China: Railroad and Highway
Networks and Freight Turnover

	Railroads		Highways	
	Length (Th km)	Turnover (Bil Metric Ton-km)	Length (Th km)	Turnover (Bil Metric Ton-km)
1952	24.5	60.2	127	0.8
1957	29.9	134.6	255	3.9
1965	35.9	213	550	7.0
1970	41.3	298	640	10.5
1971	42.8	352	670	12.0
1972	44.8	373	700	12.5
1973	45.6	403	725	13.5
1974	46.6	420	755	14.1
1975	48	458	785	15.6
1976	49.9	. . .	820	16.2

Table A.14   China: Modern Transport
Performance

Mil Metric Tons Originated

	Total	Railroads	Highways	Inland and Coastal Waterways
1949	67	56	6	5
1950	114	100	7	7
1951	134	111	13	10
1952	167	132	21	14
1953	211	161	30	20
1954	266	193	44	29
1955	280	194	50	36
1956	372	246	79	47
1957	429	274	101	54
1958	633	381	176	76
1959	864	520	230	114
1960	842	510	220	112
1961	565	340	150	75
1962	582	350	155	77
1963	634	380	170	84
1964	668	400	180	88
1965	737	440	200	97
1966	823	490	225	108
1967	690	410	190	90
1968	730	430	205	95
1969	872	510	250	112
1970	1,050	615	300	135
1971	1,229	725	344	160
1972	1,295	770	356	169
1973	1,398	830	385	183
1974	1,459	865	404	190
1975	1,598	945	445	208
1976	...	...	463	...

Table A.15   China: Gross Value of Industrial Output

Mil 1957 Yuan

	1957	1965	1970	1974	1975
Total	69,797	142,686	240,102	344,865	375,236
Northeast	15,874	32,115	49,546	66,463	72,707
Liaoning	10,078	19,090	29,497	41,349	44,202
Kirin	2,155	5,018	7,372	9,329	10,539
Heilungkiang	3,641	8,007	12,677	15,785	17,966
North	14,446	. . .	. . .	91,398	. . .
Hopeh	2,519	6,723	13,445	22,648	24,873
Shansi	1,645	. . .	. . .	6,264	. . .
Inner Mongolia	631	3,009	4,487	6,018	. . .
Peking	2,100	5,602	12,079	18,570	19,607
Tientsin	3,911	6,882	12,097	17,524	18,748
Shantung	3,640	6,174	12,565	20,374	20,991
East	21,206	. . .	. . .	99,996	. . .
Kiangsu	4,124	7,509	15,625	23,435	. . .
Anhwei	1,348	2,390	3,811	6,149	7,330
Chekiang	2,132	3,900	6,060	7,800	. . .
Kiangsi	1,100	. . .	. . .	5,242	. . .
Fukien	1,100	1,835	2,532	4,323	4,626
Shanghai	11,402	24,220	39,074	53,047	55,707
Central-South	9,995	19,923	35,679	50,011	. . .
Honan	1,560	3,737	7,173	10,612	11,960
Hupeh	2,514	4,140	7,500	9,238	. . .
Hunan	1,634	2,929	6,027	8,167	8,403
Kwangtung	3,570	7,810	12,553	17,474	20,284
Kwangsi	717	1,307	2,426	4,520	4,926
Southwest	5,843	10,799	. . .	20,494	. . .
Szechwan	4,283	6,929	. . .	13,852	17,465
Kweichow	562	2,527	. . .	3,158	4,548
Yunnan	989	1,324	2,079	3,395	. . .
Tibet	9	19	. . .	89	114
Northwest	2,433	5,924	. . .	16,503	. . .
Shensi	1,134	2,707	5,547	6,517	6,904
Kansu	694	2,172	4,381	6,769	7,732
Tsinghai	117	273	553	997	1,096
Sinkiang	465	696	1,293	1,861	. . .
Ninghsia	23	76	. . .	359	424

Table A.16a   China: Production of Selected Types
of Machinery

	Electric Generators (kW)	Machine Tools (Units)	Spindles (Units)	Sewing Machines (Th Units)	Powered Irrigation Equipment (Th Hp)	Tractors (15-Hp Units)		
						Total	Conventional	Garden
1949	10,181	1,582	...	...	...	...	...	...
1950	22,798	3,312	...	...	...	...	...	...
1951	31,731	5,853	131,984	...	...	...	...	...
1952	29,678	13,734	383,128	...	...	...	...	...
1953	59,525	20,502	287,424	257	...	...	...	...
1954	54,617	15,901	489,044	316	...	...	...	...
1955	107,595	13,708	304,400	174	...	...	...	...
1956	288,263	25,928	784,020	206	170	...	...	...
1957	312,200	28,297	484,000	278	52	...	...	...
1958	1,425,000	30,000	1,000,000	637	720	1,100	1,100	...
1959	...	35,000	1,360,000	563	1,255	9,400	9,400	...
1960	...	40,000	...	676	1,610	23,800	23,800	...
1961	...	30,000	...	...	700	16,200	16,200	...
1962	...	25,000	...	...	955	13,100	13,100	...
1963	...	35,000	...	...	640	15,700	15,700	...
1964	625,000	40,000	700,000	1,257	860	19,450	19,300	150
1965	780,000	45,000	1,400,000	1,571	1,150	23,875	23,000	875
1966	...	50,000	...	...	1,530	34,625	32,000	2,625
1967	...	40,000	...	...	...	29,100	27,000	2,100
1968	...	45,000	...	...	...	32,675	30,000	2,675
1969	...	55,000	...	1,800	...	43,200	40,000	3,200
1970	...	70,000	...	2,400	...	79,000	70,000	9,000
1971	3,000,000	75,000	...	3,000	3,089	114,625	105,000	9,625
1972	3,500,000	75,000	...	3,300	4,016	136,000	115,000	21,000
1973	4,000,000	80,000	...	3,894	5,984	166,000	138,000	28,000
1974	4,650,000	80,000	...	...	6,000	150,000	120,000	30,000
1975	5,460,000	90,000	...	...	7,000	180,000	140,000	40,000
1976	...	...	...	...	...	190,925	128,800	62,125

Table A.16b   China: Production of Selected Types
of Machinery

	Mainline Locomotives (Units)				Freight Cars (Units)	Merchant Ships (LSD Metric Tons)	Trucks (Units)
	Total	Steam	Diesel	Electric			
1949	0	0	0	0	3,155	0	0
1950	0	0	0	0	696	0	0
1951	0	0	0	0	2,882	0	0
1952	20	20	0	0	5,792	6,100	0
1953	10	10	0	0	4,501	14,800	0
1954	52	52	0	0	5,446	31,400	0
1955	98	98	0	0	9,258	50,200	0
1956	184	184	0	0	7,122	51,200	1,654
1957	167	167	0	0	7,300	46,400	7,500
1958	350	346	2	2	11,000	61,300	16,000
1959	533	530	3	0	17,000	54,300	19,400
1960	602	600	0	2	23,000	23,600	15,000
1961	100	100	0	0	3,000	18,800	1,000
1962	25	25	0	0	4,000	13,500	8,400
1963	27	25	0	2	5,900	23,400	16,800
1964	27	25	2	0	5,700	31,000	20,300
1965	50	20	30	0	6,600	50,600	30,000
1966	220	150	70	0	7,500	55,900	43,000
1967	300	200	100	0	6,900	48,200	32,000
1968	340	200	140	0	8,700	64,500	27,000
1969	391	230	160	1	11,000	93,100	60,000
1970	435	250	180	5	12,000	121,500	70,000
1971	455	250	200	5	14,000	148,000	86,000
1972	475	250	220	5	15,000	164,600	100,000
1973	495	250	240	5	16,000	209,400	110,000
1974	505	250	250	5	16,800	288,400	121,000
1975	530	250	275	5	18,500	313,600	133,000
1976	...	...	...	...	...	318,800	...

Table A.17a   China: Production of Selected Producer Goods

	Electric Power (Mil kWh)			Natural Gas (Mil Cubic Meters)	Crude Oil (Mil Metric Tons)	Coal (Th Metric Tons)		
	Total	Hydroelectric	Thermal			Total	Large Mines	Small Mines
1949	4,300	700	3,600	Negl	0.121	32,430	22,117	10,313
1950	4,600	800	3,800	Negl	0.200	42,920	32,607	10,313
1951	5,800	1,000	4,800	Negl	0.305	53,090	45,405	7,685
1952	7,300	1,300	6,000	Negl	0.436	66,490	56,184	10,306
1953	9,200	1,500	7,700	...	0.622	69,680	61,527	8,153
1954	11,000	2,200	8,800	...	0.789	83,660	75,545	8,115
1955	12,300	2,400	9,900	...	0.966	98,300	89,650	8,650
1956	16,600	3,500	13,100	...	1.163	110,360	101,862	8,498
1957	19,300	4,700	14,600	600	1.458	130,732	...	...
1958	28,000	5,500	22,500	...	2.264	230,000	...	...
1959	42,000	7,800	34,200	...	3.7	300,000	...	...
1960	47,000	9,000	38,000	...	5.1	280,000	...	...
1961	31,000	8,000	23,000	...	5.186	170,000	...	...
1962	30,000	6,000	24,000	...	5.746	180,000	...	...
1963	33,000	6,000	27,000	...	6.360	190,000	...	...
1964	36,000	7,000	29,000	...	8.653	204,000	...	...
1965	42,000	9,000	33,000	9,200	10.961	220,000	187,000	33,000
1966	50,000	10,000	40,000	...	14.074	248,000	210,000	38,000
1967	45,000	10,000	35,000	...	13.9	190,000	155,000	35,000
1968	50,000	12,000	38,000	...	15.2	205,000	165,000	40,000
1969	60,000	15,000	45,000	...	20.377	258,000	200,000	58,000
1970	72,000	18,000	54,000	20,700	28.211	310,000	235,000	75,000
1971	86,000	21,000	65,000	...	36.700	335,000	250,000	85,000
1972	93,000	23,000	70,000	...	43.065	356,000	260,000	96,000
1973	101,000	25,000	76,000	...	54.804	377,000	271,000	106,000
1974	108,000	27,000	81,000	...	65.765	389,000	279,000	110,000
1975	121,000	30,000	91,000	34,600	74.261	427,000	307,000	120,000
1976	...	...	...	...	83.608	448,000	300,000	148,000

Table A.17b   China: Production of Selected Producer Goods

Th Metric Tons

		Pig Iron			Crude Steel			
	Standard Iron Ore [1][2]	Total	Large Plants	Medium and Small Plants	Total	Large Plants	Medium and Small Plants	Finished Steel
1949	504	252	231	21	158	...	...	123
1950	2,156	978	928	50	606	...	...	360
1951	2,446	1,148	1,056	92	896	...	...	690
1952	4,218	1,929	1,812	117	1,349	1,276	73	1,110
1953	4,908	2,234	2,098	136	1,774	1,618	156	1,490
1954	6,728	3,114	2,940	174	2,225	1,979	246	1,770
1955	8,464	3,872	3,688	184	2,853	2,486	367	2,220
1956	10,462	4,826	4,674	152	4,465	3,974	491	3,220
1957	12,262	5,936	...	...	5,350	...	...	4,290
1958	27,280	13,690	9,530	4,160	11,080	8,000	3,080	6,100
1959	40,990	20,500	9,450	11,050	13,350	8,630	4,720	8,100
1960	54,920	27,500	13,750	13,750	18,670	12,450	6,220	11,300
1961	17,270	8,800	...	...	8,000	...	...	6,000
1962	17,630	8,800	...	...	8,000	...	...	6,000
1963	19,840	9,900	...	...	9,000	...	...	6,800
1964	23,840	11,900	...	...	10,800	...	...	8,100
1965	27,820	13,800	12,600	1,200	12,500	12,000	500	9,400
1966	33,520	16,600	...	...	15,000	...	...	11,200
1967	26,650	13,200	...	...	12,000	...	...	9,000
1968	30,870	15,400	...	...	14,000	...	...	10,500
1969	35,220	17,600	16,200	1,400	16,000	15,500	500	12,000
1970	43,970	22,000	18,100	3,900	17,800	16,100	1,700	13,400
1971	54,170	27,100	20,200	6,900	21,000	18,600	2,400	15,400
1972	60,770	30,400	22,200	8,200	23,000	20,200	2,800	16,900
1973	67,340	33,700	24,100	9,600	25,500	22,300	3,200	19,100
1974	61,050	31,400	22,500	8,900	23,800	20,800	3,000	17,800
1975	67,600	33,800	24,300	9,500	26,000	22,700	3,300	19,500
1976	...	...	...	...	23,000	20,080	2,920	...

[1] The standard used contains 55 percent iron ore.

[2] For a series of actual weight mined, see table A.11.

Table A.17c China: Production of Selected Producer Goods

	Cement (Th Metric Tons)			Timber	Paper
	Total	Large Plants	Small Plants	(Th m³)	(Th Metric Tons)
1949	660	660	0	5,670	228
1950	1,410	1,410	0	6,640	380
1951	2,490	2,490	0	7,640	492
1952	2,860	2,860	0	11,200	603
1953	3,880	3,880	0	17,530	667
1954	4,600	4,600	0	22,270	842
1955	4,500	4,500	0	20,930	839
1956	6,390	6,390	0	20,840	998
1957	6,860	6,860	0	27,870	1,221
1958	10,700	9,300	1,400	28,937	1,630
1959	12,270	10,570	1,700	32,022	1,949
1960	12,000	9,000	3,000	28,668	1,825
1961	7,800	6,000	1,800	19,335	1,388
1962	6,900	5,300	1,600	20,940	2,118
1963	9,100	6,800	2,300	22,971	2,599
1964	10,900	8,700	2,200	26,417	3,220
1965	16,280	10,900	5,380	27,183	3,611
1966	17,900	12,500	5,400	27,971	3,923
1967	14,200	10,600	3,600	22,044	3,246
1968	19,600	13,700	5,900	22,044	3,344
1969	22,540	14,400	8,140	26,438	4,219
1970	26,600	15,100	11,500	29,875	5,000
1971	31,000	18,600	12,400	30,741	5,066
1972	38,100	19,800	18,300	33,200	5,606
1973	41,000	20,500	20,500	34,163	6,032
1974	37,300	16,000	21,300	35,154	6,500
1975	47,100	19,400	27,700	36,173	6,941
1976	49,300	19,700	29,600	...	...

Table A.17d China: Production of Selected Producer Goods

Th Metric Tons

		Chemical Fertilizers						
		Nitrogen [1]			Phosphorous [2]			
	Total	Total	Large Plants	Small Plants	Total	Large Plants	Small Plants	Potassium [3]
1949	27	27	27	0	0	0	0	0
1950	70	70	70	0	0	0	0	0
1951	137	137	137	0	0	0	0	0
1952	194	194	194	0	0	0	0	0
1953	263	263	263	0	0	0	0	0
1954	343	343	343	0	0	0	0	0
1955	426	418	418	0	8	8	0	0
1956	663	586	586	0	77	77	0	0
1957	803	683	683	0	120	120	0	0
1958	1,354	1,010	1,010	0	344	344	0	0
1959	1,876	1,376	1,376	0	500	500	0	0
1960	2,523	1,723	1,723	0	800	600	200	0
1961	1,850	1,400	1,380	20	450	338	112	0
1962	2,775	2,220	2,160	60	555	355	200	0
1963	3,857	2,708	2,608	100	1,149	501	648	0
1964	5,785	3,560	3,329	231	2,225	600	1,625	0
1965	7,600	4,508	3,967	541	3,092	618	2,474	0
1966	9,600	5,229	4,288	941	4,281	1,141	3,140	90
1967	8,100	4,413	3,213	1,200	3,517	1,005	2,512	170
1968	9,500	5,200	3,500	1,700	4,070	1,375	2,695	230
1969	11,300	5,900	3,800	2,100	5,150	1,500	3,650	250
1970	14,000	7,810	4,450	3,360	5,900	1,550	4,350	290
1971	16,800	9,500	4,750	4,750	6,950	1,620	5,330	350
1972	19,841	11,723	5,744	5,979	7,738	1,934	5,804	380
1973	24,801	14,652	6,740	7,912	9,729	2,432	7,297	420
1974	24,875	15,810	6,956	8,854	8,615	2,498	6,117	450
1975	27,875	17,717	7,441	10,276	9,658	3,187	6,471	500
1976	...	...	...	...	...	...	...	...

[1] Production is measured in standard units of 20-percent nitrogen.
[2] Production is measured in standard units of 18.7-percent phosphoric acid.
[3] Production is measured in standard units of 40-percent potassium oxide

Table A.18 China: Production of Selected Consumer Goods

Th Units

	Bicycles	Thermos Bottles	Radio Sets	Television Sets	Watches
1949	14	...	...	...	...
1950	21	...	...	...	...
1951	44	...	...	...	...
1952	80	5,536	17	...	...
1953	165	12,007	25	...	...
1954	298	14,841	28	...	...
1955	335	17,958	151	...	...
1956	640	16,310	270	...	...
1957	806	20,870	390	...	...
1958	1,174	27,611	1,200	...	...
1959	1,479	37,000	1,560	...	...
1960	1,840	...	1,500	...	650
1961	634	...	1,250	2	...
1962	1,000	...	1,000	3	...
1963	1,101	33,216	1,000	3	...
1964	1,209	...	1,000	5	...
1965	1,792	...	1,500	5	1,200
1966	2,044	...	1,500	8	...
1967	...	...	1,500	5	...
1968	2,412	...	2,000	5	...
1969	3,026	...	2,500	10	...
1970	3,640	...	4,600	15	...
1971	4,030	...	6,000	20	6,200
1972	4,300	...	6,700	40	6,950
1973	4,859	...	12,100	75	7,800
1974	5,194	...	15,000	115	...
1975	5,460	...	18,000	205	...
1976	...	...	...	...	...

Table A.19 China: Per Capita Indicators of Consumer Welfare

	GNP [1] (1976 US $)	Grain Output [2] (kg)	Cotton Cloth Output (Linear m)	Consumer Goods Output (index 1957=100)
1949	96	206	3.5	33
1950	116	237	4.6	42
1951	132	253	5.5	55
1952	153	283	6.7	67
1953	159	281	8.0	80
1954	162	278	8.8	88
1955	173	295	7.1	85
1956	183	302	9.2	96
1957	190	298	7.9	100
1958	221	315	8.7	115
1959	205	256	9.1	125
1960	196	229	7.2	107
1961	152	242	4.8	74
1962	167	255	5.0	75
1963	183	264	6.4	97
1964	202	264	6.9	117
1965	220	259	8.5	156
1966	241	280	8.7	172
1967	227	287	7.0	161
1968	223	262	7.5	176
1969	242	262	8.0	182
1970	275	289	8.9	208
1971	287	286	8.4	203
1972	294	273	8.3	215
1973	325	297	8.5	239
1974	330	300	8.3	243
1975	346	304	8.1	252
1976	340	300	...	...

[1] These figures are derived from unrounded data.
[2] Including soybeans.

Table A.20   China: Balance of Trade

Million US $

	Total Trade				Communist Countries				Non-Communist Countries			
	Total	Exports	Imports	Balance	Total	Exports	Imports	Balance	Total	Exports	Imports	Balance
1950	1,210	620	590	30	350	210	140	70	860	410	450	−40
1951	1,900	780	1,120	−340	975	465	515	−50	920	315	605	−290
1952	1,890	875	1,015	−140	1,315	605	710	−105	575	270	305	−35
1953	2,295	1,040	1,255	−215	1,555	670	885	−215	740	370	370	0
1954	2,350	1,060	1,290	−230	1,735	765	970	−205	615	295	320	−25
1955	3,035	1,375	1,660	−285	2,250	950	1,300	−350	785	425	360	65
1956	3,120	1,635	1,485	150	2,055	1,045	1,010	35	1,065	590	475	115
1957	3,055	1,615	1,440	175	1,965	1,085	880	205	1,090	530	560	−30
1958	3,765	1,940	1,825	115	2,380	1,280	1,100	180	1,385	660	725	−65
1959	4,290	2,230	2,060	170	2,980	1,615	1,365	250	1,310	615	695	−80
1960	3,990	1,960	2,030	−70	2,620	1,335	1,285	50	1,370	625	745	−120
1961	3,015	1,525	1,490	35	1,685	965	715	250	1,335	560	775	−215
1962	2,670	1,520	1,150	370	1,410	915	490	425	1,265	605	660	−55
1963	2,775	1,575	1,200	375	1,250	820	430	390	1,525	755	770	−15
1964	3,220	1,750	1,470	280	1,100	710	390	320	2,120	1,040	1,080	−40
1965	3,880	2,035	1,845	190	1,165	650	515	135	2,715	1,385	1,330	55
1966	4,245	2,210	2,035	175	1,090	585	505	80	3,155	1,625	1,530	95
1967	3,915	1,960	1,955	5	830	485	345	140	3,085	1,475	1,610	−135
1968	3,785	1,960	1,825	135	840	500	340	160	2,945	1,460	1,485	−25
1969	3,895	2,060	1,835	225	785	490	295	195	3,110	1,570	1,540	30
1970	4,325	2,080	2,245	−165	860	480	380	100	3,465	1,600	1,865	−265
1971	4,765	2,455	2,310	145	1,085	585	500	85	3,680	1,870	1,810	60
1972	6,000	3,150	2,850	300	1,275	740	535	205	4,725	2,410	2,315	95
1973	10,300	5,075	5,225	−150	1,710	1,000	710	290	8,590	4,075	4,515	−440
1974	14,080	6,660	7,420	−760	2,435	1,430	1,010	420	11,645	5,230	6,415	−1,185
1975	14,575	7,180	7,395	−215	2,390	1,380	1,010	370	12,185	5,800	6,385	−585
1976	13,255	7,250	6,005	1,245	2,345	1,240	1,105	135	10,915	6,015	4,900	1,115

Data are rounded to the nearest $5 million. Because of rounding, components may not add to totals shown.

Table A.21a   China: Trade by Area and Country [1]

Million US$

Area and Country	1975				1976			
	Total	Exports	Imports	Balance	Total	Exports	Imports	Balance
Total	14,575	7,180	7,395	−215	13,255	7,250	6,005	1,245
Non-Communist Countries	12,185	5,800	6,385	−585	10,915	6,015	4,900	1,115
Developed Countries	8,100	2,620	5,480	−2,860	6,805	2,695	4,110	−1,415
East Asia and Pacific ..	4,305	1,565	2,740	−1,175	3,470	1,420	2,050	−630
Of which:								
Australia	441	86	355	−269	380	102	278	−176
Japan	3,828	1,459	2,369	−910	3,052	1,306	1,746	−440
Western Europe [2]	2,810	840	1,970	−1,130	2,675	985	1,690	−705
Of which:								
Belgium-Luxem-								
bourg	94	39	55	−16	92	46	46	0
France	584	150	434	−284	571	169	402	−233
Italy	280	112	168	−56	278	135	143	−8
Netherlands.................	223	70	153	−83	124	78	46	32
Norway	131	7	124	−117	28	7	21	−14
Sweden	88	41	47	−6	79	44	35	9
Switzerland	92	27	65	−38	92	32	60	−28
United Kingdom	316	112	204	−92	277	136	141	−5
West Germany	796	195	601	−406	952	236	716	−480
North America	985	215	770	−555	660	290	370	−80
Of which:								
United States	492	158	334	−176	351	202	149	53
Canada	490	55	435	−380	309	90	219	−129
Less Developed								
Countries	2,650	1,780	870	910	2,455	1,690	765	925
Southeast Asia.................	835	680	155	525	860	660	200	460
Of which:								
Indonesia	199	194	5	189	125	125	Negl	125
Malaysia	161	106	55	51	146	97	49	48
Singapore	295	251	44	207	294	254	40	214
South Asia	335	210	125	85	280	180	100	80
Of which:								
Iran	79	51	28	23	95	89	6	83
Pakistan	65	51	14	37	80	62	18	44
Sri Lanka	157	89	68	21	66	6	60	−54
Middle East	450	320	130	190	425	275	150	125
Of which:								
Iraq	136	65	71	−6	91	41	50	−9
Kuwait	56	52	4	48	75	64	11	53
Syria	65	39	26	13	79	31	48	−17
North Africa	210	130	80	50	175	110	65	45
Of which:								
Egypt	73	50	23	27	98	39	59	−20
Morocco.......................	31	24	7	17	22	19	3	16
Sub-Saharan Africa	520	390	130	260	510	410	100	310
Of which:								
Nigeria	71	63	8	55	113	108	5	103
Sudan..........................	83	42	41	1	52	26	27	−1
Tanzania	87	71	16	55	53	38	15	23

Footnotes at end of table A.21b

Table A.21b   China: Trade by Area and Country

Million US$

Area and Country	1975				1976			
	Total	Exports	Imports	Balance	Total	Exports	Imports	Balance
Non-Communist								
Countries (continued)								
Less Developed								
Countries (continued)								
Latin America	295	45	250	−205	205	55	150	−95
Of which:								
Argentina	23	1	22	−21	3	Negl	3	−3
Brazil	75	1	74	−73	10	Negl	10	−10
Chile	18	4	14	−10	66	16	50	−34
Peru	78	8	70	−62	70	15	55	−40
Hong Kong and Macao [3]	1,435	1,400	35	1,365	1,660	1,630	30	1,600
Of which:								
Hong Kong	1,405	1,372	33	1,339	1,620	1,590	30	1,560
Communist Countries	2,390	1,380	1,010	370	2,345	1,240	1,105	135
USSR	279	150	129	21	416	178	238	−60
Eastern Europe	1,010	485	525	−40	985	435	550	−115
Of which:								
Czechoslovakia	128	58	70	−12	120	50	70	−20
East Germany	220	103	117	−14	200	96	104	−8
Hungary	97	56	41	15	71	31	40	−9
Poland	103	43	60	−17	106	40	66	−26
Romania	435	215	220	−5	453	201	252	−51
Far East [4]	740	540	200	340	620	460	160	300
Other [5]	355	200	155	45	320	165	155	10

[1] Data for individual countries are rounded to the nearest $1 million. All other data are rounded to the nearest $5 million. Because of rounding, components may not add to the totals shown.

[2] Including Spain, Portugal, Greece, and Malta.

[3] Including entrepot trade with third countries; Hong Kong reexports to third countries of $351 million in 1975 and $493 million in 1976; reexports to China of $28 million in 1975 and $25 million in 1976.

[4] Including North Korea, Mongolia, Vietnam, Cambodia, and Laos.

[5] Including Yugoslavia, Cuba, and Albania.

Table A.22   China: Commodity Composition of Imports, by Area [1]

Million US $

	1975					1976				
	Total	Developed	Less Developed	Hong Kong[2] and Macao	Communist	Total	Developed	Less Developed	Hong Kong[2] and Macao	Communist
Total Imports	7,395	5,480	870	35	1,010	6,005	4,110	765	30	1,105
Foodstuffs	885	600	180	5	100	560	350	115	...	90
Of which:										
Grains	675	585	85	...	5	325	290	35	...	...
Fruits and vegetables	35	...	20	...	15	5	...	5	...	...
Sugar	145	15	50	5	80	200	60	55	...	85
Crude materials	1,040	320	510	15	195	895	245	435	15	200
Of which:										
Oilseeds	15	...	15	...	...	5	...	5	...	...
Crude rubber, natural	145	...	135	...	10	150	...	135	...	15
Crude rubber, synthetic	10	10	...	...	...	5	5	...	...	...
Wood pulp	50	50	...	...	...	60	60	...	...	...
Textile fibers, natural	260	95	165	...	...	190	15	175	...	...
Textile fibers, synthetic	95	95	...	...	...	115	115	...	...	...
Crude fertilizers, minerals	30	5	10	...	15	40	...	30	...	5
Metalliferous ores and scrap	125	35	15	5	70	125	25	15	...	85
Crude animal and vegetable materials	20	...	10	5	5	20	...	5	10	5
Petroleum and products	105	...	105	...	...	45	...	45	...	...
Animal fats and oil	15	15	...	...	...	15	15	...	...	...
Fixed vegetable oils	15	...	15	...	...	10	5	5	...	...
Chemicals	825	745	15	...	65	600	455	35	...	110
Of which:										
Elements and compounds	260	245	10	...	5	210	210	...	...	5
Dyeing materials	25	25	...	...	...	20	15	...	...	...
Fertilizers, manufactured[3]	405	360	5	...	40	230	100	30	...	95
Plastic materials	70	70	...	...	...	90	85	...	...	...
Manufactures	4,595	3,795	155	10	635	3,895	3,045	165	15	670
Of which:										
Paper and paperboard	80	75	...	...	5	45	40	...	...	...
Textile yarn and fabric	85	80	...	5	...	125	115	5	...	...
Nonmetallic mineral products	20	15	...	...	5	15	10	...	5	...
Iron and steel	1,550	1,430	5	...	115	1,445	1,335	5	...	100
Nonferrous metals	450	290	140	...	20	260	110	130	...	20
Metal products, industrial	125	120	5	...	...	90	80	...	...	10
Nonelectric machinery	1,055	900	...	...	155	1,090	905	...	...	185
Electric machinery	210	180	...	...	30	210	185	...	...	25
Transport equipment	890	630	...	...	260	470	190	15	...	265
Precision instruments	50	40	...	...	10	60	40	...	5	15
Watches and clocks	15	15	...	...	...	15	15	...	...	...
Other	50	25	10	...	15	55	10	10	...	35

[1] Data are rounded to the nearest $5 million. Because of rounding, components may not add to to the totals shown. Ellipsis marks indicate that imports, if any, amounted to less than US $2.5 million. Estimates are based on data reported by trading partners. Where data are incomplete, as for the Less Developed and Communist countries, estimates are based on fragmentary information from trade agreements and press reports and on commodity breakdowns for earlier years.

[2] Including Hong Kong reexports of third country goods to China.

[3] Excludes phosphate rock, ammonium chloride, sodium nitrate, and potassium nitrate.

Table A.23   China: Contracts for Whole Plant Imports

Nation/Firm	Type	Value (Million US $)	Contract Signed	Comple-tion	Comment
1975 Contracts		**364**			
Japan		**38**			
Nippon Seiko	Spherical bearings	3	Apr 75	1976	Progress payments
Koyo Seiko	Cylindrical bearings	8	Apr 75	1976	Progress payments
Ibigawa	Laminated board	1	Jul 75	NA	
Ataka	Air separation	11	Nov 75	1977	Progress payments; 35,000 m³/hr capacity
Mitsubishi	Friction materials	15	Dec 75	NA	
West Germany		**90**			
Linde	Benzene	20	Jul 75	NA	
Krupp	Dimethyltherephthalate	50	Dec 75	NA	Progress payments; 90,000 t/yr capacity
Uhde	Ethanol	20	Dec 75	NA	100,000 MT/yr capacity
United Kingdom		**200**			
Rolls Royce	Jet engine plant	200	Dec 75	1980	50 jet engines plus manufacturing fa-cility and testing equipment
Italy		**36**			
Mechaniche Moderne	Detergent	1	Sep 75	NA	Progress payments
Eurotechnica	Detergent alkalation	35	Oct 75	NA	Deferred payments
1976 Contracts		**185**			
Japan		**146**			
Japan Gasoline	Aromatics complex	36	Jan 76	NA	Japan Ex-Im Bank financing
Japan Synthetic Rubber	Styrene-butadiene rubber	27	Feb 76	NA	5-year Japan Ex-Im Bank financing; 240,000 MT/yr capacity
Kyokuto Boeki Kaisha	Hot scarfer	2	Mar 76	NA	Progress payments
Teijin	Polyester/polymer	40	Mar 76	NA	5-year Japan Ex-Im Bank financing; 80,000 MT/yr capacity
Nakajima Seiki	Wallpaper plant	1	Apr 76	NA	
Nippon Steel	Desulfurization plant	26	Jun 76	NA	
Mitsui	Cinder pelletizing	14	Aug 76	NA	
West Germany		**31**			
BASF	Diethylhexonol	24	Mar 76	NA	50,000 MT/yr capacity
Kraus Maffei	High reactive lime	7	Aug 76	NA	
Italy		**8**			
Nuovo Pignone	Centrifugal compressors technology	8	Jun 76	NA	
Finland		**NA**			
Tamglass	Automobile glass plant	NA	Jun 76	NA	
1977 Contracts		**59**			
Japan		**20**			
Chiyoda	Natural gas refining	20	Nov 77	1980	5-year Japan Ex-Im Bank financing
West Germany		**39**			
Zimmer	Polyester fiber and film	12	Jun 77	1980	
Lurgi	Terephthalic acid	27	Jun 77	1980	US technology from AMOCO

Table A.24 China: Imports of Grain and Chemical Fertilizer

	Grain		Chemical Fertilizer[1]	
	Million Metric Tons	Million US $	Million Metric Tons[2]	Million US $
1966	5.6	400	2.5	155
1967	4.1	295	4.3	200
1968	4.4	305	4.0	200
1969	3.9	260	4.1	205
1970	4.6	280	4.3	230
1971	3.0	205	4.2	200
1972	4.8	345	4.2	190
1973	7.7	840	4.1	220
1974	7.0	1,180	3.0	230
1975	3.3	675	2.9	455
1976	1.9	325	2.5	230

[1] Excludes phosphate rock.
[2] In product weight.

Table A.25 U.S.-China Trade[1]

Million US $

	1972	1973	1974	1975	1976	1977 Jan-Jul
US Exports	63	740	819	304	135	68
Agricultural commodities	61	628 [2]	668 [2]	80	0	0
Of which:						
Wheat	35	308	234	0	0	0
Corn	24	141	96	0	0	0
Soybeans	0	55	138	0	0	0
Cotton	0	101	186	80	0	0
Vegetable oils	2	19	8	0	0	0
Metals	0	31	22	83	47	Negl
Of which:						
Steel scrap	0	24	12	13	4	0
Aluminum	0	3	0	47	26	0
Iron and steel pipe	0	0	3	12	11	Negl
Machinery and equipment	2	69	107	119	65	42
Of which:						
Aircraft, including engines, parts, and accessories	0	63	76	2	1	0
Other	0	12	22	22	23	26
US Imports	32	64	115	158	201	116
Foodstuffs and tobacco	4	7	16	16	24	16
Textiles and apparel	7	15	36	45	69	40
Silk and other fibers	4	6	5	4	8	4
Cotton and other fabrics	2	7	25	31	43	19
Clothing and footwear	1	2	6	10	18	17
Handicrafts	8	15	20	22	32	17
Of which:						
Antiques, works of art	3	6	8	6	12	6
Bristles, downs, and feathers	8	8	10	6	24	20
Chemicals, including fireworks	2	8	18	16	18	13
Nonferrous minerals and metals	2	8	11	42	19	6
Of which:						
Tin	1	8	9	40	13	3
Other	1	3	4	11	15	4

[1] Data are from the Department of Commerce and show f.a.s. exports and f.o.b. imports.
[2] Includes agricultural reexports from Canadian ports.

Index